D0891858

Reform in China
and Other
Socialist Economies

Reform in China and Other Socialist Economies

Jan S. Prybyla

The AEI Press

Publisher for the American Enterprise Institute
WASHINGTON, D.C.

1990

Distributed by arrangement with

University Press of America
4720 Boston Way   3 Henrietta Street
Lanham, MD 20706   London WC2E 8LU England

Library of Congress Cataloging-in-Publication Data

Prybyla, Jan S.
    Reform in China and other socialist economies / Jan S. Prybyla.
        p.   cm.—(AEI studies : 505)
    Includes index.
    ISBN 0-8447-3717-8.—ISBN 0-8447-3718-6 (pbk.)
        1. China—Economic policy—1976–   2. China—Economic
conditions—1976–   3. Communist countries—Economic policy.
    4. Communist countries—Economic conditions.   5. Marxian economics.
    6. Comparative economics.   I. Title.   II. Series.
    HC427.92.P79   1990
        338.951—dc20   90-849
                                                                        CIP

AEI Studies 505

Printed in the United States of America

Contents

FOREWORD   xi
Thomas W. Robinson

PART ONE
ECONOMICS, POLITICS, AND PHILOSOPHY IN
SOCIALIST SYSTEMS

1 FOUNDATIONS OF THE ECONOMIC CRISIS OF
STATE SOCIALISM   3
The Philosophical Foundations of Marxism   3
Bureaucracy, the Institutional Foundation   11
Conclusion   15

2 SOCIALIST ECONOMIC REFORM, POLITICAL FREEDOM,
AND DEMOCRACY   16
Definitions   16
The Socialist Economic System   17
Problems of the Socialist System   18
How Bad Is It?   21
What Is to Be Done?   22
The Market System   23
The Market System, Political Freedom, and
    Democracy   25
Socialism, the Market System, Political Freedom and
    Democracy   25
Prognosis   26

3 THE RELATIONSHIP BETWEEN THE FIFTH
MODERNIZATION AND THE OTHER FOUR IN CHINA   28
The Four Modernizations   28
The Fifth Modernization   29
Economic Modernization   30
Democracy   37
Economic and Political Modernization   38

Economic Change   39
Political Change   41
Summary and Conclusions   43

4   SOME REFLECTIONS ON MAN AND SOCIETY IN CHINA   46
    Political Performances   46
    Anti-Individualism   47
    Totalitarianism   50
    Individual Fulfillment   54
    Hope for the Oppressed   56

PART TWO
COMPARATIVE SOCIALIST ECONOMIES IN REFORM

5   IS THE SOVIET TYPE OF ECONOMIC
    SYSTEM STRONG OR WEAK?   59
    Strong or Weak?   59
    The Bumble Bee Paradox   60
    Weakness   61
    Strength   63
    The Three Economies of State Socialism   64
    Spillovers   66
    Operational Characteristics of the Military–Public
       Security Economy   69
    Summary and Conclusions   71

6   SIMILARITIES AND DIFFERENCES OF ECONOMIC
    CHANGES IN CHINA AND THE SOVIET UNION   72
    Similarities   72
    Differences   78
    Conclusions   83

7   MAINLAND CHINA AND HUNGARY—
    TO MARKET, TO MARKET . . .   85
    Some Theoretical Questions   86
    Price System—Information and Coordination   87
    The Price System in Hungary   89
    The Price System of Mainland China   93
    Motivation   98
    Property   106
    The Nationalized Black Market   112
    Conclusions   112
    Bibliography   116

8   THE POLISH ECONOMY—A CASE STUDY IN THE
STRUCTURE AND STRATEGY OF DISASTER   118
    Economic Reform and Adjustment   120
    The Road to Disaster   123
    Systemic-Structural Defects   129
    What Poland Needs   131
    What Poland Is Likely to Get   131

PART THREE
THE CHINESE ECONOMIC REFORMS

9   CHINA'S ECONOMIC REFORMS   135
    Property System Reform   139
    Political Reform   141
    Failure of Price System Reform   142
    The Management Responsibility System in Industry   142
    The Future of Agricultural Reform   143
    The Way Forward for Chinese Economic Reform   144

10   CHINA'S ECONOMIC EXPERIMENT, FROM
MAO TO MARKET   146
    Policies of Adjustment   148
    Results of Adjustment   150
    Beyond Adjustment, toward Reform   150
    Some Problems in Industry   155
    Macro-Control   157
    Micro-Autonomy   162
    Prospects   166

11   CHINA'S ECONOMIC EXPERIMENT—BACK FROM THE
MARKET?   171
    Sweet   174
    Sour   175
    Conditions for a Successful Market System   185
    Measures to Eliminate Sourness   193
    Prospects   198

12   PRICE REFORM IN THE PEOPLE'S REPUBLIC OF CHINA   203
    Theoretical Positions   203
    Price System   204
    Economic Philosophy and the Price System   204
    Institutional Structure of Prices   208
    Price Policy   216

13 WHY CHINA'S ECONOMIC REFORMS FAIL 222
China's Economic Problems around 1978   222
Possible Policy and Structural Remedies   223
If Reform, What Kind of Reform?   224
Requirements for Market Reform   226
Requirements for a Successful Market System   227
China's Reforms since 1979   228
Conclusions   235

14 THE ECONOMIC CONSEQUENCES OF TIANANMEN
SQUARE 237
How Ethical Are Capitalist Ethics?   238
Socialist Ethics   239
The Stakes   241
The Capitalist's Dilemma   242
Government and International Agency Sanctions   246
Longer-Term Consequences   248

PART FOUR
COMPARATIVE ECONOMIC DEVELOPMENT IN
THREE CHINESE ENTITIES

15 THE ECONOMIES OF TAIWAN AND MAINLAND CHINA 253
The Economies Compared   253
The Record since 1979   256
Taiwan as a Systemic Model   260

16 U.S. ECONOMIC RELATIONS WITH TAIWAN
SINCE THE TAIWAN RELATIONS ACT 265
Achievements of the U.S.-ROC Economic
Relationship   265
Problems in the U.S.-ROC Economic Relationship   266
Work to Be Done   271
Bibliography   274

17 THE HONG KONG AGREEMENT AND ITS IMPACT
ON THE WORLD ECONOMY 276
Hong Kong and the World Economy   279
The Preagreement Vulnerability of Hong Kong   280
Vulnerability under the Agreement   283
Conclusion   287

PART FIVE
CONCLUSION

18 THE TRANSITION FROM SOCIALISM TO CAPITALISM   291
Economic, Noneconomic, and Antieconomic
Systems 291
The Question of Mixture 297
To Market 299

NOTES   305

ACKNOWLEDGMENTS   349

INDEX   351

ABOUT THE AUTHOR   359

LIST OF TABLES
7-1. Combinations of Public Ownership and
Private Entrepreneurial Activities   113
12-1. Categories of Prices according to Allocative
Function in China since 1978   210
15-1. Indexes of Gross National Product and
National Income, Taiwan and the Mainland,
1952 and 1985   253
15-2. Sectoral Origin of Net Domestic Product
(Taiwan) and Net Material Product
(Mainland), 1952 and 1985   255
15-3. Foreign Trade, Taiwan and the Mainland,
1952–1988   257
15-4. Annual Growth Rates of Real Gross National
Product (Taiwan) and National Income
(Mainland), 1979–1988   259
LIST OF FIGURES
5-1. The Three Economies of State Socialism   65
8-1. Growth Indicators in Poland, 1977–1987   120
8-2. Poland's Consumption and Living Standard,
1977–1987   121
8-3. Poland's External Hard Currency Debt,
1977–1987   122
8-4. Poland's Gross Ruble Debt, 1977–1987   123

Foreword

For many years, Jan Prybyla has been writing seminal articles and chapters in the general field of Socialist economics. In every case, these have evidenced several qualities: a skeptical attitude toward the attributes and propensities of centrally planned, state-owned, Communist party–run economies; scrupulous accuracy and honesty regarding the relative successes and failures of such economic systems; a philosophy of letting the facts speak for themselves and of ensuring that all the facts are brought forth; an approach that embeds "purely economic factors" (if there is any such thing) in the broader arenas of politics, society, history, and foreign relations; an assumption that the combination of a market-oriented economic system and a democratic political system (with, to be sure, a "proper," if usually minimal degree of state intervention in the economy) is both the natural and the best way to organize a political economy; and a philosophical orientation thoroughly grounded in the Western tradition, combining Greco-Roman and Judeo-Christian elements in a unique liberal-conservative blend.

Most of these writings have concentrated on the Chinese economic system, but in fact Prybyla's "model" (in the negative sense) has been the Soviet-style economy in general as found not only in the Soviet Union itself but also, until the late 1980s, in Eastern Europe as well. All that has come from his pen evinces a startling quality and unity of thought and a clear, penetrating style, that are at once appealing and arresting. But like many such authors, these attributes have not been demonstrated as convincingly as they might because of the dispersion of these articles over many publications and a considerable period. This volume is designed to heal this condition.

That by itself would, of course, not be sufficient to justify publication of even such a superb set of essays as these. Fortunately, in his case there are other excellent reasons for proceeding. For one, he is practically alone not only in studying Communist economic systems as a whole but also in having first-hand experience with both their European and their Asian variants. His writing thus carries the virtues of completeness and comparison. For another, his track record of successful prediction of economic changes in Communist states is astonishing: time and again, his forecasts have proved accurate, particularly regarding China within the six-month to two-year time frame he stated. Third, Prybyla is more than an economist, in the same sense that Adam Smith was: like Smith, he invites his readers to judge the economic worth of a system on standard economic criteria—efficiency, growth, distribution, and the like, of course, but on higher philosophical, even moral, standards as well. That he finds socialism wanting according to those standards and capitalism (generally) acceptable should challenge the reader to ask, as he does, What moral tests should be applied to economic activity, and why does capitalism usually do better than socialism? His answers go to the heart of the relationship between economics and the other social sciences and to what trade-offs modern societies must make among material well-being, political freedom, modes of social organization, belief systems, and personal evaluations of self-worth.

The organization of the volume reflects these orientations. Part one is grounded upon the notion that the Socialist economy is integral to the Marxist-Leninist political and ideological system and that the measure of success of such economies is the correspondence between Marxist-Leninist ideas and basic truths of mankind's existence. Thus, no reform of the economy can occur without thoroughgoing, simultaneous revamping of the whole Socialist ethos, including ideological assumptions, the system of party rule, and the Communist attitude toward morality and human rights. Part two details and compares the experience and prospects of economic reform in four Socialist states: the Soviet Union, Hungary, Poland, and China. Here the author argues that reform cannot be a halfway affair. Once one or even several elements are tampered with, systemic instability sets in and cannot be overcome unless the transition—rapid and complete—is made to a market system or unless reforms are abrogated completely and restoration of the Stalinist centrally planned, state-owned and -administered economy is accomplished.

Part three inspects the Chinese experience during and after the decade of economic liberalism, 1978–1988. China's experience is a graphic case study of what happens when economic reforms are half-hearted: inevitably they fail, as they did in this case, according to Prybyla. Although these reforms were not doomed to failure from the outset, with the rejection of full-blown marketization as a good in itself and the corresponding unwillingness to link economic and political reform, prospects for success were poor, and the systemic breakdown of 1988–1989 should have been expected. Part four carries further the author's inquiry into China's Socialist economy by drawing a useful comparison with the economic system of two other Chinese entities: Hong Kong and Taiwan. Here Prybyla demonstrates conclusively that it is not China in the historical or social sense that imposes impediments on successful economic development, for both Hong Kong and Taiwan are Chinese in that regard as well as in the cultural and linguistic sense. They are in fact major economic successes, and the reasons are obvious: they are export-led models of economic growth; economies whose ownership is, largely, in private hands; and polities that provide stability, freedom to do business, and a system of law and justice such that both private and public corporations can count on due process and objectivity in its application. Interestingly, Prybyla does not argue that democracy is a prerequisite to successful economic modernization, at least in the initial and high-growth stages. But once economic maturity arrives, the transition to a democratic polity is both desirable and necessary for further economic success. By contrast, China has lacked these qualities, or has been unwilling to supply them; its economic failure was thus foreordained.

Part five sums up the argument of the volume by essaying on how socialism might solve its problems and what the future might hold. His answer is the same as in the first chapters: a Socialist economy, to be successful, must essentially commit suicide, that is, replace itself with its opposite, capitalism. In 1990, the Eastern European economies were engaged in just that process, the Soviet Union was still in the throes of deciding whether and, if so, how to do so, while China had rejected that alternative, much to its own detriment.

These essays, singly and as a whole, compose a sensible, reasonable, and fearless approach to the solution of the economic crisis of socialism. Although written over many years, they demonstrate startling relevance to the economic and political transitions occurring throughout the Socialist world in the late 1980s and early 1990s. As such, they should prove of close and continuing interest to many readers.

THOMAS W. ROBINSON
American Enterprise Institute

PART ONE
Economics, Politics, and Philosophy in Socialist Systems

1
Foundations of the Economic Crisis of State Socialism

Countries ruled by state socialism ("Communist" countries) are in the throes of a crisis that, if left to its own dynamics, calls into question their survival as political and economic systems in the existing form.

The roots of the state Socialist crisis lie not in domestic and foreign subversive machinations or in the leaders' many mistakes. The crisis does not result from counterrevolutionary schemings, imperialist conspiracy, Stalinism, Brezhnevism, Castroism, Maoism, or Jaruzelskiism. It is first a problem of Marxism, of the system's philosophical assumptions and second a problem of the institutional structures built on these poor foundations. This is recognized by reformers in the state Socialist countries whenever the political climate permits. Despairing of ridding the system of its Marxist substance, they do the next best thing: search for the "young" Marx, the one with the human face. This, however, is merely the counsel of despair. The Marxist blueprint, faithfully implemented by a succession of dictators from Lenin to Mao and beyond, has no human face. Contrary to the worn cliché, Marx would not turn in his grave if he saw what has been done in his name in Russia and other state Socialist countries. The legitimate line of succession is from Marx to Lenin to Stalin to Pol Pot, not from Marx to Mitterrand or Schmidt.

The Philosophical Foundations of Marxism

The Marxist conceptual edifice rests on three foundations: relativity of truth (dialectical materialism), class hatred (dialectical and historical materialism), and emasculation of the individual person. Lies, hate, and depersonalization are poor foundations on which to build a new human order. I do not agree with Leszek Kolakowski that "communism would be such a splendid idea if only there were no people." The idea is poisoned at the source by the liberties it takes with the truth, the antagonism on which it feeds, and its aggregated class conception of the world. It is a metaphysical illusion that impoverishes the spirit while failing to feed the body. Inevitably in practice it produces totalitarian terrorism on a monumental scale. In Cambodia, in the space of three years, as many as 3 million people were slaughtered in the cause of communism: 43 percent of the population. In 1978 Cambodia was well on the way to achieving the splendid idea without the people.

Relativity of Truth. A key condition for a viable economic system is legitimacy: the acceptance of the system by those who live and make their living within it. Acceptance should be freely given rather than obtained by the use of constraint. Willing acceptance depends on the system's credibility in the eyes of its participants: the description of the system and its practical outcomes must not be seriously at odds; nor should the system function in ways that force participants into daily conflict with the law or into routine violations of moral standards accepted by the people. In other words, the system must be truthful. Lech Walesa was right when he said that "truth is as necessary for Poland as coal." Nobel Prize laureate Kenneth J. Arrow makes the same point:

> Trust and similar values, loyalty or truth-telling, are examples of what the economist would call "externalities." They are goods, they are commodities; they have real, practical, economic value; they increase the efficiency of the system, enable you to produce more goods or more of whatever values you hold in high esteem.[1]

I think one should go farther. These moral "goods" are as essential to the continued existence and development of the system as water is to fish.

Repeatedly and everywhere the state Socialist system runs afoul of popular trust. People quite simply do not believe what the system tells them. The lie is not haphazard or accidental. It is grounded in dialectical materialism, which proclaims that until the highest, the perfect stage of human societies (full communism) is reached, truth is dialectical, that is, relative. Truth is an ever-changing object, the correct historical trajectory of which can be perceived only by the most advanced elements of the most advanced class—in practice, by the minuscule upper stratum of the Communist party's bureaucracy. The reverse of this is that in all pre-Communist experience there are no bedrock, universal, unchanging values. Today's truth is tomorrow's untruth.

The relativization of truth and the placing of its definition in the hands of the vanguard elite have four practical consequences. First, dictatorship is promoted. Second, congenital lying is doctrinally legitimized. At any given moment truth is what those in power say it is; and truth can be changed to accommodate those who define it. Third, because the volatile, diaphanous official truth monopolizes the field until officially repealed, opportunism, deviousness, and sycophancy are practiced by all but the hardiest candidates for martyrdom. Fourth, because of the chameleon-like nature and unreliability of official truth, the rumor mills work overtime. Thus, most of the information flowing through the system is inaccurate. Conceptually an economy is a system of information flows about needs and costs. In state Socialist economies this flow, for the most part, consists of lies and half-truths that distort consumer, worker, and managerial behavior in Byzantine ways.

Untruthfulness in state Socialist economies manifests itself in several particulars. For illustrative purposes one need not go beyond two of the more technical ones: inflation and unemployment. In market economies these phenomena show up openly from time to time—prices rise and workers are out of work. State Socialist economies claim that, thanks to central planning, they have banished both these scourges: no inflation, no unemployment. This is not true. Suppressed inflation and hidden unemployment are chronic conditions of the system. By definition, they do not appear in the statistics, but they exist nonetheless right under the surface. Suppressed inflation—the pricing of many goods of everyday use below market equilibrium—shows up in lines outside stores, shortages of goods, rampant black marketeering, and bribery (to bribe someone is, effectively, to raise the price of the good or service sought). The freezing of the prices of many consumer goods creates what economists call a "money illusion": the real (true) prices of commodities are understated, and the real cash balances in the hands of consumers are overstated by the price structure. The procedure necessitates huge budgetary subsidies, especially in agriculture and housing. These have been rising rapidly in recent decades. In China, for example, they quadrupled in four years (1978–1981) and now exceed the state expenditure on culture, education, public health, and science and are about the same as the state's total investment outlay. Soviet agricultural subsidies, caused by the inefficiency and consequent high cost of Soviet socialized farming, are equal to the Soviet Union's very sizable defense outlays. One Polish state farm produced meat

5

at a cost of $26 a pound (the State has favored state farms in invest-ment allocations). In the stores at the time, the same meat retailed at seventy-five cents a pound. The average cost of producing a liter of milk was $1.20. A liter of milk retailed for ten cents. Of course, neither meat nor milk was much in evidence in the retail stores.[2] At fifty-five cents a pound (official price) a person cannot actually get his ration of beef in Havana. He can, however, get pork on the free market at $2.50 a pound. From time to time the Socialist state tries to shake off a part of this subsidy burden by sharply raising retail prices (200–400 percent in Poland on February 1, 1982). This shatters the money illusion, reveals the true cost of goods and the modest size of consumers' cash balances, and, as often as not, has to be backed by resort to the state's all-purpose instrument of social policy—the tank.[3] To calm disgruntled workers, the money wage is sometimes increased. This only makes goods sold at con-trolled prices disappear from the stores that much faster, however. A general wage increase means the queues are longer.[4]

Underemployment in state Socialist economies is notorious. Be-cause of the objective of full employment (in fact, quasi-compulsory employment),[5] the injunction against firing workers (except for politi-cal causes), and other systemic reasons, state Socialist enterprises are overstaffed: that is, more people are employed than are needed to do the job. This results in low labor productivity and low incomes. While in modern capitalist market economies the unemployed are paid unemployment benefits when they are out of work, in state Socialist economies unemployment compensation is paid on the job. If a wage is paid for eight hours' work when only four hours are needed to do the job or if 100 workers are on the payroll when only 50 are needed, half the wage bill is really the dole. The illusion of full employment, however, is officially promoted and used to castigate capitalism. During the Polish "spring" of 1980–1981, one manager confided that "if they scrapped the employment limit, we could reduce our workforce 30 percent."

All this cannot be rationalized away by arguing that it is simply an alternative price and employment strategy that rations goods by the queue rather than by the price and provides security of em-ployment, even if the employment rolls are padded.

The suppression of reality, the hiding of real phenomena, the burying of unpleasant truths are not, of course, limited to the state Socialist system. In the state Socialist system, however, they are the officially sanctioned and promulgated rule. The dialectical percep-tion of truth deprives the economic system of predictable and perma-nent ethical guidelines and constitutes a license for the state's propensity to arbitrariness. In the course of the post-Mao self-criticism in China, a Peking Party daily (*Guangming Ribao*) summed up the problem citing the views of university students: "Theory," the students said, "is without basis. Theory cannot be taken seriously. There is no point in studying what the line is now, because next year you will be teaching us a new line."

Truthfulness also means that the system must not function in ways that force participants (consumers, workers, managers of firms) into daily conflict with the law or into routine violations of moral standards held by the people. A system that prohibits by law voluntary, contractual, lateral, or competitive exchange transactions among potential individual buyers and sellers does precisely that. When economic transactions become matters of command, vertical communication, and sanction by hierarchical bureaucratic authorities, the tendency to fawn, cheat, lie, steal, and corrupt is much encouraged and becomes, in fact, part of popular culture and an indispensable element of personal survival. Communism like its reverse side—fascism—brings out the worst in people.

Class Hatred. The *homo oeconomicus* of English classical economic theory is motivated to enter the market and compete in it by self-interest. His self-interest as a producer drives him to satisfy the needs of the consumer expressed and synthesized in market prices. His self-interest as a consumer makes him maximize his satisfactions, that is, choose efficiently among competing alternatives. The essence of the market is the social reconciliation of competing personal interests. Both sides to the market transaction come out of it better off than they had been before. The basic motivational force of the Christian interpretation of economic life is love—personalized, individualized, and translated into concrete works. In the Marxist view, the fundamental driving force of economic life is class hatred: not self-interest catering to the wants of others; not love, empathy, and sacrifice of self for others, but aggregated hatred. Marxist history moves onward and upward in response to the clash of massive social opposites defined in relation to property in the means of production. The Marxist confrontation is antagonistic, despite tactical attempts to downplay whatever divides (one divides into two), and to emphasize those aspects of the contradiction that unite (two combine into one). It is a view of the human condition that focuses on solutions arrived at by force and violence and excludes compromise, consensus, and reconciliation. It is an ethic tailored to evil rulers, thought up by a man "seemingly filled with loathing of life and almost everyone he came into contact with."[6]

7

In the Marxist perception class hatred is the *sine qua non* of violent historical transitions. Hatred is the dynamic, dialectically constructive and creative force of every society at every historical stage of Marx's *Stufenlehre*. It does not have to be cultivated; it is a natural, material condition of aggregated man. Marx's surplus value is a theory of exploitation that furnishes the historically progressive class with the "scientific" rationale for violent action. The proletarian class, led by its most advanced detachment, is the unit of revolutionary action. A key purpose of Marxist teaching is to promote the dormant, dark side of the human psyche and to enlist it in the cause of Socialist revolution. One of the constant observations made by those who study state Socialist societies concerns the lowering of human relationships and the brutalization of society.

The division of people into progressives driven by hate and those marked for extinction (the grave-diggers and their customers) is social racism. People are cast into "correct" and "incorrect" social groups: the incorrect are destined for the trash can of history. Millions died and millions more were psychologically crippled as a result of Stalin's, Mao's, and lesser dictators' application of Marx's concept of class warfare in Russia's villages, in China's "new democratic" land reform and Cultural Revolution (hailed by many Western intellectuals as the dawn of a new era), and in Cambodia's genocide by the Khmer Rouge. The Soviet geophysicist Iosif Dyadkin estimates in his *samizdat* essay "Evaluation of Unnatural Deaths in the Population of the USSR, 1927–1958" that Stalinist terror and World War II combat had taken the lives of between 43 million and 52 million Soviet citizens: some 30 million died in World War II; 13–23 million were killed by the Soviet government in peacetime.[7] These are not random happenings due to a mistaken "style of work," the personality cult, or deviation from the line. They *are* the line.

Immediately relevant to our concern here with the crisis of state Socialist economies is the question of what happens to class hatred under socialism. According to Marx, at the Socialist stage, by reason of the socialization of property and the dictatorship of the proletariat, the dialectic is gradually extinguished: class antagonism becomes benign misunderstanding among the people. By definition, workers cannot turn against the workers' state. Since everyone formally owns everything, no one is exploited; no one is alienated. The record of all state Socialist societies demonstrates the error of this proposition. Class hatred, long nourished by the Communists, comes to full fruition under state socialism. Massive alienation of the working class from the party-state and antagonistic divisions between the people and the new privileged class of party and state bureaucrats are synonymous with state socialism. To survive and develop, an economic system must be capable of adaptation. It has to have a mechanism for the peaceful resolution of divergent and conflicting interests. It must be able to adapt to changing social and technical circumstances. Because of the Socialist state's unconditional insistence on retaining total power, its exclusion of all potentially competing organized social formations (whether labor unions or political parties), the canyons of hatred that separate the directors of the system from those directed, and the deep-freezing of conflicting positions, economic reform—even systemically innocuous readjustment—in state Socialist societies is a political issue that can be resolved only by violence. A system born of force—employing force as the principal instrument of economic policy and nourished on antagonism between rulers and ruled—is a system that courts dissolution by force. I am convinced that, in the absence of Western financial assistance, we shall witness a worldwide coming apart of state socialism as an economic system.

Emasculation of the Individual. Despite the claim that it aims at the liberation of the individual through the "real appropriation of the human essence" in communism, Marxist theory consistently diminishes the human person and reduces it to a byproduct of the mass. The individual can fulfill himself only through social labor; whatever he may think, his true perception is that of his class as defined by his property relation to the means of production. He is caught in the grand, dehumanized, impersonal sweep of history to which he must adapt in a preordained way. He is nothing now apart from his class; he becomes everything in the future conditional. The conclusion drawn from this, the leading tenet of state socialism, is that society—specifically, society's historically anointed, that is, self-appointed, self-perpetuating leaders—knows better what is good for the individual than does the individual himself. This is an arrogant thesis that diminishes all concerned. It is the stuff of which serfdom is made. It breeds tutelage of the individual by the totalitarian state. The instruments used by the state to exercise this feudal tutelage are undiscriminating and undiscerning. Little wonder that state Socialist regimes, while they manage to keep the masses reasonably well in hand, have great trouble when challenged by the human micro unit: a Solzhenitsyn, a Sakharov, or Father Ciszek. Lev Kopelev, Sakharov's friend, puts it this way: Sakharov's fate at the hands of the Socialist state is "an example how one man—one very ill, very weak man, who has already had two heart seizures—a very modest man, a very calm man—can be stronger than this super-

9

power, with all its millions of soldiers and hundreds of thousands of policemen and millions of party members . . . he is stronger than this system of might."⁸ The strength and resilience of the individual flow from what Solzhenitsyn calls the "tiny but corrosive fund of human decency, which over the ages men have quietly stored away as their most prized possession." This small change in copper is an inexhaustible treasure against which the state monolith is ultimately powerless.

The unimportance of the individual in Marxist theory is translated in state Socialist economic policy into consumer and worker deprivation and the surveillance exercised by the state over consumers, workers, scientists, and plant managers. Production for society comes first; production for individual needs comes last. People serve the system instead of the other way around. The system exists for its own sake. The socialization of the means of production and distribution (that is, the placing of broad property rights in the hands of state bureaucrats) and the institutionalized impossibility of setting oneself up in business for oneself reduce the person to a cog in a centrally run machine. They deprive the system of grass-roots entrepreneurial skills, personal initiative, and inventiveness and encourage routine, aversion to risk, and stagnation in all but the state bureaucrats' top-priority sectors (mainly armaments). Because the system breaks down much of the time and, when it works, operates against the individual interest, the only way for the individual to survive and assert himself is for him to dissimulate, cheat, lie, bribe, and corrupt on the model of the all-powerful Socialist state. Official untruth becomes a component of popular culture. Because merely to make it through the twists and turns of the system's ethics people have to demean themselves and lose their self-respect, the class hatred postulated by Marx for pre-Socialist history emerges as individual loathing of the Socialist state.

Thus the Marxist blueprint of shifting truth, class hatred, and the submergence of the individual in the mass has helped spawn a state Socialist system lacking a humanly acceptable moral code and unable to cater to the legitimate material needs of millions of individuals over whom it exercises control. It takes Western leftist intellectuals a little time, but eventually they too come around to this view. Heberto Padilla, exiled from Cuba in 1980, concludes (after twenty years) that

the theoretical model proposed by Marx and Engels seems to me now a fatal determinism, as repugnant as the Absolute

Ideal of Hegel, which ended by sanctioning Napoleon and the Prussian state. The nineteenth-century socialist utopias now seem to me precursors of the forced labor camps and the Ideal City of Man in which the New Man was to be created. Their works seem to me now like luxuriant verbal constructions no less distant from reality than those of the socialist thinkers Georg Lukacs, Herbert Marcuse, and Theodor Adorno: empty scholasticism.[9]

Bureaucracy, the Institutional Foundation

Marxist ideas are not alone responsible for the crisis of state Socialist economies. The derivative proximate cause is the institutional structure of the state Socialist system: specifically, the planning and managerial bureaucracy.

The facts of the matter are these. Systemic economic objectives can be set and resources can be allocated to those objectives in only two ways: by free markets and by administrative command. The political purpose of Communist revolutions is to eliminate the existing political order and replace it with the dictatorship of the Communist party. The economic purpose is to abolish free-market relations and private property and replace them with administrative command and social property. State Socialist economies are administrative command economies on the model of the army. Information in the system is transmitted in the form of specific physical orders and state-set prices from the top bureaucrats (the planners) to lower-level administrative authorities, and allocative decisions made by these top bureaucrats are coordinated through the central physical and financial plan. The information and the plan are mandatory for the recipients. Markets are not supposed to play any significant role in the system (although in fact they do) and are to be eventually eliminated. The job of generating, transmitting, processing, and coordinating information within the system is done by administrators. As an economic system, not only does state socialism need bureaucracy, but it is bureaucracy. And many of the system's troubles flow directly from this fact. Debureaucratization of the system is possible only if competitive market relations are introduced, effective allocative decision making is taken out of the domain of the central planners and put in the hands of consumers and independent plant managers, and property rights are privatized (that is, extensive rights over the acquisition, use, and disposal of property are granted to the actual users of assets). Such economic decentralization means a change of the system. That is why it is unlikely that it will be undertaken in state

11

Socialist societies. Other decentralizations are administrative reshuffles that do not constitute systemic reform. Nor do they much affect the bureaucracy. While those who argue for more efficient centralization of state Socialist economies see relief from bureaucracy in computerization, they may be wrong.

Bureaucracy has been the subject of bitter complaint throughout state Socialist experience. Massive assaults have been made on it by, among others, Mao Zedong during the Cultural Revolution, but with little permanent effect. (In the late 1960s, Mao almost succeeded in destroying the bureaucracy without replacing it with markets. He thus effectively dismantled the economy.) Neither Marx nor Lenin ever fully grasped the absolute necessity of bureaucracy for socialism. On the contrary, they persisted in their conviction that bureaucratless socialism was not only possible but also inevitable. The size and increase of state Socialist bureaucracy have been staggering. China, which sets 800 material balances at the center (150 of them at the planning commission level), has 1,000 ministers and deputy ministers of the central government and 20 million administrative officials. The Soviet Union sets 2,000 material balances at the Gosplan level plus 17,000 balances entering the material technical supply network (Gossnab), and 40,000 balances at the all-union ministry echelon. Economic planning absorbs the energies of 700 administrative organs (including 100 central ministries) employing 12 million people in 1970, 14.2 million in 1971, and 15 million in 1972. This means that about 11 percent of the Soviet labor force works in the planning apparatus. These people do the work of the market—only not half as well.[10]

More specifically, the four major problems inherent in an economy run by clerks rather than by spontaneous market transactions are cost, absence of automatic sensors of social need, lack of innovation, and unresponsiveness of agriculture to bureaucratic control.

Cost of Information and Coordination. Ideally, the generation, transmittal, and analysis of economic information and the coordination of economic decisions should be costless. The more it costs to get information in usable form, the fewer will be the resources left for other purposes. Real-life market information and coordination, while not costless, are much cheaper than information produced, conveyed, processed, and coordinated by vast hordes of public administrators. The buyer and seller in a market transaction are not paid salaries for trading information about costs and utilities. The necessary information (and not more than is necessary) emerges from the respective offers to buy and sell, in the form of a multidimensional market price, which automatically coordinates the particular transaction with all other transactions in the market. In a system of administration the information is unidimensional, mostly about physical quantities backed by accounting price expressions. The producer is obliged to carry out the information command. The conflict between his particular interests and the order givers' (planners') interest remains unresolved. Almost inevitably the result distorts producer behavior: that is, the producer will carry out the order in the way that suits him best, which nine times out of ten is against society's interest. Therefore, both the provision of information and the carrying out of the planners' instructions have to be monitored by yet another army of clerks, who themselves have to be supervised by others. The key issue is the widespread absence of voluntary exchange relations within the system. Information is not diffused throughout the system so that buyers and sellers can adapt as they see fit and, by virtue of this adaptation, coordinate the flow of inputs and outputs: that is, inputs and outputs are not automatically coordinated through price, thereby resolving conflicting and divergent interests between the transacting parties and between individuals and society. Resolution of market conflicts is not perfect and has to be aided by the capitalist state's monetary and fiscal policy and contract enforcement, but such resolution is there for the asking. In state socialism economic information is a command—direct, specifically addressed, and unconditional. It reinforces conflicts of interest and resolves them in dialectical fashion by one side's (usually the producer) outwitting the other (the planner and consumer). Substandard and wrong goods and services are delivered to the state and to consumers as part of the normal functioning of the system, and for this plant managers get rewarded with bonuses.

Absence of Built-in Mechanism for Formulating Social Goals. The motto of state Socialist economies is not "from each according to his ability, to each according to his work," but "if the planners don't do it, it won't get done." The marketless state Socialist system lacks institutional means for revealing—automatically, spontaneously, and continuously—what needs to be done in society. In the system, society's objectives have to be formulated consciously, deliberately, and administratively by the political leadership speaking through the state planners, in effect by an unelected, self-perpetuating bureaucracy. Social goals are set manually at both the macro- and the microlevels by the elite and their clerks (in the case of most consumer goods, for example, consumer demand is brought into line with the plan-determined supply through state-set prices, rather than the

13

other way around). The enormous size of the undertaking makes it certain that the planners cannot do the whole job. They can, at best, concentrate on a narrow range of high-priority objectives (normally heavy industry and armaments production) and relegate the rest—with all the problems created by preempting the economy of key inputs—to happenstance. Allocative errors made by the planners because of faulty information and because the job is too big are resolved at the expense of consumers, in the lower-priority sectors, or are driven into the underground economy. The absence in the system of any institutional economic means whereby customer demand can manifest itself in any allocatively meaningful way greatly increases the probability of conflict between the individual and social interest. The customer has no direct influence on prices, nor are prices in the system intended to be the primary carriers of information to the supplier on customer wants and needs. The dogmatic assumption that the central planning bureaucracy knows better what is good for the individual than does the individual himself and that it can make better decisions for the producer than the producer would make himself in the pursuit of profit compounds the problem. Bureaucratic centralization is thus not just a device: it is a leading purpose of state socialism. The reverse side of centralization is the exclusion of the great majority of people from effective participation in the system. The system is deprived of the potential benefits of broad participation by the horror with which it views spontaneity, diversity, competition, and unplanned creativity. The result is ossification, routine, class differentiation, and widespread popular resentment.

Innovation. Bureaucracy thrives on routine. It is generally averse to risk, hierarchical, and wedded to the principle of referral of decisions through many overlapping established channels. Centralized bureaucracy of the state socialist type is intent on controlling all activities, innovation included. Innovative ideas are thus generated at the top in special research and development institutes and transmitted to lower echelons in the form of plans for technical progress. Because the bureaucracy also sets gross output performance as the primary criterion of managerial success, the plans for technical innovation are usually not translated into production at the grass-roots or are applied "formally," because applying the technical plan means stopping the production line for retooling, causing a loss of current output, and hence a loss of bonuses. Because the bureaucracy as a whole is evaluated and rewarded or punished primarily by reference to short-run output and other annual or shorter "success indica-

14

tors," near horizons and the execution of immediate tasks at hand become dominant. The systemic propensity to discount the more distant future leads to a wasteful use of resources, underemphasis on pure research, and a propensity to concentrate on rather narrow, highly applied innovation, when and if this clearly carries with it immediate payoffs.

Agriculture. The patently most adverse influence of bureaucracy is on agriculture. A survey of state Socialist agricultural experience from China to Cuba confirms the debilitating effect that central administrative command planning has on farm output and productivity.

Conclusion

The economic crisis of state socialism derives from the system's philosophical and institutional foundations: from the treatment of truth as an object of manipulation, the use of class hatred as the primary agent of social motivation, the relegation of the individual to nothingness, and the all-embracing bureaucracy. In the past decade the crisis has been contained largely because of huge financial aid from Western democratic governments and private banking interests. Indications are that this aid—unprecedented in its largesse—will continue.[11] In the absence of such aid, the probability is strong that the state Socialist economic system would collapse.

2
Socialist Economic Reform, Political Freedom, and Democracy

It is all very sad.
—Irving Kristol

The chapter explores the relationship between Socialist economic reform, which like the treadmill (to borrow from Gertrude Schroeder's famous phrase) has been in near perpetual motion ever since Stalin's death, and political freedom and democracy.

Definitions

Socialism. By "socialism" I understand to mean the ideas and institutions derived mainly from Marx and given practical expression by Lenin, Stalin, Mao, and other lesser nonbenevolent autocrats, which constitute the totalitarian polities and centrally planned economies of the world and which—ominously for their longer-term survival—have produced no culture of note, but rather a pauperization of the spirit.

Political Freedom. In the positive sense, "political freedom" means the vesting in the personally responsible individual and voluntary associations of individuals of the natural, inalienable rights of moral beings, among which are the right to speak out or keep silent, to assemble peacefully, to move at will, to enjoy privacy, to act upon the dictates of conscience, and to have equal justice under the law— not just any law, but a legal order. Political freedom includes the notion that governmental power is held in trust for the governed and that a government that breaches this trust may be replaced, while the trust endures[1]—"all that Western stuff," as Deng Xiaoping put it. "Justice," says Adam Smith in *The Theory of Moral Sentiments*

(1759), "is the main pillar that upholds the whole edifice. If it is removed, the great, the immense fabric of human society . . . must in a moment crumble into dust." In a negative sense, political freedom denies to the monoparty "vanguard elite" state the possibility of materializing Nietzsche's will to power, that is of concentrating in the state's innermost elite (often in one man) all rights, unrestrained by any bounds of propriety or any external force, be it "a Deity, or Natural Law, or some absolute system of morality."[2]

Democracy. I understand "democracy" to mean the institutionalization of political freedom in a secret-ballot, unrigged electoral contest of open alternatives on the basis of universal suffrage and in representative (majority) legislative and executive organs of government and in an independent judiciary. Implicit in this definition of democracy are the notion of legal order or the rule of law and that of a constraining external moral force (both being explicit in the definition of political freedom). Their presence works against the abuse of power by the duly elected majority and for respect by the majority of minority concerns voiced by a loyal opposition. According to this understanding of the terms, political freedom deals primarily with the micro-aspect of human rights, while democracy is concerned with the aggregative aspect. According to that same understanding, political freedom is a necessary but not a sufficient condition of democracy. There can be no democracy without political freedom, but there may be political freedom without democracy (as in pre-1997 Hong Kong). Moreover, Deng Xiaoping is right (although not in the way he intended it): both political freedom and democracy are at their origin "that Western stuff," but they can be, although they have not been extensively, practiced elsewhere.

The Socialist Economic System

The Socialist economic system was created by Lenin in the aftermath of the October *Putsch*. It was subsequently "perfected" by Stalin in Russia and by Mao in China. Its explanatory theory is Marxist (hinging on the normative labor theory of surplus value) with "creative" additions or extensions by Lenin, Stalin, Mao, and a lesser breed of subintellectuals: Castro, Hoxha, Ceausescu, and the elder Kim, among others. The system reflects Marx's consistent diminution of the individual, who can fulfill himself only through identification with the grand, dehumanized, impersonal sweep of history, to which he must adapt in a way preordained by historical materialism,[3] and Lenin's preoccupation with control and contempt for absolute moral

17

order and the rule of law—his "organic cancer of power," as Paul Johnson puts it.

Diminution of the individual human person, obsession with control (the "messy art of hanging on to power"), and contempt for moral and legal order translate into an economic system of consumer neglect, centralized administrative command involving a far-reaching demonetization of the economy, and frequent resort to "teleological" planning, that is, the setting of goals unconstrained by any objective conditions, laws of value, resource scarcities, factor endowments, levels of national income, and the like—ultravoluntaristic planning subject only to the rule of the planner's thumb (production "from the achieved level").[4] The relativism and arbitrariness that define the Socialist political sphere extend with undiminished force to the economy.

Problems of the Socialist System

The system is a failure. Specifically, it fails in four respects:

• It fails to provide people with increasing quantities and qualities of goods and services that the people want at prices they are prepared to pay; that is, the system is one of chronic shortages of both consumer and producer goods.[5]

• It fails to supply goods and services efficiently; that is, the system is statically inefficient: in plain language, monstrously wasteful.

• It fails to promote economic growth by improvements of factor productivity, such improvements being due primarily to technological and social innovation; that is, the system is dynamically inefficient. Much of what it produces qualifies as instant antiques.

• It fails to provide an automatic spontaneous mechanism that would reconcile individual and social preferences and transform individual strivings into socially beneficent outcomes. In capitalist economies such a mechanism is supplied by the competitive market. In the very process of imposing on one and all the preferences of the inner vanguard elite, the system creates antagonistic relationships within the economy that have to be bridged by force of *Diktat* or by bribery. A system of involuntary transactions is not meliorist: it does not leave those engaging in them better off. True to its Leninist origins, the system is a war game and a perpetual test of who will outwit whom: a system in permanent moral disequilibrium.

Just as the fourth failure is systemic, not accidental, or due to "wreckism," or vodka, or Radio Free Europe, or some other masochistic solipsism, so are the other three.

Shortages. Because all earthly economies are subject to scarcity of supply relative to demand (that is, goods are not free), an instrument of rationing or exclusion is needed. In a market economy people are excluded only by their ability and willingness to pay the going market price (the price at which supply and demand curves intersect): they are "priced out." The decision to buy or not to buy is theirs to make: it is vested in the potential individual user of the good. Socialist regimes do not like this. They want the exclusion decision to be made by the authorities (the vanguard elite) in accordance with criteria set by the authorities (differential access to goods according to class standing, for example, or positioning on the *nomenklatura* ladder). A sure way of transferring the exclusion decision from the potential buyer to the state is to create an artificial shortage of the good or goods in question (best of all, of all goods). This can be done by fixing (and enforcing) prices below market equilibrium levels, that is, below levels at which the price would just ration out the available supplies among potential users. At such below-equilibrium compulsory prices there is excess demand for the goods. This calls for nonprice rationing, which the state is glad to provide either through allocation certificates (distributed to potential users in accordance with the state's scale of values) or through the queue. In any event, by creating a shortage (or excess demand) on the way to the Communist *Überflussgesellschaft,* the state seizes control of who gets access to what goods and how much of them. The economic system, as has been said, becomes a machine for producing state control rather than goods for use. The economics of shortage is not fortuitous. It is deliberately built into the system. Access to goods becomes a privilege that the vanguard elite doles out according to its lights. In the process, powerful, privileged constituencies come into being, a Socialist *rentier* class, whose vested interests lie in opposing all real reform that would make access to goods a function of price, the individual's budget constraint, and his maximizing decision, rather than of loyalty to hierarchical superiors, political clout, cronyism, favoritism, and other Socialist nonprice criteria.[6] The planned shortage economy is demonetized in the sense that ability and willingness to pay money really do not matter much (except to buy officials, and even here a crate of fresh eggs will do the job better), since money is not readily convertible into goods. The system reverts to the primitive condition of barter carried on with the help of an elaborate, not to say Byzantine, and crooked web of personal-political connections *na levo.* Shoddy system, shoddy goods. The shoddiness of the goods is an unintended byproduct of input shortages married to ambitious output targets and of the

19

condition of excess demand itself: why bother about quality when the goods you produce will be snapped up whether they work or not? Another unintended consequence of the economics of shortage is the collapse of incentives for ordinary people. "A very curious thing occurs," says Jacobo Timmerman. "Everybody has a job and no one works." Milovan Djilas observes that the Socialist economy is "a non-market bureaucratic economy . . . where all real values, including the value of work, are lost." Zaslavskaya, one of Gorbachev's economic mentors, deplores the "conspicuous and general tendency to passivity."

Waste. Static inefficiency or waste bordering on the truly monumental is also a systemic defect. There are five causes. First, the volume and assortment of goods produced are not the volume and assortment that users would choose were they free and able to do so. The whole operation thus has a built in rejection factor. Second, because the economic system lacks a reliable automatic mechanism to indicate the opportunity cost of using resources in competing alternative uses, the system is allocatively rudderless. Allocation based on physical criteria, technical coefficients, and political prices is clumsy, costly, and incapable of solving the multitude of simultaneous equations that have to be solved to arrive at mere internal consistency of allocative decisions, never mind at optimality. Third, the problem is aggravated by the inaccuracy of much of the information circulating in the system (in a regime of commands it pays to dissimulate) and by the treatment of information by the vanguard elite as a state resource to be dispensed on the basis of planner-determined need to know. Fourth, the very narrow and restricted property rights the system grants to the actual users of assets contribute to waste. Nobody really bothers about costs (in fact, inflating costs may be one easy way to obtain the targeted gross output value), and nobody takes care of assets that belong to everybody and nobody and that everybody steals. Fifth, the chronic tautness of the plan encourages hoarding (high inventories or "hidden reserves") by firm managers.

Stagnant Innovation. Socialism's trouble with technological innovation, especially the application of innovation to the production process, has a number of system-related causes. Innovation requires a social climate favoring individual creativity and the assumption of risk. This is contrary to the spirit of the central plan, however, which demands conformity and avoidance of risk. As an idea, central planning locks society into a set pattern of behavior for the period of the plan, a pattern that militates against rapid adaptation to changing configurations of cost and usefulness and of technical-scientific developments abroad. Despite its intent to predict and mold the future—its alleged "progressiveness"—the plan is in practice a conservative instrument. This conservatism, inherent in planning, is reinforced by the technicalities of the plan, two of which should be noted. First, in the absence of a market mechanism, a state bureaucracy must set goals and allocate resources. Characteristically, this bureaucracy is anti-innovative and anti-entrepreneurial. Second, the use of material balances in planning compounds the problem: material balances are static with respect to technology. The input-output relations they express reflect the technological coefficients at the time at which the balances are constructed; the balances do not, by their very nature, indicate the dynamics of technical progress. The technological stasis implicit in the use of material balances as coordinating tools injects an anti-innovation bias into the system.

Another reason for socialism's technological inertia is that under the central plan, innovation—like much else—becomes an order from the planners. Now, there are three things wrong with this. One, innovation normally and naturally comes from below—from the inventive individual mind and the quick-on-its-feet small and medium-sized firm, not from ponderous committees of bureaucrats at the top. Two, the planners have been traditionally (and remain to this day) interested in output: the more of it the better. Innovation necessitates retooling, that is, time out from current output, and it is untried and risky. Lower echelons thus have every incentive not to innovate, because they rightly perceive the planners' subsidiary interest in the subject, or they innovate "formalistically" wherever specific innovation targets are set. Three, coming up with bright ideas is likely to earn one a reputation for insubordination. The plan demands fulfillment, not efforts at satisfying or anticipating user preferences. The rule of conduct is: "If it's not in the plan, don't do it."

How Bad Is It?

All this sounds bad. But how bad is it really? It may be argued that, although the Socialist system is not a consumers' paradise, people have put up with shortages for long periods of time and that after seventy years of socialism the Russians must certainly be used to it. A "sellers' market" mentality has taken root, some say, in much the same way as people have accepted political monopoly. Young Russians, for example, find it hard to understand why there should be more than one candidate for each position in an election.[7] Political scientists, especially, are prone to ask: "What is so important about efficiency?" Repeatedly, the bayonet has been quite effective at harmonizing divergent preferences, fear being a powerful coolant of the rage for freedom. True, while one can put people down with bayonets, one cannot sit on bayonets for any length of time; still the Soviet vanguard has been sitting on bayonets for quite awhile. "I won the Empire on horseback! Why should I bother with the Classics?" said the emperor. To this the scholar Lu replied: "You may have won it on horseback, but can you rule it on horseback?"[8] It seems one can indeed. Two fronts on which the Socialist economy is alert and progressive are eavesdropping and the military.[9] Such high-tech Leninism, however, does not extend to the planned civilian economy.

I agree with Birman that things are actually worse than they look and that in the absence of real reform they will continue to deteriorate at an accelerated pace.[10] Without structural remedies of ideas and institutions, the Socialist system of planned shortages will hit the threshold of tolerance at which morbidity sets in. Berliner has explored this question and there is no need to restate his argument beyond noting that systemic collapse is a distinct possibility.[11] People have been known to rise up and overthrow social arrangements that denied them material goods and to throw out ideas that disputed their right to be in charge of their lives. There is, however, another, less apocalyptic side to this matter. Without real reform, the Socialist countries, the Soviet Union at their head, will revert, through a process of competitive decadence, to third world status. This is difficult for the leaders to accept, and one may expect, therefore, that they will take action to stem the trend. This action, however, depends on first altering the past and present process of elite selection, which can be described as reverse Darwinism, or survival of the unfittest to rule. The question is currently being decided in Russia and China, and at this stage it is impossible to predict whether brains, talent, and the open mind will assert themselves over concentrated stupidity.

What Is to Be Done?

If under popular pressure from below, or through a social Darwinist counterattack, it comes to be decided that the economic failures of socialism are sufficiently serious to be dealt with forthwith (and apparently such a decision is in the process of being made, except perhaps in Laos), the remedy must go beyond the usual tinkering with the system, beyond adjustment to real reform. Birman puts it well: "Some say that the economy has huge reserves. . . . It is very true that the economy is extremely inefficient, and that in this sense it has colossal reserves. But to use the reserves you need another economic system."[12]

What is this other system? We are concerned not with hypothetical, imaginary, utopian constructs, but with real-life systems that can effectively address the four failings of socialism. That being the case, electronic ultracentralization, the computer-based mathematically modeled pure dictatorship is out. In the 1970s there was an illusion about its feasibility in Eastern Europe, particularly in Hungary and Poland, and a lot of computer hardware and software was imported from the West without any tangible mitigation of the four failings but with an astronomical accumulation of hard currency debt.

The in-between solution of neither-plan-nor-market, half-plan-half-market, or market socialism does not work either. This has been hotly disputed by some Western academic economists of the Lange-Lerner tradition, but today even the Soviets are having second thoughts about it. Larissa Popkova (*Novy Mir*, May 1987) writes:

> Socialism . . . is incompatible with the market by its nature, by the intentions of its founders, and by the instinct of those who have deliberately implemented and continue to implement the appropriate principles and usages. . . . There is no third option. One cannot be just a little bit pregnant. Either plan or market, either directive or competition. It is possible to seek and apply something in the middle, but there should be no expectation of successful balancing on two stools.

She speaks of the "illusory idea of 'market socialism.'" For her "this collocation is an absurdity. Wherever there is socialism, there is not, and I repeat there cannot be any place for market or liberal spirit. . . . Socialism is incompatible with the market."[13] (It is not altogether clear whether Popkova supports the market system solution or socialism, but she does make a forceful statement against *Kathedersozialismus* and other halfway professorial constructs.)

The Market System

Since perfect electronic centralization is technically and humanly impossible and market socialism is an academic illusion, the only way for socialism to deal with its four economic failings is to yield to the market system. This idea, once considered absurd, is less shocking today than it was ten years ago when the Chinese on the mainland began flirting with it.

The two institutional pillars of the market system are transactions and property rights. Market transactions are voluntary, competitive, horizontal (symmetrical) legally binding contracts entered into by individual buyers and sellers for utility and profit-maximizing purposes, by reference to market prices, through the disbursement of money votes. Property rights give individuals broad rights to the acquisition and disposal of goods and services (transfer), to the employment of such goods and services (use), and to the fruits of the goods and services (income). The role of government in this system of transactions and property rights is twofold: laissez faire, in the original sense of letting buyers and sellers alone (capitalism is what people do when left alone) and intervening in support of market transactions and private property rights by ensuring that rules of contract (voluntariness, competition, symmetry) are observed; by providing domestic order and protection against external threats; by compensating for market failures (externalities, public goods, and taking care of people who cannot take care of themselves, for instance); by perceiving and encouraging the longer-range developmental and growth perspective (through encouragement of research and development and comparative advantage, for example); and by safeguarding private property rights. Contrary to a common view, government in the market system is not absent, nor is it passive; it is interventionist in the cause of the market—sometimes highly so. It should be noted that private property rights, in the sense stated above, are an indispensable organic part of the market system, as the Chinese are beginning to find out. No market system is "pure" in either the voluntary-competitive-horizontal transactions or the private property sense. But voluntary, competitive, and horizontal transactions and private property rights must clearly dominate the system, and governmental intervention must promote, not hinder or suppress them.

Notice the ideas that undergird these institutional arrangements. They are the idea of free association (voluntariness); of equal access, free exit, and opportunity at the start (competition); of cooperation (in the market every act of competition is also an act of cooperation under the division of labor); of nonhierarchical relations (symmetry of transactions); of individualism (decision making by individual buyers and sellers, and broad property rights vested in individuals); and of personal responsibility (personal assumption of risk, accountability for losses, and reaping of benefits). Market relations are rendered objective by the cash nexus, rather than being subjective—that

24

is, based on loyalty to one's hierarchical superiors, personal-political duties and obligations, backdoor connections, *guanxi, blat,* and other nonprice links. The market system, in short, is a system of economic freedom.

The Market System, Political Freedom, and Democracy

The ideas and institutions of the market system are similar to and dovetail with the notion of political freedom examined earlier, and political freedom, as we have seen, is a precondition of democracy. The market system is a necessary condition of political freedom, but it is not a sufficient condition. A market system can coexist with authoritarianisms of various sorts (but not with Socialist totalitarianism), but the coexistence is uneasy: it is a state of ideological, institutional, psychological, and moral disequilibrium that sooner or later has to be righted. In recent years, for example, Taiwan and South Korea (both market economies) have moved in the direction of expanded political freedom and emerging democracy. Singapore, in contrast, appears to be moving in the other direction, strengthening authoritarian rule. On the one hand, the presence of a market system (economic freedom) exerts a strong influence in favor of political freedom, but it does not guarantee the outcome. On the other hand, there can be no political freedom (hence no democracy) if the economic system is one of central administrative command planning (socialism). The two are mutually exclusive.

Socialism, the Market System, Political Freedom, and Democracy

No Socialist country to date has crossed the systemic border and adopted a market system: not Hungary, not Yugoslavia—no one. Some Socialist countries (China in deed and the Soviet Union in words) have grafted individual markets and discreetly expanded private property rights onto the body of the plan. Like importing Western computers without importing Western freedom of information, these transplants have not worked. They have not lessened, much less eliminated, the plan's four failures. The plan remains everywhere a clumsy wartime economy in peacetime. Because, erroneously, these grafts have been identified by the grafters as "reforms" and whereas they are, in fact, mere repairs and replacements of the more dysfunctional parts of the planning machine ("adjustments"), they have given reform a bad name (although at least the Gdansk shipyard workers recognize it for the fraud it is). So, as always, the chances of reversal are strong.

25

The hesitation of the vanguard elite to make a bold transition to the market system is due to many causes, among which the intuitive understanding of the logical connection between the market system and political freedom and ultimately "bourgeois" democracy (that is, real democracy) is very important. The Chinese, who since 1978 have gone farthest down the road of marketization and privatization, made some attempts at "democratization" of the monopoly party, but none of substance. Their economic system remains planned (especially outside agriculture), and so political freedom, while greater than zero, is not a serious possibility. Under Gorbachev the Soviets have approached the problem from the side of politics.

A school of thought in Eastern Europe and the Soviet Union resolves the old question of "which came first, the chicken or the egg?" by opting for the political egg that Gorbachev must lay before marketization and privatization of the economic system are possible:

> The extreme étatization of the economy and social life [writes Tadeusz Kowalik] destroyed independent social organizations, independent centers of social activity and initiative. . . . Without radical limitation of the state and without restoration of independence and spontaneity in social life, without some degree of pluralism, official and recognized by law, there is no chance for normal interaction of society with the authorities, there is no climate for rational social action on a variety of techniques.[14]

Gorbachev talks about modification and "perfection" of the political superstructure (*politicheskaya nadstroika*) in order to make the *"perestroika"* of the material productive forces (the base) possible. "Socialist pluralism," however, according to Bogomolov, "is not the notorious 'free play' of political forces, but an expansion of the platform of national unity under the leading role of the party."[15] It is not political freedom and cannot contribute to the emergence of a market system that would effectively deal with the four failures. Going at the problem from the side of economics is difficult enough. Tackling it with *glasnost* makes it almost certain that the attempt will fail.

Prognosis

In the circumstances, the prognosis is not optimistic. Since "socialism cannot be reformed without being abandoned,"[16] and given the undiminished will to power of the vanguard elite of the monocratic party, the chances of real reform from the side of economics are very slim, and the chances of reform from the side of politics are practically nil. That is to say, there is little if any likelihood that economic freedom, political freedom, and democracy will emerge as a result of reformist measures undertaken by those now in power. Tinkering with the system notwithstanding, the shortage, inefficiency, and repressed antagonism will persist and probably grow worse. The Socialist countries will thus slide into third world status. Alternatively or concurrently, reform could be thrust on the elite by popular uprisings with all the attendant worldwide tremors that a violent systemic dissolution implies.

Death from decay or by revolution can be postponed, however, and the "thievocracies" can continue to muddle along if not through, if the world's capitalists, democratic governments, and progressive intellectuals rally to socialism's aid: the first with money, the second with blessings (including credit insurance), the third with remedial ideas. Such help, given from a variety of motives (greed, détente, intellectual investment in the Socialist experiment), is the one certain thing in an otherwise uncertain world. West German banks, for instance, are in the forefront of this rescue effort, but they are not alone. Dwayne O. Andreas, the chairman and chief executive officer of Archer-Daniels-Midland Co., the world's largest processor of farm commodities, says that the late President Dwight D. Eisenhower once advised him, "Sell the Russians anything they can't shoot back." "My feeling is," says Mr. Andreas, "Gorbachev's main interest as a human being is agriculture. . . . When he talks about how to raise more chickens, he's on the edge of his chair, he's excited."[17]

It *is* all very sad.

3

The Relationship between the Fifth Modernization and the Other Four in China

The slogan "Four Modernizations" is part of the Chinese Communist glossary of easy-to-remember terms in the political arithmetic of social engineering. Other arithmetically phrased slogans have included at different times such encapsulators of mass campaigns as the Three-Anti, The Five-Anti, and the Three Great Banners; guides to Socialist ethics like the Four Points of Study and the Five Good; and synthesizers of fundamentals such as the Four Basic Principles. Benign by comparison with most of the others, the Four Modernizations refer to the updating and upgrading of agriculture, industry, science and technology, and national defense. In essence economic, they signal a shift of official emphasis from apocalyptic political transformation to more moderately paced, longer-term economic change.

The Four Modernizations

The origin of the concept of the Four Modernizations is traceable to Zhou Enlai's report to the Fourth National People's Congress in January 1975 and the translation of the modernization idea into national policy by Deng Xiaoping beginning with the Third Plenary Session of the Communist party's Eleventh Central Committee in December 1978. For reasons of ideological continuity and legitimacy, the notion of Socialist economic modernization has been attributed to the "good" Mao, specifically to his report "On the Ten Major Relationships," which predates the "bad" Mao's Three Red Banners of 1958 (popularly known as the Great Leap Forward). Empirically,

28

the Four Modernizations mirror the concerns of the "pragmatic" (as against the "ideologue") faction within China's Communist leadership that influenced policy after periods of Mao-engineered calamity, as in 1961 and 1975.

Several facts about the Four Modernizations have emerged. They are, arranged in rank order: agriculture first and national defense last; the acquisition of science and technology is pursued, at this stage, primarily through the "open door" of foreign (mainly capitalist) trade and investment; and—certainly in agriculture, less clearly in industry—modernization involves not just institutional changes but some structural alterations as well.

The Fifth Modernization

On December 5, 1978, Wei Jingsheng—the son of a Communist party official, one-time Red Guard, sometime electrician with the Beijing zoo—put up a big character poster on Beijing Democracy Wall, in which he said in part: "If we want to modernize our economy and science and defense and the like, we must first modernize our people. We must first modernize our social system." By modernization of the social system he meant the introduction of democracy.

> Is it true to say that if democratic rights were granted to the people, there would be a danger of falling into disorder and anarchy? On the contrary, newspapers in our country recently exposed all the scandalous abuses that our despots, large and small, could perpetrate precisely because we have no democracy– *that* is the real disorder, the *real* anarchy!

Wei's poster reveals that while its author did not have a textbook-perfect idea of democracy, he did have an intuitive knowledge of what freedom is and what democracy means. (The only slip is his contention that democratic rights should be "granted" to the people. By whom? The government? But it is the people as individuals who naturally possess those rights and, through voluntary agreement, delegate some of these rights in trust to the government.)

So that his understanding of the concept of democracy and of the relationship between democracy and the Four Modernizations could be rectified and his insolence in questioning the probity of the officials representing the vanguard elite could be disciplined, Wei Jingsheng was put in solitary confinement and was twice admitted to a Beijing hospital for Soviet-style "psychiatric treatment." He was then banished to a "labor reeducation" camp in Qinghai. According to Amnesty International, he had been suffering from kidney and heart ailments and had lost all his teeth as a result of "his conditions of imprisonment in Beijing during the first years of his imprisonment and the lack of medical care afterward."[1] On November 14, 1987, the *New York Times* wrote that "Wei Jingsheng . . . is reported to have died in prison while serving a 15-year sentence for 'counterrevolutionary crimes.'" On December 30, 1986, in a talk with leading members of the Central Committee, Deng Xiaoping said: "A few years ago we punished according to law some exponents of liberalization who broke the law. Did that bring discredit on us? No, China's image was not damaged. On the contrary, the prestige of our country is steadily growing."[2]

The Party, too, recognizes that modernization of the social system is necessary. The documents of the Thirteenth Congress (October–November 1987 issued at the time of the report of Wei Jingsheng's death) say that "without reform of the political structure, reform of the economic structure cannot succeed in the end." The political changes envisaged by the Party, however, are a far cry from the democracy Wei had in mind.

All this raises some interesting issues. The first concerns the meaning of economic modernization; the second, the meaning of democracy; and the third, the relationship between economic modernization and democracy. Although directly relevant to mainland China's five modernizations, these issues transcend China and apply to all Socialist attempts at economic and political modernization.

Economic Modernization

An economic system can be called modern when it satisfies the following general conditions:

• It provides increasing quantities and improving quality of goods and services that people actually want at prices they are prepared to pay. It is a system of plentiful supply that caters to the final user.

• The system makes useful supply available. The goods and services supplied are actually used, not wasted. The system is allocatively efficient.

• In the system output grows quantitatively and qualitatively, primarily through improvement in the performance of factors of production brought about by a constant flow and unhindered diffusion of technical and social innovation.

• The system maximizes the use of voluntary agreement in organizing social activity,[3] and minimizes coercion (or maximizes freedom from government).

The two leading principles of a modern system are the centrality of the individual and the freedom of individual choice. The system's purpose is to maximize the individual's material welfare and his social welfare through efficient use of resources and efficient growth. Both the two ends (more and better consumer goods, and free social activity) and the two means (efficient allocation and improved productivity) require that broad property rights to the acquisition, disposal, use, and income from goods and services be vested in the individual.

The fulfillment of the four conditions of modernity based on the two principles of individualism and freedom of choice constitutes a regime of economic freedom. A regime of economic freedom can be brought about only by a workably competitive market system equipped with extensive rights of private property. The market system is a web of voluntary, contractual, competitive, horizontal transactions carried out by autonomous, property-owning individuals, who buy and sell to increase utility or make profit. The principles of the system, which originated in the Anglo-Scottish Enlightenment of the eighteenth century, have been embodied in institutions that grew and matured in Western Europe and North America from the eighteenth century through the twentieth.[4] Both the principles and the institutions are middle-class, bourgeois creations. They contain, in their very core, the notions of rule of law and of a constraining external absolute moral force of which compassion is an important ingredient. The rule of law, which Adam Smith sees as "the main pillar that upholds the whole edifice," rests on the notion that governmental power is a trust from the governed and that if the trust is violated, the government may be replaced while the trust endures.[5] Limits on the coercive powers of the state are a key issue here. The doctrine of laissez faire does not exclude government intervention in the market. The market is subject to failures, as in the provision of public goods. That the legitimate functions of government in a market system can be quite extensive is illustrated by the economic history of most post–World War II Western European countries. It is essential, however, that government intervention support the market, not fetter it. This condition does not preclude some modification of market outcomes (for instance, in income distribution where the disparities are morally untenable and politically explosive). Strong restraints, however, have to be imposed on the taking power of government, for "when the state by punitive taxation perverts the reward system of an economy, it also weakens its capacity to adapt, to innovate, and to learn by trial and error."[6] The constraining absolute moral force works through conscience: "this judge within" deriving, in Smith's words, from "that wisdom which contrived the system of human affections as well as that of every other part of nature."[7]

Not only is the market system of economic freedom thus Western and middle class but also it requires for its proper functioning an ethic rooted in the Judeo-Christian tradition, more specifically in the tradition's Protestant manifestation.[8] That requirement does not make the system easily exportable despite its manifest material success. That it can, in fact, be exported and adapted to different cultural configurations without injury to the recipient societies' spiritual identity is shown by its healthy growth in Japan, Taiwan, South Korea, Hong Kong, and Singapore. The market system, says Peter Berger, has the

> capacity to adapt to different cultural contexts and indeed to survive sometimes remarkable cultural decadence. . . . This autonomous functioning is precisely one great advantage of capitalism over its rival systems: it is at least relatively "foolproof," because the market corrects the actions of fools much more reliably than any planning mechanism.[9]

When, however, traditional obstacles to the implanting of the market system combine with the ideology and institutions of Marxism-Leninism, adoption and adaptation become impossible.

The Socialist system of central administrative command planning—of which the mainland Chinese economy is an example—fails to satisfy the four conditions of economic modernization. The failure is rooted in the principles and institutions of the system.

The system is one of chronic shortage.[10] The shortage is deliberately created as a means of transferring decision-making power from potential individual users to the state.[11] In the *Cancer Ward* the cancer-stricken Kostoglotov sums it up: "And once again I become a grain of sand, just as I was in the camp. Once again nothing *depends* on me." In the best Socialist economy, East Germany, the waiting time for cars is typically five years, and widows can inherit a place in line formerly occupied by husbands who died waiting.[12] In the worst, North Korea, the consumer goods on display in Pyongyang's top department store are not for sale.[13] In between, in Romania food sales have stagnated in the four years 1985–1988 despite a 2 percent increase in population.[14]

The system is impressively wasteful. Given the allocative irrationality of political prices, the extent of the waste (in opportunity cost) cannot be easily quantified, but it visibly exists.[15] At the end of the 1970s an estimated one-third to one-half of the rural workers in China (100 million–150 million people) were unnecessarily employed in agriculture and should have been more productively put to work elsewhere—"a frightening misutilization of manpower in the countryside," as one French agricultural specialist put it.[16] Chinese "factories now have made 20 million watches, 7 million electric fans, and 10 million bicycles so badly that they cannot be sold even to the unpernickety Chinese."[17] In Czechoslovakia, according to Prime Minister Strougal, "Useless output in 1986 and 1987 came to $3.5 billion": more than the total growth of national income over those two years. In his speech to the special Party conference in June 1988, General Secretary Mikhail Gorbachev complained that Soviet "enterprises are being compelled by means of state orders to manufacture goods that are not in demand."[18] Several systemic reasons account for this enormous waste, three of which might be mentioned. First, the system is anchored in Marx's labor theory of surplus value. While this theory offers a normative (and inaccurate) explanation of why revolutions occur, it is of no help at all in allocating resources rationally. Second, allocating resources consistently and most advantageously is not possible if the job is controlled from the center, even an administratively decentralized center. The task is simply too big and too complex, and the technology to do it is not there. Third, the concentration of property rights in the state's bureaucracy raises transaction costs and causes rigidities, inefficiencies, and neglect of the proper upkeep of assets. Vesting the bulk of property rights in the state is the antithesis of "that wisdom" that Smith speaks of, "which . . . seems to have judged that the interests of the great society of mankind would be best promoted by directing the principal attention of each individual to that particular portion of it which was most within the sphere of both his abilities and of his understanding."[19]

The greater part by far of Socialist economic growth (not the same as the creation of wealth) can be attributed to the addition of factors and use of known technology, rather than to improvement in the performance of factors through the application of technological and social innovation. In China total factor productivity declined between 1957 and 1982 at an annual rate of 1.1 percent.[20] "Scientific research is divorced from research in China," says Ouyang Jianfe, the country's first Ph.D. in precision engineering. "For example, in this University [Tianjin] there's a lot of advanced scientific and technological projects, but after these projects are finished, they're just put away. Nobody uses them."[21] Beginning in the 1970s, despite large-scale importation of Western technology, steep reductions of labor productivity occurred in all East European Socialist countries.

The stagnation of inventiveness and the difficulty experienced by all Socialist economies in translating such innovation into civilian products are rooted in the all-embracing interpretation given to the notion of confidentiality and the consequent compartmentalization of information in the system. Different hierarchical levels have access to different amounts and kinds of information. There are, so to speak, little Berlin walls splitting apart the body of knowledge. The system operates on the prescriptive principle: only that information is released which the appropriate party authority specifically declares to be fit for release—everything else is, by definition, a state secret. The empty spaces left by the dearth of factual information on all facets of reality are filled by rumor. The rationing of information, like the rationing of goods, is a weapon in the ruling elite's drive for total control. It represents the practical application of the doctrinal conviction that someone other than the individual knows best. Innovation is further obstructed by the system's asymmetrical and highly politicized links among economic agents. Asymmetrical relations are based on constraint; they are relations of domination and submission where the qualities demanded of subordinates by superiors are those of obedience and submission. Each echelon is evaluated according to its allegiance to its bureaucratic superiors rather than by the quality of its performance in supplying useful goods to users and coming up with novel ideas for more and better goods. As Arthur Koestler has written, "There has never perhaps been a society in which a rigid hierarchical order so completely determined every citizen's station in life and governed all his activities."[22] Individual creativity and departures from the set norm are equated with disobedience and insubordination. The system encourages what Zaslavskaya calls a "conspicuous and general tendency to passivity."[23] It rewards risk avoidance, routine, and sycophancy—qualities not in tune with the creative impulse. Like the making of bricks, inventiveness and entrepreneurship are subject to the prescriptive rule: they are planned from on high, and what is not specifically prescribed by the plan is not done, or is done on the sly and diverted into sterile, redistributive, underground channels.

Most obvious is the absence of the principle of voluntariness. This results in chronic adversary relationships between order givers and order receivers (accentuated by shortages), prompting massive evasions, the forwarding of falsified information from the base up, cronyism, cynicism, and corruption. Writing in the June 1988 issue of *Novy Mir* in the era of *glasnost*, Vasily Selyunin warns that unless radical changes are made in the Soviet economy by the mid-1990s, the Soviets face the very real possibility of reversion to classical central planning of the guns-and-goons variety, in which case "the economy would fall apart with all the consequences flowing from that—social, foreign policy, military, and so on. It will be too late then to talk about democracy."[24]

The failure of the Socialist economic system to satisfy the four conditions of modernity resolves into a failure of ends and a failure of means. The ends are retrograde: on the way to his ultimate self-realization in utopian communism, the individual is relegated to last place; he is a residual of the collectivity. The purpose of the economic system is not the progressively greater and better satisfaction of individually formulated material wants but state control and the interests of the state producer. To that end, individual preferences are given no institutional way of manifesting themselves in the system, except by ruse and in violation of the rules. Nor is the purpose of the system the social fulfillment of the individual through voluntary association. All the attributes of the market system—voluntary transactions; the freedom of individuals to use their own knowledge for their own purposes, with everyone's benefiting from the knowledge others possess; improvement of everyone's opportunities; the reconciliation of the claims of different noneconomic ends without an agreement on the relative importance of those ends—are replaced by the principle of coercion, rank ordering of imposed ends, monopoly of information, and bureaucrat-to-bureaucrat links.[25] The market's generalized cash nexus with its "democratic"[26] assumption of self-interest is replaced by hierarchical relations, personal and political loyalties, administrative power fiefdoms, and a web of neofeudal social compacts. Central control, elitism, and social class consciousness designate the system as a direct descendant of the despotisms and autocracies of the past.

The failure of means consists in the advanced demonetization of the economy—a partial return to barter in both internal and international relations (in all Socialist economies the domestic currency is not readily convertible into wanted goods; nor is it, partly for that reason, convertible into non-Socialist hard currencies)—and in the use of clumsy, unidimensional, physical, engineering-oriented allocation mechanisms (for example, material balances, material-technical supply networks for key inputs, and of administered, inflexible prices) as the principal means of information and coordination in the system. Looked at another way, the system avoids spontaneity and relies on the illusion of conscious central planning. The uncertainty always inherent in the process of economizing is vastly increased.

Because perfect electronic centralization of planning is not technically feasible now, the only way for the Socialist economic system to overcome its four failures is to move in the opposite direction—the decentralizing direction of the market system. For various under-standable reasons, the reformers have been quite reluctant to carry reform through to its logical conclusion: that is, to abandon central planning and adopt the market system. Instead, they have opted for the continued leading role of planning and socialized property rights, but with a dash of markets and a whiff of private property rights.

From the standpoint of ends and means, this adjustment consists in the partial and selective use of market microtechniques and indi-rect financial macrocontrols accompanied by a discreet, strictly lim-ited privatization of property rights. Individual prices, for example, are raised where they are obviously out of line with production costs, but all prices are not freed. Rights of land use (as in China) are granted to farm families, but restrictions control the transfer of land, its size, the number of hired hands that can be employed on it, and the family's right to income from the land. To combat lethargy and ossification, Chinese planners have redefined official ends slightly more in favor of individual consumption and have loosened up on coercion somewhat. The principal intent is to improve efficiency through the incorporation of market and private property elements to achieve basically unchanged Socialist ends, among which control remains the most important.

This will not do. It will not work:

> After more than 70 years of believing themselves to be the vanguard of history, communists the world over are slowly waking up to the bitter reality that they are bringing up the rear. . . . Everywhere, communists are facing a chal-lenge to their Marx–Lenin–given right to rule. Several par-ties have started ditching the dottier economic theories of Marx. None has yet dared to debunk the political theories of Lenin. Unless they do, communism is for the scrap-heap. But, without Lenin, what is communism anyway?[27]

Even in its most advanced form of "market socialism," the pro-posed remedy of grafting selected and "pasteurized" elements of the market and private property rights onto the calcified body of the plan, is defective theoretically and has little to show for itself in practice (see, for example, Hungary and, at times, Yugoslavia).[28] Market institutions are incompatible with plan institutions, however, and market philosophies with plan philosophies. For the arrange-ment to be internally consistent, one or the other (market or plan) has to be clearly dominant.[29] The point had been made long ago by von Mises, and it is being increasingly understood these days in, of all places, the USSR.[30]

The problem facing the Socialist reformers, then, is that an effective solution to the four failures cannot be found on the way to the market and that to become modern the Socialist economic system must deny itself. This revelation is extremely difficult for the Communist vanguard elite to accept because of its implications for political culture, as we shall see.

Democracy

Democracy is institutionalized political freedom. Political freedom has to do with individual human rights. Democracy translates those rights into the nuts and bolts of political governance.

In a regime of political freedom as a matter of fundamental principle the personally responsible and accountable individual human being possesses natural ("God-given"), inalienable rights, among which are the right to speak out, keep silent, and be left alone; to assemble peacefully and organize; to move at will; to enjoy privacy; to act upon the dictates of conscience ("this judge within"); and to have equal justice under the rule of law. Individual responsibility and accountability for freely made decisions and the posited moral sense of the individual exercising his natural human rights safeguard the rights of others and help prevent individual freedom from degenerating into anarchy or dictatorship.

Democracy is the institutionalization of political freedom in a secret-ballot, unrigged electoral contest of open alternatives on the basis of universal suffrage, one-adult person one-vote, and in representative (majority) legislative and executive, and independent judicial organs of government subject to the rule of law and to a constraining external moral force (both implicit in the notion of political freedom). Democracy includes not merely the toleration of organized dissent from majority positions but the institutionalization of and respect for the loyal opposition, and a pervasive sense of fair play translated into political conduct. In this sense democracy is political modernity.

As has been argued earlier, it is possible for political freedom to exist without democracy. In other words, political freedom, while it is a necessary condition of democracy, is not by itself a sufficient condition. The coexistence of political freedom with a system of governance that falls short of democracy, however, represents a state of disequilibrium that sooner or later has to be attended to.

Economic and Political Modernization

Economic modernization, for China as for other members of the Socialist centrally planned system, requires transition to the market system, and nothing short of it:

> Not only is there an organic connection—a connection in both theory and fact—between modern capitalism [the market system] and liberal society; such a connection is also to be found between modern capitalism and modern democracy, especially American democracy. . . . Though, in the abstract, capitalism may be regarded as one thing and democracy as another, *modern* democracy—a democracy in which the individual is actually encouraged to satisfy his desires and appetites, even as he multiplies them—is incomprehensible without its capitalist underpinnings.[31]

In fact, the ideas that undergird the institutions of the market system are almost identical with those that constitute the foundations of democracy. Just as there can be no market system without private property rights, so there can be no political modernity—no democracy—without the market system. The market system is a necessary condition of democracy. For society as a whole to become modern, the market system and democracy must be conjoined.

A necessary condition, however, is not therefore a sufficient condition. A society can conceivably be economically modern but politically obsolete: that is, an authoritarian government can combine with a market economic system. Such a combination, though not uncommon, is philosophically and institutionally unstable and, in the long run, untenable. In these circumstances the economic system will exert strong forces in favor of democratization of the political order, while vigorous pressures on the freedom of economic enterprise will come from the nondemocratic polity. Sooner or later society's disequilibrium has to be corrected, either through the centralized planning and socialization of the economy or through the democratization of politics. Deterministic predictions aside, chances are that the market argument will prevail because failure to keep and develop the market system will ultimately reduce any political power to irrelevance. On the scale of human values, while the economic argument may not be the most important, it is the single most powerful. In short, once the market system is in place, protected and encouraged by even a nondemocratic political system, it will tend to permeate the political realm with its ideas of freedom and its "democratic" assumptions, eventually weaning away that realm from authoritarianism.

Although it is possible for a full-fledged market system to coexist, albeit uncomfortably and temporarily, with an authoritarian one-party political system, the combination of a full-fledged market system and a totalitarian polity is impossible. The two are mutually exclusive.

Many, but not all, democrats and an increasing number of totalitarians understand this. The Thirteenth Chinese Communist Party Congress (October–November 1987) recognized that "without reform of the political structure, reform of the economic structure cannot succeed in the end."[32] China has reached a critical juncture in its evolution toward a "commodity" (market) economy, where further advance is barred by the totalitarian political system designed to suppress such an economy. To say that the market system will emerge by itself if only people are left alone is not quite true. Although scattered market-type transactions will surely appear openly, for the market system to emerge and take root, laws have to be enacted and observed, asserting the legitimacy and inviolability of private property and of individual economic freedom as a matter of principle rather than expediency. This consequence requires political action, a change in the political system. Even the more reactionary totalitarians, like those of Czechoslovakia, seem to grasp this. With considerable poetic license the chief adviser to the Czechoslovak prime minister notes that "we [the Communists who suppressed the 1968 Prague Spring] have always emphasized that without political change there can be no economic change."[33] If we abstract from the peculiar meaning attached to the notion of "change," we see that the sequence of change in the reactionary totalitarians derives here, as elsewhere in Eastern Europe, from Gorbachev and the Soviets rather than from Deng and the Chinese: political change comes before economic change.

What meaning does the vanguard elite in charge of "restructuring" attach to economic change and to political change?

Economic Change

Nowhere, China included, does economic change entail the total abandonment of central administrative command planning and its replacement by the market system. Instead, as the Thirteenth Party Congress stated, it means the creation of a "socialist planned commodity economy . . . that integrates planning with the market . . . [and is] based on public ownership. . . . Under the new economic mechanism, 'the state regulates the market and the market guides enterprises.' . . . The key to realizing this goal is to change the highly centralized planning system and make effective use of the market."[34] In short, the intent is to exploit some market techniques to make central planning produce goods more efficiently. The intent is not, however—if official pronouncements are to be believed—to achieve this improvement in the only way possible, through the transubstantiation of the planning system into the market system. "While we will import advanced technology and other things useful to us from the capitalist countries—selectively and according to plan—we will never learn from or import the capitalist system itself, nor anything repellent or decadent," says Deng Xiaoping.[35] At the boldest, what is proposed is movement toward market socialism of the Hungarian type and the former Yugoslav type—a theoretical and practical mistake. Hungarian economists have been highly critical of the neither-plan-nor-market, half-market-half-plan, or so-called market-Socialist solution. It is true that it has reduced consumer costs compared with those monumental ones normal in other Socialist economies, but it has created other severe problems (including a huge hard currency debt) and has hardly touched, where it has not exacerbated, static and dynamic inefficiencies. Neither has it removed commandism, now going by the name of ministerial "advice" and "recommendation."[36] Most blueprints for economic change, however, stop far short of the halfway mark. After a burst of marketizing and privatizing activity in agriculture, China's economic changes have slowed on the crucial issue of reform of the industrial price system. Without a reform (that is, liberation) of the price system as a whole, the changes made so far in the economic mechanism will not overcome socialism's four failures, and the chances of stagnation and eventual retrogression to central administrative command planning remain very real.

In China (unlike in the USSR) the rapid proliferation of local cooperative and private industries outside the planned sector has reduced shortages; the supply of agricultural products has increased significantly through the de facto privatization of rural production and far-reaching marketization of distribution, including fairly advanced marketization of the agricultural price system; cooperative and private services and retail marketing have expanded in urban areas; and the industrial price system has moved toward marketization. Two- or three-tier pricing exists for both agricultural and nonagricultural goods, with free or quasi-free prices being a more important component in agriculture than outside it. The expansion of industrial and service activities outside the mandatorily planned sphere represents a de facto privatization of property rights through both the rise of private, joint venture, and cooperative businesses and the

40

vesting in local government authorities of fairly broad rights to the acquisition, use, and disposal of and income from assets under their control. Food and other prices have risen to within shelf-clearing levels, and many queues have disappeared. Partly because of the incomplete transition to the market system and especially to more widespread rational pricing, however, recurrent shortages of many key consumer and producer goods and services persist in such critical sectors as housing, energy, and transportation; waste and inefficient use of resources continue on a large scale; and factor productivity remains a problem. In addition to the continued presence of large, strategic areas of command planning, informal, corrupt commandism by local officials has surfaced; they extract bribes and other "fees" from the private sector and, in return for "gratuities" from collective industries, supply these with hard-to-come-by inputs through networks of personal and political connections. As Edward A. Gargan in the *New York Times* put it, quoting a Chinese interlocutor, "That's how things get done. And nobody can do anything about corrupt officials. They're the law."[37]

Political Change

It is a common belief confirmed by conversations with individual unofficial Chinese, that whereas the Chinese economy has moved quite a distance toward the market system, the political system has changed little:

> There remains no genuine forum for public debate and criticism. In the cultural sphere, art shows are closed if the local party bureaucrat disapproves, films are banned if they displease the censor and news reports are screened before publication. Communist Party members do not disagree with one another in public. University students are forcibly prevented from demonstrating for better food in the mess hall, or for more democracy.[38]

The economic changes of the past decade tending toward the market system suggest that change in the totalitarian political system must have taken place, some of it by design, some through an internal process of putrefaction. The traumas of the Great Leap Forward and the Cultural Revolution, on top of all the other mass campaign shocks of earlier years, had caused the Communist party and its totalitarian governmental establishment a massive loss of face and produced what in the early 1980s was judged to be a profound crisis of confidence and loss of faith.[39] The Party lost most of the support it once had outside its ranks, and it putrefied within. One result has been a nonprogrammed loosening up of political controls that had formerly been enforced with ferocity and effect. Repeated attempts by the factionalized leadership to reassert its former undisputed autocracy (as in the 1983 anticrime campaign, the campaign against spiritual pollution, and the 1986–1987 antibourgeois liberalization offensive) have not overcome totalitarian decomposition and the shift toward what Harry Harding calls "consultative authoritarianism."

In addition to this unintended adjustment, Mao's successors have already recognized that "without reform of the political structure, reform of the economic structure cannot succeed in the end." Here the limits of political reform are carefully spelled out. The proposed "democratization" is modest, amounting to the correction and formalization of the already made informal adjustment toward authoritarianism. The Thirteenth Party Congress concluded that China's "basic political system [of the people's "democratic dictatorship"] is good." It had become a little frayed with the passage of time by bureaucratism, feudalism, leftist deviations, and errors of work style. These errors can be set right by delegating power to lower administrative levels, divorcing governmental bodies from the management of firms, using indirect instead of direct levers of control to guide rather than command affairs, and separating Communist party functions from those of the Communist government. As the Thirteenth Party Congress warns, however, "The separation does not mean in any sense that the Party's tasks will be reduced and its role weakened. Rather the separation will further consolidate the Party's leadership role."[40] This view of intrasystemic repairs is consistent with Deng's thesis that

> In order to realize the Four Modernizations in China, we must, in the field of ideology and politics, uphold the Four Basic Principles. This is a fundamental prerequisite for the realization of the Four Modernizations. These Four Basic Principles that we must uphold are: the socialist road, the dictatorship of the proletariat, the leadership of the Communist Party, and Marxism-Leninism-Mao Zedong Thought.

In the same remarks in which he noted that China's image had not been damaged by dealing with the likes of Wei "according to law," Deng said,

> Without leadership [that is, monopoly] by the Communist Party and without socialism, there is no future for China. . . . We cannot do without dictatorship. We must

not only affirm the need for it but exercise it when necessary. . . . Democracy can develop only gradually, and we
cannot copy Western systems. If we did, that would only
make a mess of everything.[41]

There is an ironclad consistency to Deng's views on the subject
of modernization. There is to be no transition to the market system
("we will never . . . import the capitalist system itself"), and there
is to be no transition to democracy ("the fact of the matter is that
socialism cannot be defended or built up without the dictatorship
of the proletariat").[42] If this is more than rhetoric, and if it is adhered
to, there will be no modernization.

There is, however, a hypothetical out. The kind of political adjustments envisaged in China, while clearly undemocratic, could
conceivably make the monopoly rule by the Party less rigidly totalitarian by, among other things, institutionalizing consultation and
dialogue both within the Party and between the Party and various
Party-approved functional social strata.

Such formalized authoritarianism would at least make possible
the emergence of a market system with its democratic spillovers
into the political sphere. As already noted, the coexistence of a market system with an authoritarian polity would not guarantee the
transformation of the political system into democracy, but at least
forces would be exerted in that cause from the direction of the economy. This view of the modernization process is the most optimistic
possible given the Communist party's undiminished will to power
and its repeated resolve to stick by Leninist principles and practices
that are antithetical to those of the market system and democracy.
The achievement of political modernization via the market economy,
moreover, is a very long-term prospect at best, and one fraught
with the dangers of recidivism.

Summary and Conclusions

More than urbanization, industrialization, and the use of state-of-the-
art plant, equipment, and technology, economic modernization is,
above all, a state of mind, an attitude translated into a system of
resource allocation. Political modernization too is a state of mind
and an attitude translated into a system of civil governance. A modern society joins institutionalized economic freedom (the market system) with political freedom (democracy).

China's economy and polity, part of the broader Socialist economic and political society, has in the past failed the test of modernization. Since 1978 the stated intent has been to modernize both

the economy and the political system. To that end steps have been taken to dismantle sections of the edifice of central administrative command misplanning, move the economy in a market direction, and attenuate the rigidities and reduce the centralization of politics by "perfecting Socialist democracy."

It is not, however, the official announced intent of the Communist party of China to preside over a systemic transition to the market system in economics and to democracy in politics. It is the Party's wish to combine elements of the market system with aspects of central planning and to introduce a measure of pluralism into the political system—a process that has been initiated, unintentionally and informally, through the Party's partial ungluing in the aftermath of the Cultural Revolution. In sum, the Party intends to move toward some form of market socialism in economics and one-party authoritarianism in politics. If this intent succeeds, modernization will not be achieved. Adherence to the Four Basic Principles, even if interpreted loosely, would result in minuscule political liberalization. In such circumstances further progress in a marketizing and privatizing direction will be barred. China cannot be modernized economically on the way to the market, nor can it be modernized politically on the way to democracy. A systemic crossing of the border is needed on both fronts.

The dabbling in authoritarianism makes it at least theoretically possible for a market system to emerge in China. Such emergence is necessary even without the ruling party's rhetorical intent and despite the forces in the Party and society opposed to the very idea of systemic change. The push toward such change comes not only from the need for economic modernization but also from the inner logic of the market mechanism, which cannot function with disjointed and unconnected parts mixed in with vertical, administrative controls. The failure of all economic "reform" movements in Socialist countries since the 1950s derives mostly from the reluctance to go all the way to the market system. To modernize economically, a country cannot use markets as medicine to bring relief to the Socialist disease and rejuvenate sclerotic central planning. The poison must be gotten out of the system. To this end the economy has to be marketized, and the rights of private property must be introduced and protected to the point where they dominate the economy and find expression in free prices. It is not the often denounced bureaucracy that has sabotaged "reform," but the unwillingness of all party factions at all levels to accept the idea of economic freedom and institutionalize that idea in a network of voluntary, competitive, lateral contracts entered into by autonomous, property-owning, price-directed buyers and sellers—in a society, that is, "where private arrangements [take] priority over public, where the family [is] the favored social unit, and where the voluntary principle [is] paramount."[43] The key problem has been the rejection of real reform and the settling for half-measures: intrasystemic adjustments parading as reform. Because these adjustments have not worked, they have discredited the notion of systemic reform.

Should the market system come into being, it will inevitably exert democratizing pressures on the authoritarian political structure within which it is encased. The market system is not neutral with respect to political culture. Whether the liberalizing influences from the economy can prove sufficiently strong to overcome the opposite pressures from the authoritarian polity is an open question. The consequences for society of not effectively addressing shortages, static misallocations, dynamic inefficiency, and commandism would be serious: at a minimum, a return to what the Soviets call the "period of stagnation," that is, on an international scale, comparative decline. Thus, if a market system should emerge in China (or elsewhere in the Socialist world), the fifth modernization would have at least a chance to appear one day. Such a prospect, however, is highly uncertain and very distant. For its materialization it would require the renunciation of the Four Basic Principles in theory as well as in practice, that is, the repudiation of Marxism-Leninism and all its derivatives, not just their revisionist-opportunistic reinterpretation.

4

Some Reflections on Man and Society in China

Just over a year ago I went to Communist China with a group from Pennsylvania State University. I had studied communism and China for years before that, but here at last was an opportunity to see the faces behind the rhetoric. Because our delegation was overwhelmingly academic, we were shown around universities, colleges, and high schools and had ample occasion to talk with faculty, students, and administrators in rather elaborately stage-managed settings. At the time of our visit, China's education—both learning and the institutions of learning—was still in the process of digging out from under the rubble left by a political cyclone of unprecedented ferocity that had hit, and closed down, all schools from 1966 to about 1969. While we were in China, ideological tornado warnings were being hoisted everywhere; there was a premonition of yet another impending cultural holocaust, a foreboding in the way the nationwide campaign against Confucius and his latter-day alleged disciple, former Defense Minister Lin Piao, was carried out.

Political Performances

On arrival in the city of Soochow, not far from Shanghai, we were treated to a performance by a group of children ranging in age

This piece was written after my first visit to mainland China in February 1974 at the tail end of the Cultural Revolution. Although today the sentiments expressed therein are part of conventional wisdom, they were certainly not that then. At that time the norm in Western intellectual circles was to extol Mao's social engineering model for its alleged virtues of spunky self-reliance, egalitarianism, asceticism, and mass line, especially when contrasted with capitalism's decaying and decadent society—a pubescent adulation best exemplified in a book published in 1972 by a group from the Committee of Concerned Asian Scholars just back from a trip to China.

46

from about six to perhaps ten or eleven. The show was colorful and extremely well done. It was also almost totally political, as is everything in China. Two themes dominated the performance: first, the extinction of the individual and his dissolution in the mass; and second, the mandatory uniqueness of truth and its identification with the political line laid down by Chairman Mao. The whole was pervaded by boundless and, I must admit, contagious optimism.

In a ballet sketch called "I'm Busy Feeding a Flock of Geese for the Commune" (a sort of updated and politically conscious version of the "Story of Ping," only Ping was, as it happened, a duck), a goose chooses to leave the flock and strike out on its own in what we in the United States would approvingly regard as the spirit of entrepreneurial initiative. Such a manifestation of individualism is thoroughly criticized by the remaining goose collective. Moreover, terrible things happen to the deviant goose as it wanders blindly through the world, away from the stern but also warm and understanding group. In the end it rejoins the flock, humbly accepts the community's pointed criticism, engages in self-criticism, and thenceforth works unstintingly for the common good with no thought of self.

The moral of the tale, as I read it, is not simply that the collective is to be preferred over the individual; the message is that the self is not legitimate, the ego must be torn out and dissolved in the mass, and any thought of personal advancement is by definition at odds with the interests of the collective and is, therefore, wrong and harmful. In the "Story of Ping," the disobedient Ping finally returns to his family gaggle, a very extended family, to be sure, but still a family. In the updated version at Soochow, the errant bird staggers back to the people's commune, an entity much larger, which extends beyond blood ties.

Anti-Individualism

I have the feeling that in China today the family is tolerated, indeed surrounded with solicitous care by the authorities, because it is a useful feeding and housing unit, and where day-care centers are not yet available, a handy baby-sitting service as well. But in China today the family is not, I believe, the officially sanctioned social nucleus. Any action taken in the sole interest of one's parents, children, husband, wife, or other relatives will be not accorded social legitimacy. Least of all will such legitimacy be granted if the action is taken in pursuit of purely personal objectives. That actions of this sort occur is not, I think, in doubt. That they have to be taken

47

circumspectly, almost furtively, and that they are tracked down and rectified is equally clear. The climate of officially inspired opinion is against them.

The anti-individual, antipersonal writ is enforced through relentless, organized peer group pressure at the grass-roots. Each man, woman, and child in China is a member of at least two basic organizations guided, directed, and inspired by the Communist party and ultimately by the thought of Mao Tse-tung. There is, first of all, the organization at one's place of residence—the block, alley, street, or neighborhood collective, or the village (production team, as it is called) in the countryside. Then there is the organization at one's place of employment—the work group, shop, factory, or classroom committee. In between there are countless other organizational units that embrace the quasi-totality of life and thought. A person's everyday existence consists of movements from one organized structure to another, which is as much as to say that private life is transparent, open at all times to inspection by the collectivity. There is, to put it simply, no privacy. There is no refuge in silence because not to say out loud what is expected of one is to attract suspicion. Unity of action and orchestration of thought are brought about by a web of mutual supervision. A former Thai Communist guerrilla put it this way: "In the jungle," she said, "there is a system where each person supervises every other person." Framing the system are numerous cadres or "responsible persons" of the regime, full-time guardians of the new morality. It has been estimated that there is one cadre for every ten adults in China.

It can be argued, of course, that repugnant as the method appears to some, there is merit to the objective of a society of selfless cooperating human beings who own in common all but the most intimately personal things, consume enough but not more, and spurn the lures of personal wealth and distinction. Such vision is as old as humanity itself. It has never been realized to my knowledge, except in small religious or quasi-religious communities of like-minded people, and then only for a historically short span of time. Today, some people argue, the vision is being implemented among China's 900 million-strong multitudes. Moreover, they say, given the awesome dimensions of the economic problem, there is no other way but to mobilize, regiment, and unleash the masses against hunger, disease, illiteracy, floods, drought, and other calamities. The price, if it is that, of three meals a day, a change of clothes, a roof over one's head, basic education, and tolerably good health is the collectivization of brawn, mind, and soul. China, these people contend, cannot afford the luxury of everyone pulling in a different direction, nor can it any longer tolerate the maldistribution of income and wealth attendant on such a system.

The children in Soochow put on for our edification another little morality play, the message of which was even more far-reaching than that of the capitalist-roving goose. The action takes place in a school mathematics class. All the children except one apply them-selves with ardor to solve the difficult sums, and they do this in concert, helping and encouraging each other along the way. The one lazy, obstreperous little boy finds the whole thing a bore and a waste of his time. He fidgets and fiddles around, and time after time comes up with the wrong answer. Gradually he becomes iso-lated, alienated from his friends and comrades. The rest of the class has a heart-to-heart chat with him, but it does no good. They then collectively criticize him and struggle against him. Through this proc-ess of struggle and criticism, the deviant individual's latent proletar-ian consciousness is raised. He relents (breaks down?), publicly confesses his error, and is joyfully integrated in the group. He ceases to exist as an identifiable separate entity, merging his inner self and his outward behavior with the collective personality. The cadre at my side beamed with pleasurable approval. He explained: "There are all sorts of questions, but there is only one answer." The source of the correct answer is Chairman Mao, the embodiment of the General Will. "Chairman Mao," the children sang in unison, "is in our hearts." In life, as in math, the answer is objective. Rigorously and inevitably it flows from the elements of the problem, which is class struggle. It emerges from the deep, like Venus, beautiful and harmonious. It is not arrived at by means of competitive individ-ual solutions, through the trial and error of alternatives and compro-mises but bursts forth upon each and everyone from the accumulated wisdom of the working class, refined, synthesized, corrected, and expressed in the thought of Chairman Mao. "From the people, to the people" as the formula has it.

The same chord was struck several days earlier by a history professor at Chungshan University in Canton. At the end of what amounted to an abject, ritualized self-examination before our group, he said: "Without the correct political line, you cannot serve the people." This enlightenment, he told us, came to him as a result of the struggle and criticism directed at him by formerly poor and lower-middle peasants during the Cultural Revolution. The theme was repeated in identical terms by everyone we spoke to, wherever we went.

All this is not new. It is only more massive and thorough. Throughout the human experience spiritual and political leaders have claimed to know better what the people wanted than did the people themselves.

Totalitarianism

In its political manifestations the phenomenon is known as totalitarianism. It has its costs in the constant and unending anxiety of the individual, the fear for his person and for the fate of his family. What he does now may be right in the official scheme of things, but will it be judged right tomorrow when the definition of what constitutes correctness changes: when 2 + 2 are decreed to equal 3, not 4? In a rare street conversation with a Western correspondent some years ago, a Chinese confided that "in China everyone is afraid, but no one quite knows why." A monolithic polity also has its rewards in the strength and power it projects, the massive, if perhaps at times synthetic, enthusiasm it is able to generate and in its ability to concentrate all forces on a small number of key problems to achieve spectacular breakthroughs.

The homogeneity of values that accompanies every self-respecting totalitarian polity also has its costs and compensations. The costs accrue to those who want to think for themselves and assume the form of a painful bending of the will and wrenching of the soul, the need to live a life of dissimulation fraught with dangers. I have met people in China, the older professors at the universities, for example, who were, I sensed, alive but dead. Repeated encounters with struggle-criticism-transformation had left them an empty shell: a walking, talking, food-consuming spiritual void. But there is another side to this. In his essay "Ethics without a Moral Code," the Polish philosopher Leszek Kolakowski explains the benefits to the individual of accepting an all-embracing moral code:

> The desire to possess a moral code is . . . part of the desire for security and part of the flight from moral choice. It is the desire to live in a world in which all the moral decisions already have been made. . . . The code . . . foresees the satisfaction that is derived from properly executing moral directives as easily as it foresees the feeling of guilt which arises from violating those directives.

To some, freedom is option space, room for the exercise of one's discretionary power, limited by the important proviso that, as John Stuart Mill puts it, "complete liberty of contradicting and disproving our opinion, is the very condition which justifies us in assuming its truth for purposes of action." To others, perhaps to most, freedom means the recognition of necessity: conscious and active submission to the historically or otherwise inevitable. In the Marxist scheme of things, the individual liberates himself by first recognizing and then surrendering himself to the compulsive collective will of the toiling class. In his *Economic and Philosophic Manuscripts,* Marx speaks of communism as "the positive transcendence of private property, or human self-estrangement, and therefore as the real appropriation of the human essence by man and for man . . . the complete return of man to himself as a social (i.e., human) being—a return become conscious, and accomplished within the entire wealth of previous development." In his later work Marx emphasized the automatic and mechanistic aspects of this presumed return of man to his social essence at the expense of man's conscious and informed decision to do so. Mao has resuscitated the personal willfulness of the act, a willfulness helped along by "heart-to-heart chats" and other exercises in collective aid to the individual's correct understanding of historical necessity. At a less exalted but persuasive level of abstraction, to accept the General Will in People's China is to earn a measure of material security: the three meals a day, the change of clothes, a roof over one's head, basic education, and tolerably good health. Failure to bend to the General Will relegates one to the category of the Five Black Classes, where there is no material security but only the prospect of a life of anxiety.

I will lower the curtain on this act of my morality play with a quotation from the reported exchange between another exponent of the General Will, Joseph Stalin, and the head of the Economics Department of the Soviet secret police apparatus, L. G. Mironov, a man of unimpeachable proletarian credentials, early in the great Russian purge of the 1930s. The background is as follows. A high, and till then respected official of the regime, Lev Kamenev, accused by Stalin of having violated the General Will as formulated by the master, was being interrogated in the cellars of the secret police by Mironov and his assistants. He would not confess. He would not yield. He went against historical necessity. He was a goose straight out of the Soochow play, the bad little boy in the math class. He thought he was right, but as everyone knows, "Without the correct political line, you cannot serve the people." Here is how it went:

"You think Kamenev may not confess?" asked Stalin, his eyes slyly screwed up.

"I don't know," Mironov answered. "He doesn't yield to persuasion."

"You don't know?" inquired Stalin with marked surprise, staring at Mironov. "Do you know how much our state weighs, with all the factories, machines, the army, with all the armaments and the navy?" Mironov and all those present looked at Stalin with surprise.

"Think it over and tell me," demanded Stalin. Mironov smiled, believing that Stalin was getting ready to crack a joke. But Stalin did not intend to jest. He looked at Mironov quite in earnest. "I am asking you, how much does all that weigh?" he insisted.

Mironov was confused. He waited, still hoping that Stalin would turn everything into a joke, but Stalin kept staring at him and waited for an answer. Mironov shrugged his shoulders and, like a schoolboy undergoing an examination, said in an irresolute voice, "Nobody can know that, Yosif Vissarionovich. It is in the realm of astronomical figures."

"Well, and can one man withstand the pressure of that astronomical weight?" asked Stalin sternly.

"No," answered Mironov.

"Now then, don't tell me any more that Kamenev, or this or that prisoner, is able to withstand the pressure. Don't come report to me," said Stalin to Mironov, "until you have in this briefcase the confession of Kamenev!"[1]

Like the goose and the antimath boy in Soochow, Kamenev admitted the error of his way. He confessed. The difference is that Kamenev was physically abused and finally liquidated, while the goose, the boy, and the professor at Canton were kept physically alive but were otherwise left for dead. In their state of suspended animation, they continue to be used as teachers by negative example.

The attractiveness of the goal of replacing egoism with empathy, individual competitiveness with group cooperation, sharp income disparities with a more egalitarian scheme of distribution, and conspicuous—often wasteful and trivial—consumption of material goods with measured moderation and an interest in the finer things of life is considerably lessened, in my eyes, by the fact that the blueprint for this brave new world emerges ready-made from the brain of the master and leaves no room for debate or disagreement. Dissent, especially when organized, however reasonable and rational, is *ipso facto* immoral. The dissenter is not only wrong but evil in various degrees, depending on his obstinacy. Discussion is seen as the duty of the possessor of truth to help his opponent recognize and eliminate error and sinfulness. It is a missionary approach to dialogue. The missionaries' efforts in the Chinese instance are supported by the most massive, thorough, and pervasive behavioral engineering operation in the history of mankind. Yet it is frequently applauded by many thinkers in the West. The tune is so powerful they do not, or do not wish to, hear the words. The appeal of the vision obscures the mandatory nature of the goal and the often unsavory means used to attain it. The point is reached where to question in our own land the ultimate humaneness of the objective is to be accused of insensitivity to the plight of the masses of China, and to deplore the means is to be allegedly misinformed on the magnitude of China's economic problem. I believe one should do both: question the objective and expose the means. While we recognize the achievements, it is incumbent on us, especially those among us who have seen the process with our eyes, both to give credit and to count the costs.

I mentioned earlier that the two themes, the extinction of the self and the ineluctable uniqueness of the code, were conveyed with optimism. In the message were an intimation of strength and a conviction of the righteousness of the cause and of its ultimate victory. The absence of uncertainty lent relief to the ideal: a world without shadows, transparent, clinical, seething with confidence. To be sure, we talked only with the priests of the regime and for the most part saw only those aspects of China's society they were willing to show us. Even so, the contrast with the argumentative, free-wheeling world back home was striking. We experienced an almost total lack of sensual stimulation, a puritanical primness that, too, contrasts with manners and morals at home. Enveloping all was the sensation of inevitability, of an objective necessity sustained by an organized will. Among the "Five Constantly Read Articles" written by Mao is one entitled "The Foolish Old Man Who Removed the Mountain." It is a eulogy of the collective will's ability to crush through the most formidable barriers. At Fudan University in Shanghai, a leading institution of learning in China, I asked what books were being used in courses on political economy. Next to *Das Kapital* and some works of Lenin and Stalin came "The Foolish Old Man." One is told over and over again that there are no problems that cannot be resolved, no obstacles that cannot be removed, no enemies who cannot be conquered, on condition that one correctly grasps the political line and struggles collectively in behalf of history.

We asked about crime and the drug problem in China. The name Shanghai was once synonymous with public and private piracy. Today, say the cadres, people behave themselves. "Very few crimes," they say, "go to the courts. Most problems are settled by criticism and self-criticism in the household. Neighbors help to solve the problem. When this doesn't work, the question goes to the street committee. . . . There are no lawyers working as a profession. But, if the accused wants a lawyer, he will get one. Our policy of dealing with criminals in China is clear-cut. It is lenient with those who confess." How much does the state weigh, with all the factories, machines, the army, with all the armaments and the navy?

"Drug addiction," our hosts told us, "used to be a very serious problem in pre-Liberation China. Drugs were used by the imperialists to poison the Chinese people. After Liberation people became politically emancipated; ex-junkies were given political education; opium smoking was outlawed. Nowadays opium is used only as a pharmaceutical drug. This result was achieved because of the superiority of the socialist system." Drug pushing is classified as a counterrevolutionary crime punishable by death or lifelong imprisonment in a labor reeducation camp. Addiction was treated by political study sessions. Some made it, some did not. Those who did not no longer pose a problem.

There is a fervent, unending recitation of struggles crowned with success. The wavelike inevitability of it all is hammered home ad nauseam. A feeling of loneliness sets in, a sense of one's fragility and unimportance in this scrubbed universe of revolutionary socialism.

"The worst thing the communists did to us," an East European once said, "is to have convinced us that they are inevitable." Is there, indeed, no other way?

I, for one, reject what I consider to be a counsel of despair. There is, I believe, not one; there are many ways if only we would will them. I do not refer here to grandiose schemes for the economic and political betterment of societies. There is abundant literature on the subject of alternative models of economic development and participatory political arrangements, and practical examples of nontotalitarian growth abound. The Communist models are not the only ones, nor are they the most effective. My concern here is with a much narrower issue, but one on which all else hinges. It is also an issue about which we as private persons can do something at once.

Individual Fulfillment

The crucial point it seems to me, is to prevent further erosion of our confidence and belief in the basic humaneness and viability of our way of perceiving the moral problems of our time while keeping our minds open and informed. Despite its many drawbacks and dark spots, the assumption that societies exist for the greater fulfillment of the individual human person—and not the other way around—is a sound assumption. The hypothesis according to which individual fulfillment is not by definition contrary to the public good is a good and workable hypothesis. The purpose of collective action is not to stamp out personal drive, but to restrain those manifestations of it which in the light of open, free, and public discussion are thought to harm our neighbors, near and distant. The social preference function should not emerge ready-made from some presumed General Will embodied in a party, a central committee, or a supreme master. Its building blocks should be the free expression of opinion, freedom of association to promote divergent views, as well as the freedom not to participate and to keep silent. Mill is right when he reminds us that "to call any proposition certain, while there is any one who would deny its certainty if permitted, but who is not permitted, is to assume that we ourselves, and those who agree with us, are the judges of certainty, and judges without hearing the other side." To deny others the right to disagree with us—worse still, to put the pressure of the state's astronomical weight upon them to make them see our truth—is to do grievous harm to the very essence of man's humanity. What has been done in Russia and China and in Cambodia and Vietnam is class racism, not the dawn of a new and better man. In a letter to Maxim Gorky, the Russian peasant democratic writer Vladimir Korolenko wrote: "In the summer of 1921, the State Commission for Famine Relief . . . was arrested. They had tried to combat the unprecedented famine in Russia. The heart of the matter, however, was that theirs were the *wrong hands* to be offering food and could not be allowed to feed the starving." Describing the destruction of those simple folk who would not be collectivized by Stalin in 1929–1930, Alexander Solzhenitsyn has this to say in *The Gulag Archipelago,* the most telling documentation of man's inhumanity to man in our times:

> They burned out whole nests, whole families, from the start; and they watched jealously to be sure that none of the children—fourteen, ten, even six years old—got away; to the last scrapings, all had to go down the same road, to the same common destruction. (This was the *first* such experiment—at least in modern history. It was subsequently repeated by Hitler with the Jews, and again by Stalin with nationalities which were disloyal to him or suspected him.)

The latest chapter of the drama occurred in recent weeks in the tragedy of what the perverse code calls the "liberation" of Phnom Penh.

We must reintegrate man not by suppressing self but by gently putting together the egoistic man of Adam Smith's *Wealth of Nations* and the empathy and social consciousness that defines man in the

55

Theory of Moral Sentiments. We must, too, summon up the will to act in defense of oppressed people who call for our help rather than engage in nationwide egoism. I think the Communist way does violence to the universal nature of man, and despite the fervor and the optimism that it exhibits, it will be undone by those very individuals it purports to serve and liberate.

Hope for the Oppressed

The other day the Polish Communist party periodical, *Polityka*, published an uncommonly candid survey of young people's thoughts, feelings, and values. Surveyed was a representative sample of youngsters between the ages of sixteen and nineteen, as well as first- and second-year college students. All of them were born and bred within Poland's totalitarian polity and fed on homogenous values that prize the mass over the individual. The answers given were disconcerting to the sponsors. The young Poles, when asked what value they cherish most, replied in overwhelming majority that it is the family. "What gives sense to your life," the questionnaire asked. "Family happiness, the feeling that one lives for the good of one's nearest," was the top-ranking answer. Personal friendship and mutual respect among individuals came next. The young Poles preferred small informal groups of friends and colleagues to the structured mass organizations in which the regime had barracked them since birth. In answer to the question regarding the meaning of life, belief in some great idea, the mandatory code of so-called "scientific socialism," came in thirteenth place—next to last, well behind family happiness, one's own place in society, personal affection, human trust, work, and religious belief. There is, they seem to tell, another way.

Recalling the days when, as a young man, he was being initiated into the mysteries of the code, when as Marx would have it, "the complete return of man to himself as a social (i.e., human) being" was being dangled before his eyes, Solzhenitsyn says: "People can shout at you: 'You must!' And your own head can be saying also: 'You must!' But inside your breast there is a sense of revulsion, repudiation. I don't want to. *It makes me sick.* Do what you want without me; I want no part of it." This is, as I hear it, what the young Poles are saying, drawing, as they do, upon that "small change in copper"—the tiny but corrosive fund of human decency—which over the ages men have quietly stored away as their most prized possession.

PART TWO
Comparative Socialist Economies in Reform

5
Is the Soviet Type of Economic System Strong or Weak?

In this chapter the "Soviet type of economic system" refers to the allocation of resources through a central plan: that is, the setting by government officials of mandatory general and specific production, exchange, and distribution goals and the procedures for attaining those goals expressed in physical, technical, and financial terms and enforced primarily by administrative methods. All significant means of production and distribution are government owned, either directly (nationalization) or indirectly (collectivization).[1] Stalin fashioned this type of economic system in the 1930s on the basis of a rather loose interpretation of Marxist-Leninist doctrines, in the context of an underdeveloped country without any traditions of personal freedom or liberty. In various forms it remains to this day the economic foundation of state socialism everywhere.

Strong or Weak?

The strength or weakness of an economic system is determined by performance criteria, which must be legitimate.[2] Legitimate performance criteria fall into two fairly fluid groups: a group of conventional indicators that can be applied to different types of economic systems and a group of less conventional norms regarded as important by a particular socioeconomic and political entity.[3] Conventional indicators include wealth, growth, stability, security, efficiency, equity, technological innovation and diffusion, and national defense. Less conventional indicators include military power (going beyond defense to expansionism); economic freedom (freedom of enterprise, freedom of choice of a job, freedom of consumer choice) versus central control (a Leninist imperative); economic sovereignty (consumer sovereignty versus leadership sovereignty, or who sets the system's goals); political freedom and pluralism versus absolutist unity; and environmental quality.

Conceptually, the evaluation of a system's overall performance is beset by philosophical and methodological difficulties. These arise from two causes: the fact that the system of economic organization is only one of several factors that influence economic performance and that the goals and hence the performance criteria are so numerous. The way an economy behaves will be affected by the economy's resource endowment, the political and legal systems of which it is a part, the configuration of beliefs, national history, cultural experience, and the like. The precise contribution to overall economic performance of the economic system itself cannot be easily isolated in these circumstances.[4] The existence of many competing, unequally weighted, alternative, sometimes incompatible goals simultaneously pursued and of the relevant performance criteria means that

> evaluation of the total performance of a system is possible only if the relative importance of these criteria can be unequivocally established; that is to say, if all the criteria are unequivocally weighted and rank-ordered. Without such a ranking, it is impossible to determine whether or not a system that excels in criterion A but does poorly in criterion B is doing better or worse than another system that does well in criterion B but fails in criterion A. The ranking of various criteria, however, depends on the value preferences of the evaluator, and, as such, cannot be unequivocally established by reference to rational calculus.[5]

These difficulties are compounded by the question of what time spans are chosen for comparison.

The Bumble Bee Paradox

The difficulties inherent in evaluating and comparing the performance of economic systems are among the reasons for disagreement and an occasional acrimonious exchange among Western economists about the perceived strengths and weaknesses of the Soviet type of economic system.[6] I think it is fair to say that today most Western comparative systems economists agree that by reference to most conventional benchmarks and some less conventional ones (for example, environmental quality), the Soviet type of economic system has performed poorly—so badly, in fact, that it has lost credibility as a possible model for developing countries. It has also shown itself increasingly unsuitable for a modern society; its users risk being left behind in the worldwide technological race. Within the majority of those who agree with this assessment, many—perhaps most— qualify their negative judgment in various ways.[7] Others conclude that the Soviet type of economic system has, in some of its local manifestations (for instance, Poland and Romania, and at a lower development level, Vietnam and Ethiopia), already reached the stage of degenerative collapse where the basic institutions of the system (information, coordination, motivation, and property) cease for all practical purposes to function.[8] The full realization of economic collapse is prevented in these instances by force of arms, police terror, external subsidies, and, in Ethiopia, by resort to the tested Stalinist weapon of man-made mass starvation. Other Soviet types of economies, it is argued (the Soviet Union itself, for example) are approaching this critical stage, their progression toward systemic collapse being cushioned by the participants' (the Russian people's) exceptional, not to say sheepish, tolerance and acceptance of extraordinary economic mismanagement and morally offensive economic abuses. After nearing the brink, the smart or lucky ones (Communist China and Hungary) have made far-reaching adjustments that are beginning, in some sectors, to resemble structural reforms (agriculture in China, for instance).[9]

If the Soviet type of economic system represents some sort of reverse Darwinism, however, how is it that we talk about it so much and worry too, as if it were a threat to our own superior system? Surely, the account of the system's weakness is not the whole story. This line of questioning has come to be known as the "bumble bee paradox." Briefly, it is said that according to the laws of aerodynamics the bumble bee cannot fly. But it does. There are no such laws applicable to the bumble bee; so the paradox is just a clever rhetorical device. At a less frivolous level the question posed by the paradox is legitimate, however. Why fuss about a system that does not work? In what follows, I look at the system's weaknesses and strengths and suggest some tentative answers.

Weakness

Back in the dark ages of Sovietology (the 1950s and early-to-mid-1960s), it was commonly thought that although the Soviet type of economic system did not do well (not yet, anyway) by the criterion of wealth (especially per capita consumption) and was rather inefficient, its performance was creditable—indeed superior to the market system—in growth and quite good in stability of output, price, and employment, as well as security and even (despite Stalin's anti-egalitarian bias) distributional equity. By and large, it was not a bad showing so far as fallible human systems go. There was a great deal of concern about "catching up and overtaking," and there was the vision, whipped up by the Soviet Union's 1961 program, of the Communist millennium to have been inaugurated no later than 1990.

Later more rigorous and better informed analysis revealed flaws in this generally upbeat picture. It was shown that many of the ills of the Soviet type of economic system were simply suppressed, not readily visible to the naked statistical eye. This was particularly true of the alleged stability of output, employment, and prices, but it also applied to most of the other conventional indicators of performance, including technological innovation and diffusion. It was sluggishness on this front, ephemerally relieved by massive Western credits for the transfer of technology from West to East, that in the end failed to relieve the secular decline in the system's growth rates caused by the exhaustion of extensive sources of growth. Security of employment and the budget-guaranteed immortality of Socialist firms came to be viewed in the context of motivational breakdown, entrepreneurial failure, and pervasive risk avoidance. To the system's planning and managerial elite, risk is truly anathema. The comparative distributional equity of the system came to be questioned as analysts began to understand that in the Soviet types of economies the distribution of money income is much less important than the distribution of political power and that political power is skewed beyond all reason in favor of the *nachalstvo* (the leadership principle). Even more disturbing is the evidence adduced by a recent study of poverty and patterns of deprivation in the Soviet Union:

> The existence of poverty some six and a half decades after the revolution must be counted as one of the greatest failures of the Soviet experience. . . . In the late seventies some two-fifths of the non-peasant labor force earned less than the sum needed to achieve the minimum level of subsistence proposed by Soviet scholars for a small urban family. This compared with about a ninth of the population reported to be under the "cut-off" level in the USA. A tentative comparison of the poverty thresholds suggests that the Soviet threshold is much lower.[10]

The cultural and political environment within which the Soviet type of economic system operates (or, as in the case of Poland, fails to function) is not conducive to curing the economy's ills or helping the system modernize.

While I have tried to demonstrate the difficulties of evaluating and comparing the performance of economic systems and the care and attention that should rightly be given to this problem, I wish to offer an observation that, however intuitive it may appear, rests on good sense. Preoccupation with the difficulties of evaluation and comparison, if overrefined, can result in intellectual paralysis. While admittedly it is not easy to judge economic systems on their overall performance, such a judgment can be made without doing violence to scholarly care and academic integrity. In fact, the fundamental purpose of any economic system is to provide those who make a living in it with a decent and rising standard of living. An economic system should supply the goods that people want, at prices they are prepared to pay, in rising quantities and qualities, at a declining cost. A system that does not do that is a failure. In that basic and common sense, the Soviet type of economic system is indeed a failure.

Strength

When we think of the strength of the Soviet type of economic system, what is it that comes to mind? Two things, I believe: military might and the system's enormous capacity to repress domestic opposition—the army and the public security apparat. As of the time of this writing, except for the early Soviet withdrawal from Austria and for Grenada (where the system had not fully taken root before it was pulled out), state socialism and its centrally planned economies have not retreated one inch anywhere in the past forty years. On the contrary, the Soviet realm has expanded so that by now it embraces a large part of the earth's surface and a significant and growing proportion of the world's population. The expansion has been brought about in every case with the help of arms. The gains have been preserved and retreat has been prevented by the same means. Except for the latest Chinese experiments—the direction of which is contradictory and whose outcome remains in doubt—and for the inconclusive Yugoslav affair with markets and workers' management, there has been no instance of structural economic change: the old Stalinist economy has been repaired, upgraded, and renovated, but not abandoned and replaced, not even in Hungary. The more terroristic and overtly barbaric mechanisms of the political machine have been deactivated but not dismantled, and some slight movement has been at times discernible on the claustrophobic front of cultural mediocrity. The oppression of the spirit, however, remains as severe as ever. In 1986, asked for her feelings on boarding a return plane for Russia, Yelena Bonner summed it up this way: "Anyone who is in a sound mental state would not want to return from freedom to a prison."

The biggest advance has been in military posture, weaponry, and the refinement of the instruments of domestic surveillance, intimidation, and suppression.

The Three Economies of State Socialism

The Soviet type of economic system comprises three distinct but related economies: (1) the official centrally planned civilian economy (which includes, in a subsidiary way, a legal market economy confined largely to agricultural produce; a legal economy of special unmarked stores for top members of the leadership in which the Communist nobility is able to purchase at cut-rate prices goods unavailable elsewhere in the system and unimaginable for the ordinary citizen; and hard currency stores in which imported capitalist goods and the best domestic products unavailable in the stores of the planned civilian economy are sold to those equipped with hard currencies); (2) a "second," parallel, shadow, underground market economy; and (3) the military–public security (secret police) economy. (See figure 5–1.) By now our understanding of the operational principles and mechanisms of the official planned civilian economy is good. Investigations into the formerly neglected "second" market economy have made big strides in recent years thanks largely to the work of Gregory Grossman at Berkeley and Vladimir Treml at Duke University.[11] Our knowledge of the military–public security economy—its structure, principles, and procedures—remains deficient for reasons that are understandable given the sensitivity and obsessive secretiveness of the subject. Because of the importance of the third economy, both in its volume and the quality of inputs it absorbs and in the awesome output it produces, our limited knowledge of its institutional arrangement and *modus operandi* represents a serious and dangerous defect.

The presence of structurally different economies within a particular economic system is not, of course, limited to the Soviet type of economic system. Our own market economy has its administratively planned civilian and military component (the government sector, the public educational establishment, and the "military-industrial complex" that received much attention from the radicals of the 1960s and 1970s), and an underground economy estimated in the United States at some 10 percent of the gross national product.[12] There are, however, at least three important differences between state so-

FIGURE 5–1
THE THREE ECONOMIES OF STATE SOCIALISM

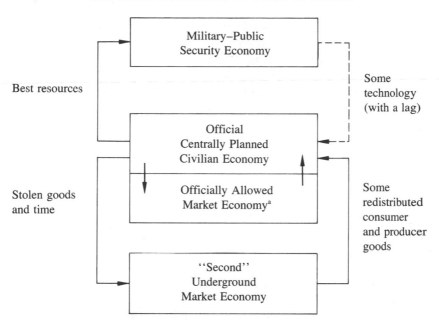

a. Time and inputs partly appropriated from the planned civilian economy are indicated by ↓ :
Some agricultural goods and some consumer goods and services redistributed to the planned
civilian economy are indicated by ↑ .
SOURCE: Author.

cialism and capitalism in this regard. First, the size of both the
military–public security and the underground economies in the Soviet type of system is larger than it is in the market system. A
study by the U.S. Defense Intelligence Agency concludes that the
Soviet military industrial base "is by far the world's largest in number
of facilities and physical size and it produces more individual military
systems in greater quantities than any other nation." The number
of people employed in Soviet military industry was 9 million in
1981, up 64 percent from 1965. Defense spending since 1970 grew
at an estimated annual rate of 6–7 percent. In constant 1970 prices
the military burden probably reached 21 percent of gross national
product in 1985 (17 percent in 1985 prices, or more than two and
a half times the comparable U.S. figure for 1985).[13] This does not
take into account outlays on the secret police. The amount of effort,
time, and money expended on shadowing people, jamming foreign
broadcasts, scrambling television receptions, monitoring telephone

calls, censoring the written and spoken word, collating, classifying, and checking denunciations, building walls and manning them around the clock must be staggering.

The size of the underground market economy is also great in every state Socialist country. The Hungarians say that they earn 4,000 forints a month, spend 7,000, and bank the rest. In fact, the most distinctive feature of the Hungarian New Economic Mechanism (NEM) is that it has come to terms with the underground economy by legitimizing it—the official euphemism is "extending the state sphere." The large size of the second economy is due in part to the kind of goods and services traded on its market, and this constitutes the second difference between the underground economy under state socialism and that under capitalism. Most goods traded on the Soviet type of system's underground market are "ethical" goods: blue jeans, spare parts, plumbers' services, housing construction, and the like; some would perhaps call them "necessities," which the official planned economy does not supply in sufficient quantities and qualities. True, many of the goods are stolen from the official economy, as is the time spent in procuring and disposing of them, but the goods themselves are ethical in the sense that they do not—as they do in the underground economy of the market system—involve primarily narcotics, prostitution, gambling, extortion, and other products of organized crime. What is unethical is the inability of the Soviet type of civilian economy to provide its citizens with ethical goods, like prime meat and fresh vegetables. Third, the Soviet type of planned civilian economy is an economy of chronic supply shortages (one is almost tempted to say planned shortages). It is certainly not one whose problem (like that of the market system) is the recurrent deficiency of aggregate demand. The scarce—and the best— resources of the civilian economy are diverted to the military–public security economy, second to the underground market economy: in the first case by the government, in the second case spontaneously by the people.

Spillovers

Because hermetic secrecy surrounds the military–public security economy, apparently few, if any, innovations spill over from that economy to the planned civilian one:

> As far as spillover of military technology per se into the civilian sector is concerned, one can state with confidence that it barely exists. The dissemination of such innovations

is strictly prohibited, and the secrecy that pervades Soviet military industry serves to prevent infringements of this prohibition. Technological advances that are not strictly military in nature are eventually permitted to filter into the civilian sector, but this process takes so long that it is easier and more profitable for civilian industry to draw on foreign sources of information. . . . What exchange of production technology know-how does exist between the civilian and military sectors is generally one-directional, from the civilian to the military.[14]

On this (not universally shared) view, the civilian economy is, on balance, a loser in the transaction.[15] It is impoverished by the transfer. The demand of the military accentuates the systemic shortages inherent in the civilian economy. As Mikhail Augursky points out, however, there is some gain because of a curious twist. The secrecy restrictions imposed on the employees of the military–public security economy are so stringent and oppressive that the best talent is apparently not attracted to that economy or quits as soon as it can. Secrecy and bureaucratic and security tangles also slow down the introduction of technical and managerial innovations into the military–public security economy, whereas the obstacles to such innovations (most of them "borrowed" from the West) are less in the civilian economy, especially in those segments of it devoted to the manufacture of hard currency exports. In this way, the military–public security economy becomes dependent on the civilian economy, which might be described as a case of the blind leading the lame.[16] These reflections are a useful corrective to the common assumption that just giving the military–public security economy top priority in almost everything automatically makes it progressive and efficient. During their post-Mao introspection the Chinese came across many instances of slackness in their military economy, which used to receive the best of everything, including protection from Red Guard excesses at the height of the Cultural Revolution. A study carried out by the Yunnan Economic Research Institute in 1982–1983 showed that the province's military industries had two to three times as many trained technicians as did the civilian industries—a ratio that probably applied to mainland China as a whole. The productivity of cutting machines in the military factories, however, was only half that in civilian factories, and labor productivity was almost two-fifths lower.[17] One should not, however, push this argument too far and conclude, as Augursky does, that the "military industry [in Russia] cannot by any means be considered efficient; it is in fact primitive and unsophisticated in terms of produc-

67

tion methods and development."[18] In the end, the generosity with which the military and the KGB receive all kinds of superior inputs surely overcomes the inefficiency and other problems created by this very abundance.

Rigid secrecy strictly applied means that there are no spillovers from the military to the underground market economy. For all practical purposes there is no link between the two. In most civilian factories workers use their work time and state-owned equipment to make goods for the underground market, the earnings from such activity frequently exceeding the official wage. Because of the tight discipline in military factories, such activity is unheard of there.[19]

How about spillovers between the official planned civilian economy and the underground market economy? Here the mutual relationship is complex. As already noted, resources are diverted by employees of the planned civilian economy into the underground market system where they are redistributed in accordance with the dictates of supply and demand (consumer preferences), not according to plan. Some of the resources return to the planned civilian economy, but the recipients are not the ones designated by material balances, allocation certificates, the state budget, and credit and cash plans. There is probably a net gain in consumer and producer welfare as a result of the underground activities of the market economy. The supply of consumer goods and services is more nearly consistent with actual consumer preferences (the leaking faucet gets repaired right away, even though the repair is not in the plan, and if manufactured in the underground economy, the faucet would probably not leak in the first place), and producers are enabled to fulfill their output targets by using market-produced inputs and thus get their hands on official bonuses. Everybody is better off, except the tax collector. So in this sense the official civilian economy gains from the operation of illegal markets. In fact, without the underground market economy, the planned civilian economy would probably be paralyzed by its own internal inconsistencies and the inherent absurdity of the central planning task.

At another level of analysis, however, the planned civilian economy is a loser. Take the planned distribution of the labor force, for example. By virtue of the income they derive from underground market activities, those who cannot find officially sanctioned employment in areas of the country they prefer are resistant to wage differentials, bonus schemes, housing amenities, and other enticements proffered by the planners and designed to move labor from labor-surplus to labor-deficiency areas, or more generally in directions dictated by the planners' preferences with regard to the civilian economy. Since the profits reaped in underground activities cannot be legally invested in plant and equipment or research and development, they are used to buy officials and consumer goods.[20] Entrepreneurial ingenuity, creative in a free market system, takes on a street-smart, redistributive quality in the illegal market economy of the Soviet type of system.

The large-scale diversion of resources from the planned civilian to the shadow market economy through stealing testifies to the failure of planning. Everybody knows that without such transfer the planned economy would function worse than it does, if it functioned at all. What we have here, in other words, is not just a movement of resources from one economy to another but the loss of legitimacy of the official plan—an erosion of economic ethos that affects the motivational system by fostering indifference, cynicism, and resentment. The major psychological spillover from the underground economy to the planned civilian economy is the mentality and ethics of *blat* (corruption). On balance, the planned civilian economy is a loser again.

Everyone is aware of that, leaders included. Their reaction to the ubiquitous presence of the second economy fluctuates between repression (unleashing the public security economy on the underground) and co-optation. The first increases the chaos in the civilian planned economy and raises consumer costs. The second, practiced most clearly by Hungary, consists in coming to terms with the market economy, bringing it up to the surface (where some of it can be taxed), and learning to live with it while calling it socialism and proclaiming the superiority of central planning. This solution of half-plan half-market, neither plan nor market, makes life more livable but creates a systemic disequilibrium and a moral instability that afflict society, a sense of alienation, pretence, and void.[21]

Operational Characteristics of the Military–Public Security Economy

Despite the problems besetting the military–public security economy, due mostly to that economy's insulation from information flows for reasons of secrecy, there is no question but that the economy performs satisfactorily when judged by its twin objectives of creating military might and an effective apparatus of domestic political control. Whatever the opportunity costs involved, the ability of the Soviet type of economic system to produce arms and police people's lives is not in doubt. What are the major operational characteristics of the military–public security economy in the Soviet type of setting, and how do they differ from the characteristics that define the planned civilian economy?

Absolute Priority. The military–public security economy receives the highest priority in every area of operations, but especially with regard to the quantity and quality of its inputs. Contrasted with the planned civilian economy, particularly that economy's consumer goods and services segment, there are no shortages here, no limits.[22] While this might prompt some wasteful practices, the best ultimately does get produced, no matter what the cost.

Consumer Sovereignty. The military–public security economy borrows certain operational principles from the market economic system. The most important of these is sovereignty of the consumer—in this case, of the monopsonistic state (Defense Ministry). Unlike what happens in the planned civilian economy, consumer demand is dominant here.

Quality Control. Technical quality control is much more thorough than it is in the civilian planned economy. It includes stringent specifications incorporated into every set of guidelines, subject to review by several inspection levels, all generously staffed with qualified personnel. Unlike what happens in the civilian planned economy, the organs of quality control are not subordinate to the manufacturer's supervisory ministry but are directly under the control of, and responsible to, the consumer (the state through the Defense Ministry). These organs have veto powers. No consideration is given to production schedules, and no replacement of materials is allowed, even if such replacement would not adversely affect the product. While this raises the cost of the product, it does tend to ensure its quality, certainly when compared with most goods turned out by the civilian planned economy. Notice that quality control in the military economy is not an automatic byproduct of the operation of a market price mechanism but of a thorough application of technical and administrative inspection procedures lacking elsewhere.

Research and Development. Aron Katsenelinboigen and Herbert Levine make the useful distinction between the treatment of uncertainty in routine and that in creative processes. Although uncertainty of outcomes is present both in routine production processes and in creative processes of science and technology, it is much greater in the creative processes. The resolution of the high degree of uncertainty in creative processes requires parallel competitive research, preferably in the context of horizontal relations. The Soviet type of planned civilian economy, however, uses vertical institutional organizations in science and technology, with parallel research being reduced to a minimum by the planners: "Only in the military sector, is parallel, competitive research normally pursued in the framework of a vertical mechanism."[23]

Secrecy. While the whole Soviet type of economic system is security conscious, the consciousness is carried to its ultimate limits in the military–public security economy. The net effect is to neutralize or undo many of the advantages that could accrue to that economy from its top position on the planners' scale of preferences, the prevalence of state-consumer sovereignty, strict technical quality control, and some parallel, competitive research pursued in the framework of a vertical institutional mechanism. This point emphasizes that elements of weakness lie even within the strongest component of the Soviet type of economic system.[24]

Summary and Conclusions

The Soviet type of economic system consists of three distinct but related economies: the centrally planned civilian economy, the underground market economy, and the military–public security (secret police) economy. The military–public security economy—the purpose of which is to create military might and ensure domestic control over the citizenry—is by far the most important to the leadership. Both objectives have been achieved with notable success, although at a sizable opportunity cost. The military–public security economy represents a drain on the planned civilian economy; it gives little, if anything, in return. The civilian economy experiences chronic resource shortage, efficiency problems, and substandard quality for reasons integral to the system of central administrative command planning, aggravated by the drain of its resources to the military–public security economy. The planned civilian economy is an unmitigated failure. In some of its local manifestations it is already in a state of degenerative collapse. It produces goods that neither consumers nor planners want. The full realization of collapse is postponed by a lively but essentially redistributive "second" underground market economy, which, while it raises material welfare, contributes to the system's internal inconsistencies and gives rise to serious disequilibrium in the society's value system. The planned civilian economy is popularly perceived as a trick at the service of the military and the secret police.

6
Similarities and Differences of Economic Changes in China and the Soviet Union

From the early 1980s through the middle of the decade, first China then the Soviet Union embarked on a course of economic change: the "Four Modernizations" in China and *perestroika* in the USSR. Some Western observers regard these changes as potentially revolutionary, that is, capable of structurally transforming the system of central administrative command planning. Others, in contrast, see in them the makings of yet another failed attempt to deal fundamentally with the system's chronic shortages, static and dynamic inefficiencies, and abysmal quality.

The Chinese and Soviet diagnoses of their respective economic ills and the proposed as well as implemented remedies reveal certain instructive similarities and differences.

Similarities

Changes from the Top. In both countries the changes have originated at the top, by the grace of the uppermost echelons of the Party. If, indeed, what is involved is a revoluntionary transformation of the economy's essence (still an open question), the revolution comes from above, and the ruling elite intends to control it and to determine its course, scope, and pace. If the change involves some genuine transfer of decision-making power from the monocratic party elite to consumers, workers, firm managers, foreign equity holders, and other economic agents, the Party elite's "democratic instinct" is all important. History shows that such instinct is alien to Communist party elites everywhere. Hence, if the contemplated economic changes are of a decentralizing temper, the fact that they originate at the top, among hardened autocrats, poses serious dangers to their eventual materialization.

Qualified Recognition of Systemic Causes. Both the Chinese and the Soviets—the first with Deng's return to power in 1978, the second with Gorbachev in 1985—recognized that the problems troubling their economies were caused by more than just "erroneous work style" ("bureaucratism," "formalism," and other types of deviationist behavior) that allegedly made it difficult for the doctrinally posited superiority of the Socialist economic system to manifest itself in the form of a plentiful supply of technologically progressive, high-quality goods and services at accessible prices. The recognition that not wrong policy alone but that the system itself may be at fault is mostly implicit, defensive, qualified by assurances about the instrinsic strength and vigor of the system, and far from generally shared among the elites. Indeed, the whole reformist episode has added to the inherent factionalism and divisiveness of the Party's leadership. Even so, the admission by some leaders, however hesitant, that the economic base of socialism—its very core—may be flawed, represents an achievement of sorts for a party wedded to doctrinal certainties. If it is true that a system consists of three main elements—ideas, institutional structures, and policies—a dent in set ideas is a welcome preliminary to institutional and policy change.

Common Disabilities. Because they do, in fact, stem from the same systemic defects, the major ills that beset the Chinese and the Soviet economies are remarkably similar, despite the two economies' many obvious differences (for example, in level of development). These common ills are chronic shortage of consumer and producer goods; massive waste, caused by both resourse misallocations of imposing proportions and wasted motion; and low quality, not only of goods and services, but of motivation, morale, and human relations in general. Included in this short list is the problem the system experiences with technological innovation and diffusion, particularly in the civilian sector.

Qualified Consensus on General Direction of Change. Acknowledgment that structural reform is needed has been accompanied in both countries by recognition, however grudging, that the reform should be decentralizing and that it should bring about some diffusion of decision-making power regarding production, exchange, and distribution. The reform has to marketize, to some unspecified degree, the institutional arrangements of information, coordination, and incentives and to privatize property rights.

Absence of General Theoretical Blueprint for Change. Neither in China nor in the Soviet Union has the rather fragile leadership consensus on the broad direction of change been informed by a comprehensive theory of systemic transition. No blueprint can indicate to those in charge of the reform what the final outcome will be, what turns to make at which time, how much disruption is avoidable, and how much is inevitable and necessary to get to the root of the problems of shortage, waste, and inferior quality. This unpredictability derives partly from the deficiency of economic theory—both Socialist and market—in intersystemic change but also partly from political and ideological considerations. It is extremely delicate for a regime not only to admit the failure of its economic system but also to map out transition to another system—indeed, to one that is not only opposite but that had always been portrayed as self-destructive, bankrupt, and unjust. In the circumstances virtue is made of necessity and the improvisational nature of the changes is presented as newly found pragmatism: "crossing the river while groping for the stones," as the Chinese put it. Emphatically asserted in both countries is the claim that the transition is not to capitalism (the market system), but to a new kind of socialism: a socialism "with Chinese characteristics" for the Chinese; a "renewal and regeneration of Socialist principles" after years of distortion and stagnation for the Soviets. Both agree that this new kind of superior socialism will contain market elements and broader-than-hitherto property rights exercised by the actual users of assets (privatization). These market-private property grafts are justified as part of the process of paying attention to the "law of value" in a Socialist "commodity economy" and are contrasted with adventurist "teleological" planning and the largely demonetized "natural" (physically planned) economy practiced by Stalinists and left deviationists (Maoists) in their "blind" headlong rush toward full communism. The new Socialist commodity economy, however, is still seen as a planned economy dominated by socialized ownership of the means of production. Markets for individual commodities—mainly for consumer goods and services—but not the market system are to be used to demonstrate the inherent superiority of Socialist arrangements, to complement and supplement—but not replace—central planning, which is now to be more flexible; less physical, direct, and imperative; and more financial ("value inclined"), indirect, and indicative (giving "guidance" rather than orders). In sum, the absence of a well-thought-out theoretical blueprint of systemic transition, the insistence on step-by-step pragmatism so-called, the demonstrable lack of a genuine understanding of how the market system works, and the continued hostility of even the more enlightened reformers toward capitalist institutions and philosophy, combined with a vague vision of Lange-like academic socialism, do not bode well for the Chinese and Soviet reforms.

Zigzag Courses, Half-Measures, and Recidivism. Thus far in both countries (ten years of changes in China and four in Russia), change has followed a zigzag course with a strong tendency to back away from reform and find refuge in policy adjustments as soon as any sizable obstacles appear. The stones encountered in the river crossing are often seen not as necessary footholds for further advance but as boulders that bar progress and prompt retreat. The failure to distinguish genuine problems from disruptions that are a necessary and indispensable part of the cure for the centrally planned system's ills arises largely from the absence of a theory of systemic transition and the theoretically uninformed mixing of market and planning instruments and state and private property rights. The resulting indigestible neomercantilistic mélange of neither-plan-nor-market, a little bit of this and a bit of the other without any clear notion of how they fit in or whether they go together at all, and the seeming purposelessness of the circuitous motions and their indecisiveness and irresolution have led to widespread popular disappointment with reform and calls in some quarters for a return to the known inconveniences of the past. Ad hoc policy, which is not really an informed, purposeful structural reform, is giving marketizing and privatizing reforms a bad name. Moreover, the many incompatibilities of selected parts of market and planning instruments of information, coordination, and incentives and of public, ill-defined, and often harassed private property rights invite massive corruption. Corruption there has always been, but like much else under the neo-Stalinist regime of the central plan, it was frequently hidden or disguised. Now it is in the open (like inflation, unemployment, and income differentials), operating in the canyonlike cracks of the unfinished, neither-this-nor-that semi-system.

Price System, Factor Markets, and Private Property. Nowhere have the hesitations surrounding the reform movement been more clearly demonstrated than in the reformers' approach to three key elements of change: the price system, factor markets, and private property. Solution, or at least significant alleviation, of the triple shortage-waste-quality problem crippling the Socialist economy requires that the senseless, allocatively irrational, politically motivated price system be thoroughly changed and revolutionized—that is, freed. The liberation of the price system must extend to all price categories: industrial, agricultural, consumer goods, materials, and factors (land, labor, and capital). Given the administratively created price distortions in the context of chronic shortages, freeing the price system is synonymous with open inflation. Understandably, the prospect of significant inflation alarms the leadership, who will seek means of reducing inflationary pressures to politically tolerable proportions.

Since the macroeconomic market infrastructure of inflation control (tax systems and an independent central banking system) are not in place, the leadership resorts naturally to known administrative levers of control, implying recentralization and rebureaucratization of the economy and a partial return to the regime of direct, mandatory physical planning. What little progress had been made in rationalizing the price system is lost. Sensitivity to inflation and hesitation on the whole subject of price reform are exemplified by attempts to ease the pain through the introduction of multitrack prices for a number of key commodities: fixed state-set prices for planned deliveries and flexible prices for above-plan production. The multitrack price solution is no solution at all. It adds to the disarray by promoting behavioral distortions of all kinds and encouraging political bargaining and corruption. Both China and the Soviet Union, then, refuse to bite the politically explosive bullet of price system reform. Without it the reform is as good as dead.[1] Marketization of the price system requires as its precondition the elimination of, not just reduction in, the system of central physical rationing: that is, the abolition of the material and technical supply network.

This has not been done either in China or in Russia. Marketization of the price system also means marketization—that is, freeing—of factor markets. This, too, has not been done or has been done minimally for labor and above-plan capital. The free pricing of factors presents conceptual difficulties greater even than those involved in the pricing of consumer goods because of the Marxist theoretical position on the nonproductive nature of capital and land and the consequent absence of the concept of a scarcity price for these factors. (This again illustrates the necessity for systemic reform to embrace not only institutional change but also change in ideas: both positive—economic theory—and normative—economic ethics. It calls for a rejection of Marxism.) Marketization of the price system also requires that property rights be privatized; very broad rights to the use and transfer of and income from goods and services must be vested in the users of those goods and services as individuals or freely formed associations of individuals. While the connection between allocatively rational resource employment and private property rights is better understood today than it was a few years ago, the understanding is incomplete and continues to be obfuscated by doctrinal *idées fixes.* Officialdom in China and the USSR continues to view private property as a necessary evil, an exploitative and dirty thing, to be reluctantly tolerated, harassed, and squeezed. This hostility is not limited, however, to party and government officials but is common among the citizenry (the "red eye disease" of envy, as the Chinese call it).

Defense of Socialist Ethics. Marketization and privatization of the ossified centrally planned command economy are made more difficult than they otherwise would be because both the Chinese and Soviet leaderships adhere to ethical Socialist principles that have become deeply embedded in the popular psyche in the past several decades and that today are embodied in powerful special interest lobbies for the defense of the status quo. These principles, which are inimical to economic calculation and efficiency, represent a payment made by the regime to the citizens as consumers and workers in exchange for state control, citizen obedience, shortages, waste, poor quality, and a low rate of improvement in living standards.

As *The Economist* puts it, "For all its faults, old-fashioned central planning has its attractions: stable prices, job security, egalitarian (if miserly) pay."[2] If these are removed, something better has to be put in its place quickly. Price stability enforced by price freezing, job tenure irrespective of performance, and egalitarian low wages, however, are the very opposite of the spontaneous flexibility required by an allocatively rational and technologically progressive economic system. They are a denial of the market principle. While some progress has been made in the Socialist understanding of price flexibility, this understanding is limited to downward and occasional flexibility, not to upward and continuous price adjustments.

Some slight advance has also occurred in the understanding of the need for the liquidation of parasitic firms and the positive efficiency role of eliminating nominally full and permanent employment of the underemployed work force. Here again, as with inflation, the necessary market-related social infrastructure (in this instance of unemployment insurance) is missing from the half-reformed economics, and so, quite naturally, in times of difficulty the instinctive leadership reaction is to bail out failing firms with subsidies and pay unemployment compensation to unneeded workers on the job.

Political Changes. The proponents of economic change in China and the Soviet Union understand that even a partial and disjointed marketization and privatization of the economic structure require some liberalization of the political "superstructure." The Thirteenth Congress of the Communist Party of China (October–November 1987) noted that "without reform of the political structure, reform of the economic structure cannot succeed in the end." Similar sentiments have been expressed in Gorbachev's Soviet Union. Given the close relationship everywhere between economic and political systems, economic decentralization requires some correlated movement toward political pluralism. In both China and the USSR the party has interpreted this pluralism in the narrowest terms as a shift away from totalitarianism toward some form of hard authoritarianism. In China the Four Basic Principles define the limits of the Party's "democratic instinct." In the USSR, "Socialist pluralism" is interpreted not as "the notorious 'free play' of political forces, but [as] an expansion of the platform of national unity under the leading role of the party." The Chinese agree. They talk about separating the functions of the party from those of the government, and of the government from the daily business of economic enterprises. "China," however, "is a socialist country under the people's democratic dictatorship and its basic political system is good." The separation of Party-government and government-enterprise functions "does not mean in any sense that the Party's tasks will be reduced and its role weakened. Rather, the separation will further consolidate the Party's leadership role."[3] In short, political decentralization in China and the USSR is envisioned as a means to the end of more efficient party dictatorship, not as a structural transformation, the end product of which is democracy. The Party's will to retain its monopoly on political power has not discernibly weakened.

Differences

Response from Below. In sharp contrast with the Soviet Union, the economic changes initiated from above in China initially met with enthusiastic popular response. The trauma of the Cultural Revolution in China exceeded by far the effects on the Soviet citizenry of Brezhnev's "ten years of stagnation." Whereas in China the response of the citizenry to calls for radical economic changes was like a groundswell, carrying all before it, Gorbachev's impassioned pleas for restructuring the economy have fallen on deaf ears. The Soviet response is partly explainable by the longer reign and the greater success of socialism in implanting its value system in the Soviet Union (particularly in Russia) than in China. War communism, Lenin, Stalin, and their successors have first managed to eradicate physically the entrepreneur from the land and then to benumb what little was left of the entrepreneurial spirit by bartering it against the promise of price stability, employment security, and money income (not power) equalization.[4] By and large, despite the Socialist ravages of the Great Leap Forward and the Cultural Revolution in China, the demoralization of the citizenry in the early through the mid-1980s was greater in the Soviet Union than in China. For the most part, Chinese peasants responded eagerly to the marketization and de facto privatization of the rural incentive structure (accomplished through the so-called household production responsibility system, whereas to this day Gorbachev has trouble persuading more than 1 or 2 percent of his proletarianized collective farmers to exchange their current low-level security for productive work and possibly higher income. In sum, the social anomie appears to be much worse in the USSR than in China and the lethargy, apathy, and sullenness—not to dwell on drunkenness—more widespread. Although we know relatively little about the inner workings of the Communist party's higher reaches in either country, intraparty bureaucratic opposition to even a modest marketization and privatization of the economic system appears distinctly stronger in the Soviet Union than in China.

Action versus Talk. The Chinese began their economic changes with actions rather than words. The Soviets under Gorbachev started with a progaganda barrage about the revolutionary nature of the proposed reforms and an outpouring of legislative acts. Since Soviet citizens by now tend to be somewhat skeptical about oratorical promises and paper laws, the incentive effect of all this preliminary agitprop activity has been nil or negative. The one thing that might positively change the climate of Soviet public opinion on the subject of *perestroika* is the prompt appearance on store shelves of consumer goods that people actually want at prices they are prepared to pay. This happened initially in China. It has not happened so far in the Soviet Union and is not likely to occur in the foreseeable future. An opinion poll published at the end of 1988 in *Komsomolskaya Pravda* revealed that one-third of the respondents thought long lines for food and most other goods would not be done away with "during their lifetime, if ever." Only 0.3 percent believed the lines would disappear within a year ot two.[5] For a while even vodka, an indispensable component of the Russian diet, vanished from the shelves, followed by sugar, meat, cabbage, and the rest. This is no way to start a reform.

Economics First versus Politics First. The Chinese began their changes with economics; the Soviets, with politics. In China the period of political liberalization was very brief and treated by the reformists as a tactical weapon in factional struggles for power. Once fully in charge, Deng Xiaoping (a leading author of the Anti-Rightist scourge of 1957) put a quick end to demands for the "fifth modernization"—political democracy. By contrast, in the Soviet Union the Gorbachev era began with calls for and some movement toward *glasnost* and *politicheskaya nadstroika* (political superstructure), which, though modest affairs by Western standards of democracy, represented a political thaw compared with Khruschev's later years and the Brezhnev decade. Although welcomed by sections of the Moscow intelligentsia, the partial opening up of formerly taboo political and intellectual areas was and continues to be resented by irredentist groups (including Russian nationalist elements) both within the party and in society at large. They see it as catering to the demands of minority nationalities within the boundaries of the USSR and as encouraging anti-Soviet and anti-Russian sentiments in Eastern Europe. An honest, factual reexamination of the history of socialism in both countries, moreover, shows the citizens that the Communist elite was, for the most part, either incompetent, cruel, crooked, or all three at once. This does little to raise public morale or restore confidence in the vanguard party. In any event, *glasnost* is food for thought, not food for the table.

Beginning with Agriculture versus Beginning with Industry. The Chinese changes began quietly and technically with structural transformations—partial marketization and bold decollectivization—of agriculture. Peasant families received restricted de facto private property rights in land and farm capital subject to delivery to the state of certain portions of output at state-set prices and the payment of some communal levies. The peasants made production and income distribution decisions with respect to all output above the contractual and tax obligations, consuming the surplus themselves or selling it at relatively free market prices. The incentive effect of combined marketization and privatization was very positive: output and productivity rose rapidly and substantially, providing the reform effort with a foundation of increased peasant prosperity (particularly of peasants near large cities) and larger and better-quality food supplies for urban consumers. In industry, the Chinese stressed the long-neglected consumer goods and services sector. They allowed the importation of foreign consumer goods to ease pent-up demand and help translate rising money incomes of both the peasantry and the urban workers into wanted goods. They altered the property structure of industry by transferring the many medium-sized state enterprises to the less rigidly and bureaucratically controlled cooperative sector, by expanding the scope of private ownership of small-to-medium industrial and service activities and by experimenting with mixed property forms (state-cooperative, cooperative, private, state–foreign private). The Chinese considerably reduced (but did not eliminate) the central physical rationing of inputs and legally sanctioned residual markets in materials and producer goods. They also conducted experiments with stock ownership in cooperative and state enterprises. As reform of the industrial price system became more elusive in the late 1980s, bold theoretical proposals were advanced for the denationalization of all industry and the transformation of state industrial enterprises into publicly owned stock companies. By contrast, the Soviets began their economic changes not with agriculture but with industry, and heavy industry at that, particularly machine tools; this approach does not translate into immediate tangible benefits for the consumer. The massive Soviet Law on the State Enterprise (effective January 1, 1988) does not change in any fundamental way the economic structure and property relations of industry, heavy or light. An initial expansion of private service activities in the cities has been the object of subsequent stifling restrictions. A belated proposal to lease land out to groups of *kolkhozniki* (collective farmers), even to individual peasant families, has met with little response.

Adjustment and Reform. A study of the Soviet legislation on economic change leaves an impression of *déja vu*.[6] It looks for the most part like the already tried (or half-heartedly tried) Kosygin-Liberman scenario of the 1960s, which failed not because Brezhnev replaced Khrushchev but because it did not go far enough to market—because 99 percent of it was surface tinkering with a diseased system and the remaining 1 percent reform consisted of disjointed pieces of the market mechanism, unable to function in their truncated condition, uncoordinated among themselves, and at odds with endlessly reorganized administrative mechanisms of the command plan. As noted, the Soviet Law on the State Enterprise contains little that could be called structural reform. Harking back to Kosygin-Liberman in its emphasis on greater accountability and expanded decision-making latitude of state sector firms, the law specifies numerous organizational and other superficial changes that have been tried in one shape or another before and have failed each time to provide the needed cure. In the absence of structural and systemic reforms of the industrial price system (marketization), the abolition of physical rationing of all materials and investment goods, the dismantling of ministerial branch empires, and the introduction of varied ownership forms (including private property rights on a large scale), Gorbachev's *perestroika* will be just another in a long line of ineffective adjustments that produce stagnation at best.

The first response of Soviet firm managers to the greater rights given them to fix prices of new products has been to raise the prices of substandard currently produced products and pass the old stuff off as innovation. Then, to stem rising prices, the state—as expected—increased its subsidies for various consumer goods, not only adding to its formidable budget deficit but further distorting an already highly irrational price structure. The heralded Soviet "reform" of the price system is nothing but a recalculation, on the basis of an allocatively meaningless Marxist value theory, of Brezhnev's old cost-plus prices, a gigantic and ultimately futile bureaucratic exercise for which there are several precedents in the USSR. It is merely another example of waste. The Soviet agricultural price system is equally flawed and equally in urgent need of reform, but reform is not anywhere on the horizon. By contrast, the Chinese did marketize their agricultural price system, not fully but significantly, and carried out de facto, if restricted, privatization of property rights in the farming sector. They have failed in their attempt, begun in 1984, to inject some allocative rationality into the industrial price system, including industrial wages and capital goods. Despite a small increase in industrial labor mobility and the emergence of markets for some above-plan producer goods (and the appearance of a rudimentary market for urban real estate), reform of the industrial price system had not proceeded far before inflation struck and "retreat into caution" was ordered in 1988. The result has been contradiction between a substantially marketized and privatized agriculture and a still largely administered and socialized industry and, within each sector, between market and administered prices and between conflicting state and private property rights. In 1988 China decided to postpone industrial price reform for at least two years, signaling the possibility of permanent retreat from the marketization resolve of 1984. Still, on balance, China has gone farther on the road of reform than the USSR. Thus far, at least, the Soviet Union has very little to show for all the grand talk about revolutionary structural economic change.

The Open Door. The system of central administrative command planning is essentially a closed system tending toward self-sufficiency, avoiding foreign economic involvements as much as possible, and insulating the domestic economy to the maximum extent feasible from the influence of the world market. Once considered a strength, the system's very marginal participation in world trade and finance is now seen as a costly failing. The insulation of domestic industry from foreign competition (the USSR has an estimated 3,000 secret exchange rates protecting its industry) and of the domestic price system from world prices contributes to the calcification of domestic industry, retards technological advance, and makes calculation of comparative advantage and participation in the international division of labor very difficult. Since the early 1980s the Chinese have stolen the march on the Soviets in opening their doors to international trade and finance, including joint ventures within the country. On this front, too, reform has its limits. After a certain point, which is rapidly being reached, participation in the world market means acceptance of the rules of the market system, or domestic marketization through the open door. As expected, this type of back door marketization has its opponents in both countries and has thus far proceeded by fits and starts. In the forefront of the opposition are coddled state industries threatened in their gross inefficiencies by the specter of foreign competition.

Conclusions

While acknowledging that the problems of chronic shortage, waste, and low quality are in their origin very largely systemic and that to address them effectively they must restructure the system in a marketizing and privatizing direction, the Chinese and the Soviets refuse to accept the proposition that the system's ills can be removed only through a complete changeover to the market system. Complete transition to the market system means that the successor system is one in which information, coordination, and incentives arise from horizontal, competitive, voluntary, utility-maximizing and profit-making buyer-seller transactions guided by spontaneously generated free market prices for consumer goods and services as well as factors. These transactions unfold in a context of private property rights. The principle of voluntariness of transactions expressed in a workably, not perfectly, competitive market and the principle of vesting in individuals and voluntary associations of individuals broad rights of transfer, use, and income with respect to goods and services must clearly dominate the system. Their presence does not exclude an active role for government in behalf of the market and private property and in areas of market failure. Any attempt to stop halfway, to use bits and pieces of markets and restricted rights of private property in conjunction with bits and pieces of central administrative command planning and state property, will cause systemic breakdown and build up strong pressures for a return to the old system. Frequent attempts to supplement central planning with a market here and there and some circumscribed private ownership—that is, onto the body of the plan—will certainly not solve the Socialist system's chronic shortages, waste, and inferior quality. They will probably make these matters worse.

Only a clear conceptual and practical recognition that to cure the ills of the plan one must travel all the way to the market system and that "taking the capitalist road" means going to capitalism, not to some Socialist inn one-third of the way down from the plan or stopping at a desert place halfway down the road, will enable China and the Soviet Union to catch up with the advanced countries of the world. Such a recognition is, on historical evidence, hardly to be expected from Communist party elites in either country unless they are forced into it by mounting evidence of a decaying society and insistent pressures from below.

7

Mainland China and Hungary—
To Market, to Market . . .

[In China] we are developing a socialist commodity [market] economy which is fundamentally different from the capitalist commodity economy.

T'IEN CHI-YUN

[In Hungary] we have moved in the direction of the market but the economy has not yet completely arrived there . . . I am confident that more influence of the market on economic decisions would improve the Hungarian economy even more.

JÁNOS KORNAI

Hungary since 1968 and mainland China since 1978 have been experimenting with their economic structures, which both had originally adopted from the Soviet Stalinist model of central administrative command planning and comprehensive socialization of property rights in assets. The reason for this experimentation is that the model of command planning and socialized, highly centralized property is probably the world's second most inefficient way of economic decision making, the first being the model's radicalized variant known as Maoism. In Hungary the model reached the point of degenerative collapse in the revolution of 1956. It took the Hungarians another eleven years to get rid of much of it, but even now it keeps pounding at the door and occasionally, as in 1972–1979, breaks down the door and makes a fine mess of things. In China the decision to dump the model (together with its Maoist outgrowth) took only two years, but then the Chinese did not have to worry about what the Russians thought, nor were they hampered in their resolve by membership in the Council of Mutual Economic Assistance (CMEA), the Warsaw Pact, or other Moscow-sponsored impedimenta. What the Chinese have most to fear is themselves. As in Hungary, sections of the ruling party and of society are not fully convinced of the nefariousness and alleged bankruptcy of the old model, although—visibly at least—there is not much support these days for the model's Maoist variant of barefoot industrialization and development by paroxysms. In certain well-placed quarters there is a good deal of nostalgia for (as they now recall them) the dynamic, spiritual, pollution-free times of the neo-Stalinist First Five-Year Plan (1953–1957). Born-again hardliners like Chen Yun believe that with a little twiddling of policy knobs on the rusty machine, the old model could be made to work again in a reincarnated form of enlightened Stalinism.

Some Theoretical Questions

A few conceptual hurdles must be cleared at this time. There is, first of all, the question of comparability. Hungary is small, resource deficient, short of labor, heavily dependent on foreign trade, saddled with a large hard currency debt, and handicapped by a small domestic market. China is none of these. There is a big difference between the two in level of development, about as big as between the mainland and Taiwan. While these and other differences are real, they are also essentially "technical," that is, nonsystemic. What we are interested in are systemic arrangements for the generation, conveyance, and processing of information about costs and utilities in the economy, the coordinating mechanisms, the motivational subsystems, and the nature of property rights with respect to assets. On this level of economic organization comparisons between national entities are legitimate and instructive no matter how great the technical differences. In their attempt to rid themselves of economic decision-making models inherited from the past, mainland China and Hungary have much to learn from each other.

This happens to be so even more because the direction of economic experimentation in Hungary and mainland China is similar. Despite ideological disclaimers, the fact is that, as of now, the economic structures of China and Hungary are moving in the direction of the market. Inevitably, the marketization of information, the coordination, and the motivation in both economies have been accompanied by an expansion of rights vested in the actual users of assets with regard to the assets they use. Another name for it is privatization or property rights on the level of the firm.[1]

To accomplish their purpose of apportioning relatively limited resources to competing alternative uses, both plan and market use institutional arrangements for the generation, transmission, and analysis of information about the changing relationship of resources and objectives (costs-utilities, supplies-demands); the coordination of such information into a coherent pattern of production, exchange, and distribution; the motivation of the principal economic agents; and the extent and distribution of property rights with respect to assets.

I propose to handle the comparison of Hungary and mainland China by looking first at the role played by the price system in performing the information and coordination functions in the post-1967 Hungarian New Economic Mechanism (NEM) and the post-1978 mainland Chinese economy. Next, I shall take up the changes made in the motivational (incentive) arrangements in both economies, that is, the reward mechanisms directed at peasants, workers, and managers. Next, I shall examine property rights in assets: their privatization and increasing diversity, then the peculiar case and place of the so-called second economy in the new scheme. Finally, I shall try and draw some useful conclusions.

Price System—Information and Coordination

Importance of the Price System. There can be no real reform of administrative central command planning without a profound qualitative change in the nature and role of the economy's price system. Changes that do not touch the vitals of the price system are adjustments of the existing economic system, repair jobs, and replacements of worn-out parts that do not address themselves to the core of the efficiency problems of the economic engine.

In the command economy, information about what is to be done and coordination of decisions take the form of quantitative orders issued by the planners, cast in physical and technical terms, backed by administratively determined accounting prices, and sent to specific recipients. These addressee-specific, unconditional commands are coordinated at the central and lower levels of the administrative hierarchy through a process of bureaucratic iteration known as the method of material and financial balances. The whole process is vertically structured and involves substantial transaction costs.

A word about the "prices" that supplement the system's *Tonnenideologie* (concentration on physical magnitudes): the two sets of prices backing up physical and technical commands are prices at which the state buys agricultural produce from the nationalized or collectivized peasantry under compulsory physical delivery quotas (quota agricultural procurement prices), and industrial wholesale prices,

87

that is, prices at which state firms transfer goods among themselves. Both categories of prices are set by the state, usually on a cost-of-production plus profit-margin basis, with little or no regard to supply and demand. Since the allocation of quota farm produce and industrial producer goods is determined by physical rationing, the prices attaching to these goods are merely accounting devices intended to be allocatively neutral (which, in practice, they are not). They are allocatively irrational, divorced from the scarcity relationship (supplies-demands, costs-utilities) prevalent in the economy. There are other categories of prices in a command system that take some account of supply and demand forces, mainly to make less burdensome the planners' job of physical rationing. Retail prices are of this kind. They are usually set at levels that are supposed to clear the market, and they are moved up and down by the planners—often with considerable lag—in response to planner-perceived changes in the relationship of demand and supply in particular commodity markets. Wages of labor (in most command economies, except mainland China for many years) are also partly, but very imperfectly, cognizant of supply and demand in the labor market, but they too are altered by the planners at infrequent intervals.

A conservative change—or "intrasystemic adjustment"—in the command system, the kind that has been implemented by the Soviet Union and most East European countries since a little after Stalin's death, consists of two parallel movements. There is, first, a movement away from physical and technical norms to price indicators. Second, there is a movement away from mandatory planning by direct orders to "guidance" through price and price-related indicators. It should be noted that the obsession with tonnage and the compulsion to dictate in minute detail are reduced but not done away with. Firms are now instructed to fulfill profit, profitability, and sales targets and to pay more attention to costs. The instructions are less openly administrative and commandist, more indirect and clothed in generalized price expressions. There is, in other words, marginally less economic physics and *Diktat*. Some relative prices are adjusted up, some down; the methodology of cost accounting is slightly improved; and profit margins are altered. The systemically crucial point, however, is that while individual prices are changed and the importance attached to prices and price-related phenomena (for example, profit) as indicators of a firm's success is increased, the price *system* remains unchanged. It continues to be unrepresentative of the cost and utility relationships in the economy. It remains allocatively irrational. Since it does not reflect the opportunity costs of the economy, it cannot be used as a guide to allocatively meaningful (rational, optimal, efficient) decisions by economic agents. But it is, in fact, expected to do just that. The profits that firms are urged to make, deriving as they do from a constellation of daft prices, are not a synthetic mathematical expression of the reconciliation of the microinterests of the firm and the macrointerests of society. In terms of efficiency of resource use they mean nothing. There are, therefore, some substitutions of new allocative distortions for old and some additions.

If improvement of allocative efficiency is to be achieved, the movement away from physical indicators toward price indicators and from mandate to guidance must be accompanied by a movement away from administratively set accounting prices toward market-determined, workably competitive, opportunity cost prices. In other words, the price system must be liberated; that is, people must be freed so they can make their own decisions in accordance with their own maximizing calculus. As carriers of information, prices must emerge from untrammeled, lateral, buyer-seller transactions voluntarily and competitively undertaken. For the price system to act as a coordinating mechanism, the volume and structure of production must respond to the profitability signals emanating from the system. Price fluctuations—price flexibility—must be recognized as a necessary condition of market coordination, and there must be constant, spontaneous adaptation to price changes by buyers and sellers. This is something many Socialist economists (never mind the professional *apparatchiki*) have trouble understanding. They have by now grasped the need for relative price changes carried out once in a while (in a "planned manner") to bring prices more in line with supply and demand conditions. But they have yet to assimilate intellectually the need for continuous price fluctuations and the ongoing automatic adaptation of the volume and structure of supply and demand to such "anarchy."

The Price System in Hungary

Agricultural Prices. Agricultural prices consist of agricultural procurement (producer) prices and retail prices of agricultural products. Under the NEM there are no administratively set compulsory quota deliveries or sowing plans for collective and state farms. State trading companies are commissioned to buy some portion of the total farm output (mainly grain, animal products, and sugar beets) at long-term, state-fixed prices. These assignments, however, have to be carried out by means of contracts negotiated by the companies with the farms, and the purchase prices can be adjusted with an eye to general market conditions. Moreover, selling to state trading companies is only one way of disposing of farm produce. The farms can sell many agricultural products directly to state processing concerns on the free market, or—in some cases—they can export their products directly to Western firms. Producer decisions in this multichannel sales system are guided by expected profit based on relatively flexible, market or market-related prices. A cooperative's decision to sell to state trading companies at below market equilibrium prices may be dictated by a desire to bring some safety into its transactions, a course of action that may concurrently contribute to greater overall agricultural price stability. The multichannel sales of produce consumed for the most part (for example, early vegetables), are calculated on the basis of domestic input costs and are not directly related to nonruble import and export prices. This attempt to base domestic farm product prices partly on international prices is another manifestation of the trend toward the marketization of the agricultural price system.

One must not be carried away, however. Although efforts are made to reduce the disparity between the structure of the agricultural producer and consumer prices through the reduction or partial removal of differential taxes and subsidies, such disparities persist, particularly for agricultural staples with elastic demand curves, because the state perceives the need to protect urban real incomes. Another problem is that the calculation of correct farm costs of production is hampered by the system's inability to determine the appropriate scarcity charges (rent) for land use. In addition, one may ask how voluntary, lateral, contractual, and competitive is the relationship between cooperative and state farms on the one hand and the state trading or processing companies on the other when it comes to purchasing such key commodities as grain.[2] In monoparty states with significant remnants of command institutions and commandist philosophy, the borderline between mandate and guidance is not well defined. One may also ask how reliable are the "uniform foreign trade multipliers" and associated exchange rates in translating world market prices into domestic prices. The answer is, They are not reliable.

Industrial Prices. With few exceptions, the setting of output targets for firms and the physical rationing (central funding) of key inputs by planners and supervisory ministries have been abolished. The physical-technical supply network has been replaced by multiple-channel trade in the means of production.[3]

Industrial prices—both wholesale (producer) and retail—have

been freed from central control in varying degrees. There are (1) state-fixed prices, which can be changed only by the government Price Office; (2) maxima prices, which are allowed to float in response to changes in market supply and demand, but only below a state-determined maximum ceiling; and (3) free market prices.

An attempt has been made to align the structures of industrial producer and consumer prices through the removal of various taxes and subsidies to clear the information channels between buyers and sellers.

Because of Hungary's heavy reliance on foreign (including hard currency) trade and the consequent need for the domestic price system to reflect worldwide scarcity values to arrive at a notion of comparative advantage, an effort has been made, since 1980, to align some domestic industrial producer prices with world market prices. The share of such "competitive" prices is 80 percent in machine building, 50 percent in the chemical industry, and 20 percent in food processing.[4] Firms whose prices are subject to such links are those exporting more than 5 percent of their output in hard currency trade and those using a high proportion of materials imported in such trade.

As with agricultural prices, the formal steps taken to marketize the industrial price system do not tell the whole story. In actuality marketization of industrial prices has been hesitant, partial, and fitful. This has given rise to an information and coordination network that, in the words of one Hungarian economist, is neither market nor plan, or is "half-market, half-bureaucratic control"—an incompatible combination.[5]

The checklist reads as follows. First, regarding the changeover from mandate to guidance, it is true that since 1968 the party government has been (though by no means consistently or unanimously) more favorably inclined toward the idea of competitive, lateral, contractual information and coordination spontaneously generated by buyer-seller transactions. But old commandist habits die hard, and the temptation to dictate remains strong. What can be said in good conscience is that the once highly visible hand of the planners has become less visible: firms are advised rather than ordered to do certain centrally desired things. In practice, however, the advice is as binding as the former orders, norms, balances, and allocation certificates. In the opinion of one Hungarian economist, the firms subject themselves "almost voluntarily to patronage."[6]

Second, just as the degree of firm independence under the NEM is less than meets the eye, so also is the degree of price freedom. The ratios of free to controlled prices are somewhat misleading because they do not take into account the relative weights of free and controlled prices in the economy. Many prices of key commodities (fuels, raw materials, basic intermediate products) are fixed, while prices of "luxuries" are not. Then there is the problem of nominal versus effective control over prices. Calculation of the effective control over output prices should include the degree of control over the prices of inputs that go into output.[7] Moreover, the "free" trade in and free pricing of producer goods (the 80 percent) take place in highly imperfect, near-monopolistic markets in which buyers' free choice remains a formality and the crucial ingredient of competition is missing. Finally, numerous regulations inhibit the free movement of prices in the free sphere. Perceptive Chinese observers of Hungarian pricing practices have remarked that:

> On the surface, enterprises [in Hungary] seem to have a lot of decision-making power to fix prices. But actually this is not so because the floating prices, which follow the maximum limited prices, have actually become fixed. Both the floating prices and the fixed prices must be authorized by the commodity price control office. The enterprises only have some power to fix their floating prices at the lower levels. The free prices also have restrictions. While fixing the free prices, the enterprise must follow government regulations. . . . If the price of the free-price products is to go up, the factory must submit its application to the price control bureau six months in advance. Six months later the price will be raised automatically if the bureau has no objections. If the bureau has complaints about the price, then the application is shelved for future study. The government has set up a strict control system to supervise the retail prices set by commercial enterprises. When we visited a private clothing shop, the owner told us that the price of goods was a free one, which he could set by himself. But according to government stipulations, the differential rates of all clothing should be set ranging from 8 to 20 percent. When setting a price the shop should not exceed this rate. Otherwise it is an offense against the law. Punishment includes a warning, a fine, and revocation of business license.[8]

Kornai agrees:

> There are still many areas where prices are centrally fixed. Again in other areas prices are not fixed, but there are very detailed instructions issued by the price office telling the firm how to calculate the price on a "cost plus" basis and constraining the seller and the buyer in deciding on the price in a free contract. There are still many arbitrary,

non-market-clearing prices. And since all prices are interdependent, the arbitrariness of some important prices has a spillover effect and leads to severe distortions in the whole price structure.[9]

The multichannel wholesaling of industrial producer goods is still obstructed by rules that limit its scope, and informal interventions by state authorties in the wholesale market are common. While they are not blanket interventions, they distort the intent and execution of market-type allocation. In sum, the right of Hungarian firms to set and vary the prices of their products (even where these prices are in the free sphere) is quite limited, restricted by many specific legal and administrative rules. In this regard the basic relationship remains by and large vertical—between the firm and the government price office—but the verticality is less formal than it was before. Kornai characterizes the new relationship as a "regulator game," repeated matches in a game in which the players try to outsmart each other.[10]

Third, industrial wholesale (producer) and retail prices remain separated by a variety of taxes and subsidies—fewer than before 1968, but still to an extent where one cannot speak of unobstructed information flows and unhindered structural adaptation between the two.

Fourth, the alignment of domestic with convertible currency world trade prices in the "competitive" sphere of the economy is imperfect and frequently violated. World market prices do not act directly on domestic prices, but instead are simulated through "a rather peculiar pricing procedure."[11] Moreover, whenever the profitability of exports declines, obliging export firms to reduce their domestic prices accordingly and thereby reduce their profitabilities with adverse effects on the firms' management and workers' profit-sharing salary and wage supplements (and perhaps even employment), the state steps in with tax and subsidy measures designed to compenstate the firms for the adverse effects of foreign competition. In fact, there is no import competition to speak of, although Hungarian firms do have some latitude with regard to convertible currency area exports. In the absence of such import competition there is no perceptible alignment of domestic industrial producer prices with world market prices.

The Price System of Mainland China

Agricultural Prices. Until 1985 (with increasing relaxation) the state maintained a monopsony (first introduced in 1953) with regard to grain, oil-bearing crops, cotton, and timber. Grain, cooking oil, cotton wadding, and cotton cloth were rationed to urban consumers (the last two being rationed to both urban and rural consumers). The retail prices of these goods were below their state procurement prices, entailing a heavy burden of budgetary subsidies. In addition, there were compulsory delivery quotas for more than 100 other categories of farm and sideline products. After Mao's death and until 1985, rural production teams and households had four marketing channels for their products (two for products subject to state monopsony) and four sets of prices (two for monopsony goods). First, products subject to compulsory delivery quotas were sold at state-fixed quota prices. Second, some portion of output over and above the quota was sold to state procurement agencies at higher, above-quota prices fixed by the state. Both of the above were mandatory prices. Third, after the fulfillment of quota and above-quota obligations, extra output could be sold to the state at negotiated prices. Fourth, anything left over after that, and goods not subject to quotas, could be sold on rural markets at "free" market prices, the freedom being restricted by allowable price ranges set by the state.[12]

In what was billed as the "second stage of rural structural reform," the state monopsony and fixed-quota purchase system were to be gradually phased out. The movement was to be away from physical mandate, toward guidance and the market. Except for certain stipulated products, state quotas for the delivery of products at state-fixed prices have been abolished and replaced by a system of contracts based on negotiated targets and paid for at state-fixed prices. Any surplus remaining after the targets have been met can be sold on the open market at market prices. The state is to buy a stipulated 75–80 million tons of grain every year at its unified price (also known as the "preferential" price). This price is a weighted average made up of 30 percent of the former quota price and 70 percent of the former above-quota price. The rest of the crop is to be regulated by market forces. When the market price "goes low" (below the old quota price), however, as it did in 1985–1986, the state will purchase any surplus grain (as well as surplus cotton and oil-bearing crops) from the peasants at "protective" prices, higher than the market prices. When the market price "goes high," however, the state will sell appropriate quantities of its reserves on the market to bring the price back down.[13]

Prices of fish, poultry, eggs, vegetables, meat, and other non-staple perishable products have been partially decontrolled, meaning that the state "gave localities the go-ahead to fluctuate prices."[14]

The partial decontrol of nonstaple product prices resulted in initial sharp increases in those prices.

As in Hungary, what happened in mainland China by mid-1986 was a movement away from the regime of economic physics and compulsion, accompanied by significant marketization of the information and coordination functions of the agricultural price system. As in Hungary, voluntary, lateral, competitive, contractual transactions carried out through multiple trade channels increased, and the size and composition of farm output were affected more than before by a freer price system, together with taxes, credits, state subsidies, and other indicative, financial instruments. In 1984 25–30 percent of retail and agricultural procurement trade in mainland China was transacted in a marketized and privatized context, both marketization and privatization, however, being restricted in various ways.[15]

As in Hungary, the dematerialization, decompulsion, and marketization of the agricultural price system have been far from complete. For staple commodities, a direct link between state procurement prices and state retail prices has not been established. The agricultural tax and many more or less arbitrary, sometimes capricious local levies in China (in Hungary the land tax, collective income tax, labor remuneration tax, personal income tax, and production taxes on nonagricultural rural production) interpose themselves between producer and consumer with distorting effects on economic calculation. In China, like Hungary, the lateralness, voluntariness, and competitiveness of the contractural relations between tenant farm households and the state procurement agencies may be questioned. Commandist habits are alive and well. Fluctuations of the decontrolled prices in response to changing supply and demand forces in China, as in Hungary, remain subject to numerous administrative restrictions.

Industrial Prices. Until recently, industrial producer prices in mainland China were set by the state along familiar Soviet-style lines. They were cost-plus prices (average planned cost of production in the given industrial branch plus a profit margin) and paid little or no heed to the underlying conditions of supply and demand. The cost was calculated according to a peculiar Marxist costing procedure (no allowance for the scarcity cost of land and capital); the profit margins were economically arbitrary, determined for the most part by the planners' sociopolitical preferences; and no account was taken of demand. The allocative usefulness of these prices was zero.

In fact, as noted earlier, industrial wholesale prices were not supposed to exercise allocative influence, being simply accounting backup devices to physical apportionment through material balances. In the immediate post-Mao period an effort was made to adjust individual producer goods prices—the more blatantly distorted ones—the adjustment being limited to making individual prices reflect average branch production costs more accurately. Industrial retail prices were insulated from producer prices by commercial and industrial taxes (positive for most goods, negative for some). The taxes were adjusted up and down from time to time, thus raising or lowering retail prices for particular goods in order to ease shortages or eliminate surpluses in individual goods markets, mainly by bringing consumer demand for such goods into rough concordance with the planner-determined supply. Domestic prices were divorced from world market prices. The whole system was allocatively irrational and very wasteful of scarce resources.

The verticality of the information and coordination network has varied over time but has always been dominant. The number of centrally determined material balances covering the first two categories of goods (widely used and specialized materials allocated by the State Planning Commission and central "branch" ministries) has been reduced from a peak of 592 in 1964 to around 60 at the present time (and there is talk of bringing these down to 30). Concurrently, there has taken place a large increase in local government (provincial, municipal, prefectural, even township) control over physical and financial allocation of resources. This is not necessarily indicative of a significant lessening of the verticality of the information-coordination network.[16] These trends continue. In other words, the scope of mandatory physical planning is to be reduced, and the scope of administratively decentralized financial guidance planning is to increase as is the sphere of market transactions. Mandatory planning, however, will not be dispensed with altogether. It will be retained for "major products" and "major economic activities that affect the overall situation" (a catch-all caveat). Presumably, major products include primary energy, key raw materials, steel, large machinery, synthetic fibers, newsprint, and some other materials and semifabricates. The right of firms to enter into lateral contractual relations with one another is to be enlarged.[17] The Hungarian experience suggests that even where mandatory planning is abolished for the bulk of products, the propensity persists for governmental authorities at different hierarchical levels to mandate guidance.

The blueprint for industrial sector change is contained in the "Decision of the Central Committee of the Communist Party of China on Reform of the Economic Structure" adopted by the Twelfth Central Committee at its Third Plenary Session on October 20, 1984.[18] The decision—which was put on the back burner in 1986—also envisages marketizing changes in the industrial price system. The intent is to reduce gradually "the scope of uniform prices set by the state and appropriately enlarge the scope of floating prices within certain limits, and of free prices." Since the prices of many key inputs are to remain centrally fixed, however, the "Hungarian" question of the weights to be attached to the controlled versus "free" prices and the effective control over the price system through control of input prices is posed. There is, further, the question of the incompatibility of fixed, semi-fixed, and free prices both across products and for the same products.

As matters stand now, industrial prices consist of state-fixed prices, floating prices, negotiated prices, and free market prices.[19] Each category is supposed to apply primarily to a particular sphere of the economy. Thus, the stable state-fixed prices apply mostly to goods produced and transferred within the command sphere (that is, under the mandatory state plan) but also to some goods produced and traded outside the mandatory plan, in the guided sphere. Moreover, once the mandatory quota is filled at the state-fixed price, the producing firm can apparently dispose of any surplus at either floating, negotiated, or perhaps even free market prices.[20] One result has been dual pricing. Abram Bergson reports that the basic state-fixed price for steel is 600 yuan per ton, but the same steel outside the plan can sell for 1,300 yuan a ton, which does not make for improved economic calculation.[21] Negotiated prices and free market prices apply primarily to goods produced and traded outside the state mandatory plan (the so-called self-disposal goods). They are mostly small goods and sideline commodities. Some evidence suggests that the attitude of local authorities toward the non–fixed-price sphere is at best ambivalent and that while it is generally understood that the price structure must be changed, the indispensable complementary understanding that the change must be a continuing one (temporal price flexibility) is missing. The authorities' inclination to freeze producer as well as consumer prices when these prices move up in search of a market-clearing equilibrium level is well known. It is related to the Socialist (including Hungarian) politically induced imperative to prevent price increases from adversely affecting living standards. This puts a damper on the reformist quest for improvement in allocative efficiency.

The industrial system of mainland China is in a state of transition and flux. Indications are that the decision of October 20, 1984, to reconcile the rigid industrial economy with the marketization changes carried out in the agricultural economy slowed in late 1985 and in 1986 as the size and complexity of the task came to be better understood.

Information and coordination in the Chinese industrial economy remain primarily vertical, that is, characterized by still-considerable physical-commandist elements. The institutional contradictions between the Chinese industrial and agricultural price systems appear to be greater than they are in Hungary. So far the Chinese changes in the industrial information and coordination system have been more modest and conservative than the Hungarian and more internally inconsistent. (But then, the Hungarians have been at it, on and off, for more than eighteen years.)

Finally, where do the Special Economic Zones and related experiments with liberalization fit into all this? These zones are controlled experiments expected to serve as both positive and negative role models in the search for Socialist allocative efficiency—with "Chinese characteristics" and capitalist input. The zones are special, encapsulated phenomena in the learning process, and their didactic contribution to China's long march to the market may turn out to be quite marginal.

Motivation

A serious problem of centrally planned administrative command economies has always been the insufficiency and perverse working of positive incentives to peasants, workers, and managers and the considerable component of compulsion and fear (negative incentives). Next to a thorough reform of the price mechanism, reform of the motivational structure of the command system is indispensable if the system's allocative efficiency is to improve.

Peasant Incentives. The Hungarian NEM, apparently with success, provides incentives to farmers at several levels. Members of agricultural cooperatives and state farm workers are paid guaranteed state-set wages (which constitute a sort of safety net), bonus payments linked to farm profits (6–20 percent of members' earnings from the collective), and the social wage (social benefits). These are made credible by the (near-) voluntary nature of membership in the socialized farms, the farms' relatively wide rights of decision making (in which members are associated, and not just pro forma), and the not overly demanding amount of yearly working time that has to be put into the collective by individual members. An additional incentive is the opportunity for collective and state farm workers to set up small cooperatives of various kinds and subcontract land and specialized farm and farm-related off-farm jobs from the parent collective, even to own land and other productive assets. These subunits work strictly on the basis of profit and loss. Members share profits and losses and are not rescued by the parent collective if they experience persistent losses. Members of collective farms and state farm workers own small plots, the produce of which is sold at market prices. Earnings from this source are believed to double, perhaps as much as quadruple, peasant income derived from collective/state sector work. The plots can be rented out to the cooperative at fixed money payments. Thus, in the case of a private plot, small cooperative, and big cooperative/state farm, a direct link (strongest in the first two instances) is established through the profit motive between the volume and assortment of production and a partly marketized price system. The result is a reasonably accurate and frictionless reconciliation of the private and social interest at a fairly "low" (micro) societal level. In general (except for occasional bureaucratic outbursts of antiplot mentality, as in 1975), the authorities have pursued a constructive policy with respect to private plots and private initiative. They have supported them with bank credits and comparatively liberal access to modern inputs (chemicals, small machinery). Finally, cooperative and state farmers have availed themselves of opportunities to work in or, in fact, to run a variety of local industries and businesses, some closely connected with agricultural production, others not. This has become an important source of income for many farmers. In short the successful motivational apparatus of Hungarian agriculture owes its success to flexibility, multiplicity of forms, voluntariness, participation in decision making by members of collectives, and the importance of market-determined profit as a guide to production.

One should, however, keep these qualities in perspective. As noted in connection with the discussion of the agricultural price system, many questions of bureaucratic interference, hostility to markets and private initiative, and distortion of economic calculation through subsidies, taxes, and strange costing methodologies remain unresolved. On balance, however, the distance traveled by the Hungarian rural economy in the direction of market reform of the motivational system has been substantial, if not always proceeding in a straight line.

In mainland China since 1980 agriculture has more formally decollectivized. The *baogan daohu* (household production responsibility) system, with its fifteen-year leases of collectively owned strips

of land to individual peasant families in return for contractual produce deliveries at unified or protective prices and the household
payment of the agricultural tax and other levies, is in essence a
system of family tenant farming operating in a still imperfect but
widespread market setting.[22] The central motivation is the households' net income from sales of produce over and above the contractual part at market or near-market prices, that is, the profit motive.
While profits and profitability rates are distorted by the continued
presence of administrative rules, haphazardly determined levies, and
dictatorial modes of thought and behavior on the part of local officials, the net incentive effect on household producers has been positive as evidenced by increased output and labor productivity. Since
the peasant household's production surplus above the contracted
portion goes to the household to be disposed of freely, the household
will tend to increase its output until its marginal cost equals its
marginal revenue at the market price, thereby maximizing its profit.
The structure of farm production has undergone changes to conform
to demand signals emanating from the market; the movement has
been from cruder to finer grains, from grain to more profitable cash
crops, from general farm production to specialized production, and
from agricultural work to nonagricultural service and industrial activities, mainly in the area of food processing and industrial consumer
goods.

There are also problems with the newly marketized and privatized motivational system, however.[23] The problems, I think, reside
in the present incompleteness of the changes. Marketization has
an inner logic that requires that it be carried out in toto. Halfway
arrangements will not do. Two examples drawn from the Chinese
experience will illustrate the point.

First, collectively owned land has been leased to peasant households in narrow strips (some good land, some not so good, some
with access to roads, some not) for reasons of fairness. The total
size of these strips per family depends on such nonmarket criteria
as the number of people or the number of able-bodied workers in
the family. "Excessive" consolidation of land holdings and "excessive" hiring of farm labor by individual landholders are frowned
upon as evidence of emerging landlordism. (More generally, labor
mobility remains restricted.) So there is a remarkable fragmentation
of land holdings, which makes it difficult to take advantage of economies of scale and inhibits mechanization. In addition, "large" investment in rural infrastructures (irrigation and drainage works, roads)
is reportedly neglected under the regime of miniholdings and short
and narrow investment horizons, when what is already there is

not altogether dismantled and put to private use. Since people are still apprehensive about the durability of the marketizing and privatizing changes, there is a tendency to go for quick production payoffs through, for example, overchemicalization of land. All this raises questions about the permanence of the output and productivity upsurge of the past several years. To remedy the situation, the market has to be allowed to determine the optimal size of holdings, and property rights in land have to be further privatized. At the same time cooperative arrangements freely entered into by the entrepreneurial farmers could be encouraged through fiscal and credit policy to help take care of larger infrastructural investments.

Second, some evidence shows that income and wealth differentials in the countryside are increasing—as they tend to under the regime of the market—and that instances of jealousy and harassment of the better-off farmers by their poorer neighbors and unreconstructed cadres are on the rise. The pursuit of efficiency within the setting of markets will necessarily produce inequalities of outcomes. Tax measures can be taken to reduce some disparities (those arising from economic agents' acting in restraint of competition, or the socially and politically more intolerable ones—but here one has to be discreet in what is labeled intolerable), but they cannot be eliminated.

Industrial Wages. Under the classical administrative command plan the motivational system applied to industrial (or more generally, nonagricultural) workers has the following major characteristics: wage levels are pressed down to ensure high rates of investment and to keep consumption (hence inflationary pressures) in check, and elicit high labor participation ratios; consumer goods are in chronic short supply and of inferior quality and assortment; occupational choice and labor mobility are administratively controlled; the use of administratively enforced negative incentives is widespread; in the Stalinist version wide money wage disparities are permitted (in fact, encouraged under the shock-worker system), while in the Maoist variant they are compressed; much attention is given to nonmaterial, "moral" prods, particularly in the Maoist variant; each (state-sector) firm's wage funds, wage categories, and wage scales are determined at a high level of the central planning hierarchy (that is, firm managers have minimal discretion in setting basic wages and only a little more when it comes to the distribution of bonuses); hiring and (especially) firing of workers are largely out of managerial hands (full employment constraint).

Changes in the industrial wage system under the Hungarian

NEM are in the nature of an adjustment rather than reform of the old system. Stalin's "law" of rational low wages is repealed: basic wages are raised, the raises being usually linked to increases in the firms' profits. Through an intersectoral reallocation of investment, consumer goods become more plentiful but are mostly high priced. As one Polish traveler put it: Poles have money but nothing to spend it on, while Hungarians "can look but not touch"; that is, many Hungarian goods are too expensive for the average wage earner.[24] While the quality and assortment of industrial (consumer and producer) goods are better than before, the goods are still not competitive on hard currency world markets (though a few make a big splash on the CMEA market). Compared with the situation in Hungary before the NEM and with other centrally planned economies today, there is—whatever the reservations—a net lowering of consumption costs: less lining up, less hassle, more goods. There are more occupational choice and labor mobility, but administrative restrictions persist, some of them connected with urban housing shortages. Money wage differentials are significant, due not only to differential bonuses but above all to some workers' access to very remunerative registered and unregistered employment outside the official economy. Different earning possibilities when linked to consumer price increases (in the free market and floating spheres) have resulted in the emergence of an economically deprived class composed of some 1.5 million pensioners, blue-collar workers, young people, and others living on fixed incomes, without or with only limited access to extra-official sources of earnings.[25] The rising income gap poses a worrisome political threat to the continuance of the NEM's marketizing and privatizing changes.

The state continues to exercise considerable control over the industrial wage system by both indirect and direct means. Indirect means include the use of taxes to determine what portion of retained firm profits is to be allocated to the firm's bonus fund and price supports/subsidies that influence the size of firm profits and, hence, basic wages. There are three kinds of direct wage controls.

• Relative wage level: here the state limits increases in the average wage of individual firms. Increase in the average wage is linked to the growth of wages and profits per worker.
• Relative wage bill: here the total wage bill is regulated on the basis of increases in value added, limited by the prescribed increases in average wages.
• Centrally determined wages on the basis of either the average wage or the total wages bill of the firm: most common is the regulation

of the relative wage bill (55 percent of firms) followed by centrally determined wages (30 percent of firms), and relative wage level (15 percent of firms).[26]

While this regulation is important for motivation, less controlled or uncontrolled income from outside the official system is also very important. In Hungary under the NEM "Almost everyone lives partly, or—even more exactly—to a very small extent from his formal wage or salary. To a far greater extent they live from other activities, from those activities associated with the secondary, parallel, hidden, or more simply market economy."[27]

In mainland China changes brought about so far in the industrial wage system are also adjustments, not reforms. Money wages have been raised, and overtime and bonus pay has been reintroduced after a hiatus during the Cultural Revolution. Bonus funds linked to profits have been instituted at the firm level, but there has been a concurrent tendency for managements to distribute bonuses in an egalitarian fashion, as across-the-board wage supplements. Attempts have been made to introduce a responsibility system, whereby basic wages and bonuses are linked to the workers' productivity rather than seniority. The state has intervened with various kinds of money grants to compensate urban wage earners for steep increases in nonstaple food prices and public transportation.

In 1984 there was bold talk about going beyond adjustment toward reform. The Soviet type of eight-grade tariff wage system was to be abolished in state firms, the firms were to have more control over wage determination, and total payrolls were to be allowed to float according to individual enterprise performance.[28] Such practices, however, would require the freeing of industrial labor (marketization of the labor force) so that labor could move spontaneously in response to fluctuating wage differentials. So far this has not happened except at the margin (some collective sector and free sector labor). The greater part of the labor force continues to be assigned to their work places by labor bureaus, and both inter- and intrafirm labor mobility are subject to mandatory administrative planning; there is fear in official quarters about the possible consequences of "anarchic free flow" (that is, market allocation) of labor.

Increase in money wage differentials (especially when bonuses are included) has occurred. It has been praised as necessary from an efficiency standpoint. In China like in Hungary, however, such differentials cannot exceed certain rather narrowly defined limits without giving rise to political difficulties. Redistributive mechanisms (such as progressive income taxes linked to transfer payments) are not yet in place, so wage control has to be more direct. The Hungarian experience with state wage controls suggests that however "liberal" the changes as compared with the old plan, the state is unlikely to relinquish its hold over the industrial wage system, occupational choice, labor mobility, or all three. This is so partly out of fear of inflation and partly out of the already noted concern over the ethically permissible degree of income disparity in Socialist society.

So far the result has been that in terms of marketization of the motivational system the changes in the industrial economy lag behind those in agriculture, thus injecting an element of intersectoral disharmony to the system.

Incentives to Managers. Under the old Stalinist motivational arrangement managers of industrial and other state sector firms were rewarded and punished primarily by reference to indicators of gross output—the infamous *val* (*valovnaya produktsiia*, or gross value of output). Under both the Hungarian and the Chinese new economic regimes, the leading indicator of managerial success becomes the firm's profit (even though remnants of the *val* mentality haunt ministerial couloirs). Various schemes are devised to give managers broader rights to make profits, retain profits, and dispose of them; and to link managerial compensation to profit performance. It should be noted that such schemes are not overly innovative; they draw on Yevgeni Liberman's ideas of the early 1960s and usually involve various firm-based funds among which the retained portion of profits is distributed, both the amount of profits and their precise interfund distribution being affected in different degrees by government fiscal actions and administrative regulations. In mainland China before the changes, 100 percent of firm profits reverted to the state budget. Under the new policy, instead of remitting all profits, state firms pay a tax on profits (tax-for-profits scheme). This and other taxes are used by the state as "economic levers" to induce the desired firm behavior (including investments) with respect to the after-tax profits retained by the firms. In Hungary, the firm's management committee decides how much of the after-tax profit is to be put into the firm's bonus fund. Normally, out of the share going to the firm's development fund, 60 percent is taxed away, 10 percent goes into a reserve fund, and the rest (not very much) is available for autonomous investment by the firm.

The fatal flaw in this new preoccupation with profit as the indicator of the efficiency of firm operations is that the profit emerges from a still very distorted industrial price system and is not, therefore, in any way a summation of socially felicitous outcomes. It is not reflective of costs and utilities in the system, and it does not represent a reconciliation of individual and social interests. Like its predecessor under the regime of central administrative command planning, it is just a number, and the rest is dross. The underlying price distortion arises, as we have seen, from the internally inconsistent and conflicting coexistence of state-set (cost-plus), floating, and free market prices and from the absence of real market competition (this is particularly true of the Hungarian economy noted for its highly concentrated, amalgamated, and monopolistic industrial structures).

Realizing this, the Chinese and the Hungarians have introduced numerous taxes intended to correct the distortions. These probably add to the confusion. The Chinese taxes include a tax on products, which is applied uniformly throughout the country but is differentiated among products, its purpose being to confiscate that part of (windfall) profits on certain goods that arises from "wrong" pricing (for example, profits on some consumer durables and cigarettes). There is also a resource tax designed to eliminate rent differentials among extractive industries and mining and an adjustment tax whose purpose is to remove differences among enterprises in the same industrial branch, whenever such differences arise from "undeserved" causes. A capital charge is levied on fixed and working capital. A bonus tax is in effect to help curb the "blind" and "wanton" disbursement of premiums. An eight-grade progressive income tax (long used in collective undertakings) is being applied to state firms.[29] Needless to say, what is "undeserved," "wrong," "wanton," or "blind" is answered by reference to all sorts of criteria (mainly those relating to the Socialist ethical code), among which market tests of efficiency are notable by their rarity and weakness.

In Hungary the situation is similar. When firm profits and profitabilities emerged from the changed system of "competitive" prices, they were quickly annulled by differentiated taxes and subsidies, the result of which was to restore the *status quo ante*. Of a total of 1,135 industrial units, 971 (85.5 percent) reverted to the old allocatively useless profitabilities within less than two years of the introduction of the "competitive" price system. Between 1968 and 1980 more than 100 orders and legal rules were introduced to regulate the profits and profit-sharing decisions of the firms. About two-thirds of the firms' gross profits were taxed away and redistributed by the ex-planners. What kind of redistribution was involved? As in mainland China, the redistribution tended to equalize profits across firms by taxing away the profits of highly profitable firms and using them to cover the losses of unprofitable ones.

The last action is indicative of what Kornai has repeatedly denounced as the "soft budget constraint" of firms in Socialist economies, whether of the old Stalinist or the NEM type. Just as Socialist
workers do not get fired, Socialist firms do not go bankrupt. They
can almost always count on the state bureaucracy for a handout.
Their budget line is not binding; it is expanding. This leads to care-
lessness with costs, inflated investments, and other behavioral distortions that entail inefficiencies on a grand scale.

> We see here a vicious circle. Prices are distorted. Therefore
> profitability measured at the incorrect prices is not a true
> reflection of efficient performance. Not even in a stochastic
> sense do profits measured this way reflect the degree of
> efficiency statistically in most of the cases. Profitability does
> not have much prestige under such circumstances. A firm
> lobbying for subsidies may argue that the loss occurred
> not because of poor performance but because of incorrect
> prices. All right, it receives a subsidy, and others also get
> them, each of them bargaining for better treatment in the
> complicated network of fiscal redistribution. As a conse-
> quence, we arrive at dozens or hundreds of taxes and tax
> exemptions, highly differentiated, sometimes almost tailor-
> made tax and subsidy rules. And that inevitably leads to
> price distortions. The soft budget constraint is both a cause
> and a consequence of the price distortions.[30]

Property

By "property" is meant a socially enforced bundle of economically
valuable rights to the acquisition, use, and disposal of assets. Privatization involves the enlargement of these rights with respect to the
actual user of the assets (the operator of the farm, the manager
of an industrial firm, the worker with regard to his labor). Property
rights are important in the overall scheme of economic organization
because of their effects on the motivation of economic agents, the
distribution of income and wealth within the system, and the distribution of power.

Agriculture. Characteristic of both the Hungarian and the Chinese
economic changes is the de facto privatization of property and the
proliferation of property forms.

Privatization of property has taken the form of enlarging the
use rights of the operator of assets including the right to distribute
the income generated by the assets. In Chinese agriculture this is

manifested by the extension of land leases from the former one to three years to the present fifteen years (thirty years for grasslands and woodlands) and the vesting of those leases in the family. Subject to payment of the quasi-rent (contractual deliveries of produce at state-set prices), the agricultural tax, and some collective levies, the family is free to decide on its production pattern and schedule, disposal of its produce, and distribution of its income. Although land parcels cannot be bought or sold by the family tenant farmers (there is no free, rent-bidding, market for land), the contracts can be transferred and land strips consolidated with the permission of the collective; instances of individual contracts involving 750 *mu* of land (more than 100 acres) have been reported. This has been accompanied by the individual tenant's right to hire a limited number of workers: at first it was six to eight people, then any number so long as they were family members, now—apparently—unlimited numbers, family or not.[31] Acquisition and legal ownership of productive equipment (tractors, machinery, trucks, processing equipment, draft animals) are permitted and widespread. Many formerly collectively owned and operated assets have been leased to the highest bidder, either an individual, a family, or a group of individuals or families (voluntary association). This includes not only ponds, pastures, forest, commune, and brigade (now township and village) industries, transportation, and many services (including trading), but also dispensaries, clinics, and even schools. Although restrictions on labor migration to the larger cities are in effect (with some evidence of decreasing effectiveness), the right of the individual peasant to his own labor has been expanded in the sense of greater mobility for those who wish to leave farm work and seek employment in rural industry and the newly burgeoning services sector in rural towns. (The slogan is "leave farming but not the countryside.") Since 1980 roughly 100 million peasants have abandoned farm work— roughly one-third of the agricultural labor force. Many of them have found employment in industrial and service establishments in rural towns.

In Chinese agriculture privatization has been unabashedly to the private family unit with, so far, relatively little development of mixed property forms (voluntary cooperative arrangements). Legal social ownership of land has been maintained. As suggested earlier, for infrastructural investment reasons, either these de facto private farms will have to find freely their own market-dictated optimal size (including the extent of private ownership of productive assets other than land and the size of the privately hired labor force), or forms of voluntary cooperation in certain undertakings (infra-

107

structural investment included) will have to be developed.[32] In the absence of such developments a reversal of rural structures to neo-Stalinist collectives cannot be ruled out.

Hungarian agriculture under the NEM has opted for an interesting solution. On the surface, Hungarian agriculture looks highly socialized. Some 85 percent of the land is under state and cooperative farms yielding 66 percent of the gross value of agricultural output. The cooperative farms (about 1,400) range in size from 50 to 60,000 acres. The socialized sector allows, however, significantly privatized de facto property rights: there is a strong element of voluntariness, a relatively wide scope for decisions by the cooperative or state units, and a not unimportant degree of participation by members in the decision-making process. Members receive land rent for land that they own but that is collectively cultivated; the privately owned land can be inherited by the owner's children, but if they are not members of the cooperative, they must sell the land to the cooperative. Within the state and large cooperative farms, various forms of subcontracting or outright sale of land and specialized tasks to small cooperatives have been developed. There are about 3,000 such small co-op units employing more than 200,000 workers. They do work that for one reason or another the parent cooperative or state farm finds unprofitable.

In addition, special organizations have been established to diffuse modern farm technology and agribusiness mentality within a region (Technically Operated Production Systems or TOPS). Last but not least is the private sector consisting of 1.5 million privately owned plots and minifarms. These occupy 15 percent of the land and produce 33 percent of the gross value of agricultural output. Restrictions on the sale of tools, small machinery, fodder, fertilizer, pesticides, and other production inputs to households for use on the plots have been lifted, and legal restrictions on the number of animals permitted on the plots have been abolished. Credit has been made available to households for livestock purchase, acquisition of equipment, and modernization of structures. The average area (0.6 hectares per plot) can be doubled by leasing from the collective or state farms land that these farms find unsuitable for large-scale cultivation.

The success of Hungarian agriculture in output, quality, factor productivity, and export performance is due in large measure to the privatization of social property in a variety of sizes and forms. De facto privatization of state and collective farms and small cooperatives has been combined with the de jure privatization of plots and small farms. The privatization process at the state farm and large cooperative levels is far from complete and conflict free, as we have seen. But the degree of privatization appears to be sufficient to limit the damage caused by the continued contradiction of market and plan instruments in agriculture.

Industry. Privatization in Chinese industry is less advanced than in agriculture. The most important development so far has been the destatization of state firms and their de facto collectivization, a change that involves less direct state intervention in the affairs of these firms. The official intent is to get government bureaucracies out of the business of running industrial firms (separation of ownership and management).[33] Many industrial and service activities have been leased to private individuals or cooperatives, most of them in the consumer goods and services sector (restaurants, repair, maintenance, construction). In the period 1985–1987 all firms with fixed assets of less than 1.5 million yuan (US$500,000) and annual profits of under 200,000 yuan were to be contracted out or leased to individuals or cooperatives for periods of up to five years. The leased firms are required to pay rent and taxes to the state. They are granted relatively broad rights of business decision making, including decisions about the distribution of their profits. Firms operating under the leasing arrangement are allowed to avoid restrictions on the hiring of labor applicable to private sector enterprises. It was expected that by the late 1980s most industrial output value would be produced under the leasing cooperative arrangement. Various joint state-collective, state-private, and collective-private ventures have been reported, practices reminiscent of an earlier united front, the New Democracy (pre-1953) age. It is also intended over the next several years to extend the lateral ties between various firms and to establish lateral associations of firms gradually. Unless carefully managed, this could lead to the Hungarian type (or for that matter Soviet type) of amalgamations and a reduction rather than an increase in competition. The legal urban private sector has been much expanded—more than fifteen times in employment between 1978 and 1985. The legal private sector, however, accounts for only a very small proportion (less than 3 percent) of total urban employment. There has also emerged a considerable but not easily quantifiable amount of semilegal and illegal business activity, including the proliferation of so-called briefcase companies set up by party and government bureaucrats with access to scarce materials and connections, but also by academics and others. The official attitude toward these shadowy formations fluctuates from tolerance to sudden violent campaigns of repression. Unlike Hungary, mainland China has not yet come to terms with the Socialist black market.

In China, as in Hungary, equity participation in industry by foreign investors is permitted. It takes various property forms ranging from coproduction agreements through compensation trade arrangements and joint equity ventures, to outright foreign ownership (limited in time).

As we have seen, the Hungarian firm has been significantly liberated on its input acquisition side through the commercialization of producer goods and materials supply. On the output side, too, the abolition of mandatory targets set by the planners has resulted in the expansion of firm autonomy. The central authorities, however, still keep a tight grip on contractual delivery obligations ("sales" performance) of enterprises, so that on this side room for maneuver by the firm is more limited. The firm has gained some rights to set prices (particularly of new products) and to invest its retained profits, but such rights remain residual. Still, as compared with the past, the sphere of prices determined by direct agreements between buyer and seller has been considerably enlarged. While investment by firms remains comparatively small, investment decisions have been pluralized. Instead of being determined by a central planning board, they are now the combined responsibility of the central authorities, the state banking system, and the firms.

While many organizational forms exist, the problem is primarily one of the size distribution of state sector industrial enterprises. Hungary has one of the highest industrial concentration ratios in the world: a very small number of very large firms.[34] This concentration is the result of policy measures pursued throughout the 1960s and 1970s for reasons of ease of control, economies of scale, and technological diffusion. In fact, the Hungarian enterprise or firm is more like a trust or a Soviet "association." One of the consequences of this high concentration is the absence of competition over wide areas of the industrial economy, which in turn reduces the possible efficiency-producing effects of marketization of information and privatization of property rights. Since 1980 attempts have been made to break up these industrial dinosaurs, but progress has been sluggish. In 1982–1983 there were 700 state-owned industrial enterprises, more than half of them with an annual output value of over 50 million forints. Of these 700 firms, 275 produced 73 percent of the total industrial output value. In the following two years some 80 to 90 smaller firms were created by breaking up the large enterprises. Hungarian industry thus continues to suffer from the rigidities of large size, especially in light industry where flexibility is highly desirable. Fewer than 19 percent of all industrial workers are employed in enterprises with a total work force of under 100 each; in Sweden the equivalent ratio is 45 percent.

Small and medium-sized firms can be created in Hungary not only through the breakup of large firms, but by the establishment of new ones from the top down or—more interestingly—from the bottom up. In 1982 regulations were issued allowing ministries, local councils, and state-owned enterprises to set up affiliate firms. These are of two kinds: "enterprise business work partnerships" (EBWP) and "business work partnerships" (BWP) or simply "small cooperatives." The EBWPs come in several variants. One of the more imaginative involves the new affiliate unit's subcontracting a part of the parent enterprise's operations including use of the enterprise's fixed assets, paying a fee for it, but keeping its own profits. These profits may be distributed as bonuses among the affiliate's workers. The affiliate workers' basic wages, however, are paid by the parent enterprise. The BWPs or small cooperatives can be set up by ministries, local councils, large enterprises, or individuals. There are fewer administrative and other restrictions on them than on the larger firms, as is the case with cooperatives generally, but at the same time they cannot ask for help from the founding authority in the event of financial difficulty. In 1980, with 3 percent of the industrial capital stock, they employed 14 percent of the industrial labor force and accounted for 6 percent of gross industrial output and a much larger share of net output. Small co-ops formed by individuals are common. They range in employment size from two to thirty people and are primarily concentrated in the service trades, including professional services (management consulting and writing computer software, for example). The partners who supply the bulk of the capital— earned, no doubt, in the underground economy—are legally liable for all debts incurred by the co-op. Despite very progressive taxes imposed on the co-ops' profits, the lack of infrastructural facilities for small business in a land of giant enterprises, and bureaucratic foot-dragging, the productivity of these private co-ops is high: the per capita income of small private cooperatives is four times that of the orthodox ones. Unlike the typical traditional service cooperatives, the BWPs provide badly needed services (for example, plumbing and auto repairs) when they are needed, not two or three years later. Another novel organizational and property form consists of "new operational systems" (NOS). The NOS involve the awarding to individuals through auction of the right to lease small businesses of all kinds (restaurants, food stores, barber shops, and tourist lodgings). The lease typically runs for five years but can be renewed. With rare exceptions, each entrepreneur is limited to operating only one business unit; no chain stores here. The NOS are given considerable latitude in obtaining inputs and setting prices and are fully responsible for their profits and losses. They do very well, their services being responsive to demand through the market.

The public-private property enterprise combinations are shown in table 7–1.

The Nationalized Black Market

Perhaps the most interesting characteristic of the Hungarian economic experiment is the co-opting by the half-plan, half-market official economy of the shadowy "nonplanned sphere" (or the "second economy") where legal public and private enterprise imperceptibly merges with manifold money-making pursuits of various degrees of illegality and moral shadings. Altogether 1.2 million man-years are believed to be expended in the legal private economy by an economically active population of 5.2 million people. Many more million man-years are spent in extralegal and semi-public, semi-private, and private activities. Much of the success of the Hungarian NEM in regard to consumer material welfare through reduction of consumer annoyance has resulted from official toleration, indeed, integration, of the shadow economy in the official economy on the principle that "if you can't beat them, join them." In official phraseology this is known as the "extension of the state sphere." The state settles for its citizens' wheeling and dealing even—perhaps mainly—on government time and with the aid of discreetly appropriated (stolen) government assets. The Hungarian Party and state have come to terms with this condition to a greater extent than their Chinese counterparts. The Hungarians were really the first to practice quietly Deng Xiaoping's dictum that it doesn't matter whether a cat is black or white so long as it catches mice. The result is an unstable mixture of pretend-socialism and pretend-capitalism that, however, generates much more income than revealed by the statistics.

Conclusions

The mixture of plan and market elements, of quasi-socialism with quasi-capitalism, of notions of legality and illegality, of Socialist moral codes and principles of market efficiency—in short "market socialism"—is an unstable condition economically and ethically.

TABLE 7–1

COMBINATIONS OF PUBLIC OWNERSHIP AND PRIVATE
ENTREPRENEURIAL ACTIVITIES

Owner of the Means of Production	User of the Means of Production	Arrangement for Use of Capital Equipment	Typical Branches
State enterprise or cooperative	Private person or group of private persons (in some cases the lessee is chosen through auction)	Leasing fixed capital for a definite rent[a]	Catering, trade
State enterprise or public institution	"Economic team" formed from the employees	The team works under the protection of the employer and uses part of the fixed assets for which it pays rent	Maintenance, repair, fitting (as yet preliminarily planned)
Partly state enterprise or public institution, partly the user	Workers of the enterprise or institution in question	Illegal informal work done during regular working hours, perhaps with the use of employer's equipment	Construction, maintenance work, repairs, trucking

a. A related form is the so-called contractual operation; in this form the owner enterprise or cooperative also procures a portion of the materials.
SOURCE: János Kornai, "Comments on the Present State and the Prospects of the Hungarian Economic Reform," *Journal of Comparative Economics*, vol. 7, no. 3 (September 1983), p. 239, table 6.

Sooner or later either plan and centralized social property or market and private property must prevail and dominate the system. There has to be further movement in the direction of marketization and privatization or there will be retrogression to one or another variant of the central administrative command plan.

This is so despite the achievements of the Hungarian and the Chinese experiments on the front of consumer welfare—the reduction in not easily quantifiable consumer costs (shorter lines or no lines outside stores, less of a seller's market, plentiful food, more and better quality consumer durables, and so on).[35] Hungary's achievements under the NEM according to more orthodox measures of success have been questioned. Peter Murrell, for example, argues that although the visitor to Hungary "sees bustling restaurants . . . direct observation cannot provide an accurate picture of economic performance." Compared with other East European countries by measures such as per capita gross national product and its growth rate in the 1970s and 1980s, per capita net debt to Western commercial banks, and the rate of this debt's reduction, Hungary does not come out well, which—Murrell concludes—"will certainly convince other East European leaders that market-oriented reforms are not the route to economic success and independence."[36]

Although Murrell's argument is flawed in that it appears to ignore the composition of per capita national income in Hungary and other East European countries and omits the sizable contribution of the co-opted Hungarian shadow economy, there is an element of truth to it. The Hungarians, like the Chinese, have not gone far enough on the road to market; not by a long stretch. Kornai is right:

> The main cause of [the Hungarian] slowdown is not in too much but in too little decentralization—that is, in too little confidence in and reliance on the market. We didn't adjust quickly enough to the changing world situation. I think many of the market economies respond better to the changing world trade situation than Hungary did, with its half-market, half-bureaucratic control.
>
> In my judgment, we could advance still farther toward a shift in the combination of vertical interaction in the planning bureaucracy with horizontal coordination through the market system, in favor of the latter, to bring greater economic benefits, more efficiency, and better productivity.[37]

And because marketization has not moved far enough, the economy remains in a state of systemic disequilibrium. This disequilibrium has two main causes.

First, market institutions of information, coordination, and motivation and private property rights in assets are incompatible with the institutions of central administrative command planning and centralized public property rights. Each set has its own internal logic that requires that it be dominant within the system. One has to accept, if not the whole package, at least enough of it for its contents to determine the structure of the economy. Otherwise one runs the risk of getting the worst of both world.[38] In this analytical sense, "market socialism," which I take to denote a compromise of market-plan and private-public property fairly evenly balanced, is not a viable remedy for the command economy's efficiency troubles. The construct is prone to contradictory pulls in market and command directions.

Second, there is a contradiction between the dictates of economic efficiency and what has come to be known as the "Socialist ethical code." The code is one part of a neofeudal social contract that Communist authorities (at least since Stalin's death) enter into with their subjects. Kornai lists the principles that make up the code as being: (1) Socialist wage setting—to each according to his work and equal pay for equal work; (2) solidarity—help the weak to rise rather than punish them through "blind" competition; (3) security—full employment guaranteed by society and immortality of Socialist firms guaranteed by state budgetary bailouts; and (4) priority of the social interests as interpreted by the state over "partial" (individual) interest.[39] These principles are inserted by the Party-state into the *contrat social féodal* in return for the citizens' acceptance of very modest rates of increase in their standard of living, tolerance of daily frustrations associated with a permanent seller's market and retail void, restrictions on personal mobility, and, above all, strict limitations placed on freedom of expression and organization. The dictates of economic efficiency, in contrast, read as follows: (1) an incentive mechanism designed to stimulate better performance from all individuals participating in production; (2) careful calculation of costs and benefits and termination of nonefficient production activities; (3) fast and flexible adjustment to the current situation and external conditions (spontaneity); (4) entrepreneurship, implying freedom of individual initiative; and (5) personal responsibility.[40] Only in the academic imagination of Oskar Lange is the contradiction between the values of economic efficiency and the ethical values of socialism resolved in the context of a "decentralized market economy along Walrasian lines, which functions efficiently and at the same time fits without difficulty into a system built on socialist ethical principles of justice." "In light of our experience in the real world," however, "there are

115

conflicts when we have to make choices."[41] Soon after markets and privatized property rights make themselves felt in the cause of efficiency within an economic structure that still contains powerful elements of central administrative command planning and centralized public property, cries of anguish are heard from a variety of adversely affected interests. Before the efficiency results have a chance to materalize in more and more productively produced goods, the four Socialist guarantees are likely to be broken and with them the social contract. The long march toward the market is stalled for "digesting" purposes, and there is some or much retrocession benefiting central command.

In addition to systemic disequilibrium of the economy, a moral instability afflicts society, a sense of alienation, void, and purposelessness, a "live for the day" mentality, a feeling of deception and malaise. There is deep cynicism about society, the leadership, and much else fed by the knowledge that things are not what they appear or what they are officially said to be. The moral malaise of the half-and-half solution is shared by Hungary and mainland China. So far the tangible economic benefits have obscured the moral crisis from Western eyes, with a few exceptions.[42] One hesitates to end on this depressing note.[43] It is, however, appropriate, for it reinforces the overall conclusion that market-type changes applied to a centrally planned administrative command system cannot stop halfway; they have to proceed to their logical outcome of systemic transformation or else they run the risk—through the inherent instability of halfway solutions—of being pushed back to some form of modernized Stalinism.

Bibliography

Bauer, Támás. "The Second Economic Reform and Ownership Relations." *Eastern European Economics* (Spring–Summer 1984), pp. 33–87.

Berend, Ivan T., and György Ránki. *The Hungarian Economy in the Twentieth Century.* New York: St. Martin's Press, 1985, especially chaps. 6, 7, and 8.

Bornstein, Morris. "The Soviet Industrial Price Revision." In *Socialist Economy and Economic Policy: Essays in Honour of Friedrich Levcik.* Edited by G. Fink. Vienna and New York: Springer-Verlag, 1985, pp. 157–70.

Crook, Frederick W. "The Reform of the Commune System and the Rise of the Township-Collective-Household System." Working paper, U.S. Department of Agriculture, Washington, D.C., 1985.

Csikós-Nagy, B. "Further Development of the Hungarian Price System." *Acta Oeconomica*, vol. 32, nos. 1, 2 (1984), pp. 21–37.

Friedländer, Michael. *Die Ungarische Wirtschaftsreform*. Forschungsbericht der Wiener Institut für Internationale Wirtschaftsvergleiche, Nr. 99. (October 1984).

Furgeri, I., and J. Betlen. "The Past, Present and Future of the East-European Economies: The Hungarian Case." *Acta Oeconomica*, vol. 31, nos. 3, 4 (1983), pp. 297–326.

Hartford, Kathleen. "Hungarian Agriculture. A Model for the Socialist World?" *World Development* (January 1985), pp. 123–50.

Hsu, Kuang-t'ai. "Property Rights in Mainland China's Common Rules of Civil Law." *Issues & Studies*, vol. 22, no. 5 (May 1986), pp. 7–9.

Liu, Guoguang. "Changes in Ownership Forms: Problems and Possibilities." *Beijing Review*, May 12, 1986, pp. 17–22.

Marer, Paul. "Economic Reform in Hungary: From Central Planning to Regulated Market." In *East European Economies, Slow Growth in the 1980s*. Selected Papers, U.S. Congress, Joint Economic Committee. Washington, D.C.: U.S. Government Printing Office, 1986, pp. 223–97.

Myers, Ramon H. "Price Reforms and Property Rights in Communist China since 1978." *Issues & Studies*, vol. 21, no. 10 (October 1985), pp. 13–33.

Prybyla, Jan S. "China's Economic Experiment: From Mao to Market" *Problems of Communism*, vol. 35, no. 1 (January–February 1986), pp. 21–38; chap. 10 in this volume.

8
The Polish Economy—
A Case Study in the Structure
and Strategy of Disaster

Key aspects of the internal and external dynamics of the Polish economy between 1977 and 1987 are shown in figures 8–1 through 8–4. The decline in the growth rates of the major indicators turned into negative growth rates in 1979 through 1982. The absolute declines were very significant for gross investment (54.6 percent during the period), average real monthly wages (38.1 percent), and net material product (NMP) used (30.7 percent). The depression of 1979–1982 was the most severe in all of Europe since the end of World War II. The severity of the downturn was compounded by the timing: it occurred when levels of real income were already modest and unacceptable to the population, as reflected in repeated social disturbances, particularly in 1970 and 1976.[1] The subsequent recovery to roughly the levels of 1977 has been, in fact, smaller than suggested by the statistics. This is so because the quality and mix of the goods produced by the economy are inferior to what they once were, more out of tune with demand, partly because of restrictions on the purchase from the West of high-grade inputs and partly because of the collapse of work incentives and a consequent decline in standards of workmanship.[2] Lower quality, assortment mismatched with demand, substandard workmanship, and pseudo-innovation (by enterprise managers eager to fulfill the output plan with the least bother) are manifestations of hidden inflation that should be subtracted from the officially published growth rates. More ominously, the postdepression recovery "is not due to any fundamental change in the way the Polish economy operates, but

. . . is attributable to continued large inflow of resources from abroad."[3]

The absence of structural changes has been a constant of the Polish economy since the first outburst of popular discontent in 1956. The continued inflow of resources from abroad is not matched by exports. Unlike a number of other countries that became heavily indebted in the 1970s when Western bankers, flush with recycled petrodollars, were eager to lend and Western governments, in the spirit of détente, were ready to offer credit guarantees and other financial help, Poland has had great difficulty in generating a sufficient volume of exports to hard currency areas to make a dent in its growing debt. Debts to Western banks and governments rose from $14.9 billion in 1977 to $39.2 billion at the end of 1987 (figure 8–3), a sum unthinkable a few years ago. Stagnating output and living standards, chronic shortages of numerous basic goods, enormous waste, inflation no longer suppressed, high energy and materials utilization rates, and a huge foreign debt in hard and soft (ruble) currencies lie behind figures 8–1 through 8–4.

Not revealed graphically is the estrangement of Polish society from the system, a massive loss of trust, the "deliberate encouragement of political apathy and social anomie."[4] A poll conducted by the Polish Center for Public Opinion Research in 1985 showed that three quarters of the industrial workers and managers interviewed rated the Polish economy as unsatisfactory to hopeless, and virtually none of those questioned thought the government's economic policies were correct.[5] The only remaining discourse between the authorities and the citizens, erratically pursued, is the dialogue of misunderstandings.[6] "Hopelessness," writes one Polish economist, "begets cynicism and cynicism begets corruption, contributing to a further decline."[7]

The cynicism, apathy, pessimism, and withdrawal of society into itself (the phenomenon of the "alternative society") bode ill for the future. There is "a widespread feeling that not just the economy but the whole theocratic system is no good."[8] "The present situation," says a Polish economist, "must lead to a catastrophe of the country's civilization."[9] Another writes, "The socialist economy will be either radically and fundamentally reformed, or it will quite simply collapse."[10] "In 1990 the structure of production will be worse than it was five and ten years ago,"[11] predicts another. "There is surely some solution," says economics professor M. Mieszczankowski, "but I can't quite see it."[12] A West German economist agrees: "At present there is no sign of a solution."[13]

FIGURE 8–1
GROWTH INDICATORS IN POLAND, 1977–1987
(annual increase in percentages)

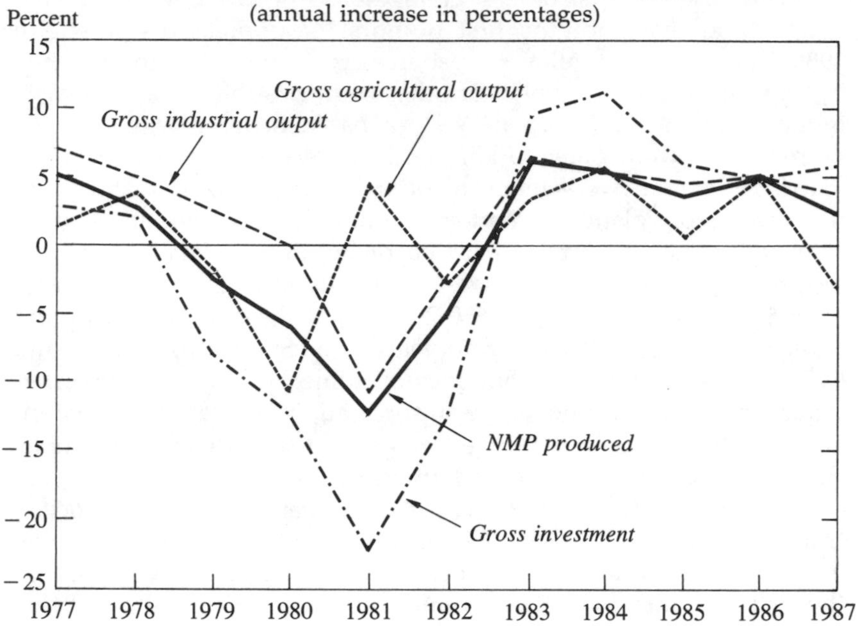

Percent

SOURCE: Polish statistical data.

Economic Reform and Adjustment

An economic system is composed of two major elements: institutional structure (undergirded by economic theory and economic ethics) and policy. Changes in the institutional structure and principles of the system constitute economic reform. Changes in policy (for example, rearrangement of the systems's goals, repair or replacement of some institutional parts, or theoretical revisionism) without change in the institutional structure and principles as a whole, constitute economic adjustment. The distinction between reform and adjustment is important. When the institutional structure and principles of the system are basically sound but the system nevertheless underperforms in some respect, adjustment may be enough to bring about the desired performance improvement. If, however, the institutional structure and principles—the genes—of the system are defective, policy adjustments will not provide a solution and may, in fact, make the problem worse.

For a Socialist centrally planned command system (the Soviet type of system), economic reform is made more difficult by the fusion of the economy and polity. While all economies are in various degrees political, the Soviet type of economy is identical with politics. Structural economic changes urgently necessitate concurrent changes in political structure: in the "leading role" (monopoly) of the Communist party. If the Party refuses to share its leading role with other autonomous sociopolitical formations, economic reform will be aborted, structural problems will fester, and there will be a temptation to seek refuge in policy adjustments. As of 1988 no Communist party to date (with the possible ephemeral exception of Slovenia[14]) had freely agreed to share power, although at least since Deng Xiaoping there is now some slight willingness to concede that the core economic problems are of systemic origin. Poland in 1988 was not an exception. According to Zdzislaw Sadowski, chairman of the State Planning Commission: "All previous attempts to introduce reforms proceeded largely on the assumption that you could change

FIGURE 8–2

POLAND'S CONSUMPTION AND LIVING STANDARD, 1977–1987
(annual growth in percentages)

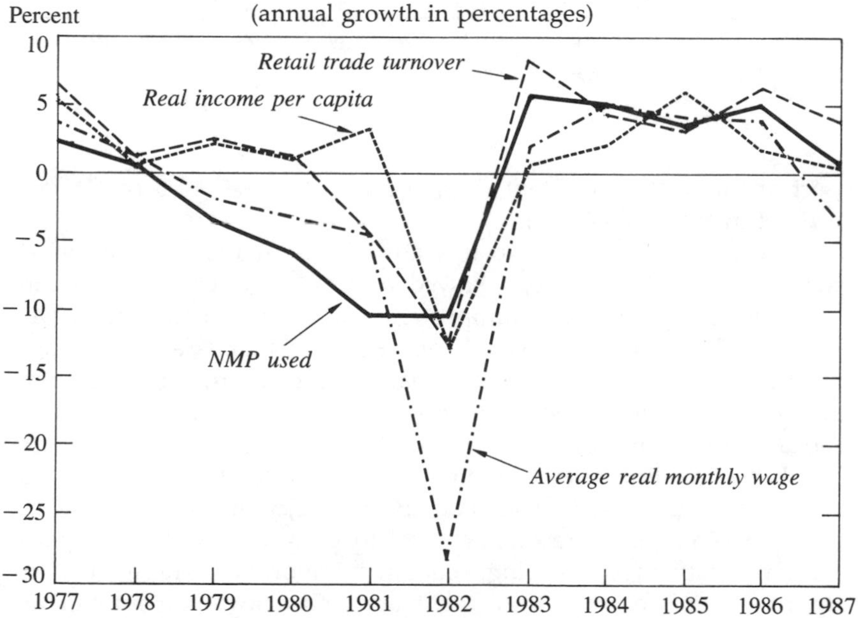

SOURCE: Polish statistical data.

121

FIGURE 8–3
POLAND'S EXTERNAL HARD CURRENCY DEBT, 1977–1987
(billions of dollars)

SOURCE: *PlanEcon Report*, April 15, 1988, p. 5.

part of the system without changing the whole." As a result, "we are not in the best of health."[15]

Poland's economic problems are structural first and foremost, that is, due primarily to a flawed economic system. In addition, in a subsidiary but not unimportant way, they are due to flawed policies. Bad policies flowing from a bad system are made worse by the shoddy character traits (venality, corruption, arrogance, and stupidity) and unprofessionalism (economic illiteracy and incompetence) of policy makers.

When dealing with economic changes, one should not be distracted by legalisms. Socialist Poland, in particular, but by no means alone, exhibits an extraordinary zeal to pass laws and issue quasi-legal regulations concerning economic "reforms." These give the impression of forward movement and mass involvement but are in fact rubber-stamped by an unrepresentative legislative chamber, the Sejm, or issued by a nominated bureaucracy. Between January

1982 and December 1987, for example, the Sejm passed 320 legislative acts to regulate the latest economic "reform." Over 12,000 supplementary regulations and interpretations (most of them internally inconsistent) were issued by administrative authorities at various levels—8,000 by the Ministry of Finance. In the absence of the *rule* of law, mere laws are made to be bent, amended, fudged, forgotten, ignored, or broken to suit the monocratic party's perception of what at any given moment best serves the preservation of the Party's "leading role." Dialectical legalistics should not be taken for reform. They are not even bona fide expressions of reformist intent.

The Road to Disaster

There are four calendar signposts on the Polish economy's road to what is now taking on the dimensions of disaster: 1956, 1970, 1976, and 1980–1981. Each was marked by popular disturbances and

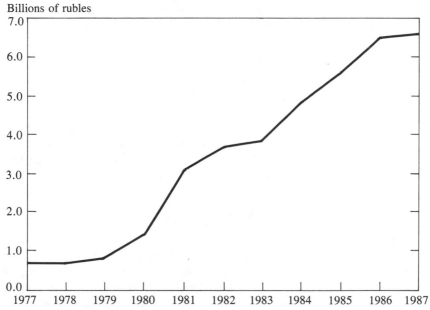

FIGURE 8–4
POLAND'S GROSS RUBLE DEBT, 1977–1987

Source: *PlanEcon Report*, April 15, 1988, p. 15.

labor uprisings, followed by official promises and sometimes attempts at bringing about change, followed, in turn, by recidivism.

The revolution of 1956, which brought to power Wladyslaw Gomulka (a "national" Communist, it was thought), was a violent reaction against the exploitative Stalinist model imposed on Poland shortly after World War II in 1949. The model consisted of massive socialization of assets; forced industrialization that emphasized producer goods industries and resulted in crippling sectoral disproportions; high rates of investment; postponement of consumption; elimination of the market mechanism and market prices and their replacement by central administrative command planning; agricultural neglect verging on exploitation; import substitution aimed at achieving autarky and redirection of trade into intra-Socialist channels; and a reign of fear. W. Brus, a former Party economist now with Oxford University, believes that for those (like himself) who in 1956 counseled change,

> Decentralization of economic decision making necessarily combined with some kind of market mechanism within the planning and management system, was not only an instrument for raising economic efficiency, but at the same time an indispensable condition and factor of political change of a pluralistic nature (democratization, as popular language had it at the time).[16]

The aim was to build market socialism or some kind of marketized planning system accompanied by political change of pluralistic tenor and, interestingly enough, to introduce a form of worker coparticipation or self-management on the pattern of the Yugoslav model. The demand for workers' self-management in Poland, which has been recurring ever since, was, according to Brus, a spontaneous phenomenon "reflecting traditional endogenous tendencies." At the level of economic analysis, it was counted on, says Brus, to improve the economy's X-efficiency.

The new government responded by issuing two legal acts: a Workers' Council Act and an Enterprise Fund Act, the first for management sharing and the second for profit sharing (November 1956), as well as a regulation granting substantial autonomy to state industrial enterprises. At the same time, however, the authorities rejected giving up the "leading role" of the Party, the Party's monopoly of power, and there were no projects to reform the irrational administrative price system. By 1958 when the changes were to have been fully implemented, they were, in fact, dead. "This was in my opinion," says Brus, "not a case of rejected transplant but a refusal to carry out the operation."[17] Brus may be right, but even had the transplant materialized, chances are it would have been rejected, as it has been in other Socialist countries that have experimented with partial marketization and privatization, because of the conceptual and practical untenability of market socialism, the inherent inconsistency of halfway solutions, and the incompatibility of plan and market institutions and philosophies. The 1956 changes included one that was potentially structural and systemic. It was the decollectivization and privatization of agriculture. The institution of property in land was changed in a potentially reformist sense. But the potential was never realized. By 1958 "private" agriculture had been surrounded by a wall of restrictive regulations that limited private property rights almost down to the narrow right of use and discriminated against private farms in the supply of credit, machinery, building materials, fertilizer, and other inputs. Privatization remained nominal, and marketization less than nominal. Poland's "private" agriculture continued to be as inefficient as any collective one, because it was collective in everything but name.

The economic mess of the early 1950s continued through the early 1960s when (1964–1965), in imitation of the "Liberman" adjustments in the USSR, Poland tried some minor tinkerings of its own. These included ministerial reorganizations; reduction in the number of centrally set material, technical, and other indicators; stress on enterprise profitability as a planned indicator (shades of Liberman) but within an unchanged structure of allocatively irrelevant administered prices; and the introduction of export incentives to firms. Brus characterizes these measures as a "half-hearted response to mounting economic difficulties . . . scattered and superficial . . . absorbed by the traditional system, which was impervious to efforts devoid of any political muscle."[18] Even these modest adjustments, it appears, remained by and large on paper:

> The economy proved continuously incapable of securing increases in the standard of living, the main foundation of the regime's legitimacy after the frustration of the hopes for the "likeable socialism" of October 1956. The official data on the dynamics of real wages over the period 1960–70 showed Poland worse off than any other East European country.[19]

In 1968 (the year of the Prague Spring) there was much unrest in Poland among intellectuals and students who demanded real economic reforms and were promptly accused by the authorities of "market deviation." Instead, the government came up with its own solution. It proposed to raise (planned) prices to levels that would cover costs and show a book profit (these included huge increases in food prices) and to invigorate the wage incentive system by linking enterprise wages funds to a set of renovated indicators such as output, productivity, and materials utilization. To compensate for the steep increases in the prices of necessities, it was proposed to lower the prices of some secondary industrial consumer goods that were not in big demand. The first effect of the wage changes would have been to freeze money wages for two years. The package was presented (the price increase intent was concealed until the last moment) as a "reform" designed to move the economy onto a path of modern, intensive, productivity-based growth through internal changes, that is, through a more rational use of the country's own hitherto wasted resources. It was met with worker riots that began on the Baltic coast and were put down with much bloodshed. Gomulka went out; Edward Gierek came in.

Gierek's prescription for the structural ills that beset the Polish economy was more adjustment, but more attractively packaged. The main idea was to modernize the economy (improve factor productivity and technology), which was what Gomulka had finally tried to do; but instead of the Polish people paying for it, he would have capitalist bankers and governments pay for it. Internally, after some brief talk about "in-depth" economic and political "reform," the changes settled down into the usual rut of intrasystemic adjustments that included increased autonomy of firms with a reduction in centrally set plan indicators, a new wage incentive scheme linked to value added, the forging of more direct links between the domestic economy and foreign trade, and the creation of large economic organizations—in systemic, reformist terms, nothing much. The program included something for everyone. It was intended to promote consumption and a higher standard of living for the broad masses of the people, invigorate agricultural investments and investments in consumer goods industries, reduce the gap between the growth rates of producer and consumer goods (that is, reorder the planners' goal priorities), raise housing construction, and expand social insurance.

All this was to be done without much pain because the expansion was to be financed not by domestic savings but by foreign capitalist loans that Western bankers, with recycled petrodollars to invest, would and did provide. With such loans and credit guarantees and other supports from Western détente-minded governments, Poland would import large amounts of modern technology, both capital goods and licenses. When put in place and rolling, these, it was thought, would generate a flow of top-of-the-line exports that would pay off the debt in no time. The strategic idea was one of import-led increase in domestic consumption financed by foreign credits in a weak structurally defective economy without systemic reform. For a few years, until 1976 or thereabouts, investments rose through the importation of modern capital equipment paid for by foreign bankers, and domestic money incomes were allowed to rise rapidly while prices were kept steady by administrative order, so that real incomes rose together with investments without reallocation from current consumption. Private farmers initially benefited from the removal of compulsory produce deliveries to the state, large increases in procurement prices, the introduction of free medical care, and improved supply of inputs long denied them. From 1971 through 1975 (after which the attractive package began to unravel), national income (net material product) rose at an average annual rate of 9.7 percent (exceeded in Eastern Europe only by Romania, but Romanian statistics are not to be believed), annual investment that had been 27 percent of national income in 1966–1970 rose to 36 percent in 1974, and consumption increased by 8.7 percent a year compared with 5.5 percent during 1966–1970.[20] Then the bottom fell out, just like that.

By 1977 when the slide into the abyss began in earnest, the expansionary drive had brought about inflation, at first suppressed but later open. By 1976 aggregate consumer demand exceeded aggregate consumer goods supply by an estimated 150 billion zlotys. In 1982 inflation on consumer goods was running above 100 percent. The chronic shortage of both consumer and producer goods became worse than ever. In the fall of 1981 the only commodity readily available in Polish shops was vinegar.[21] Even in 1988 20 percent of the people lived at the social minimum: "too many, 43 years after the war."[22] To have a telephone installed required a wait of ten to twelve years. At the end of 1987, in the world as a whole there were twenty-four telephones per one hundred people; in Poland there were 12.2.[23] "Almost universally," writes one analyst, "there is beginning to be a shortage of tools in enterprises, supply shortages persist, not much has changed with regard to decapitalization, income from work is less and less satisfying."[24] Output is being forced out of the economy and investment forced into it, regardless of the output's final importance or the investment's yield—which in the absence of a rational price system cannot even be measured. Eighty percent of the borrowed capital in the 1970s was channeled into the neo-Stalinist system's favorite heavy rust-belt industries instead of into export-oriented projects, because of the political influence exercised by these industries through their ministries and associations. This may be called "junk industrialization."

In 1971–1975, more than 60 percent of investment went into the electrical machinery, metallurgy, and energy industries, 80 percent of that into new installations rather than into upgrading existing ones. Agriculture got only 13–17 percent of investment, and most of that went into inefficient state and cooperative farms. The massiveness of the capital imports and the newness of the technology proved beyond the capacity of the economy to absorb. Already long construction periods lengthened. Because of the advanced technological content of the imported installations and the rapidity of technological change in the non-Socialist world, the rate of obsolescence of the new projects accelerated as gestation periods slowed, rendering the final products, when they finally appeared, noncompetitive on world capitalist markets. At the end of 1986 unfinished investment stock came to 2.6 trillion zloyts, a figure roughly the same as that year's total investment in the economy (2.7 trillion slotys), of which sum 85 percent was earmarked for the completion of this stock—most of it useless from a hard currency export standpoint.[25] All the unfinished projects require for their completion inputs that have to be purchased with hard currencies or much less desirable substitutes produced in the Socialist world, and the finished projects need capitalist parts and licenses. Because all Polish exports to non-Socialist countries should go to pay interest on the outstanding debt and to repay the principal and since Poland's creditworthiness is questionable, the means to complete the aging projects and keep the finished ones going are not likely to materialize in abundance. In fact, from 1981 through 1983 none were forthcoming.

The economy is thus experiencing serious capital decumulation and growing technical retardation. The inefficiency of resource use, now fed by net raw material and energy imports, is staggering. Granted that most prices are allocatively meaningless and that, therefore, profits or losses measured in such prices say nothing about efficiency or the lack of it, it is still interesting to note that without government subsidies, all Socialist enterprises combined would have experienced net losses in the years 1982–1984 and that the situation is not much improved today. Subsidies for financially troubled Socialist firms accounted for 44 percent of enterprise profits in 1982 and represented the largest single item in the government's civilian budget expenditures.[26] The intensity of resource use in Polish industry is two to three times what it is in Western Europe. In 1979, for example, in Poland 1,515 kilograms of coal were expended for every $1,000 of gross domestic product (GDP) compared with 502 kilograms for France. That year in Poland 135 kilograms of steel were consumed per $1,000 of GDP compared with 42 kilograms in France.[27] The reasons were obsolete technology, faulty coordination of allocative decisions, and the absence of a cost constraint on Socialist firms.

Exports then have lagged behind imports, and hard currency debts have swelled from $15 billion in 1977 to 39.2 billion in 1987, while the ruble debt went up from 0.7 billion rubles in 1977 to 6.6 billion 1987. Repayment of the hard currency debt is among the Polish government's lowest priorities. Reschedulings are arranged with private bankers and Western governments, and more loan funds are sought. The Polish attitude is one of injured innocence. Foreign credit restrictions are blamed for Poland's economic troubles, and the rule seems to be: first give us the money and then we will be able to do something about the economy. On the policy front the situation is reminiscent of the worst cases in Latin America:

> The profligacy, inefficiency, and corruption of the Latin governments and state agencies that did so much of the borrowing also are central to the story. There are Mexican steel complexes where production costs are twice those in South Korea; uncompleted Peruvian irrigation schemes that will be the world's most expensive watering projects if they are ever finished; and Brazilian nuclear projects that have cost overruns totaling billions of dollars.[28]

In Latin America, at least, the neomercantilist system of economic organization, a precapitalist system relatively open to world market influences, is potentially capable (with some prodding from the World Bank and the International Monetary Fund) of reforming itself and evolving into a modern market system. In Poland, the systemic obstacles to reform are more formidable, and the contribution of the system itself to the problems is larger and more direct. What are the systemic and structural defects?

Systemic-Structural Defects

Irrational Price System. The system lacks a mechanism that would automatically, accurately, expeditiously, and continuously indicate to decision makers what needs to be done in the economy, how much what needs to be done will cost in alternatives sacrificed, and what the optimal way of doing it is. It lacks a rational price system. There are three types of prices in Poland's official economy: administratively fixed, regulated, and contractual. They are based vaguely on a cost-plus-profit principle but do not take demand into consideration. They are, allocatively speaking, a farce. Foreign exchange rates are phony, and the zloty is overvalued. More than 50 percent of inputs by value are allocated by administrative quotas and 80 percent of the foreign exchange. The domestic market is in a state of permanent disequilibrium (excess demand), and export incentive schemes actually encourage imports. There is a huge underground market.

Prices are not flexible. They do not help to reduce the domestic and external disequilibriums. They continue to disinform buyers and sellers and make all financial results of an enterprise and its economic calculations meaningless or even misleading.[29]

In the absence of a price system that would reflect the marginal social costs and utilities in the system, the system is rudderless, and investment and other allocative decisions become determined by the comparative strength of special interest lobbyists. The system, says one Polish observer, is "politicized to a degree bordering on absurdity."[30]

Poor Information. The system lacks an automatic mechanism for the continuous reconciliation of private and social interests. The competitive market provides such reconciliation and harmonization. In Poland, as in other Socialist economies, social consultation must be politically organized, and, by virtue of the Party's leading role, it is always—when it exists—a dialogue between unequals, a dialogue of misunderstandings leading to frequent confrontations. Confrontational situations between order givers and order receivers have devastating effects on the quality of information in the system. In a system of commands it pays to dissimulate: lying is raised to the level of universal principle. Much, if not most, of the information circulating in the system is debased. A good deal is never released.

The system lacks a mechanism for spontaneously detecting and automatically correcting mistakes and quickly adapting to changed cost and utility (supply-demand) conditions. Errors cumulate, and when spotted through sociological and administrative investigation, they tend to be overcorrected at random, usually too late. While troubles were piling up during 1971–1975, no warning signals were flashing; in fact, information on the rapidly accumulating hard currency debt, for example, was not properly known and when known, was not communicated to the key decision makers, and, when finally communicated, was not acted upon.

Quantity over Quality. The system prefers extensive growth of output irrespective of cost and quality. The system provides producers

130

with no incentives to save on costs (the "soft budget constraint" phenomenon), and it has a strong anti-innovation bias in the setting of high output targets and chronic excess demand. In Poland, as in other Socialist economies, no state firm goes bankrupt because it exceeds its cost and underfulfills its quality and assortment plans or because it produces instant antiques.

Central Control. The system is interested above all in preserving control in the hands of the central Party and state authorities, even if often the control, by reason of resistance from below, is less than it looks. Control is the system's most important output to which all else is subservient. One result is high industrial concentration (fewer units being presumably more subject to central control than a great many units) and associated monopolistic behavior by producers.

What Poland Needs

What Poland needs is systemic reform: the dismantling of the system of central administrative planning and its replacement by a market system with dominant private ownership of the means of production and distribution. That is the only way to put an end to the chronic scarcity, to reduce static inefficiency (monumental allocative waste), and to spur growth through innovation and factor productivity improvements. Such reform necessitates the marketization and privatization of the existing sclerotic structure on the whole front, not just here and there. Most important, it requires a freeing of the price system, removal of physical and technical rationing, the demonopolization of the industrial structure, and the decollectivization of the "private" farmer. What Poland does not need—if it genuinely seeks abundance, static efficiency, and qualitative growth through innovation—is market socialism, syndicalism, or other halfway, half-baked solutions. Given the identity of economics and politics under socialism, economic reform requires political democratization and power sharing, with the distinct possibility of the Communist party's eventual demise. Given the apocalyptic dimensions of necessary reform, it is no wonder that observers in and out of Poland feel no solution is in sight.

What Poland Is Likely to Get

Reform necessitates a painful transition during which the market takes hold and private property takes over. With the enormous distortions that the planning system has produced in the economy,

131

the pain is going to be great, probably unacceptable to society in its present demoralized and destitute condition. The government will recoil before it, and for "leading role" reasons, the Party will resolutely oppose it. The Party and state most likely will offer more of the same: ineffectual adjustment that leads back to 1956, 1970, and 1981. But the government is not alone in eschewing the only workable systemic reform. Paradoxically, the democratic forces of society, the independent labor union movement, for one, muddy the waters by insisting on transition not to the market system but to "humane socialism" with workers' self-management as the leading management form. The disarray of the Yugoslav model demonstrates that this does not work if efficiency is the goal. Given the Poles' proclivity toward centrifugality, market syndicalism à la Tito is not going to do the job that needs to be done: the elimination of economic disorder or at least a very significant reduction of it. The Catholic church, too, is not enthusiastic about a transition to a market system. What it wants is social justice, a just wage, and dignity of the individual, but not the crasser aspects of capitalism, the "blind" pursuit of profit. But to have just distribution, there must first be something to distribute, and there is no substitute for modern capitalism when it comes to producing goods to distribute. Albeit reluctantly, because the meaning he attaches to "economic" is not to be trusted, I for once agree with Sadowski, chairman of the Polish Planning Commission, who believes "that the economy should be governed by economic considerations. Worrying about justice only makes sense in the context of an efficient economy, not as a substitute for economics."[31] But it may be too late for Sadowski and his planners. Justice is on the political agenda and has to be dealt with, even though it may mean going at the efficiency problem from the wrong end.

Because Sadowski, his commission, and the apparat that spawns them will not destroy themselves and invite the market to take their place and because Solidarity and the church are interested more in socially proper distribution and worker participation than they are in cold market logic, the prospects for effective marketizing and privatizing reform in Poland are dim indeed. Social justice can be injected into the market system and into private ownership, but the market system must be constructed first and must be allowed to apply its harsh economic calculus to the mess left behind by the plan.

PART THREE
The Chinese Economic Reforms

9
China's Economic Reforms

Reform of the price system, reform of the property system, and reform of the political system are the key steps in China's economic reform at the present stage.

Reforming the price system does not mean occasional adjustments of selected relative prices, which then remain fixed for long periods of time. What is needed is structural change of the whole price system, the purpose of which is to make prices the principal indicators and coordinators of relative scarcities, that is, of the relationships between marginal social costs and utilities in the economy.[1] For the price system to perform these basic information and coordination functions rationally, with the least feasible resource waste, and at the same time to act as the principal instrument of incentive, prices must be marketized. That is, prices must respond automatically to changes in supply and demand in the economy, and they must do so continuously.[2] Prices must therefore be free to move all the time, not just once in a while, and upward, not just downward. This requirement applies not only to prices of consumer and producer goods but also to factor prices: wages, interest on capital, and rent on land. Goods and services as well as labor, capital, and land must be exchanged voluntarily, horizontally, and competitively.[3] This implies the acceptance and application of the principle of free mobility of production factors. The principle of free mobility applies to agricultural and industrial prices, both wholesale and retail. Its operation cannot be restricted to one sector only, without distorting information, coordination of decisions, and incentives. Moreover, there must be a single price for each good or factor sold in the market. Multiple-track prices (fixed, negotiated, floating, free) cause similar problems of erroneous economic calculation and distorted allocative behavior. Among others, they encourage corruption and the black market.

On the other side of the coin, freeing prices entails dismantling the network of mandatory, vertical, administrative, largely physical and technical indicators of economic performance and administratively set cost-plus planned profit prices (the old-style plan) and replacing them with macroeconomic fiscal and monetary indirect means of social intervention suited to the new market relations. This change necessitates, among others, the creation of a new system of direct and indirect taxation and a restructuring of banking and financial institutions.[4]

One more point is that the price system is not a neutral mathematical construct but the expression of an underlying philosophy of life. A system of workable competitive market prices expresses the philosophical position that people are free to make their own decisions regarding the allocation of resources under their control in competition with others; that they are the best qualified to do it since they themselves know best what is good for *them* and that buyers and sellers can voluntarily conclude transactions to the benefit of both. In other words, what is affirmed is economic freedom. As a result of the voluntary and competitive nature of transactions, together with mutually maximizing behavior, each party is better off after the transaction than before, and society is better off as well. Intervention in this transaction between buyer and seller, consumer and producer, is limited to cases of market failure, of which there are several; some of them, like external costs and public goods, are quite important.[5] Competing individuals and voluntarily constituted groups of individuals (firms, partnerships, and corporations) in the market consider this intervention secondary and subsidiary to the free exercise of choice, however. Indeed, economic freedom and consumer sovereignty are among the more important social objectives of the market system, which itself is often referred to as the price system.

The idea of economic freedom and consumer sovereignty suggests further that the fundamental purpose of an economic system is to provide participants in the system with increasing quantities and qualities of goods and services at prices these people are prepared to pay. The economy exists to cater to individual material welfare.[6]

This market philosophy has two main components: a normative part grounded in concepts of moral philosophy and jurisprudence[7] and a positive part expressed in neoclassical economic theory. Both help explain the principles of market economics, and both find their practical manifestation in the system of market prices. Reform of the price system, I suggest, is not simply a technical operation but involves a change of philosophy: both of normative perceptions and of positive economics, especially as they apply to price theory. Without substantial modifications, the labor theory of surplus value, for example, is quite useless for rational allocation of resources in a market setting. Such modifications—served up as verbal reinterpretations to propose, in effect, a totally different marginalist theory—have been attempted in the past by Soviet mathematical economists, but without any visible practical results so far.

The main purpose of reforming the price system in China in a market direction is to remedy three problems that seem to be inherent in the system of central administrative command planning. These problems, if not remedied, threaten to slow down attempted improvements in the people's living standard and leave China behind in the worldwide developmental and modernization drive. These problems are: (1) goods shortages or a quasi-permanent sellers' "market";[8] (2) resource misallocations, long construction cycles, and the production of useless products—many of them useless because of quality defects; and (3) difficulties with generating and diffusing technological innovation, particularly in the economy's civilian sector. Resource misallocations arise most directly perhaps from the central planning system's faulty mechanisms for revealing constantly changing scarcity relationships in society. All three problems are related to the planned price system's dampening influence on the structure of incentives, particularly entrepreneurial initiative, but on ordinary labor performance as well. The inadequacies of information as transmitted to the participants by both physical commands and administered prices account largely for problems of innovation in the system. For innovation to occur from the bottom up (that is, from individuals), information in the system must be treated as everyone's natural right. Information must be seen not as a privilege to be dispensed by the planners on a need-to-know basis, with the planners determining the need on criteria only partly economic. Not only technological innovation but also economic modernization as a whole is not primarily a matter of up-to-date equipment but rather of the way such equipment is used. Modernization depends especially on attitudes toward the right to know and to apply and disseminate knowledge.

Theoretically, the marketization of the price system is not difficult. All that needs to be done is to let prices find their own level, to let go of price controls, to give an order not to take orders. In practice, however, things are more difficult. Specifically, in the Chinese case the sudden freeing of all prices and the mobility of labor, entrepreneurship, and capital would very probably—given the present highly subsidized condition of most Chinese industrial wholesale and retail prices—lead to an inflationary surge and to massive redistribution of the labor force and income patterns. In particular, the inflationary threat seems to be behind the step-by-step approach to reform. While the reluctance to plunge into price system reform is understandable, however, it carries its own dangers: the stretching out of the process of reform allows those elements opposed to reform to marshal their forces and try to slow down, halt, or reverse the reform movement. This has happened in Hungary and other centrally planned economies.

Several constituencies in society might not take kindly to the marketization of the price system. First of all, marketization of prices, together with property and political reforms, will certainly help solve the shortage, efficiency, and innovation problems, but it is not a universal remedy because it creates some problems of its own, and when mixed with planned prices and unreformed property and political structures, it only redefines the old problems and causes novel behavioral distortions everywhere. That marketization of the price system is not a panacea is obvious. The new price system might give rise to open unemployment, rather than disguised unemployment as under the plan, and open instability of the general price level, instead of suppressed instability. The fact that the combination of market and plan prices creates new distortions in the half-reformed economy is beyond doubt, as the Hungarians and others have repeatedly found out. Problems in the reform of the price system create an intellectual stumbling block for the reformers, whose efforts, and the concepts underlying those efforts, reform opponents will claim cause more trouble than the undertaking is worth. A "don't rock the boat" and "we told you so" school of reform critics quickly develops, and a myth of the "good old days" takes hold. Moreover, opponents of marketization often believe that whatever moves should be regulated, because spontaneous movement, especially of prices, is chaos. The opposite view, proved, I think, by experience, is that free markets are not as a rule chaotic; instead, they create spontaneous order at a relatively low transaction cost. In addition to opposition on intellectual grounds, the implications of price system reform are likely to raise reservations in some ideological and political quarters, among those who find it incompatible with particular notions of Socialist ethics and power alignments. Then again, living with a competitive market price system is a stressful experience requiring reeducation from skills learned in a centrally planned society. The market experience is one of risk taking rather than risk avoidance, and it is one opposed to bureaucratic routine. It calls for a fundamental departure of managerial outlook, skills, and behavioral patterns from those acquired under, and effective in, a system of central planning. Some managers are bound to oppose it, since they had learned how to use the old system for their benefit through personal and political connections and other means. Some workers in the state sector may object to the sacrifice of formerly guaranteed lifelong employment (even if, in fact, it was underemployment) and resent the probability of losing their jobs under the new system for cyclical or structural reasons, or simply because they do not perform according to the marginal revenue product rules of the market price system. More generally, anyone whose real income declines by, say, 5 percent or even rises by 5 percent while his neighbor's rises by 10 percent, can easily catch the "red eye disease" and oppose reform.

So, all in all, as every reformer who has tried it knows, system reform is not an easy task, and, if the tide should turn, the reformers may themselves end up being reformed.

Property System Reform

By "property" I mean legally protected rights to the acquisition, use, and disposal of goods and services and the fruit of those goods and services. A distinction can arise between the nominal legal proprietor (whether a private person, voluntary association of private persons, or the government) and the actual manager or user of goods and services (private or public manager or director of an enterprise). In Socialist centrally planned economies an additional complication arises with the Communist party, whose representatives at different levels of government and society claim broad property rights in many goods and services, including most producer goods.

The range of property rights may be broad to include acquisition, use, and disposal, subject only to some social restrictions necessary to protect the property rights of others, or they may be narrow, limited to the right of use.

The crucial issue is the locus of property rights in the means of production and distribution (in whom the rights are vested) and their breadth. When broad property rights are vested in the nominal legal proprietor who at the same time is the user-manager of the goods and services (individual ownership) or these broad rights are voluntarily delegated by the nominal legal proprietor to the actual user-manager, there is, in my opinion, private property.[9] In this formulation, private property exists when broad rights to the acquisition, use, and disposal of goods and services are vested in the actual

139

user-manager of those goods and services. Such broad rights constitute effective control over the goods and services in question, and
private property in this sense is a necessary condition for the functioning of the market system. The right to buy, use, and sell goods
and services, immediately if need be in response to changing market
price signals, without asking hierarchical superiors for permission,
is the essence of the market.

If China decides to marketize its price system, it will have to
privatize its system of property in the sense outlined earlier. The
two reforms have to be carried out simultaneously, because otherwise
the functioning of the price system as an information, coordination,
and incentive device will be compromised, and economic calculation
will be meaningless.

A partial marketization of the price system and de facto privatization of property rights have already occurred in agriculture. The
agricultural price system, however, has not been fully marketized,
and the property has not been fully privatized. The peasant user's
right to purchase and sell the land he rents from the nominal legal
owner, the state, for example, is very imperfect and bureaucratized.
While the recent experiments with land-use certificates point in the
right direction, they represent only a very small dent in the land
immobility problem.[10]

Property rights outside agriculture have not been privatized to
the same degree as in agriculture, although there is the possibility
that they may become so under the manager responsibility system
now being implemented. The denationalization and collectivization
of some state enterprises and the leasing of collective enterprises
to individuals tend in the same direction.

Still at the present time, a triple institutional contradiction exists
in the partially reformed Chinese economy. The first contradiction
is between market prices and fixed, negotiated, or floating prices.
The second is between privatized and nonprivatized (economically
centralized) property rights. The third is between the more marketized and privatized agriculture and the much less marketized and
privatized industry. The Chinese economic system, therefore, is in
a state of institutional disequilibrium that sooner or later will have
to be corrected in one direction or the other. In the absence of
further reform or retreat, market and plan institutions of information,
coordination, motivation, and property will work at odds, and economic calculation will continue to be distorted, although in different
ways from the plan. Because of these distortions, the reform movement itself may become discredited. After thirty years of half-

measures, even some Soviet economists have come around to this view.[11]

Political Reform

What is called "political reform" was approved in China by the Thirteenth Party Congress (October–November 1987). "Without reform of the political structure, reform of the economic structure cannot succeed in the end," the congress declared. The congress documents then clarify that "China is a socialist country under the people's democratic dictatorship and its basic political system is good." The defects concern questions of leadership, organization, and style of work, finding expression in overconcentration of power, bureaucratism, and feudal influences. To correct these, the congress proposed to take a number of policy measures, the chief of which is the separation of the functions of the party from those of government. According to the congress documents, however, "The separation does not mean in any sense that the Party's tasks will be reduced and its role weakened. Rather, the separation will further consolidate the Party's leadership role."[12]

In addition to this separation of party and government functions, and subject to the same principle of maintaining, strengthening, and consolidating the party's leadership role, the congress proposed to delegate power to lower administrative levels, especially to big cities, enterprises, and institutions, and to separate governmental bodies from enterprises and shift the functions of those bodies from direct to indirect control.

The subject of political reform is, of course, of the utmost sensitivity. The recognition of the longer-term dependence of economic reform on reform of the political structure is an important first step in the correct direction. What remains at issue is the interpretation of the content of political reform. There is, I think, a conceptual distinction to be made between "adjustment" and "reform." The term "adjustment" should be reserved for changes that do not affect the fundamental structure of and the principles underlying the institutions that make up a system. Adjustment consists of intrasystemic changes, "perfecting" the procedures of existing institutions as, for example, correcting the style of work. "Reform," in contrast, means changing the fundamental structure of and the principles underlying the institutions that make up a system. Reform is institutionalized change or intersystemic change. As I read them, the documents of the Thirteenth Party Congress outline a program of political adjustment. They reduce the degree of political concentration but do not pluralize the political structure. Should the economic changes continue along their reformist course, a fourth contradiction will be added to the ones now existing within the economy: the contradiction between economic pluralism and continued (if less than before) political centralization. In this state of disequilibrium, chances are that the old planning principle and structures will reassert themselves.[13]

Failure of Price System Reform

Given the importance of price system reform, failure to implement it would jeopardize the whole reform, consequently calling into question the solution of the shortage, efficiency and innovation problems that have been the main impetus behind China's economic reform. Because of the practical difficulty of marketizing all prices at once and the conceptual difficulty of accepting the philosophy behind it, marketization of the price system is likely to proceed step by step—the steps being uneven, some forward and some back. So long as there is foward movement, there is hope. The longer it takes to marketize the price system, however, the smaller the likelihood that the price system will be marketized and the economic system reformed. Timidity and understandable caution in regard to price reform will solidify the internal contradictions now discernible in the economy and encourage forces opposed to system reform on intellectual, ideological, vested interests, and other grounds. Postponement of price reform, even though "compensated" for by reformist efforts on other fronts (property, for example) should be viewed with considerable misgivings. Temporary postponements have a way of becoming permanent. Permanent postponement means the abandonment of reform and reversion to largely ineffective adjustment measures.

The Management Responsibility System in Industry

From the standpoint of systemic reform, the changes in industrial management responsibility represent a movement toward the privatization of property rights. In this respect they are all to the good for two reasons: first, they place fairly broad property rights in the hands of those with the best information to use those rights and, second, they bring industrial property rights more in line with those in agriculture, thus helping to reduce somewhat the resource misallocations and the problems with technological diffusion. Property rights, however, can be realized and become effective only with marketized industrial prices and the separation of government from party functions and enterprise management from direct government intervention—that is, with political reform. Even assuming independent management, to give managers broad decision-making powers will not promote supply, efficiency, and innovation if those powers are exercised in the context of an irrational industrial price system. That had been the great flaw of the Liberman experiment in the Soviet Union. It makes no sense to tell managers to make profits, if these profits derive from allocatively irrational prices. Industrial price system reform and the system for industrial management responsibility, then, must be implemented simultaneously.

Even in its narrow version (without a comprehensive price reform), the idea of industrial management responsibility in its present form continues the soft budget constraint on state sector firms and does not provide for the unemployment that will surely occur when managers dismiss workers who do not perform according to contract. Of course, enterprise bankruptcy and dismissal of surplus labor make sense only within a rational price structure, including wages. This again illustrates the necessary logical connections of economic reform and the weakness, not to say ineffectiveness, of half- or quarter-measures.

The Future of Agricultural Reform

The major measure now, in my opinion, is to create a market in land, that is, to extend and legitimize the de facto changes in the property structure that have already been carried out, by permitting peasant households to buy, sell, and sublease the land over which they have responsibility. This is necessary to bring about an economically rational size distribution of farms that allows economies of scale in farming. The average size of household production responsibility farms is now too small, and the determination of farm size by noneconomic criteria (such as, for example, the number of people in the household) reduces or negates some of the output and productivity gains obtained through the new system's better incentives. The establishment of a market in land (which, I think, is now being done) presupposes the consolidation and further marketization of the agricultural price system capable of providing the signals needed to determine optimal distribution of farm size. Another measure is the creation of truly voluntary cooperative arrangements that would help take care of large infrastructural investments, especially irrigation and drainage, as well as provide agrotechnical services of various kinds—especially "agricultural extension" services, including information on scientific farming. A third measure is increased marketization of farm production, including provision of farm credit and marketing services and the progressive removal of interprovincial and other administrative barriers to agricultural trade. A fourth measure is the development of new economic levers to permit social intervention in the market process, including the establishment of a tax system that would reduce market-generated income inequalities without dampening or extinguishing incentives to individual producers. While not simple, the task is made easier by the currently unsatisfactory, rather haphazard, and arbitrary system of locally levied fees. Liberalization of the market for labor is also needed to achieve optimal employment of labor per farm and rational distribution of the labor force between farm, auxiliary, and nonfarm occupations. Finally, individual and voluntary and cooperative property rights in agricultural capital should be further consolidated.

The Way Forward for Chinese Economic Reform

Although the pre-1989 Hungarian economic system no longer appears to be the best model for Socialist reform in China and elsewhere, much can be learned from Hungary's experience with economic change, some of the learning being by negative example. The fundamental weakness of the Hungarian effort at reform is that it ended up being just another adjustment, bigger to be sure than in other European Socialist countries, but an adjustment all the same. Another way of putting this is that the marketizing and privatizing changes introduced as part of the so-called New Economic Mechanism stopped halfway, resulting in a system that is neither planned nor spontaneous. This has been particularly true of the price system, which remains highly imperfect and hemmed in by all kinds of "corrective" administrative interventions, and to property rights, which have been privatized more on paper than in fact.[14] The only really imaginative feature of Hungary's half-reform has been the co-opting by the state of the black market: numerous business activities and property structures that were formerly illegal are now merely unofficial. This is not enough, however, to overcome the distortingly miscontrolled instability of the half-plan, half-market, neither-plan-nor-market mixture. The latest remedy has been to replace turnover taxes with value-added and personal income taxes. These are intended to help the government lower enterprise profit taxes now running at 90 percent of gross profits. These "economic levers," however, superimposed on a still very imperfectly marketized economy, are likely to cause more distortions in addition to a predicted 14–18 percent fall in real incomes in 1988, with inflation expected to run at 15 percent at the least. Hungary's external hard currency debt stands at $9 billion, higher per head than Poland's.[15]

The solution, in Hungary as elsewhere, is to push economic reforms of the Soviet-type planning system to their logical pluralistic conclusion in both prices and property rights, a conclusion that necessitates pluralizing changes in the political system. The lesson of Hungary and Yugoslavia is that a borderline combination of plan and market will not solve the problems of shortages, efficiency, and blocked innovation. That lesson shows any reform will result in domination of either market or plan. If market relations and privatized property rights are dominant, they can—indeed must—be supplemented by macroeconomic control and corrective measures taken by the state, measures structurally suited to the market system. Such measures will be primarily of the indirect, "guidance," or indicative kind, working primarily through the institutions of the market, including motivation and property. This does not exclude resort to administrative, mandatory control instruments that work primarily outside the market, but these should be kept to an absolute minimum. The institutions of a system need not work with theoretical perfection, but the system must be pure in its institutional composition. Market and plan institutions are incompatible conceptually and in practice. Happily, in the state of "primary" socialism, the predominance of market relations and economically decentralized property rights need not, perhaps, pose too troublesome theoretical problems.

10
China's Economic Experiment, from Mao to Market

After a brief, turbulent period of a market-plan economy with mixed private-socialized property in the early 1950s (the political equivalent of which was Mao's "New Democracy"),[1] the Chinese adopted Stalin's model of a centrally planned command economy with comprehensive state-collective property. The installation of this model was completed in 1956, toward the end of China's First Five-Year Plan (1953–1957). Almost as soon as it was in place, however, the model was found to be ill suited to China's conditions. The Stalinist emphasis on capital-intensive heavy industrialization at the expense of agriculture produced many problems: sluggish agricultural output and labor productivity; sectoral disproportions; shortages of consumer goods and low consumption; bottlenecks in the supply of key inputs; retarded services; urban unemployment (25 percent of the urban labor force, or 8 million people, in 1957); and rigid, overcentralized bureaucratic structures and procedures. As a result, between 1957 and 1976 the model was subjected to "right" (1957, 1961–1965) and "left" (1958–1960, 1966–1976) adjustments that caused violent swings in the economy, as well as in the political and social lives of the Chinese people.

By 1976, the Chinese economy was in a bad state. While the poor quality of the country's economic performance was not new and had many dimensions, it was summed up in low and, for sometime declining, factor productivity.[2] Indeed, the ten years of profound political upheaval during the Cultural Revolution merely added to the already long-term negative trend of productivity, which had averaged −1.5 percent annually since 1957.[3] The growth in the net domestic product that had been obtained since the introduction of the planned economy in the mid-1950s (4.4 percent annually)[4] was due primarily to the addition of factors, especially labor, rather than to improvement in the efficiency of factor use. In fact, great damage was inflicted on land (through ecological abuse), labor (through educational obscurantism), and capital (through technological retardation), particularly in periods of leftward adjustment, such as the Great Leap Forward (1958–1960) and the Cultural Revolution (1966–1976).[5] The result was poverty verging on destitution in large areas of China's countryside.

The search for the causes of China's economic problems proceeded in two stages. The first, from 1976 through 1980, was characterized by political housecleaning, ideological reinterpretations, and piecemeal economic adjustments. The formal beginning of the end of the first stage came in December 1978 with the holding of the landmark Third Plenum of the Party's Eleventh Central Committee at which Deng Xiaoping consolidated his hold on the party leadership. The consensus that emerged from the plenum was that China's economic problems lay in the Party's and government's erroneous "style of work," which, it was said, had produced leftist distortions of the system of central administrative command planning. Thus, it followed that if this work style were rectified—through replacement of personnel plus some "education"—things would fall into place. In other words, what was needed was a simple adjustment. With time, the simplicity of the remedies and their lack of effectiveness became apparent. The second stage began in 1981 and is still going on. The consensus, apparently fragile, now seems to be that China's economic troubles are rooted in the system of central planning and that what is needed is reform.

An important conceptual distinction between "adjustment" and "reform" must be made at this time. Adjustment means policy changes *within* the framework of the given system. Adjustment type changes do not alter in any fundamental respect the basic operational principles and institutional structure of the system. The opposite is true of reform. Reform changes the principles governing the system and the system's institutional arrangements for the generation, conveyance, processing, and coordination of information about cost and utility, motivation, and distribution of property rights. Reform alters in a qualitative way the locus of decision making in the system and the criteria for making the decisions. Thus, it marks the system's transformation into something qualitatively different. For reform of a centrally planned economy to deserve its name, the market and private property must become the dominant determinants of production, investment, and the distribution of income shares in the system.[6]

Policies of Adjustment

Between 1976 and 1980, four major adjustment policies were implemented. First, the administrative structure of the plan, flattened by the leftist hurricanes of the Cultural Revolution, was rebuilt and righted. Among other things, administration of the economy was simplified and decision making was devolved to local authorities and industrial managers.[7] Second, the system's priorities were reordered primarily to benefit agriculture and consumer goods industries, as well as to create a more open economy (in particular *vis-à-vis* the West). Third, emphasis was put on the importation of modern engineering technology from capitalist countries to help modernize the technologically retarded Chinese plants and equipment. Fourth, and potentially most significant, selected elements of capitalist social techniques[8] were imported and used as supplements to the command plan ("using capitalism to build socialism").

The fourth adjustment policy raises the interesting question of whether social techniques are systemically and culturally neutral. Is it possible to graft markets and de facto private property rights onto the central administrative command plan to improve the plan's efficiency, without reforming the planned system *as a whole*? Indeed, can capitalist social techniques be used to build a more efficient state socialism? Or is it necessary to truncate such techniques, emasculate them, and restrict them to prevent them from fundamentally changing the state Socialist system? More broadly, does the importation of capitalist social techniques produce behavioral ripples that transcend the economy and cause "spiritual pollution," for example, or "unhealthy tendencies"?[9]

The answer, of course, is that social techniques cannot be completely separated from the system from which they have evolved. Nor, in my opinion, can they be used disjointedly. They must be applied as a system, their organic connections unbroken. Capitalist social techniques, it can be argued, are the products of a pluralistic culture and as such need a pluralistic, competitive, free-wheeling, free-choice environment to do their job of efficient resource allocation. If such an environment is denied them, or if their essential connections are broken, they either atrophy or work in a perverse way. Indeed, ever since Nikita Khrushchev came to power in 1957, the Soviet and East European economies have borrowed capitalist social techniques, only to devitalize them and hem them in by the bureaucratic plan. Consequently, the efficiency results have been very small, nonexistent, or even negative.[10]

In China, like elsewhere in the world of the plan, the use of capitalist social techniques during the period of adjustment was intended to maximize reliance on "economic levers" rather than on "administrative levers." Unlike administrative levers, which are arbitrarily imposed from above, economic levers are indirect, general inducements to economic agents expressed in financial terms. Economic leverage means using prices (including wages and interest rates), profits that depend on prices, and taxes to motivate workers and managers and to influence the spending patterns of consumers. The economic agents adapt to those inducements at will; within the parameters set up by the levers, the agents have free choice. To do the job of raising the efficiency of resource use, however, prices must be market prices, and markets must be workably (not necessarily perfectly, in a textbook sense) competitive. If prices are administered by government or party authorities—whether central or local—and thus do not originate in reasonably competitive buyer-seller transactions, then they are merely administrative levers masquerading as economic levers: arbitrary prices arbitrarily imposed.[11] Administrative levers, whether in the form of physical commands or administered prices, cannot convey the multidimensional opportunity-cost information needed for efficiency of operations. In fact, they produce troublesome motivational effects.

The use of capitalist social techniques during the period of adjustment in China had two major characteristics: the various measures adopted were not organically linked into a logical, internally consistent system; and many of the measures were confined to certain geographical areas or to selected experimental enterprises.[12] In other words, the capitalist social techniques were fenced off from one another and thus did not constitute an organic entity.

Nonetheless, the adjustments were quite comprehensive and affected urban as well as rural policies. State agricultural procurement prices (and above-quota prices) were raised, as were industrial wages and salaries.[13] Later, the salaries of teachers and other "intellectuals" were also raised. Overtime and piecework pay and bonuses to enterprise managers, workers, and employees were reintroduced for the first time since the mid-1960s, and strict administrative restrictions on labor mobility were relaxed through a de facto termination of the rustication program, the gradual removal of rightist labels, and the encouragement of unemployable youths "awaiting work" to find work for themselves in the newly revived urban private sector or in cooperative industry and services.[14]

There were important structural changes in industry as well. Instead of the state appropriating 100 percent of state enterprise profits, experiments with profits taxation, partial profit retention

by enterprises, and enterprise incentive funds were initiated in selected places and firms. Special economic zones equipped with various legal forms of joint venture or capitalist coproduction were also
begun, and similar arrangements were made in the case of individual
projects outside the zones. In the countryside, rural fairs (where
near-market prices prevail) and household subsidiary plots were res-
urrected and expanded somewhat, and a production responsibility
system subject to contract between the rural collectivity (production
team) and small groups of households was initiated in 1979.

Results of Adjustment

Although the use of selected capitalist techniques has generally
proven unsuccessful in the long run, such adjustments of the plan
are not invariably a waste of time. They can, and sometimes do,
improve certain dimensions of the planned economy's performance.
They did that in China. Indeed, by 1980, quantitative performance
of industry and agriculture had shown marked improvement from
the levels of 1975.[15] The economy's qualitative ills, however, remained
by and large unaffected. In fact, the ad hoc use of emasculated
and disjointed capitalist social techniques side by side with administrative orders of all kinds made the qualitative deficiencies if not
worse, at least more visible and less tolerable. Thus, hitherto suppressed inflation came more into the open; hidden unemployment
came out of hiding; subsidies continued to rise at fast rates; budgetary
deficits appeared, as did balance of payments disequilibriums; investment (especially outside the state budget) continued on its runaway
course despite the central authorities' efforts to curb it; the production
process was disrupted by persistent energy and transportation bottlenecks; a significant portion of state firms operated in the red; quality
of output was deficient; and factor productivity showed little or
no gain. In addition, social indiscipline was on the rise, some people
demanded more freedom of cultural expression and political democracy, and many people, especially the young, began to question
the relevance of Marxism-Leninism.[16] In these respects, by 1980 China
had begun to encounter many of the same problems advanced Socialist economies had experienced during their numerous experiments
with adjustment of their highly centralized plans.

Beyond Adjustment, toward Reform

The year 1981 marks a turning point in China's post-Mao economic
history, although the turning had been some two years in coming.

The period 1981–1985 can be divided into two subperiods. From 1981 until the end of 1984, the agricultural economy underwent important changes in market relations and privatization of labor and property that skirted, and perhaps even crossed, systemic frontiers. While this was going on, the nonagricultural, or urban, economy (industry, commerce, services, transport, communications) was still functioning primarily under a policy adjustment, with experiments of a reformist temper being tried only in a selected but growing number of enterprises and geographical locations. Beginning in 1985, however, while the reformlike changes in agriculture were consolidated, the movement toward reform in the nonagricultural sector was stepped up, though not without stops and retreats. In 1985, therefore, experiments with free markets and privatization of labor and property began to be extended throughout the other sectors of the economy.

The decision taken by the Party's Central Committee in October 1984 to move beyond adjustment in the urban sector is official recognition of the need to bring the two major sectors of the economy into institutional harmony.[17] It is also an implicit admission that qualitative improvement of economic performance must be sought through the use of market and privatization measures of reform, rather than through a return to the Stalinist plan in either its original (First Five-Year Plan) version or in its modified 1961–1965 form. A return to the no-market, no-plan solution of Maoism is not even under consideration.

Agriculture. The keystone of the institutional changes in agriculture, the element of change that constitutes a transition from adjustment-like tinkering with the parts to a reformlike replacement of the economic mechanism, is the contractual system of net-output delivery by households.[18] It is the culmination of an evolutionary process initiated in 1979 (but present in a somewhat different form in China during 1961–1965)[19] whereby the rural collective's operational unit, the production team (of some thirty to forty households), signs contracts with its smaller component units for the delivery of given quantities and assortments of output at stated prices. These smaller units may be groups of up to half a dozen households or individual peasant families. The production responsibility contract may be either an output contract or a net-output delivery contract.

Under the terms of the output contract, the noncollective producing unit (the group or household) delivers the contracted-for output to the collective and receives work points for it. The value of a work point is determined by the collective effort of all production team households in the context of the state's pricing policy, and the income distribution function rests, as before, with the production team (the collective). Under the net-output delivery contract, no work points are involved. The contracted-for output is delivered to the collective and paid for at prices specified in the contract. The balance remaining after the delivery obligation is fulfilled, the agricultural tax is paid, and a number of collective deductions are made remains the property of the household and can be consumed by the family, sold on the free market, or sold to the state at "negotiated" (near-market) prices. From the standpoint of the noncollective contracting unit, the evolution since 1979 has been from group to household. From the standpoint of the nature of the contract, the movement has been from output contract to net-output delivery contract. In other words, between 1979 and 1981, the progression was clearly in the direction of free market and the privatization of labor and use of land.[20]

The details and precise modalities of operation of the household contractual system have been publicized and widely discussed and analyzed.[21] Our interest here is in the systemic implications of this arrangement, that is, in its reform potential.

The arrangement amounts to family tenant farming, the landlord being the state (via the collectivity). Although no actual rent payment is involved, there is a quasi-rent element implicit in the net-output delivery obligation at state-set prices, which in the past were typically below—sometimes appreciably below—equivalent market prices. Legally, the land remains the property of the collective, and it cannot be bought or sold by the noncollective units. Such units, however, can obtain extensive (and exclusive) rights of use to the land, typically for a fifteen year period (longer in the case of pastures and woodlands). Draft animals, farm machinery, and means of transportation can be owned privately by the families. Limited numbers of helpers (three) can be hired, but this restriction seems not to be closely enforced. The contract can be transferred to another family with the collective's permission, and compensation must be paid to the transferor by the transferee for any capital improvements made to the land. Consolidation of land parcels is also possible, again with the collective's consent. Under the contract, households may specialize in particular tasks, regardless of whether such tasks are agricultural or not (for example, transportation, machinery repair, merchandising).

From the standpoint of the system, the importance of the household contractual system resides in the de facto (not de jure) privatization of landed property (both de facto and de jure in the case of draft animals, machines, carts, trucks, and so on); the devolution of extensive (though far from unlimited) decision-making power, including decisions about income distribution and the voluntary establishment of cooperatives, to the level of a private production unit (the family); and the significant resort to market prices and near-market prices (negotiated prices) by both parties to the contract in deciding on the volume, assortment, and disposition of output. The last is to become even more important with the proposed phasing out of the state's monopoly of purchases of key farm products (for example, grain, oilseeds, cotton) and the concurrent removal of state-set procurement prices and the contractual delivery quota. This decision has been taken in consequence of the upsurge in farm production and the resultant decline, in some cases, of market prices below state procurement prices.[22]

No doubt since 1981 a considerable marketization of information and coordination have taken place in agriculture through reasonably competitive market prices and direct lateral buyer-seller transactions, and an equally impressive de facto privatization of property rights (involving greater flexibility of cropping patterns, work schedules, specialization, and marketing), resulting in improved motivation.

Results in Agriculture. Proponents of going beyond adjustment naturally attribute the favorable situation in agriculture over the past several years to the contractual household net-output delivery arrangement. The results in agriculture are impressive (despite recent estimates of a fairly sizable reduction in grain output for 1985).[23] Production of grain, cotton, and other commodities has risen spectacularly, albeit from low levels.[24] Yields have increased, and labor productivity has risen to the point where from 15 to 30 percent of the labor force has been released from land-related work. Per capita rural incomes have risen sharply,[25] and household expenditure patterns have shown qualitative improvement. The marketed portion of agricultural output has been expanded, and town and village industries (cooperative as well as private) have mushroomed, absorbing some of the displaced farm labor.

There have also been a few troublesome results connected, it would seem, with the system. Nonetheless, so far at least, the positive developments in agriculture outweigh the negative ones. Most important, the problem of the deficient quality of economic performance in the agricultural sector has been addressed with remarkable success.

Two questions arise in this connection. The first concerns the source of the agricultural success story. Are the partial decollectivization and movement away from central command planning represented by the household contractual system? Or is it the contribution of other, less reformist, more technical factors? The more technical factors include a succession of good weather years; increased use of chemical fertilizers; reversion to traditional cropping patterns (that is, the abandonment of the Maoist policy of commune and provincial self-sufficiency and of the policy of "grain first") and a consequent rise in interprovincial trade in farm produce, and the hike in procurement prices, which falls under the rubric of adjustment. It should be noted, however, that it is not easy to draw a line between institutional changes and technical ones. For example, the increased use of chemical fertilizers by household producers is due in large part to an improvement in the system's motivational structure; it is simply now worth the peasants' while to use more chemicals whereas it was not under the old work points system.

This leads to the second question: Is the household system a reform or an adjustment? The answer is that it is an almost reform. The degree of individual choice involved is far from minor. That choice is exercised to a large extent on the basis of market price information; it is coordinated in large part by the market; and it is motivated by the lure of market gain. Property rights to assets—including land—are clearly and significantly privatized.

The liberation of individual choice under the regime of the household system, however, is not nearly complete. Limitations on that choice are pervasive and significant regarding both state intervention in the market process and state restrictions on private rights of use of assets. The coexistence of market prices, "preferential" (quota and above-quota) prices, and negotiated prices—a multitier price system—encourages market manipulations and distortions, of which quality of produce is the first victim. But there is a more fundamental problem. Even though the Chinese peasant understands instinctively and fairly accurately the principles of the market mechanism and the rights inherent in private property use, such understanding seems to have eluded the officials in charge of markets and property supervision. The attitude of these officials toward fluctuating prices (especially upward fluctuation, which is seen as "profiteering") and market equilibrium prices in the context of commodity shortages ranges from unsympathetic to hostile. In this view, what is not controlled is seen as "arbitrary" and "blind."[26] Such attitudes have had real consequences. The sharp rises in retail prices of deregulated farm goods on China's city markets in 1985, for example, led to a flurry of administrative price controls, rollbacks, and subsidies.[27] Even more dangerous, the theoretical grasp of how a market price system operates is still quite elementary on the part of many financial cadres.[28]

But it is not just a question of deficiency in theoretical comprehension of how market prices allocate resources. In practice, even for those who understand basic market principles, it is not easy to distinguish between price changes that are a result of granting greater freedom to buyers and sellers to bargain competitively and arrive at equilibrium prices in the market and price changes that stem from "wrong" sources such as speculation, cost-push, or demand inflation. Given the magnitude of this practical difficulty, the financial bureaucrats will most likely do what comes most naturally: they will administratively control prices.

Reform of the plan requires the mobility of factors of production. This is still not the case in China under the household contractual system. Even though factor mobility has increased compared with the post-1957 past, land and labor remain largely tied, and capital equipment (as well as crucial current inputs) must be purchased from the state monopolist. Although peasants are now permitted to leave the land in response to market signals, they are not permitted to leave the countryside (though many do).[29] Thus, the household system, despite its thrust toward free markets and privatization of property use and labor, is still only a half-reform, perhaps a little better than half. Even the reformist half, however, has so far operated in the broader context of the administrative command plan that still dominates the nonagricultural sectors of the economy.

Some Problems in Industry

Beginning in 1985, and lasting until 1990, this administrative command dominance over the nonagricultural economy (over "industry," or the "urban" sector for short) is to be relaxed and reduced in scope. The aim is to create a "planned commodity economy" in the urban sector, a code name for marketization and privatization. Reform-minded changes in industry are thus designed to bring the urban economy in harmony with the already accomplished reformist changes in agriculture.

Movement from adjustment toward reform in industry, however, is likely to prove more difficult than it did in agriculture. For one thing, whereas agriculture was a collective sector economy, the industrial economy is primarily a state sector economy. The state sector is characterized by a comparatively greater rigidity of administrative (ministerial-type) structures. Unlike the collective sector, it is the preserve of the bureaucrats who inhabit it in great numbers and

155

benefit greatly from the privileges flowing from its administration. There is bound to be resistance to the expanded use of the market mechanism because it takes the bread out of the bureaucrats' mouths. Ironically, there is also likely to be considerable opposition to privatization of property rights from those who would seem to benefit most from such privatization—the enterprise managers, since most of them are neither professionally nor intellectually equipped to make the kind of property-related decisions and take the entrepreneurial risks required by market rules. Like their cousins in the countryside (the commune, brigade, and team officials), but on a more grandiose scale, these urban bureaucrats and enterprise managers are prone to react to the step-by-step relaxation of direct administrative controls in a highly "feudalistic" and corrupt way that distorts and ultimately undermines the intent of the reform. Indeed, according to numerous reports in the Chinese press, a number of urban officials have taken advantage of commodity shortages, privileged administrative position and access to information, and the incompatible mixture of administrative commands and emerging markets to line their own pockets.[30]

This has happened in China on a very impressive scale. Instead of market competition and useful output and innovation, what emerges is the old-fashioned bureaucratic squeeze, mutual back-scratching, parasitic payoffs, and bribes. One of the earliest reactions to the October 1984 decision and the consequent relaxation of central controls was the emergence of countless so-called briefcase companies set up by individual officials, groups of officials, and work units to take advantage of the fluid situation and to do business in the cracks between plan and market. It is important to point out that these "unhealthy tendencies," as they are officially called, are not manifestations of competitive market ethics that demand adherence to contractual law freely arrived at. Such tendencies are rather the expression of bureaucratic privilege let loose in a setting characterized by supply shortages, demand inflation, and a combination of highly imperfect markets and administrative commands—the "commoditization" of long-standing malpractices. Instead of a market economy, what mushrooms in such a situation is "feudal socialism," that is, bureaucratic baronies operating in markets of various shades not only of impropriety and illegality, but of textbook market imperfection.[31]

The second reason why the movement toward reform in the urban sector will be more difficult than reform in agriculture is an extension of the first. In agriculture, the devolution of decision-making powers has been to the level of the private firm (the family).

In the urban sector, this devolution will be made to the level of the lowest bureaucratic unit: the state enterprise, with all that this implies in bureaucratic bad habits and modes of behavior.

Then there is the practical matter of experience. During most periods agriculture in China has operated partially in a framework of market prices (in village fairs) and de facto private property (household subsidiary plots). The private (family) property mentality promoted briefly by the agrarian reforms of the late 1940s and early 1950s has never been quite extinguished. Such has not been the experience of industry. Except for black-market prices, industry after the mid-1950s operated exclusively in a setting of state-set prices. All institutional manifestations of private property were eventually obliterated, first by the Great Leap Forward and then, more thoroughly, by the Cultural Revolution.

An important philosophical principle that has to be kept in mind when discussing adjustment and reform of the plan is that those in charge of the plan, the top leaders of the Communist party, do not intend to relinquish control over the economy but to make that control more efficient. Their goal in doing so is to facilitate maintaining political control. Direct control of the economy through administrative commands and highly centralized property rights has proved increasingly counterproductive. The only apparent alternative, therefore, is decentralization with the help of markets and privatized rights of property. The big question is thus how to combine efficient central control with such decentralization—in short, how to create a decentralized monopoly.

It cannot be done, but most state Socialist regimes in the past thirty years have given this impossibility their best shot. What is involved in this quest is the reconciliation of private and social interests. The market accomplishes such reconciliation by enabling the dominant influence of consumer demand to determine the volume and assortment of output and the basic configuration of income shares. This the philosophy of decentralized monopoly cannot allow. Reform of the plan, therefore, is caught from the start in a Catch-22 conundrum of economic philosophy. Be this as it may, the Chinese leadership's decision to initiate changes in the urban economic structure clearly tries to address this problem by concentrating on two fundamental issues: macro-control and micro-autonomy.

Macro-Control

Macro-control concerns the relationship between the state (at whatever level) and firms or enterprises. Under the Stalinist model, practically all enterprises are socialized—nationalized or collectivized—and are directly controlled by the administrative command plan, which is also highly centralized. Under modified versions of this model, the role of administrative commands expressed in physical and technical norms (for example, output targets set in tons) is somewhat reduced, and the role of indicators expressed in financial terms (for example, output performance judged by profit and profitability rates, or by sales volume) is increased. At the same time, the financial indicators are less directive and more indicative than the physical and technical norms. There is thus a double transition: from physical to "value"[32] instruments of control, and from mandatory to more "guidance" planning (plus some free production and exchange on the periphery). The financial indicators ("economic levers") continue for the most part, however, to be based on state-set, cost-plus, allocatively irrational industrial prices. This double switch, therefore, does not advance the cause of economic efficiency by much, if at all, as can be demonstrated by examining the thirty-year-old Soviet and East European experience with economic levers. From the standpoint of efficient resource use (which is the crux of the planned economy's problem), economic levers are only as good as the price system from which they stem. The Chinese are beginning to understand this, but their understanding is as yet imperfect.

In China, changes in the macro-control mechanism involve not only the double transition from physical to "value" instruments of control and from mandatory to guidance planning (which is in essence an adjustment), but also, since 1984, proposals for and some attempts at altering the industrial price system *vis-à-vis* the market mechanism. In the remainder of this section, I shall examine the key components of the Chinese planners' efforts to carry out this transition.

Planning. The idea is not to abolish mandatory planning but to reduce it, while at the same time increasing guidance planning. Reduction of mandatory planning in the Chinese case involves cutting from 120 to 30 the number of products regulated by the plan and streamlining the number of administrative echelons of economic decision making.[33] A potentially important development is the distribution of some producer goods outside the state material and technical supply network, that is, outside the centralized system of producer goods rationing. A primary mechanism for accomplishing this task is the holding of producer goods fairs, which have been reported from various places, most notably Shanghai. At these fairs, capital goods can be purchased and sold at prices negotiated by the buyer and seller within certain limits. This is a "Hungarian" development.

In Hungary, under the New Economic Mechanism, the Soviet type of material and technical supply system has been replaced by multiple-channel wholesale trade in the means of production. Increasing guidance planning, that is, the use of financially expressed incentives and disincentives, appears to involve primarily augmenting the economic role of lower-level authorities (provinces, municipalities, economic zones) compared with that of central authorities. Goods of minor or purely local importance are to be subject to the interplay of supply and demand forces in the market. The markets, however, are not to be completely free but subject to various forms of supervision by local authorities.

There are two major problems with this arrangement as it has been adopted in China. First, mandatory planning, although reduced in the number of commodities regulated, continues to apply to strategic products (for example, raw materials, steel) that enter into the manufacture of most other products. So long as mandatory planning is not completely abolished, it will, by its presence, however small, significantly limit and inhibit any and all reformist movements outside the area in which its writ runs. Second, there is reason to believe that shifting the responsibility for guidance planning from central to lower-level bureaucrats will result in merely making guidance planning mandatory at the lower levels. There is evidence that mandating guidance at lower levels has, in fact, already happened.[34] The short-term result of this propensity to dictate guidance has been an overheated economy with runaway investment and a further lowering of the quality of output. The situation is also unsatisfactory with respect to the local authorities' attitude toward the "free" market sphere. Indeed, according to reports in the Chinese press, it seems that local authorities have been wont either to turn the market into an underground operation benefiting relatives and associates in the bureaucratic power edifice or to restrict it in various ways.[35]

Price System. A largely unnoticed and unsung epic feat of bureaucratic futility occurred in the Soviet Union in 1967 when several million industrial whosesale prices were recalculated by hand and published in massive volumes as part of the USSR's proposed transition from mandatory-physical to guidance-"value" planning.[36] Although the new prices were updated and a little better calculated (in an accounting sense), they virtually ignored demand. Thus, they were instantly obsolete. Like the old prices, they gave the wrong signals, and the waste went on.

Chinese policy makers today, unlike their Soviet counterparts in 1967, are aware of the need not merely to readjust the industrial price system but to reform it, that is, to make such a price system a mathematical expression of competitive business transactions in a market in which the parties involved maintain wide rights of choice. Without such reform, guidance planning, even if carried out in the spirit of guidance rather than mandate, is a trivial pursuit. Intellectual understanding extends to the formidable difficulties—economic, political, and psychological—inherent in freeing industrial prices. Caution and gradualness characterize the leadership's approach to the task of price reform ("We must grope for stones while crossing the river"). Unfortunately, by stretching out the price distortions over time, this pragmatic, step-by-step handling of change may itself undo the intent of reform. At the back of the policy makers' minds seems to be lodged the idea that a comprehensive freeing of industrial prices should await a significant increase in the supply of goods, that is, the advent of a buyers' market (as has happened with grain and some other farm products). The arrival of such a happy state may, however, be obstructed by the present continued irrationalities of the shackled industrial price system.

So far, relative prices of some products have been readjusted, and others will be readjusted later. Still, a lot of prices (for coal, steel, short-distance railway rates, housing rents, and public utilities, for example) are "too low," while other prices are "too high." These readjustments of relative prices have several important constraints imposed on them. One is that the prices of products produced and distributed by the mandatory state plan should be left basically unchanged. What is meant by "basically" is not altogether clear, but it would appear that the prices of such products when "marketed by enterprises through their own channels according to specific regulations" are to be determined by market forces.[37]

An initial result has been the emergence of a dual price system for a number of key commodities (for example, coal and steel), which does nothing to make the price system allocatively more rational. The existence of the dual price system compromises economic calculation. Another constraint on price reform is the regime's commitment not to affect urban living standards adversely, not even temporarily. Thus, relative price adjustments and price deregulation (as with some farm products) have been typically accompanied by cash subsidies to urban wage earners or by the introduction of new price controls.

And so the present situation is marked by the incompatible and distorting coexistence of state-set cost-plus prices, floating prices, white-market prices, and black-market prices. These various prices are supposed to be restricted to their respective spheres of mandatory planning (state prices), guidance planning (floating prices), and market sector (market prices), but they are not. They overlap and conflict. Not only is there a badly insulated three- (or four-) tier price system, but there is a multicurrency system as well: one for local people and one for foreigners (foreign-exchange certificates or foreign—non-Socialist—currencies). Here, too, there are leakages from one sphere to the other. Chinese renminbi mingle with foreign exchange certificates, Hong Kong dollars, and U.S. dollars, and there is a rampant black market in foreign currencies.

The debate continues. A question that has not been unequivocally answered is whether those who advocate fundamental changes in the industrial price system realize that price flexibility is not a one-time operation, that prices must be continuously flexible, that they must move spontaneously over time. But, as already noted, economic spontaneity is equated with arbitrariness and blindness, and political pluralism is seen as unhealthy bourgeois factionalism.

At present, worker mobility in industry, particularly in the state sector, is insignificant. With the exception of private sector employment (which has risen substantially since 1978 but still constitutes a very small percentage—2.5 percent in 1984—of total urban employment) and freer movement of labor among jobs in the cooperative sector, urban workers continue to be assigned to their work units by labor bureaus, and both inter- and intra-enterprise labor mobility are subject to mandatory administrative planning. Although there have been some successful experiments in loosening up the mobility of scarce skilled labor, in general such efforts have met with theoretical incomprehension and bureaucratic opposition:[38] there is need, it is said, to distinguish between "rational flow and anarchic free flow [that is, market allocation] of talented people."[39] There have been numerous official announcements heralding future change: the Soviet-type eight-grade tariff wage system will soon be abolished in enterprises;[40] enterprises will have more control over wage determination;[41] wage rates will be determined more by individual workers' productivity-related criteria than by seniority;[42] and total payrolls will be allowed to fluctuate according to individual enterprise performance.[43]

But such practices require the freeing of industrial labor so that it can move spontaneously in response to wage differentials. The central authorities have made it patently clear, however, that they will not abandon their control over wages altogether, thus rendering the changes meaningless. (Even the "liberal" Hungarians have not done this.) The central government's interest in retaining a measure of wage control no doubt stems from its concern with the possibility of runaway consumption and inflation, as well as a concern about the skewing of the pattern of income distribution.[44] Despite talk about the need, from an efficiency standpoint, to increase income differentials, in China such differentials cannot exceed certain rather narrowly defined limits without giving rise to serious political difficulties. Redistributive mechanisms (such as progressive income taxes linked to transfer payments) are not yet in place, so wage control has to be more direct. In other words, part of the problem with the price of labor, as with other prices, is the transitional incompatibility of the plan and market institutional arrangements of motivation, that is, the coexistence of administrative controls over labor mobility with not fully marketized incentive levers, with the two sets of instruments frequently working at cross-purposes.

Because the 1985 floating of wages by enterprises was to proceed from the payroll base figures for 1984, enterprises hurried to raise wages (especially through the less easily controllable bonuses) before January 1, 1985.[45] In December 1984, wages jumped an unprecedented 46 percent, most of the increase having been paid for by borrowing from state banks. That month, bank loans rose 48.4 percent, and government expenditures on payrolls went 70 percent over the budget. To foot the bill, the treasury printed 8 billion extra yuan in 1984.[46]

Interest rates, one of the economic levers on which the government has increasingly relied to guide the nonmandatory spheres of the economy, are not market determined and have not proved effective so far in allocating capital funds rationally or in cooling down the overheated economy. Differentiated and floating interest rates are being tried, but any resemblance to market rates is coincidental.

Micro-Autonomy

Micro-autonomy means three things: experimentation with mixed public-private forms of property enfranchisement at the enterprise level; resort to partial or total foreign ownership of firms; and enlargement of the decision-making powers of state enterprises with regard to production, supply, marketing, pricing, labor, or investment. To constitute meaningful reform (that is, to raise the quality of economic performance), micro-autonomy must occur within a setting of marketized macro-control. Otherwise micro-autonomy becomes merely an exercise in administrative decentralization—a tinkering with the bureaucratic apparatus. This has been the fate of micro-autonomy in the Soviet Union and most East European state Socialist countries.

Mixed Property Forms. The coexistence of public and private forms of enfranchisement at the enterprise level is not new in the People's Republic of China. Mixed public-private enterprises existed in China before the mid-1950s, some of them even surviving until the Cultural Revolution in 1966. What is new is the direction and magnitude of change outlined in recent proposals. For example, under the proposed industrial changes, in the years 1985–1987, *all* enterprises with fixed assets of less than 1.5 million yuan and annual profits of under 200,000 yuan are to be contracted out or leased to individuals or groups (cooperatives) for periods of up to five years. As in Hungary, such enterprises tend to be concentrated in the service trades, catering, maintenance, repair, construction, and local transportation. The arrangement is broadly similar to the household system in agriculture, where legal social ownership is combined with broad privatization of the rights of use. The leased enterprises are required to pay rent and taxes to the state. They are granted relatively broad rights of business decision making, including decisions about the distribution of the firms' net income. As an added benefit, public firms operating under the leasing arrangement will be allowed to avoid restrictions on the hiring of labor applicable to private sector enterprises.[47]

It appears that most enterprises so far denationalized have been turned over to cooperative groups. The kind of small enterprises involved in this change currently account for a little more than half the total value of gross industrial output (a count that includes enterprises in rural towns and townships). As has been noted, the movement involves the de facto privatization of industrial property rights primarily to groups. The question is whether these groups will be bona fide cooperatives or neo-Stalinist collectives—which are simply a lowlier species of state enterprises. Much will depend on the taxing and rent-collecting attitudes and policies of local authorities and on whether there will be enough capital and current inputs outside the plan for the "autonomous" firms to do something with their newly acquired money. Will the leased firms compete with state firms for scarce materials, maybe even for custom? If so, what will be the state's reaction? Will the new arrangement further encourage an already active underground economy and contribute to the well-established propensity of officials to be corrupted?

In addition to the establishment of various forms of contracting

163

and leasing arrangements, the legal private sector in urban areas has been significantly expanded. This trend, however, must be kept in perspective. Although the number of people employed in this sector (mostly in services, retail trade, and catering) has increased more than fifteen-fold since 1978, such workers still constitute only a very small proportion of total urban employment (2.5 percent at the end of 1984, compared with 3.2 percent in 1957 at the end of the Stalinist First Five-Year Plan).[48] Even if one assumes considerable undercounting of this essentially amorphous backpack sector, legal private activities in urban areas are quite marginal and are likely to remain that way.

Foreign Ownership. There has been foreign equity participation in Socialist development of Communist states in the past—in the pre-Stalin Soviet Union during the 1920s and since then in some other countries (for example, Hungary); the practice has the doctrinal sanction of no less an authority than Lenin himself. In China, since 1978 various forms of foreign participation have been encouraged. Two remarks have to be made in this regard. First, foreign industrial participation—whatever the precise form, and there are many—has as a rule been isolated from the rest of the economy either through special regulations or outright zoning. Second, the high hopes that such an arrangement would attract advanced technology and generate hard currency exports (especially with respect to the special economic zones) have not yet been realized. Actual (as distinct from contemplated) foreign investment in joint ventures of all kinds has been relatively modest, made largely by "Hong Kong compatriots" for tourism-related projects, industrial assembly work (assembly of television sets, for example), and real estate speculation (and perhaps for political insurance as well).

State Enterprises. The enlargement of the previously minimal decision-making prerogatives of state-owned enterprises is also a form, albeit more limited, of denationalization and privatization of collective property rights (including, prominently, greater rights by an enterprise to its profits). Collective firms, while disadvantaged in many respects, have typically enjoyed greater independence from planning indices and ministerial intervention than state firms have. Such an increase in state enterprise "autonomy" is the micro end of the macro use of economic levers.

At the heart of the enterprise autonomy scheme is the question of profit retention.[49] In the past, state enterprises remitted almost all their profits to the state treasury. The state then allocated nonreturnable grants for the enterprises' capital needs out of the state budget and sent detailed instructions for the use of these funds. Under the new policy, however, instead of remitting all profits, enterprises will pay a tax on profits. These and other taxes will be used by the state as an economic lever to induce the desired enterprise behavior with respect to the after-tax profits retained by the enterprises. The self-interest of the enterprise, it is now believed, can be reconciled with the country's "social" interest (as perceived by the state) through the state's taxation policy. But such a view may be overly optimistic. The Soviet experience with profit retention shows that this assumption is correct only if the price system within which profit arises and taxes are deployed is market rational.[50] Without a revolutionary marketization—that is, a freeing and debureaucratization of the industrial price system—the partial privatization of property rights in the form of profits to state firms remains an adjustment that will, in my opinion, keep generating allocatively wrong signals. Indeed, Soviet experimentation with tax-for-profit formulas (and the associated "enterprise funds")[51] has now been going on for thirty years, and there are no indications that it has been at all helpful. In fact, there has probably even been some net regression.

Knowing this, the Chinese have introduced an array of corrective taxes to compensate for profit distortions due to the continued presence of an irrational price system. Among these taxes is a product tax, which is applied uniformly throughout the country but differentiated among products. The purpose of the tax is to confiscate that part of (windfall) profits on certain goods that arises from "wrong" pricing, as, for example, the profits on some consumer durables and cigarettes.[52] There is also a resource tax designed to eliminate rent differentials among extractive industries and mining and an adjustment tax whose purpose is to remove differences among enterprises in the same industrial branch, whenever such differences arise from "undeserved" causes.[53] Moreover, to remind enterprise managements that capital is not free and to correct for profit distortions due to capital intensity, a capital charge is now levied on fixed and working capital. And a bonus tax is in force to help curb the "blind" and "wanton" disbursement of premiums. The use of taxes, including the most important, the eight-grade progressive income tax,[54] shows that Chinese planners have a far better theoretical grasp of the issues involved in using economic levers with noneconomic prices than the Soviets have ever been able to manage.

But many questions are still unresolved. The most important of these is who will determine what is "reasonable" profit and what is not, and what criteria will be used to make that determination. When prices are allocatively distorted, it is not easy, even with the purest of intentions, to pinpoint what part of profits or profitability rates is due to erroneous economic calculation and what is due to other factors. In such conditions, there is bound to be considerable administrative fiat in the decision to tax, which may compound rather than lessen the problem. The Hungarians are familiar with this problem.

In addition to the right to a portion of profit and greater latitude in the use of retained profit, enterprises are to gain new rights with respect to their labor force. This includes, notably, the right to hire and to dismiss workers for cause, and the right to determine wages in relation to performance.[55] These rights, too, will almost certainly be circumscribed by the state's taxing policy and bureaucratic suasion. Other important rights granted to enterprises include the right to enter into lateral transactions with other firms, not as a general rule, but supplementary to the plan, and on a larger scale and with less administrative fuss than was possible under the mandatory plan; the right to increase the scope of production outside the plan and of "self-disposal" goods; and the right to purchase certain producer goods and materials on a more or less open market.[56]

It is interesting but not surprising to note that the introduction of the tax-for-profits scheme has right away given rise to complaints in the Chinese press about large-scale tax avoidance and evasion.[57]

Prospects

Instead of speculating on the future course of economic changes in China, I shall list some dangers that lurk along the reformist path. I assume that the current leadership, or an important and influential part of it, is committed to the improvement of the qualitative performance of the economy. I further assume that such improvement requires reform of the economic system rather than adjustment. In the Chinese context, as noted throughout this chapter, this means that markets and privatized property rights would have to become dominant in the system. This would require the marketization of the plan's institutions of information, coordination, and motivation (in short, the establishment of competitive market relations among buyers and sellers), and the de facto privatization of property rights in the means of production, exchange, and distribution.

Three interacting and interrelated groups of dangers lie in the way of the reformist movement in China. The components of these three groups have been active elsewhere in the world of the plan.

They have succeeded in all instances in bringing the reform movement to a halt either early on (as in the Soviet Union) or a bit later (Hungary). The three groups are economic, political, and ideological.

The economic dangers come from three sources: first, from the nature of the market mechanism itself; second, from the basic incompatibility of market and administrative command institutions where these coexist because the reform is introduced incrementally rather than all at once; and third, from the behavior of those unacquainted with the operational rules and ethical requisites of the market and privatized property rights.

The market mechanism is very good at equilibrating supply and demand in individual product markets (and, incidentally, at resolving conflicts at a fairly low systemic level), but it is less good in achieving equilibrium on the macro level. This means that the introduction of markets and privatized property rights might bring with it bouts of open unemployment, open inflation, booms and recessions, balance of payments disequilibriums, and wide differentials in the distribution of income and wealth. This has happened in China. These problems are also present in the system of central administrative command planning, but most of the time they manifest themselves there in a suppressed or disguised form. Their openness in a market setting provides opponents of reform with excellent issues around which to mobilize resistance to the marketization and privatization process. This has been the case in Hungary.

The incompatibility of market and plan institutions during the transitional period has been discussed here and elsewhere.[58] The effects of the cure of a little bit of market and more than a bit of planning, with partly privatized and mostly socialized property rights, have in general proved worse than the disease. A good instance of this unhappy mixture in China is the attempted extension of urban micro-autonomy in a system still dominated by an irrational industrial price system. This institutional working-at-odds has been instrumental in subverting the reformist movement (never very strong) in the USSR and most Eastern European countries.

Operating within the market environment brings rewards to many. It is not an easy or restful task, however; nor is it one with which all are familiar or toward which everyone is temperamentally and professionally predisposed. Moreover, the market is governed by stringent rules of the game. Observance of contract terms and abstinence from all action in restraint of trade, for example, are among the rules of market conduct, and a predisposition for risk taking (not gambling) is among the chief qualities of the market

167

entrepreneur. But the qualities required of government bureaucrats and state enterprise managers in a plan setting are quite different from those of the market entrepreneur. Where the entrepreneur is bold and adventuresome, the bureaucrat is obedient and staid. Where the former seeks to maximize gain, the latter tries to minimize loss.

Thrust into a market environment, bureaucrats tend to behave not like capitalists but like black marketeers, lining their pockets, stealing, and generally acting not according to the rules of the market but according to the street-smart, corrupt codes of the underground economy. Their behavior is partly connected with the high degree of imperfection found in markets created by something that is neither adjustment nor reform. Mostly, however, it is due to the incompatibility of (even modest) pluralism in the economic marketplace and continued monopoly of political power.

It should be added that bureaucrats and managers are not the only ones who experience difficulty operating in a market environment. There are other groups as well: the nonentrepreneurial peasants, for example. The market, after all, is not responsive to nonpecuniary considerations. Those unable to operate in it according to the rules, or those excluded from it, may add up to a sizable political constituency.

The political danger stems not only from this ill fit of market and centralized planning but also from other sources. The market is a labor-saving device in the sense that it generates, transmits, and analyzes information about what needs to be done in the system; coordinates the disparate pieces of information; and provides the requisite motivation to get the job done. The market does all this at a comparatively low transactions cost; there is no need for bureaucrats to do this work deliberately and manually. In other words, the market threatens the bureaucrats in their capacity as "producers"—planners, supervisors, enforcers, double-checkers, and so on. The market also endangers the consumer privileges of the bureaucratic elite. Under the regime of the market, what matters is money, not political privilege. Reform thus threatens the bureaucracy on both counts.

Ideological dangers to reform come from two doctrinal sources: Marxism and Leninism. From the standpoint of Marxism, there are two issues connected with economic reform. Clinging to Marxism are Socialist ethical codes (developed mostly after Stalin's death) that include the right to employment (regarded as more important than the right of free speech), interpreted in the state sector as the right to a lifetime job (in China, the right has traditionally extended even to children of many state sector employees). Other rights associated with the Marxist ethos are access to basic necessities of life at low (subsidized) prices, "equality," stability, and others.[59]

The quest for market efficiency inevitably comes in conflict with these ethical desiderata and creates resistance in the adversely affected quarters. The codes are part of an implicit social contract between the monoparty state and the citizenry. The citizens receive these economic guarantees but at a sacrifice: they lack mobility, experience chronic shortages of desired goods and services, put up with low quality of products and other consumer frustrations, and accept a slow increase in their standard of living. Economic reform, with its competition, high-risk quotient, and short response time to rapidly changing market conditions, breaks that contract. Some firms have to close, some people have to be dismissed from their jobs, rents rise, and so on.

The second issue connected with Marxism and affected by economic reform is that of social classes. Marketization and de facto privatization of the economic system benefit not one class but many, and these are not the ones chosen as "progressive" by Marx's laws of history. Although in the long run, reform benefits the urban proletariat—in fact, transforms it into a middle class—the short- and medium-term benefits, and some of the longer-term ones as well, accrue primarily to the entrepreneurial and independent segments of urban and rual society: the "rich" peasant, the shopkeeper, the enterprising businessman, the broker, and the venture capitalist. Reform changes not only the output structure of the economy but its class structure as well and in the process redefines class in a non-Marxist sense.

If Marxism is associated with the Socialist ethical code, Leninism is identified—much more accurately—with party control over all spheres of life. Marketization and privatization reforms diffuse economic power among many centers; production, exchange, and distribution relations tend to function best when horizontally integrated rather than vertically and tend to diversify and be made more indicative and indirect—all of which goes against the Leninist imperative of absolute power absolutely concentrated. On this Leninist issue of control, economics, politics, and ideology converge. Marketization and privatization, the opponents of reform argue, cause not only macro-economic woes and aberrant behavior ("spiritual pollution"). They threaten the planning, supervisory, and managerial elites both as "producers" and consumers; they are ethically repugnant on a

Marxist interpretation; and, above all, they are a menace to unified monopolistic control by the Leninist party.

These are serious counts that have to be carefully considered in arriving at a perception of the odds for and against the reformist movement in China.

11

China's Economic Experiment—
Back from the Market?

In a review of China's economic changes from 1979 through 1988, economist Liu Guoguang, a vice-president of the Chinese Academy of Social Sciences, divides the decade into three stages: (1) from December 1978 (Third Plenary Session of the Eleventh Communist Party of China Central Committee) to October 1984 (Third Plenary Session of the Twelfth Central Committee); (2) from October 1984 to October 1987 (Thirteenth National Congress); and (3) from October 1987 to the end of 1988.[1] The review, titled "A Sweet and Sour Decade," suggests that in the first stage, 1979–1984, policy adjustments and structural reforms in agriculture resulted, by and large, in improved quantity and quality of food supply, labor productivity, yields, and per capita income in the countryside. Liu's assessment is accurate. Not only did higher state purchase prices for farm products create positive incentives for farmers, but also—more important—the agricultural price system became significantly marketized (that is, allocatively rationalized), and property rights were restructured so that the farm sector was greatly decollectivized and the system of family tenant farming emerged. The family gained extensive use rights to land (fifteen-year leases) and de jure rights of ownership of farm implements, including small tractors and draft animals.

By 1984 the number of agricultural commodities subject to compulsory state procurement had been reduced from twenty-nine to ten. Subsequently, contractual purchases replaced compulsory procurement quotas for grains and cotton; the state, however, was still setting the prices. By 1987, according to Liu, market forces determined 65 percent of all farm and sideline products prices "to varying degrees." The positive influence of the marketizing and property privatizing reforms on output, productivity, and income made its way through improved marketing of produce (including the expansion of local and interregional trade), greater and more attentive work effort, better farm organization, and improved custody of farm assets. The gratifying agricultural results of this stage gave a good press to market-related reforms and contributed, no doubt, to the October 20, 1984, decision of the Central Committee to use this type of approach in the industrial and, more generally, urban sector. Although a clear positive correlation exists between the growth of China's farm production during the first stage and the marketizing and privatizing reforms, the improvement in output, productivity, and income must be measured against the very low levels of the preceding collectivist decade. These improvements were perhaps a one-time motivational shot, whose replication in the future and in a differently structured urban-industrial sector would be much more difficult.[2]

The "sourness" of China's economic experiment began shortly after the October 1984 decision. As some Western and Chinese economists anticipated, the urban-industrial economy—particularly the large, highly bureaucratized, demonetized, privileged state sector— has proved resistant to structural change in the two areas that really matter: the industrial price system and property. A nonscarcity, allocatively nonsensical price system and a highly bureaucratized, rigid form of nationalized (state) property still dominate the urban industrial economy.[3] This domination continues despite the reduction of the state sector's share of total industrial output from 81 percent in 1978 to 70 percent in 1987, a decrease from 120 to 60 in the number of industrial products planned and managed directly by the state, a reduction in the number of materials subject to "unified" distribution by the state from 256 to 26, a decrease in the percentage of fixed investment handled through the state budget from 77 to 32 percent, and an increase in the proportion of the prices of consumer goods and industrial materials determined to varying degrees by the market. Compared with the situation before 1979, there has been expansion of the collective industrial sector (from 19 percent of industrial output value in 1978 to 27 percent in 1987) and of private industry (from 0 to a very modest 2.4 percent). More important, the instrumentalities of central administrative command planning have weakened without a concurrent strengthening of market instrumentalities of information, coordination, and incentive. Whatever the reasons, things began to go sour after 1984. This sourness has three main ingredients according to Liu: inflation, skewed ("unfair") income distribution, and corruption (including "profiteering," bribery, and abuse of power for personal gain), contributing to "a drop in social morals across China."[4] Unfortunately for the reformers, the difficulties in changing the structure of the industrial economy coincided with a leveling off in the farm production upsurge, particularly of the always politically sensitive grain output.

During Liu's third stage (beginning in October 1987), the sourness grew measurably worse, especially in the cities. While technical debates continued on what to do about the economy, a theory rationalizing in ideological terms the marketizing and privatizing changes was put forward, and proposals for adjustments of the political structure were made. The third stage, as it turns out, has been mainly a holding operation, presumably intended by the reformers to catch breath, correct dislocations, prevent the structural changes from being rolled back too far, and, they hope, regain the momentum lost during the previous stage. Since mid-1988 forces unsympathetic to the reform have dominated.

An interesting and relatively novel feature of the third stage, especially since mid-1988, has been the degree to which the debate on what to do has been, at least outwardly, professionalized. Earlier attacks on the reform movement were thinly disguised ideological assaults carried out under the banner of resistance to "spiritual pollution," "unhealthy tendencies," and "bourgeois liberalization." This time, everyone is rhetorically for pushing ahead with economic restructuring along "Socialist commodity economy" lines in concert with the theory of the primary stage of socialism, and the focus of official concern is, at least overtly, on inflation, widening income differentials, unemployment, erosion of urban living standards, excessive industrial and lagging agricultural investment, growing subsidies, "overheating," and other technicalities. Remedial policies suggested by various leadership groups, directly or through affiliated academic economists and others, have also been notable for their nonideological tenor compared with the past, centering on the comparative merits of different macroeconomic levers of control. One should be careful not to exaggerate the significance of the change in the semantics and tone of the debate on economic modernization. The change may reflect the dominance of the media by the liberalizers, despite occasional backsliding. The technical remedies for the perceived "crisis," indeed, the very perception of economic crisis (how bad it is, how inevitable, how tolerable, of what parentage), derive from and articulate divergent ideological concepts of the relationship of the individual to society in China and the nature of "socialism with Chinese characteristics." While intraparty ideological disagreements and personal rivalries continue to abound, they now take the form of overt concerns about the country's economic disease. As Lu Xun once put it: "When you want to drown a dog, charge him with rabies."

Sweet

Even in the midst of the troubles that have beset the Chinese economy since 1985, the achievements have been significant.

Agriculture. The gross value of agricultural output has grown impressively: 6.5 percent per year from 1978 to 1987 compared with an average annual growth of 2.6 percent in the twenty-six years preceding 1978.[5] During the decade 1978–1987, the output of meat more than doubled, that of oil-bearing crops increased more than one and a half times, cotton production rose by 75 percent, aquatic products by 84 percent, and grain by 19 percent. The value of nonagricultural output produced in the countryside increased 6.5 times, an average annual increase of more than 23 percent in real terms. Whereas in 1978 the value of nonagricultural rural output (rural industries, construction, transportation, and commerce) was 30 percent of China's gross national product (GNP), in 1987 it was 50 percent. The gross agricultural output value per capita in 1987 (at 2,400 yuan) represented a real increase of 2.5 times over 1978. Per acre output of grain during the period increased 43 percent, of cotton 93 percent, and of oil-bearing crops 66 percent. The composition of farm output moved away from grain (80 percent of farm output in 1978; 77 percent in 1987) toward more profitable cash crops (10 percent in 1978; 14 percent in 1987), with a parallel shift toward the production of higher-quality grains. Some 80 million peasants were relocated to higher value-added employments in rural industries. The monetization and marketization ("commoditization") of the rural economy increased notably. In 1978, 45 percent of farm and sideline products were sold "as commodities," nearly 60 percent in 1987 (65 percent, according to Liu). Peasant per capita net income (in current prices) rose from 134 yuan in 1978 to 463 yuan in 1987. The average annual increase in peasant consumption (1979–1986) was 8.7 percent, 5.8 percent for the nonagricultural population. At more than 390 kilograms per year, per capita grain consumption comfortably exceeded the 1979–1981 developing-country average of 213 kilograms. By 1987 peasant households owned 70 percent of all large- and medium-sized tractors in China, 94 percent of walking and small tractors, and 61 percent of generators for irrigation and drainage.

Industry. The 1978–1987 record in industry was also impressive. The gross output value of state industry doubled during the period, while its share dropped from 80 to 60 percent (70 percent according to Liu).[6] The gross output value of collectively run industry increased four times. In real terms, total industrial output value during the decade rose at an average annual rate of 11.8 percent (11.3 percent during 1952–1977). One of the leading imbalances within industry was partly corrected: whereas in 1978 the ratio of heavy to light industrial output was 57:43, in 1987 it came to 50:50. State sector industrial labor productivity, according to official sources, increased during the decade by almost 50 percent. In 1978, 40 percent of the industrial output value was produced under mandatory planning; compared with 20 percent in 1987. In 1988, the physical rationing (material and technical supply) network distributed 47 percent of steel products, 44 percent of coal, 14 percent of cement, and 26 percent of timber—substantially below the shares of these key products distributed by the network in 1978. During the decade, energy consumption for every 100 million yuan of output value fell by 30 percent and the amount of steel products consumed by 23 percent. Between 1978 and 1987 industrial products valued at U.S. $145.5 billion were exported, accounting for 83 percent of China's total exports. This value of industrial exports was 5.5 times that of the period 1973–1977. The volume of foreign trade almost quadrupled.

From 1978 through 1987 more than 10,000 foreign joint ventures were established involving about $30 billion in contracts ($9 billion actually spent). Foreign loan contracts came to almost $40 billion ($27 billion spent), and various barter trade and assembly operations agreements amounted to $3 billion ($2 billion spent).[7]

Sour

The record of quantitative accomplishment tells only part of the story. Although in 1987 China was indisputably better off economically than it was in 1978 after years of Maoist misrule, the blessings have not been unmixed. The problems that accompanied the economic changes have become more bothersome since 1985 and, if not properly handled, could undo the reforms and many of the material benefits gained thus far. In general, demand still exceeds supply at the present irrational prices, and neither the old administrative nor the emerging market control levers work.

Overheated Industrial Economy. In 1988 industrial production expanded by 18 percent, more than double the government's goal, a situation close to being out of control. In August 1988, eleven provinces and municipalities registered industrial growth of more than 20 percent over the same month in 1987, with Fujian chalking up 32 percent and Guangdong 36 percent. Consumer goods led the way, with refrigerators (82 percent increase in August 1988) and color television sets (65 percent) in the forefront. This production put enormous strain on scarce raw materials, energy, and the badly overburdened and bottlenecked transportation system. It fueled inflation and also contributed to an already thriving black market with its concurrent political corruption.

Inflation. Officially, the retail price index in 1988 rose 18.5 percent over 1987, compared with 7.3 percent in 1987. Unofficially, and more realistically, the inflation rate was close to 40 percent. Even at official rates, the inflation (which began in 1985) has been the longest since 1949 and the most severe since Mao's Great Leap Forward (1959–1961). In the first half of 1988 vegetable prices in large cities rose by about 50 percent. In September 1988, the prices of meat, poultry, and eggs rose 46 percent compared with August 1987, and prices of traditional Chinese medicines jumped 52 percent.[8] Some prices doubled, others (for example, machinery prices in some large cities like Canton) rose as much as 200 percent. Rumors of further sharp price increases and projected bank restrictions on personal savings withdrawals precipitated panic buying and runs on banks in some cities, notably Shanghai in late July 1988.

Price inflation was accompanied and in part stimulated by wage inflation. The state sector wages fund expanded by 20.1 percent in the first three quarters of 1988 (19, 22, 22 percent respectively for the whole of 1984, 1985, 1986), with the bonus component rising 46.6 percent. Money wage increases greatly exceeded increases in labor productivity. (Already wage increases 1981–1985 were nearly twice as great as increases in the productivity of industrial labor.)[9] To maintain social peace in the face of surging retail prices for food and industrial consumer goods, urban subsidies were handed out liberally; the Beijing subsidy in the first half of 1988, for example, exceeded that of the first half of 1987 by 60 percent. The officially counted wage increases probably understate the actual situation, because a good part of compensation takes the form of in-kind fringe benefits (for example, free lunches or clothing allocations), some not strictly legal, which have been rising rapidly in recent years.

Nor do they take into account earnings from moonlighting in the second (legal, semilegal, or illegal) economy on government time, often with the aid of "borrowed" government-owned tools. Such additional income may equal or even exceed the statistically captured wage income, according to some. Still, despite the rising urban wages and subsidies, many urban dwellers found their real incomes declining. In Guangdong Province half the urban population was officially estimated to have experienced real income erosion in the first half of 1988, 40 percent in Shanghai. Nationwide, in 1987 the share of urban and rural households whose real income had been eroded by inflation was 40 percent, up from 20 percent in 1986.[10] This situation has led to work slowdowns and strikes—some 200 strikes, each involving more than a thousand workers, are believed to have occurred in the first half of 1988 alone.

The burden of subsidies is heavy and rising, now accounting for about one-seventh (30 billion yuan) of total state budgetary expenditures. The subsidies are paid, as we have seen, partly to assuage the dissatisfaction of urban workers with rising prices and partly to keep rents and the prices of utilities and transportation paid by urban users well under market-clearing levels.[11] Subsidies contribute to inflationary pressures. Spent largely on food, they drive up food prices on the free market. In the currently unsatisfactory state of the price system and of marketing, and in the presence of various contractual and other constraints (size of family land plots, for example) on the farmers, the rising prices either bypass the producers or reach them in distorted form. Whatever the reasons, the rise in urban food prices has not resulted in sufficient increases in the food supplies to moderate or halt price increases.

Inflation has also been stimulated by a seemingly uncontrollable hunger for industrial investment, a phenomenon common to all Socialist economies. This has been particularly true of fixed investment by provincial and lower-level government authorities and enterprises that account for roughly two-fifths of total fixed investment in China. The plan for 1988 called for a decrease of 14 percent in state sector industrial fixed investment, but in the first quarter of the year alone the increase was 11 percent (15 percent in 1987). Uncoordinated investment by localities has resulted in wasted resources through, among others, the duplication of industrial capacities. The technological level of many locally constructed plants is low, materials utilization rates are high, and managerial expertise is poor.

Another contributor to the inflationary surge has been the rapid increase in consumption by organizations. This was supposed to decrease by 20 percent in 1988 compared with the preceding year but instead increased by roughly that proportion, by more than 30 percent in some provinces.

The central authorities have in fact lost control of the money supply. In 1988, according to the central government's plan, the money supply was to have increased by 15 percent; instead, it jumped 40 percent. This uncontrolled growth has been going on for some time, the money supply rising at an estimated yearly rate of 30 percent between 1984 and 1986. One reason for the rise is the increasing monetization of the economy—a necessary and welcome ingredient of China's economic modernization. Other reasons include the probably too far-reaching decentralization of economic management combined with the banking system's lack of independence from governmental authority. China, says Li Yungi, an economist with the People's Bank,

> has no independent central bank and no banks operating as independent entities. . . . [In the absence of such independence] monetary policy . . . completely reflects the behavior of the government. Consequently almost every year the Chinese government has covered its budget deficits through bank overdrafts. At the same time, government at all levels often forces banks to finance pet projects and meet excessive working capital requirements regardless of economic results. . . . Compounding the problem is the fact that specialized . . . banks also do not operate as independent entities.[12]

Like the rest of the banking system, these banks are not responsible for their own profits and losses (that is, they operate under a mushy budget constraint with no economic penalties to speak of). Consequently, they have no incentive to deny money for often quirky ventures and every incentive to accommodate their customers who also happen to be the banks' political bosses. Li is quite right in saying that "the expectation that decentralized decision-making will lead to more efficient investment decisions depends heavily on the efficiency with which the financial system mobilizes and channels resources."[13] Such efficiency is crucially dependent, one should add, on the existence of market-determined interest rates.

Widening Income Differentials and Unemployment. Since Stalin's death (but ideologically since Marx), Socialist societies have been concerned with "fairness" in the distribution of income, understood as money income, not the income (including access to desirable goods) that comes from the exclusive possession of political power. Since in all Socialist economies, under conditions of chronic scarcity, people's earnings are not readily convertible into goods and the distribution of political power income is very unequal, distributive "fairness," understood as absence of wide income disparities among various groups, is really quite meaningless. Still, the egalitarian principle, as it applies to money income, is taken seriously by policy makers and, by now, by most citizens as well, who attribute inequalities of money income mainly to large differences in political connections, given the monopolistically politicized structure of Socialist "markets." Wide income disparities have political consequences everywhere. Such consequences become particularly important and explosive in an economy, such as China's, where people perceive them as organically linked to a highly elitist distribution of political power.

Not surprisingly, therefore, next to inflation, official China is concerned about large and expanding income disparities among various groups of citizens. First is the disparity between incomes earned by people on fixed wages and salaries, who under the existing system cannot as a rule change jobs without government permission, and the new private sector entrepreneurs. The average urban employee's wage is equivalent to about U.S. $48 per month (for two people) plus some $20 in bonuses for a total of $68, or an annual income of $816. A private businessman (in the construction business, for example) can make $10,000 or more a year. For reference, a color television set retails for about $700, nearly what the average employee and his wife earn in a year, bonuses included. The "private" entrepreneurs comprise not just rural folk (specialized householders in the vicinity of large cities) but officials who set up "briefcase companies" with politically facilitated access to scarce materials, factual information, and the chops needed for permissions and authorizations of all kinds. Second, urban workers differ in their ability to obtain bonuses, to gain access to the second economy, and, connected with this, to privatize informally (steal) socially owned assets. The existence and size of the bonus depend on whether the worker is employed in a profitable or unprofitable state enterprise, whose profitability depends largely on the firm's access to extrabudgetary funds. This access, in turn, hinges more on personal and political connections than on efficient management, given the monstrous distortions of the prices by which profitability is measured. One group that appears to be particularly underprivileged in earning power, access to political influence, and opportunity to appropriate state assets for personal gain is rank-and-file academics (those not affiliated with official research institutes and commissions), although opportunities to engage in consulting and crypto-commercial activities are not altogether absent.

It remains true, however, that the academic community has so far benefited mainly from the relaxation of the intellectual climate after Mao. Its status, as measured by both social prestige and the ability to purchase worldly goods, remains low. In 1978 state workers in knowledge-intensive occupations earned on average 2 percent more than manual workers. In 1986 manual workers earned on average 10 percent more than brain workers, and the disparity has grown since then. For the long-term the implications for China's modernization of this continuing neglect and disparagement of the intellectuals promise to be very serious. The brighter young people's great hope is to go abroad. Of the 40,000 or so Chinese students who have gone to the United States since 1979, reportedly only one-fourth have returned to China.[14]

While numerous peasants on China's eastern "gold coast," particularly those living near the large coastal cities, have prospered as never before, others—100 million of them, or one-tenth of the population—remain malnourished by official admission. Interprovincial income disparities are large and growing: Guangdong with 63 million people has an income twice that of Hunan with 57 million people; wage rates in Guangdong are 20 to 30 percent higher than in Hunan.[15]

Besides wide income variations, open unemployment has made its appearance, with perhaps 20 million unnecessary workers in the cities out of a total urban industrial labor force of about 150 million.

Agricultural Problems. Partly because of poor weather, but for policy and systemic reasons as well, agricultural performance since 1985 has given signs of running out of steam, particularly with regard to the production of grains and cotton. As already noted, farm output has not responded appropriately and expeditiously to the rising demand for food, with the result that rationing of various formerly deregulated commodities (pork, for example) had to be reinstituted in the larger cities in 1987–1988. Grain production in 1988 was 394 million tons, 9 million tons below 1987 and 4 percent under the state-set target. For the fourth consecutive year grain output failed to reach the peak production of 1984, when marketizing reforms were extended. Contributing to the decline are insecurity of land tenure, unclear rules governing family land leases, official suspicion of private property and individual decision making, harassment of family farmers through capricious and exploitative local levies and brutal enforcement of the one-child family planning policy, low state purchase prices for contracted products, the occasional failure of the state to pay cash for contractual deliveries and the attempt to pay off suppliers with IOUs, shortages and high prices of chemical fertilizer supplied by the state, excessive parcelization of land, insufficient mechanization of farm operations, neglect of communal infrastructures (such as irrigation and drainage facilities, schools, and clinics), and inadequacy of local storage and transportation.

Corruption. By official admission, corruption—defined as "abusing positions of power for personal gain, extortion and blackmail, graft and bribery, squandering public money, and indulging in luxury and extravagance"[16]—is rampant at all levels of the party and state administrations. Repeated anticorruption campaigns, clean-up investigations, and harsh penalties (including death) have done little to stem the tide of graft and bribery.

When China's leaders debated the sourness of the economy during their annual summer retreat at Beidahe in 1988, reformist zeal dramatically cooled. They decided to "retreat into caution," a pullback that could turn into a defeat for the reformists unless the nature of the problems and the systemic repercussions of the remedies are clearly understood. The battle cry of those that some observers both inside and outside China see as waging a "war on the entire reformist enterprise"[17] is: "Improve the economic environment and adjust the economic order."

A few cautionary remarks may help put the perceived economic problems in perspective. The Chinese economy, like other Socialist, centrally planned economies, had suffered in the past—before the implementation of the changes in policy and structures—from chronic excess demand for both producer and consumer goods, inflation, sharp income disparities, unemployment, corruption, and generally low quality of goods, services, and human relations. In contrast with the past, when these ills were largely suppressed or disguised by administrative commands, they have now surfaced, as they tend to do whenever markets come into play. Inflation, for example, there has always been, but by reason of almost universal price controls administratively imposed, it did not manifest itself in price increases, but rather in lines outside stores, shortages or lack of wanted goods, and corruption. Even when money income differentials narrowed as they did during the Great Leap Forward and the Cultural Revolution, enormous inequalities in actual access to goods existed, such access having been, and remaining to this day, primarily a function of a person's or group's position on the political power ladder and of the accompanying bureaucratic connections. The same applies to the distribution of wealth. Indeed, one of the reasons for the party and state bureaucrats' resistance to the marketization (and concurrent monetization) of the system is their fear of losing private rents, which they draw from public property under the system of monopolistic party and state power.[18]

Second, unemployment, always present under the old system, despite denials, was hidden too. Although everyone had a "job," irrespective of personal preferences between work and leisure and regardless of the job holder's marginal contribution to production, chronic overstaffing in most branches of the economy, low labor productivity, and massive loitering on the job had resulted. In effect, under the old system, a good part of the worker's wage was an unemployment compensation payment made on the job. These problems, though known to everyone, were disguised, visible only in queues and empty shelves instead of high prices, and loitering instead of job hunting. Even a partial and modest marketization of the system brought these conditions out into the open in China and is beginning to do the same in the Soviet Union. The first effect of this exposure has been shock. Reformers are shocked by the high cost of economic restructuring in rising prices, emergent unemployment, wide income disparities, eroding living standards of some key social groups, the lean and mean way in which wealth is pursued and, most of all, by their own apparent inability to bring these under control through the use of such market instrumentalities as they have managed to put in place. The opponents of structural reform are shocked by the nakedness of the phenomena but even more by what they believe is grievous damage to the institutional foundations and guiding ideas of Leninist socialism. Disturbed by spontaneity under the changed system, they interpret it as "chaos," "anarchy," and erosion of the party's "leading role." Ordinary people's confidence in marketizing and privatizing reform is undermined, giving way to passivity or outright hostility. "Facing so many problems," writes one Chinese economist, "people, including many young people, almost lose their confidence in our reform."[19]

Because shortages, inflation, unemployment, income distribution, and the like now express themselves openly, remedial measures different from the analysis and prescriptions used when all unpleasant phenomena were suppressed are demanded. For a number of reasons (including constraints on freedom of thought), such new analysis has been slow in making its way in China, and the remedies applied in times of acute stress have tended to be the old administrative command ones.

One result of the country's greater openness and interaction with the outside world and the availability of better, more timely, accurate, and reliable information is that today China's economic problems are more visible and measurable than they were earlier. To an extent, therefore, these problems represent the enhanced ability of statistical tools to capture them.

Any restructuring of a complex system is disruptive, sometimes painful. If the general direction of the reformist changes is judged to be correct—and China's improved economic condition today compared with 1978 (the "sweet" side of the experiment) suggests that the reform is headed in the right direction—the questions to be addressed are: Which among the problems are avoidable, due to policy mistakes, and which are the unavoidable price of change? What is the minimum critical mass of reforms (and their attendant disruptions) that have to be introduced if the objectives of reform are to be achieved? Answers to these questions, shared with the population at large, will help reduce the propensity to panic at the first encounter with serious difficulties and to take shelter in pseudo-remedies that invite Brezhnevite stagflations—the fate of Soviet economic experiments over the past three decades.[20]

China's major economic problem today is that changes in supply and demand are not translated into prompt reallocation of resources. One cause of that is technical: advanced degradation of soil, neglect of irrigation and drainage facilities, critical shortage of trained personnel, scarcity of residential housing, locally administered rationing, obsolete industrial equipment, and deficient transportation, for example. But the most important causes are systemic, deriving from the nature and extent of the structural changes made so far.

Limitations of the Market Solution. Like the Czech marketizers before 1968, many Chinese reformers saw marketization and privatization of the economy as a way to banish the problems inherent in central administrative planning without acquiring too many troublesome new ones and to grow rich quickly and painlessly into the bargain. But the market, even at its best, is not a panacea. It experiences breakdowns and has at least three structural failures (externalities, increasing returns, and lack of information) that have been thoroughly explored in the literature at least since J. S. Mill outlined a theory of market failure in his *Principles of Political Economy* (1848). The market, too, has delicate problems with ethics, some of which can be addressed only through the judicial agencies of the state. "Normal" market disabilities (business cycles, inflation, unemployment, politically or ethically unacceptable patterns of income and wealth distribution, and balance of payments disequilibriums) can be addressed with varying degrees of success by resort to such macroeconomic monetary and fiscal instruments as manipulation of the money supply via the interest rate, and tax policy. Such market control levers are just as indispensable a component of the market-price system as are legal rules for contract and tort—and more generally, observance of the rule of law. In their absence, the market system dissolves into a stateless and lawless society or libertarian anarcho-capitalism.[21] Laissez faire does not mandate the absence of state intervention in the market but merely the limitation of such intrusion.

The trouble is that after ten years of policy and structural changes the Chinese system is not a market system, nor is it any longer a coherent, centrally planned system either. It is, as they say, neither fish nor fowl, neither plan nor market, a condition recognized as such by many Chinese economists. Even if such an in between construct were equipped with the market type of macroeconomic instrumentalities of control (an independent banking system and a market-effective system of taxation), which it is not, the efficacy of such instruments to deal with the economy's present problems would be questionable for the reason just stated: the economy is not a market economy but a dismantled planned economy with uncoordinated, unlinked, and imperfect markets here and there for individual goods. Similarly, one can question the effectiveness of administrative levers to deal with problems that are partly administrative in origin, partly market related, and partly due to the incompleteness of markets and administrative command and the uncomfortable coexistence of the two: two parts dismembered command, one part disjointed infantile market. What China has today is not a mixed system, but a mixed up one, a logical collapse. The danger is that the instinct of the Communist authorities to try and "improve the economic environment and adjust the economic order" by resort to administrative command (the regulatory mentality of why permit when you can forbid) will not improve the environment but might produce a Socialist stagflation with Chinese characteristics.

China's economic changes, like Gorbachev's *perestroika*, have so far proceeded in a conceptual vacuum rationalized as "pragmatism," which the leadership describes as "crossing the river while groping for stones." Lacking are a blueprint for change, a theory of systemic transition, and a sense of direction or goals beyond the fuzzy and meaningless "socialism with Chinese characteristics." The only definite statement of objectives is a negative one: the object of the changes, the final destination, is not capitalism, not a fully fledged market system. Unless thoroughly rethought, this formulation could be fatal to the Chinese (as to Soviet) reform efforts.

The market system with dominant private property rights has demonstrated that despite problems it can successfully supply people with increasing quantities and qualities of useful goods that the people want at prices they are prepared to pay, which is the essence of economic modernity. China wants that result but continues to reject the system that brings the result about. A system is a logically consistent whole of mutually compatible, supporting, and interacting ideas and institutions. It must be accepted as a whole, as a package, or not at all. In this case half a loaf is not better than none.

Conditions for a Successful Market System

To be successful, a market system must have the following attributes:

• There must be free markets for goods and factors (land, labor, capital, and entrepreneurship). This means free access and exit for buyers and sellers and no physical rationing of inputs and outputs. Voluntariness of transactions is the operational principle.

• Prices must reflect relative scarcities. Market prices must be the core information, coordination, and incentive device of the system.

• There must be workable competition among and between buyers and sellers, that is, the presence of alternatives—with few, strictly circumscribed exceptions, no monopolies, central or local, private or public.

• There must be rational economic behavior by sellers and buyers. Sellers must want to make profits by responding to buyer demands expressed in competitive prices, and buyers must seek to maximize their satisfactions.

• Private property rights must be dominant. Private property rights require the vesting of very broad use, transfer, and income rights in individuals or freely constituted associations of individuals.

• Macroeconomic instrumentalities of intervention in the market must be in place, as well as institutionalized arrangements (social security and unemployment insurance, for instance) to deal with market disturbances and structural market faults.

These six conditions do not exist in China ten years after economic restructuring began. (They are not even on the horizon in the Soviet Union.) The fundamental theoretical questions of economic reform are how far? how fast? how much? And the answers are all the way, at once, as much as the political traffic will bear. Insofar as possible, the reform measures should be far-reaching, fast, and simultaneously applied.[22] Half-measures accentuate the basic incompatibilities of market and plan philosophies and institutions and psychologically compromise the reform movement: they give rise to disillusionment, make for loss of momentum, and encourage recidivism. A slow and graduated pace, while it may lessen the pain of systemic transition, also enables those adversely affected by the changes (the formerly privileged bureaucrats and coddled state sector workers, for example) to organize powerful constituencies opposed to reform. Lack of synchronization and comprehensiveness disrupts the logical institutional links of the old system without creating workable new ones. What emerges is a nonsystem, which is what China seems to have arrived at after a decade of zigzagging decentralization. "For several reasons," writes Liu Guoguan,

> China has proceeded in a piecemeal fashion, so at present the old and new systems coexist alongside each other. The aim of introducing reforms gradually was to avoid massive social and economic upheaval. However, this blending of two systems has undoubtedly generated a series of thorny problems. For example, with neither the old mandatory system nor the new market system effectively dominating the distribution of resources, the defects of both systems have been magnified. Confusion has arisen in production, circulation, and management, creating much leeway for speculation and racketeering. This has led many Chinese and foreign economists to suggest putting an early end to the coexistence of the two systems and establishing the dominant position of the new system as soon as possible. However, such a transformation is no easy job.[23]

China's Contemporary Economic "System." For China (as for the Soviet Union) economic decentralization requires marketization of information, coordination, incentives, and the privatization of property rights. It has also meant in practice an unwillingness to carry marketization and privatization through to their logical conclusion, that is, refusal to transform central administrative command planning into the market system. Despite a good deal of revisionist thinking on the meaning of socialism (what Marx really meant, how far Marxism is relevant to present-day conditions, whether and how much Mao and others distorted the essence of socialism), the stated determination not to go all the way to the market system remains the official Chinese position and should be taken seriously.[24]

In contemporary China marketization and privatization are more advanced in agriculture than in industry, and they are greater for goods than for factors. In fact, with the exception of a rudimentary market for urban real estate, there is practically no market for land; there exists a partial and very imperfect market for labor; and there is only a residual market of sorts for capital goods. Despite the publicity given them by Western media, financial markets are very underdeveloped, and Chinese stock exchanges are rather pathetic affairs. The continued, extremely limited mobility of factors violates the first condition of a successful market system. Resources cannot be reallocated quickly, if at all, in response to shifts in demand; and the demand-supply disequilibrium that has long plagued the economy, promoted inflation, and contributed to hidden unemployment and low labor productivity is perpetuated. The continued presence of central physical rationing of key inputs and outputs also violates the free market condition. Although fewer goods are subject to such rationing than before 1978, their number and, more important, their strategic significance distort the functioning of both the residual "free" markets for such goods and markets for other goods. At present, 40 percent of the capital goods requirements of Chinese industrial firms are supplied through commercial channels, the rest through centrally planned allocations.[25]

Although some freeing of individual prices has taken place (again, more in agriculture than in industry), the process has been staggered and uncoordinated, and the liberation of the price system (as distinct from individual prices for this or that) is not in sight. To ease the transition to a freer price system, a two-track price arrangement has been implemented under which some prices for a particular commodity or factor are set by the planners (with little or no attention to supply and demand), while others are determined by imperfectly articulated market forces. This is an unsatisfactory compromise that does little to improve the allocative rationality of China's price system and probably increases the old system's formidable behavioral distortions. It certainly encourages corruption as well-connected entrepreneurs obtain scarce inputs earmarked for planned production at low state-set prices and resell them to input-hungry firms at higher quasi-market prices. The seller manages to sell the inputs because he has secured excess supplies from the state by overstating his needs or failing to fulfill his state production contract: "As the government has control over all fixed-price raw materials, factory managers find any way they can to 'get to the mayor' rather than 'get to the market.'"[26] In other words, unwillingness or inability to pay the going market price is not the only criterion of exclusion from access to goods, as it is under the rules of a successful market system. The schizophrenic arrangement applies to prices of agricultural as well as industrial goods, payments for labor, currency values (renminbi versus foreign exchange certificates), and other exchange activities. The far-flung ramifications of the two-track arrangement are succinctly summed up by Bela Balassa:

> The two-tier system of sales and prices increases the freedom of decision making for the firm, but may have adverse effects on the national economy. Since raising the quota allocation of inputs and reducing that of output may affect the firm's profits to a much greater extent than any improvements in production, bargaining and influence-peddling are at a premium. Nor should it be assumed that profitability at the prices of above-quota sales represents social profitability, in part because these prices differ from equilibrium prices that would be obtained in the absence of quotas, and in part because the prices of capital and labor do not reflect scarcity relationships.[27]

Thus, under existing conditions, even the so-called markets in China are to a critical extent markets in favors, and buyer-seller bargaining is often soaked through with politics, not the sort of "higgling and bargaining" Adam Smith had in mind.

Most Chinese economists and many officials are aware that "the key to reforming the economy is price reform. Until China's distorted pricing system is straightened out it will remain impossible to lay a proper foundation for the establishment of a socialist commodity economic system."[28]

This awareness is qualified and tempered by fears of social upheaval if, in the context of excess demand for almost everything usable, prices were freed overnight. "Price reform," notes Ge Wu, "must not be carried out impatiently or in isolation. It requires favorable conditions and coordination with other reforms."[29] There is circular reasoning involved in this assessment because the "favorable conditions" (demand-supply equilibrium) will not be achieved so long as the price system remains irrational, rigid, and schizophrenic. The upshot is that China's two-track construct of neither plan nor market violates the second condition for the successful operation of a market system: prices must reflect relative scarcities, and they must be the core information, coordination, and incentive device of the system. The condition that buyer and seller behavior must be economically rational is also violated. The behavior of Chinese buyers and sellers is, indeed, rational within the context of allocatively irrational price signals. It involves considerable political bargaining, a running self-accounting of favors received from and rendered to one's hierarchical bureaucratic superiors or otherwise well-connected persons—Socialist feudalism one might say. It breaks, moreover, the indispensable real market link between private and social interest brought about by the depoliticized competitive market mechanism, of business profit and social profitability and of private and social use values—not always but most of the time. This absence of a spontaneous mechanism for the reconciliation of often divergent private and public strivings is what makes the centrally planned economy and its half-reformed, two-track, in-between nonsystem into adversarial societies in which private profit and utility maximizing get a bad name for being pursued at the expense of the public good: from each according to his ability, to each according to his greed, through political pull.

Because of the difficulties in completely marketizing the price system, attention has shifted to what appears at first sight to be the less politically explosive issue of property reform. The problem of excessive state ownership of assets has long been recognized in China, and some cooperativization of state property has been carried out since 1978 alongside the expansion of private property and of various mixed property forms. Privatization can be justified as giving enterprises greater use, transfer, and income rights to the assets they employ (greater enterprise autonomy—a safe and agreed to adjustment), including greater than zero retention of profits and more latitude in matters of investment. Shareholding in firms can be advocated as "reestablishing the individual rights of workers," a legitimate Socialist operation if the shares are sold to the firms' workers and even if they are purchased by the general public, since everyone in China today is by definition a worker. In addition, since most of the stock floated to date resembles bonds more than equity shares, the delicate question of private ownership can be even better explained away. Enterprise stock issues and bonds can also be defended on anti-inflationary grounds, as drawing purchasing power out of the pockets of individuals and then taxing enterprise profits for which enterprise directors are responsible to their worker stockholders. Private savings and money that would have been spent on immediate consumption can be put to productive use. Worker proprietors will have the incentive to work harder and better, plant and equipment will be well taken care of, labor productivity and output will rise, market equilibrium will be achieved, and, at that point, the price system can be freed without fear of social disturbances. Several Chinese economists who see in privatization the last chance to get the reform moving again have made this argument. The best known among them is Li Yining, professor of economic management at Beijing University, whose report recommending

189

postponement of price system reform for two years and a resolute push to liberalize property was released in May 1988 and seems to have served as a fallback position for the reformists at the Beidahe meeting that summer. Li includes agriculture in his property privatization argument. "Farmers must feel," he says, "that they have control over the land. Nowadays farmers use their lands carelessly and make little effort to improve soil fertility. They act as if they don't expect to live off the land too long." In Li's view, clearer, more secure and extensive private property rights should be legally granted to peasant families, including the right to sell and subrent family allotments.[30]

Li's thesis is contested by, among others, Wu Jinglian, director of the Technological and Social Development Research Center under the State Council. Wu argues that postponement of price system liberalization and retention of the two-track price arrangement pose the risk of an indefinite shelving of all meaningful economic decentralization reform. So long as prices are so distorted that they are useless for rational allocation of resources, granting greater decision-making powers to firms will merely cause the firms, instead of central planners, to make allocatively irrational decisions. Wu predicts more waste, which will reinforce the position of those unhappy with the reform. "I worry," says Li, "that China's problems may strengthen the hand of our most cautious economic thinkers. If the next few years go badly, China will wind up like the countries of East Europe, saddled with an inefficient, half-reformed economy."[31] "Reforms in these two fields [property and price system] . . . are interrelated," writes Liu Guoguan. "The former is aimed at creating doers of market activities, while the latter is aimed at establishing a competitive market environment. Reforms in these two fields should be carried out in close coordination."[32]

Meanwhile, the third condition of a successful market—competition—remains unfulfilled or operates in twisted ways. Giving directors of firms greater input procurement, output disposal, hiring and firing, and profit retention powers does little if anything to advance the cause of market efficiency if the newly autonomous firms are monopolies, central or regional. On the surface, the size distribution of Chinese industrial enterprises favors competition, especially when compared with other Socialist economies, including those (Hungary and Yugoslavia) farthest on the reformist road. In number of employees, for example, the proportion of large firms (over 243 employees) is 0.6 percent in China compared with 65 percent in Hungary, and the proportion of small firms (5–33 employees) is 59 percent in China and 2 percent in Hungary. Such comparison, however, is deceptive. Chinese firms in key industries (coal, petroleum, steel, nonferrous metals, timber, cement, electricity, chemicals, synthetic fibers, newsprint, cigarettes, machinery, and munitions) remain under the jurisdiction of central or provincial ministries, industrial departments, and "corporations," and a smaller portion than before but still significant amount of their supplies is directly controlled by these kingdoms, as is the distribution of a portion of their output (with corresponding state price controls). These governmental supervisory bodies interpret their legal ownership of firms in a narrow and an exclusivist way. They protect "their" firms from the competition of enterprises under rival jurisdictions and dispense favors irrespective of performance or any notion of social utility. Frequently these favored firms happen to be big, with large assets, many workers, and good networks of social connections. Under this neomercantilist arrangement enterprises compete not to maximize profits (which, given the daft state of China's prices, may be just as well), but to maximize costs and resources under their control—a phenomenon common to centrally planned and half-reformed Socialist economies. Under the present structure of property rights tied to administrative hierarchies, "decontrol" of prices makes state monopolies into enterprise monopolies.[33]

The monopolistic compulsion is accentuated by administrative-regional decentralization, something that the Soviet Union experienced briefly in the wake of Khrushchev's *sovnarkhoz* (regional economic council) experiment many years back. In recent times provincial authorities in China have been known to put up all kinds of institutional (and, on occasion, physical) barriers to interprovincial trade and factor movements to protect their enterprises and local economies. Such actions create decentralized monopolies and promote regional autarkies. Indeed, barriers to interregional trade, together with locally financed and directed overlapping investment—uncoordinated nationally through either the market mechanism or a central plan—seriously inhibit competition and make it difficult for China to reap efficiency benefits from interregional specialization.[34]

The "competition" that does materialize in these circumstances is rivalry among speculator-bureaucrats out to make a quick killing from the combination of regional monopoly (including monopoly of political power and information), two-track prices, and the absence of automatic mechanisms for the reconciliation of individual and social interests.

The devolution of many decision-making powers from the center to the provinces and lower-level authorities would not undermine efficiency as seriously as it does, if the power devolved from central plan to market and from socialized-bureaucratic to private property. In such cases the government could use macroeconomic fiscal and monetary instruments to cushion market breakdowns and correct market failures. Alternatively, purely administrative decentralization of the central planning apparatus, without the introduction of market and private property elements, would permit the central government to reverse gears quickly if it thought it was advisable to do so (as the Soviet government has done many times), because such bureaucratic decentralization would simply deactivate the administrative controls available to the central planners without removing them. Where, as in China, the economic changes are at an in between, neither-this-nor-that stage, the center has no effective institutional levers to use when things go sour. The propensity of the central state to use the infant macroeconomic market-type levers that have been created does not make matters easier. The state, for example, has used the expanded banking system and financial markets in heavy-handed commandist, political, and administrative ways; and it has, through the Ministry of Finance, ordered the banks to freeze or reallocate credit, thus destroying the substance and subverting the purpose of these financial instrumentalities.

Serious lever problems are also caused by the inadequacy of the plan's social infrastructures under changed conditions. China in common with other Socialist countries, for example, has no institutionalized way to handle open unemployment, since the very existence of unemployment had been officially denied under the system of central planning (that is, no unemployment insurance). This absence encourages the bailing out of firms by the government, irrespective of the firms' performance, to prevent the eruption of social disturbances consequent on the dismissal of millions of redundant workers. In effect, each "working unit" (*danwei*) is, in addition to a work place, a social security cell providing its members not only with wages and bonuses (still largely tied to seniority) but also with the unemployment compensation component of the wage; subsidized housing and meals; recreational, health, and day-care facilities; public assistance; public surveillance; and the like. Whatever the merits of this cocoonlike arrangement, there are economic costs in labor mobility (for instance, workers, even if they legally could, would be reluctant to change jobs since in doing so they would have to part with extremely scarce *danwei*-supplied housing). With broad social welfare responsibilities, no threat of bankruptcy, little if any competition, and a chronic sellers' market, it is no wonder that Chinese firms are not paragons of efficiency.

In the old days of Mao and the early days of Deng Xiaoping, weaknesses of the institutional structure could be overcome to a degree by the sheer will, personal power, and prestige of the leader and, before 1958, of the Party. But today the leader is old and semi-retired (perhaps physically and mentally weakened), the leadership is divided, and the prestige of the Party has been squandered. The economic changes carried out so far are neither fully institutionalized nor any longer personalized. What was described a few years ago as rational economic pragmatism and contrasted with the mad spasmodic development of the Maoist era (and hence accepted by the people and most cadres who had suffered from the madness) now gives the impression of a thrashing about in a conceptual void. In sum, the sixth condition of a successful market system—the presence of effective market-oriented control levers—remains unfulfilled in present-day China.

Measures to Eliminate Sourness

The reaction of the central authorities to the latest spate of difficulties (like the response to the 1985–1986 problems, only more so) has been to dust off the levers of administrative control and apply them to an economy that can no longer respond to this type of intervention without serious damage to its fragile market component—indeed, some argue, without doing irreparable harm to a promising marketizing and privatizing experiment. The Soviet syndrome, they say, is making its appearance in China. With regard to solving the Socialist problems of chronic shortage, waste, technological backwardness, and disharmony between private and social interests, Russia's present may turn out to be China's future. Some reform-minded Chinese economists share this pessimistic assessment.

Party leader Zhao Ziyang gave a foretaste of things to come in his report to the Central Committee in September 1988. The emphasis, he said, would be on keeping the reform's risks to the minimum; the new slogan is "Be safe." Keeping down the risks and being safe mean, according to Zhao (formerly an enthusiastic proponent and practitioner of bold marketizing and privatizing reforms), improving administration and central control ("unified guidance of the central government") and strengthening the supervisory role of planning organs. Instead of getting the Party out of the business of running the economy, provincial Party secretaries are to be held responsible to the central government for unified economic guidance: "The Party's leading, supervisory, central role should be strengthened." That is bad news for reform and for economic efficiency.

How to put an end to bank runs and panic buying? Issue a circular from the Central Committee, pass it out to Party organizations, and "mobilize the whole Party to play a major role" in ridding people of their bad habits. Problems of "price hikes . . . unfair social wealth distribution, and . . . corruption" are to be cured through a mass "educational drive . . . the most practical and welcome part of our political and ideological work." "To exercise macro control," says Zhao, "it is necessary to make comprehensive use of economic, administrative, legal, and disciplinary means, as well as conduct extensive political and ideological work. In the transitional phase, in particular, it will be unwise to abandon administrative means prematurely or offhandedly. Otherwise, economic chaos will ensue." Although "the purpose of strengthening administrative means is to better promote the reforms, not to return to the old system," the degree of the latest turn suggests a high probability of precisely such a return to commandist origins.[35]

Specific Measures. The current euphemism is that "price reform has been temporarily moderated, not cancelled."[36] What this means is that price system liberalization is postponed for "five or so" years (according to the Central Committee's 1988 "Initial Plan for Price and Wage Reforms"). Prices of key commodities (food grains, edible oils, cotton, some other farm goods, and steel) are to be frozen by administrative order or are to rise only at government-sanctioned rates. The Soviets, it might be recalled, have been postponing price decontrol for "five years or so" since the 1950s. If the marketization of the price system is put off for five years or so (even for two years), a delay probably accompanied by a rollback of free agricultural prices, the Chinese reform is likely to go into a coma from which it might not recover in the lifetime of the present leaders. One sign of the prevailing trend is Zhao Ziyang's statement that "the double-track pricing system . . . cannot and shall not be abolished in the near future."[37] The property-reform-first economists like Li Yining (to whom the reform bureaucrats seem to be turning out of frustration with the recalcitrant price system) are willing to put up with two-track prices until the year 2000, maybe longer. Their reasoning is that half a reform is better than none and that the second-track (relatively free) prices are an outpost of reform in increasingly hostile territory, which must be defended despite all its weaknesses.

Other measures the central authorities have taken to combat inflation and cool the economy down combine austerity economics and recentralizing politics, policy adjustments and reform "destructuring." These include the reintroduction of rationing for grain, pork, some nonstaple foods, chemical fertilizer, herbal medicines, and most raw materials. To conserve scarce resources, manufacturers of soft drinks have been ordered to cease their production immediately, an order that has been widely defied, at least during the hot summer.

To slow industrial growth to a projected 8 percent rate in 1989, planned government investment in fixed assets is to be cut by 22 percent, while agricultural investment by the state is to rise 14 percent to stimulate lagging agricultural performance. These are, of course, just projections, which in the past have often failed to materialize. These projections refer to investments within the plan, whereas the major problem in the past decade has been with runaway industrial and "nonproductive" investment outside the plan, financed by enterprise-retained earnings, bank credits, and peasant savings. To take care of such unruly investment, instructions have been issued to the central bank, and through it to the banking system at large, to hold down credit issuance strictly to government-set limits. In effect, new bank loans, other than those specifically approved by the state plan, have been temporarily forbidden.[38] This freeze does not affect loans denominated in foreign currencies, foreign investment projects, and foreign trading financing, but, in fact, the ripple effect of credit tightening is felt in those areas.

To conform to the central bank's austere monetary restrictions, local and specialized banks not only have reduced their lending activities but also have blocked the deposits of enterprises. This move has produced a severe temporary cash shortage affecting, among others, state agricultural procurement agencies, which found themselves compelled to pay for their purchases with IOUs to the tune of $1 billion. The peasants reacted promptly within the decision-making space they had gained through the agricultural reform by withholding contractual supplies (which are marketed by the state in its shops at subsidized prices) and exerted themselves in producing cash crops for the profitable, higher-priced free market. This development forced the People's Bank of China (the central bank) to relax its squeeze on lending to the Agricultural Bank of China, the principal credit source for the farm sector. All this has led to calls from antireform quarters for the elimination of urban markets for food and to attempts to teach the peasants a lesson by threatening them with collectivization.

Rumors of recollectivization under a different name have been rife in China for some years, contributing to the reluctance of many family farmers to make long-term investments in their land. Talk of merging family land parcels under a collective umbrella has been translated into action in some places. The action, however, was subsequently reversed under pressure from the dispossessed peasants who, when they did not beat up the offending cadres, took the recollectivization zealots to court and won, in a rare display of Socialist legality.[39] Measures are also under consideration to compel farmers to switch from cash crops to grain production. This has happened in a number of places, albeit informally under the leadership of local cadres eager to set their sails to what they think are the prevailing political winds. However isolated, such instances of Socialist recidivism in the bastion of the marketization and privatization experiment—the countryside—should give pause to those Western observers who argue that the changes made since 1978 in the structure of agricultural property are by now irreversible because the peasants like them, the World Bank advocates them, and some fashionable Chinese economists support them.

Curbs have been administratively imposed on the purchasing power of organizations such as government departments, schools, hospitals, enterprises, "companies," "corporations," and army units. Fanning out over the country, investigators pore over account books and slap heavy penalties whenever an organization's frozen bank deposit shows signs of melting (usually under the heat of political influence). Big ticket items on the spending list of these groups include "luxury" products (limousines, for example), banquets, extensive and feverish travel on what purports to be official business, and "nonproductive" (in Marxist terminology) investment in hotels, rest homes for cadres, convention halls, and other places of proletarian entertainment. Special investigative ire has been reserved for trading companies that have proliferated in recent years, some under provincial sponsorship, others fronting for all sorts of social groups.

Interest rates on personal long-term savings deposits have been raised, being loosely linked to the retail price index—so loosely, in fact, that the real rate remains negative. The interest rate increase was carried out to halt runs on savings deposits in anticipation of what the depositors thought would be reform-connected massive price increases. Even with the runs, personal savings deposits and savings rates in China (as in the Soviet Union) remain relatively high, being in large part forced by the absence or shortage of goods and services in the quantities, qualities, and assortments desired by consumers. While interest rates on investment loans have also been raised, they remain too low to discourage institutional borrowing for investment outside the state plan in preference to the use of enterprise-retained earnings. When, as in China today, manipulating the (nonmarket) interest rate fails to produce the intended results, the state simply resorts to administrative compulsion.

Wage reform (the scheduled phasing out of the Soviet-type, labor grade, basic wage system and shift to flexible contractual wages) has been put on hold.

What has been called by some "the jewel in the reformers' crown," the so-called gold coast strategy of pushing ahead with marketization and privatization of the already relatively prosperous coastal provinces and municipalities and turning them, in effect, into large, special economic zones (SEZs) is being reconsidered and might be abandoned, at least for the time being. The strategy, associated with Zhao Ziyang and Deng Xiaoping, is based on the trickle-down theory. The riches of the coastal region (with its fourteen open cities and five special economic zones), acquired through relatively open and autonomous contacts with capitalist world commodity and financial markets, would eventually spread to the poorer inland provinces. The powers granted to the gold coast's provincial, municipal, and special zone authorities, however, appear to have been used for autarkic provincial, municipal, and special zone development and did not trickle down to the poorer provinces at all. And so, instead of further gold coast liberalization—that is, closer association of this huge area with the world market—the present intent seems to make the gold coast march to the centralizing beat of the drummers in Beijing. One of the objectives of the gold coast strategy was to introduce competition into an important segment of the Chinese economy by opening up the coastal area to world trade and finance (letting in competition through the open back door, so to speak). This stratagem hinged on the authorities' willingness to establish realistic exchange rates for the yuan and to let inefficient state firms go out of business. It is not at all certain that such willingness existed before the gold coast strategy was put on hold.

Finally, reform of the political system, which has never been high on the agenda but was being toyed with in 1987–1988 in the guise of a shift from totalitarianism to hard authoritarianism, has also fallen victim to economic retrenchment.

Some fear that retrenchment will adversely affect employment. Officially, the unemployment rate in 1989 was estimated to rise to 3 percent from 2 percent in 1988. Unofficially, the real jobless rate is closer to 10 percent, with hidden unemployment in the urban sector of 20 percent.[40] Because of the clampdown on investment, jobs in the construction industry will be significantly reduced. It is possible that small- and medium-sized labor-intensive enterprises will be most affected, particularly the hundreds of thousands of rural ones. These firms, employing millions of peasants displaced from the land by the early labor productivity and yield improvements following agricultural decollectivization, do not have nearly the political clout needed in China's semireformed system to obtain regular supplies of scarce raw materials, equipment, and access to transportation facilities and bank credit.

The crackdown by the center, and the center's resort to both administrative command and economic levers to make its preferences stick, is being resisted tooth and nail by provincial bureaucrats and enterprise managers in the more economically successful provinces and regions, including the special economic zones on the gold coast. In this resistance, Guangdong province leads the way, followed closely by the Shenzhen SEZ and places like Shenyang. This resistance is not necessarily promarket; it is pro-oneself, which in the currently gelatinous structure of China's economy means protecting what one has irrespective of considerations of systemic logic. One grabs what one can by any means at hand. The effectiveness of the resistance to central intervention will have an important influence on the direction that economic experimentation in China takes in the future. It could lead to greater relaxation of central controls or—more likely—induce the central authorities to deploy the full array of repressive administrative weapons still available to them, including the public security apparatus, to try to preserve unity even at a high cost in economic efficiency.

Prospects

The review of China's economic problems and the remedial measures taken to deal with them raises an interesting question. China's economic difficulties since 1978 are not much different from those experienced by most other developing, and several industrialized, countries in a world undergoing rapid change and in a state of systematic confusion. Chinese inflation, while in the double-digit range, is not as bad as Israel's, Argentina's, Yugoslavia's, or Nicaragua's (35,000 percent in 1988). Its poverty, although still severe, is not so grinding as that of numerous other countries throughout the world. At least there is in China an awareness of that poverty, and steps have been taken to combat it. Much the same is true of unemployment and underemployment; overheating; relative ineffectiveness of fiscal, monetary, and administrative instruments of intervention in the economy; corruption (from which even prim and prosperous Japan is not immune); and most other disabilities. Why, then, the fuss about China?

Part of the answer is that China is at a crossroads of choice between two very different, arguably incompatible, economic systems. The systemic choice is between plan and market, with nothing that is theoretically coherent and practicable in between.[41] In practice all economies are in between in the sense that they combine dominant plan and public property institutions with subsidiary market and private property elements or dominant market and private property with subsidiary elements of plan and public property. As systemic arrangements, the first represents a system of central administrative command planning; the second, a competitive market system. The first system (plan) has structural defects (chronic shortages of consumer and producer goods, monstrous static inefficiencies, low quality, and technical lassitude in the civilian sector), which are now considered to be intolerable by both people and leaders alike. The remedy agreed on, albeit reluctantly, by the Communist leadership is economic decentralization, which means movement toward the market system. This agreement, however, does not include complete transition to the market system, that is, to a condition in which markets and private property are the dominant institutions of the reformed economy and in which administrative instruments and socialized property rights play a secondary role, correcting market breakdowns and compensating for market failures. Such systemic transition would not only transubstantiate economic institutions and Socialist economic theory and ethics but also require a concurrent transformation of the political order and its philosophical underpinnings. It would necessitate the renunciation of Marxism-Leninism at every level of human experience, not just the denunciation of Stalinist and Maoist crudities, which are the organic manifestations of Marxism-Leninism and not, as is still argued, errors of work style. Notwithstanding pockets of optimism on this subject in the West, such revolutionary change of concepts is now and in the foreseeable future out of the question. Although (as noted at the outset) the problem is less acute today than it was not long ago, it is still there, just under the surface.

The first element of the Chinese problem is how to transform the ideological and political system fundamentally and deal effectively with the difficulties of modernization. What would normally be a debate on technical means quickly turns into a dispute about ultimate ends: socialism versus the capitalist order. The debate is secularly theologized, so to speak, if not always in the terminology used, at least in insinuations of moral error. This approach inhibits

199

the analysis of all relevant facts, perpetuates the stifling presence of intellectually taboo areas, and prevents the emergence of a comprehensive and internally consistent blueprint for reform.

The second element of the Chinese problem, which distinguishes it from other Socialist economies that have tinkered with systemic reform over the past thirty years, is that in China since 1978 marketization and privatization have gone as far as they can without raising questions of radical systemic transformation. China is, roughly speaking, at a midway point where crucial decisions have to be made at once about the nature of the economic system. More precisely, the point was reached in late 1987 and 1988. At that time the newly established market relations could not perform their efficiency-promoting functions without further expansion and coordination of market institutions. Both the reformers and their critics intuitively saw such expansion as a crossing of the systemic border that separates plan from market. Concurrently, the institutions of central administrative command planning and socialized property had been weakened, their cohesiveness undermined by regional administrative decentralization, so that they, too, lost much of their former influence.

In the summer of 1988 the decision (still contested) to halt movement toward the market system appears to have been taken. The focus of the retrenchment measures taken since then has been on administrative compulsion. The resurgence of command is inflicting considerable damage on the frail and increasingly isolated market instrumentalities that have been created over the past ten years. In the name of protecting urban workers from the scourge of inflation, unemployment, uneven income distribution, and corruption, forces antipathetic to reform have been attacking market institutions and disparaging the market idea, while concurrently tightening up political and administrative controls. Under this onslaught, lacking unequivocal support from Deng Xiaoping, the marketizers have fallen back on writing articles about the need to push ahead with the privatization of apartment space in the cities and on the need for greater enterprise autonomy. They give the impression of theoretical disarray in the face of the simplicities propagated by the administrative centralizers. China, some say, is on its way back from the market again, heading for another Socialist dead end.

The trip back from the market can still be halted and the economy resume its course toward modernization. But to do this, China will have to make up its mind about systemic transition. It will have to discard the illusion that chronic shortages, inefficiency, and shoddy quality of goods and services can be cured by the application of halfway remedies. It will have to go all the way to the market system: no ifs, no buts. This requires the prompt freeing of the price system (including factor prices and exchange rates), breakup of monopolies, dissolution of physical input rationing, significant enlargement of the sphere of private property, and the acceptance of pain. While economic in form and substance, these are also, perhaps mainly, matters of political nerve and will. Unless a market rescue operation is launched soon, the retreat from the market could easily turn into a long march back to nowhere.

Discussing China's future possibilities, Liu Guoguan considers three courses of action advocated by different groups of Chinese economists. "Some people" hold that given China's "confused economic order," it is difficult if not impossible to move ahead with reform and preferable to "exercise strict macroeconomic control by administrative means." "It is widely feared," Liu comments, "that too much economic retrenchment, as these people advocated, would lead to economic deflation. It is also not certain whether a free economic environment would necessarily emerge as the final outcome," as these people assert, for they claim to be merely cautious and not at all against reform. Others disagree with the pessimistic assessment of China's present economic condition and oppose economic retrenchment. "Stabilizing the economy," they argue, "can only be realized by deepening reform," specifically by restructuring enterprise management and developing the contract responsibility system, followed in two or three years by price reform. "The proponents of this view estimate," Liu says, "that the new system [will] occupy the dominant position in around eight years." The recommendations of a third group of economists fall in between the first two but nearer administrative retrenchment. They would combine retrenchment with "well devised reforms to promote stable, sustained economic growth." The reform measures would include improvement of the instrumentalities of macroeconomic control, a strengthening of the enterprise contract responsibility system "in preparation for a transition to a joint stock system" (clarification of property relations "so as to switch macroeconomic management from direct to indirect control and regulation"). Liu opts for the third alternative, the one that in present circumstances is politically most feasible and that would perhaps enable the reformers to hold onto some of their past gains.[42] Reasonable as it appears, the third solution carries with it great dangers because it proposes to remedy the present systemic confusion by using the ineffective administrative and "economic" control levers of the current halfway nonsystem. A more effective solution would be one nearer to the first option:

201

continued marketization of the price system and privatization of property rights and the concurrent expansion of market-type instrumentalities of macroeconomic intervention.

This course, however, has only a slim chance of being followed. The third alternative seems more likely. If it is, the system will tend to slide back into administrative command; its shortages, waste, and technological backwardness will remain unsolved and its objective of modernization unrealized.

12
Price Reform in the People's Republic of China

I believe that the success of China's economic reform hinges on rationalizing the price system.

XUE MUQIAO

This chapter examines some concepts underlying price reform in a system of central administrative command planning such as China's and the way these issues have been addressed in the wake of the Cultural Revolution.

Theoretical Positions

An economic system consists of three related components: philosopy, institutional structure, and policy.

Economic philosophy comprises two parts: ideas on the relationship of the individual to the system and an economic theory of the system's institutional structure and the operation of economic policies within that structure. Economic philosophy thus justifies the system's institutions and policies and explains the economic laws governing their operation.

The structure of an economic system consists of four institutions: information, coordination, motivation or incentives, and property.[1] Together, the four elements help determine what the system will do and how it will do it: what will be produced, how, and for whom—that is, the structure and pattern of production, exchange, and distribution. They are the core of the system.

Economic policy consciously articulates the system's goals and the methods used to achieve those goals.[2] Ordinary policy operates within the system's institutional structure and philosophical boundaries. Reformist policy changes the system's institutional structure

203

and breaks through the philosophical boundaries. Economic philosophy, especially the relationship of the individual to the system, and the institutional structure of information, coordination, motivation, and property determine the locus of economic policy-making power in the system.

Price System

What is conventionally referred to as the price system is in reality a subsystem of the system of markets or of central planning. Like its parent stem, the subsystem of prices consists of three related components: price philosophy, institutional structure, and price policy.

The similarity between the price subsystem of the market system and the price subsystem of the centrally planned system ends here. More significant are the differences between the two price subsystems. Except in their philosophical manifestation, prices are less important under the system of central planning than under the market system. This is true of both the institutional structure of prices (that is, of prices as information, coordination, and incentive devices) and the price policy. The centrally planned system has a marked inclination to use prices as mere tools for counting, passive with respect to allocation. This inclination derives from Marxist economic philosophy, the practice of war communism, and Stalin's shell theory of commodity economy. It has been particularly pronounced in China during periods of "left" dominance over the economy.[3]

Economic Philosophy and the Price System

The economic philosophy of central planning (Marxism-Leninism and its Stalinist and Maoist extensions) has two important characteristics. First, it is a closed system of ideas, an approved Party-state dogma or official ideology that can be altered only with the consent of the highest Party-state authorities. Largely as a consequence of this, its ability to explain reality is problematical. Second, it is highly prescriptive, even in its theoretical part. Thus, for example, the factor labor becomes the proletariat, the tribe chosen by history. The factor capital is transformed into capitalists, a class of oppressors destined by history for extinction. Value become surplus value extracted by the capitalists from the proletariat. Hence the economic philosophy of the centrally planned system, including its economic analysis, is designed primarily as an instrument for changing reality in a predetermined direction.

Herein resides a serious weakness. The ideology of central planning attempts to change economic reality without analytically comprehending it. This misunderstanding frequently leads to negative consequences, some of them (forced Soviet collectivization, the Chinese Great Leap Forward) of apocalyptic dimensions.

Price Ethics. According to the centrally planned system's price philosophy, prices are to be determined mandatorily by the central planners from above, not by numerous spontaneous buying and selling transactions from below; this determination is to be made in consonance with the planners' decisions on the physical rationing out of resources, prices being used as subsidiary backup devices for such physical allocation decisions; and for control and economic accounting purposes, prices should in general be characterized by stability, any changes in relative prices or the general level of prices being initiated solely by the planners on instructions of the political leadership.

Should it be found that the planner-determined price system is not performing satisfactorily, that it is too rigid or wasteful of scarce resources, and that it must therefore be thoroughly reformed, one of the first victims of such reform must necessarily be the philosophy of elitist price fixing. Reform requires a revolutionary change in ideas regarding the distribution of decision-making power.[4]

According to some, a second message emerges from the central planning system's price ethics, one that made its appearance in the mid- to late 1950s, following the death of Stalin and the relative ebbing of the concept of rule by terror. As part of a new social compact tacitly arrived at between the Party-state and the citizenry, the former obliges itself to keep the prices of basic consumer necessities low and stable.[5] Consumer necessities include some staple foods (in China, for example, food grains and vegetable oil), some items of clothing, housing rents, and charges for public transporation, to which the state commits very sizable subsidies. One of the troubling results, in China as elsewhere, has been the creation of money illusion among urban consumers and their strong opposition to any attempt to bring the prices of subsidized goods and services more in line with costs. Another aspect of the social compact, one that has been particularly important in China, is the attempt to keep money income differentials "fair," that is, relatively narrow (what the Dengist leaders in China nowadays denounce as the bane of "equalitarianism," accompanied in the state sector by guaranteed lifelong employment or the "iron pot"). Here there have been two troubling results: erosion of work incentives and emergence of an envy-ridden society, the envy being directed against anyone who moves ahead of the pack in income and wealth. In the name of "fairness" he has to be pulled down.

Price Theory. As mentioned before, the normative element of economic philosophy spills into economic theory, which purports to elucidate the workings of the system. Marx's labor theory of value is an indispensable part of the revolutionary arsenal to be used in the overthrow of the capitalist system. It is the linchpin of Marx's five laws of capitalist motion of self-destruction and as such serves a useful propaganda function.[6] As a device that would help central planners (or anyone else) distribute resources rationally among competing alternative uses, however, it is useless. In fact, because of its defective organic composition, it encourages allocative inefficiency.

Allocatively rational prices may be expressed as follows:

$$\frac{MSC_a}{MSC_b} = \frac{P_a}{P_b} = \frac{MSU_a}{MSU_b}$$

where MSC is marginal social cost, MSU is marginal social utility (use value), P is price, and a and b are commodities. The notion of social cost and social use value covers private and external costs and use values. Prices are allocatively irrational where either the cost or the use value side of the equation does not hold.

Prices determined administratively in the centrally planned system by reference to Marxist value theory will be allocatively irrational for three reasons. First, Marxist labor value theory does not recognize the marginalist principle; it operates on the basis of averages. Second, it does not take into account the opportunity cost of land and capital (rent and interest). In other words, it is flawed on the cost side of the equation.[7] In the circumstances, it provides no theoretical basis for evaluating the efficiency of land and capital use in different employments. Third, it takes no account of utility, that is, it does not hold on the use value side of the equation.

In the context of allocatively irrational prices, the advice of a Soviet Liberman or a Chinese Sun Yefang to use profit as the primary criterion of successful enterprise performance and as the bridge linking individual, enterprise, and social interests is misleading, a point grasped by some Chinese economists. Contrary to Sun's assertion that catching hold of profit norms was just like catching hold of the "ox's nose," these economists point out that "when a rational pricing system and other conditions do not fully exist, highly profitable enterprises are not necessarily a reflection of high economic benefits."[8] In these conditions the lengthy discussions in Russia and China (1961–1963) on how the profit rate should be computed—whether in relation to production cost or investment—take on a purely bookkeeping interest.

Goods bought and sold on the world market pose a theoretical and policy valuation problem. What constitutes the socially necessary labor time in such cases? Should domestic prices be aligned with world prices for goods traded on the world market, or should they be insulated from world market prices by the state's foreign trade monopoly?

When workably competitive, supply-and-demand prices do not fully exist and dynamic mathematical optimizing operations are out of reach or simply do not work,[9] one tends to fall back on two "laws": the basic economic law of socialism and the law of planned proportional development, which are in essence expressions of intent rather than analytical guides to optimizing action. In China the works of Hu Qiaomu represent this tendency.[10]

Other Chinese economists recognize that in the context of their closed system of ideas the Marxist theory of value hinders reform of the price system, as witnessed by their repeated wrestling with the theory's metaphysical complexities.[11] The scholasticism and inconclusiveness of much discussion of Chinese value theory reflect the extreme political sensitivity of the issue. Movement toward allocative rationality, productivity-based growth, and the elimination of chronic shortages and quality problems require a theoretical recognition of the concept of the margin, the productivity of land and capital, and the influence of demand on value determination. It requires, in other words, retirement of Marx's labor cost theory of value. But this theory supports the whole Marxist intellectual edifice, not just the economic chambers. It is, therefore, unlikely that the theory will be retired outright in the foreseeable future. If the practical inconveniences of misallocation, shortages, poor quality, and technological torpor prove sufficiently acute, however, what may occur is the theory's death by "creative" reformulation along lines earlier traced in Russia by Novozhilov, Kantorovich, and Fedorenko.[12] (So far, the theoretical efforts of these perceptive Soviet optimizers have had hardly any effect on the irrational Soviet price system.)

If ideas have consequences, then in this instance the combination of Leninist price ethics and Marxist value theory contributes to the static misallocations, dynamic inefficiencies, shortages, and quality problems for which the centrally planned system has come to be known.

Institutional Structure of Prices

In a market system flexible prices are the synthetic mathematical expression of lateral, contractual transactions—protected by law— voluntarily entered into by competing, property-owning, utility- or profit-seeking, buying and selling units. In such a system prices are the principal suppliers of information about costs and utilities in the system. They are the principal coordinator of the production, exchange, and distribution activities of the system's many autonomous agents. This coordination includes, most important, the reconciliation of private and social interests. Prices of factors are the principal means of motivation in the system. Together, the information, coordination, and motivational functions of market prices constitute the system's spontaneous governance by invisible hands. Because of the centrality of prices, the market system is often called the price system.

As noted earlier, the information, coordination, and incentive role of prices is less in a centrally planned system than in the market system. Historically prices have been subsidiary to planners' physical decisions. They were designed to be auxiliary instruments of such decisions, passive with respect to allocation (with a few exceptions) and helpful with respect to measurement, planner control, and evaluation of how lower-level agents (workers, consumers, and firms) carry out the plan. In actuality, prices have never been as subsidiary, passive, and subservient to the "natural" plan as conceptually envisaged. They have always exercised sub rosa allocative influence, often opposite from the planners' intent. It remains true nevertheless that their role under central planning has been restricted. Partly because of their primary function as planners' helpers in measurement, control, and evaluation and partly because of the difficulty of administratively adjusting prices to constantly changing cost and demand conditions without any automatic indicator of what these changes are, prices in the centrally planned system have been relatively rigid, unchanged over very long periods of time. The stability of prices has meant that the economy's adjustment to changing cost and utility conditions took place in nonprice ways, in disguised forms such as shortages and surpluses of particular goods, lines outside stores, black markets, barter exchanges of favors, and underemployment. The once much sought-after stability of planned prices undoubtedly contributed to the system's overall rigidity and its sluggishness in technological innovation and diffusion, including business management technology. To Socialist economists in the late twentieth century, in China as in the Soviet Union and Eastern Europe, price stability no longer has the theoretical charm and policy attraction it once possessed.

In the centrally planned system the principal source of economic information consists of physical and technical statistics supplied from below and addressee-specific, detailed, mandatory, physical and technical, input and output targets sent to plan executors from above through administrative channels. Financial and price data accompany both flows acting as backup unidimensional information in conformity with Hu Qiaomu's dictum that "planning comes first, and prices second." The principal means of coordination has been the system of material balances formulated at the center and lower levels (branch ministry and provincial and local authority), supplemented by financial balances. The absence of payments for land and capital reflecting the relative scarcities of those factors, the policy of constricting wage differentials, chronic shortages and inferior quality of consumer goods on which money wages could be spent, and the relative importance of nonprice incentives for certain groups restrict the incentive function of prices in the system.

For allocative purposes, Chinese domestic prices (like those in other centrally planned economies) fall into three groups, ranging from the group whose allocative function is supposed to be zero (and is, in fact, extremely restricted), through the group whose prices perform various limited allocative chores, to the group whose prices allocate the goods to which they are attached (see table 12–1).[13] The composition of each group has changed over time, as has the extent of the allocative competence of the prices. Marketizing changes in the price system increase the allocative function of prices. They reduce the number, proportion, and strategic significance (although this has been slow in materializing) of prices in the first group, and increase the number, proportion, and importance of prices in the other two groups.

Group 1 Prices. Planners set Group 1 prices mainly on the basis of cost, with little attention to equalizing supply and demand. In industry, the "cost" is average planned cost in each functional industrial branch (the steel industry, for example). In agriculture, the cost is presumably the average production cost of collective farms in the production of various products. Group 1 also includes the prices charged by state stores for basic necessities, including staples such as grain and cooking oil, and residential housing rents. Both have been fixed well below cost and kept unchanged for long periods. In each case commodity allocation is by physical rationing: "Even when there was no supply of certain goods, prices remained low."[14]

TABLE 12–1

CATEGORIES OF PRICES ACCORDING TO ALLOCATIVE FUNCTION
IN CHINA SINCE 1978

Group 1: No Allocation by Price

Industrial wholesale prices
  basic and intermediate materials
  energy
  transport
  telecommunications
  producer goods
Quota agricultural procurement prices (before 1980)
State retail prices for basic necessities
Housing rents

Group 2: Limited Allocation by Price

Prices set to equate demand (buyer's free choice) to planned supply
  retail prices of non-basic necessities (fixed)
  agricultural producer goods sold to collective/family tenant farmers (fixed)
  "interest" rate on bank loans to enterprises (floating)
Prices set to equate supply (seller's free choice) to planned demand
  wages (fixed)
  above-quota agricultural procurement prices
  agricultural purchase contract prices, after 1984 (floating)

Group 3: Allocation by Price

Market prices for consumer goods (mainly food) on rural and urban fairs,
  and for materials and producer goods sold by state and cooperative
  enterprises over and above the plan.
Black market prices

SOURCE: Author.

The Chinese historical context calls for two qualifications. First, the calculation of production cost requires a workably competent statistical apparatus, in addition to the conviction that costs count and that they are important to price formation. During lengthy periods of Chinese Socialist history (the "left" periods of the Great Leap Forward and the Cultural Revolution), this conviction was lacking (costing was considered a bourgeois pursuit), and the statistical apparatus was in ruins, as was the training of statisticians. Hence prices in Group 1 were often set not just without attention to equalizing supply and demand but with little reference to cost. They were not only nonallocative but also noncost. This feature of Group 1 prices was particularly pronounced in the case of state-fixed agricultural purchase prices. Since under the collective system, payment for labor was a residual of unknown value, it was not possible to calculate labor costs or identify the profit element, that is, to apply cost accounting to collective farms or communes. This was, however, merely a technical inconvenience since state agricultural procurement prices for compulsory quota deliveries were philosophically unconcerned with covering farm costs and profit for accumulation. They were in China, as they had been in Russia earlier under Stalin, forced savings-extraction devices, a form of taxation—perhaps not as confiscatory in China as in Stalin's Russia, but harsh enough.

Second, as already noted, cost based on Marxist labor theory is peculiarly calculated in that it excludes two important opportunity costs of production: the opportunity cost of land and that of capital. If pre-1967 Soviet practice was followed, there could be other, less serious problems with cost accounting, for example, whether geological prospecting and forest maintenance costs should be included in prime cost and how to determine a rate of depreciation on fixed capital.

The two major categories of prices falling into Group 1 are state industrial wholesale prices, comprising ex factory prices (the price the producing enterprise charges other enterprises) and industry wholesale prices and the already mentioned state-fixed prices for the procurement by the state of collective farm produce under the compulsory delivery quota.[15] Ex factory prices comprise average planned cost of production of enterprises in the industrial branch (that is, average of high- and low-cost firms—meaning that at the established prices some firms operated at a loss), a profit (or planned loss) margin, and industrial-commercial taxes. Based on Marxist labor theory, costs cover cost of materials, depreciation charges, wages and salaries, and administrative expenses of various kinds. The profit rate is typically calculated on total current costs. Industrial wholesale prices, which include in addition to ex factory prices, the selling expenses of the wholesale organization and the wholesaler's profit margin, are prices at which the wholesale organization transfers ("sells") goods to state retailers, marketing organizations, and commercial agencies of agricultural collectives.

Since Group 1 prices take no account of supply and demand (relative scarcities) and their relationship to production costs ranges from relaxed to nonexistent, they cannot be, and are not, used for allocative purposes. The allocation of goods subject to these prices is by physical rationing, through the Bureau of Supplies.

To this day, despite efforts to marketize or partially marketize some Group 1 prices (especially the agricultural procurement prices,

211

but also some industrial wholesale prices), Group 1 industrial prices include goods of key importance to the economy such as basic and intermediate materials, energy, transport, telecommunications, and producer goods; and their allocative function remains extremely modest. These prices directly or indirectly affect all other prices in the system, and the goods and services to which they are attached are produced by the larger state-owned enterprises. According to Liu Guoguang (vice-president of the Chinese Academy of Social Sciences), writing in August 1986, inflexible state-set prices of this kind covered nearly half the total industrial and agricultural output at the time.[16] The proportion has certainly not diminished since then.

Group 2 Prices. Group 2 prices are state determined, but, unlike Group 1 prices, they perform various limited allocative functions for the planners. The reason why Group 2 prices are vested with such functions is that in the instances in which such prices apply, it is difficult or cumbersome to use administrative or physical allocation. Two subgroups may be distinguished: first, where for a given commodity the price is set so as to equate demand to planned supply and second, where the price is set to equate supply to planned demand. In each case "set" can mean either fixed and changed by the state as and when it sees fit to bring about rough equality of demand and supply or the setting of ranges within which the price can float, or the giving of "guidance" on, for example, the permissible rates of price differentials between different stages of production and distribution, or the specification of the lowest guaranteed buying prices and the highest selling prices for some products. While Group 2 prices are more flexible than those in Group 1 (Group 1 grain purchase prices remained unchanged for twelve years, 1966–1978, for example), the flexibility is comparatively greater where the second procedure is used.[17] It is, however, still state-determined flexibility, one built into the plan, not spontaneous, competitive, lateral, market flexibility.

Two examples of the first subgroup of prices are state retail prices of industrial consumer goods and of agricultural producer goods sold to collective or (nowadays) tenant family farmers. State retail prices include the industrial wholesale price (taxes included), selling expenses at retail, and retailers' profit margin. The retail profit margin can be adjusted up or down so as to equate consumer demand to planner-determined supply at the state-set and adjusted price. Since until recently practically all profit reverted to the state treasury, such (infrequent) adjustment was equivalent to the adjustment of the turnover tax in the Soviet Union with the same result: the insulation of retail prices and consumer demand from the production process. Goods are allocated by the state through retail prices more flexibly if the retailer (under local state authority) is permitted to make the necessary adjustments in the price, as he perceives them, under a regime of floating or guided prices. In the case of floating or guided prices—in addition to increased state-sponsored price flexibility—decision-making power devolves to lower administrative levels.[18] After 1978 the appropriation of all profits by the state was replaced by taxes on profits, (that is, a portion of profit was left to the factory, wholesaler, and retailer). The share of profits retained by state enterprises rose from 3.7 percent in 1978 to 42.4 percent in 1986—25 percent in real terms after deducting energy and communications costs, construction tax, and education fees levied by the state. In the context of chronic consumer goods shortages and increased use of floating and guided prices, upward price adjustments were made more frequently by sellers to raise their profits and their retained share. Although this helped alleviate rationing through the queue for many goods, it caused concerns in some party and state quarters about price instability. In fact, the planning mind, in China as elsewhere, has great difficulty reconciling itself to the fact that to perform allocative functions prices must be permanently flexible, not just occasionally and down only.

Under the family tenancy arrangements, the state may sometimes use the prices it charges tenant family farmers for fuel, chemical fertilizers, pesticides, farm machinery as a lever to make farmers produce more grain crops. Such inputs and capital goods are supplied at lower prices if the farmers agree to do the state's bidding with respect to grain and at higher prices, or not at all, if the farmers are obstructionist in this regard.

The prices set to equate supply to planned demand include state-determined wages (price of labor) and the above-quota state agricultural procurement prices—prices at which the state bought produce from the collective farm sector above the compulsory delivery obligation. State-set tariff and bonus wage differentials can be used to try to bring about rough equilibrium between the supply of particular labor types and skills in particular locations and the planned demand for such labor in the short run. In China the use of wages-bonuses as limited labor allocation devices has been much rarer than in other centrally planned economies, and, conversely, resort to administrative labor allocation has been more important. Like other prices, wage rates in the state sector remained almost unchanged for twenty years after 1957. Above-quota procurement prices, higher-than-quota procurement prices, were a rather crude device to stimulate additional supplies of agricultural products. They were normally fixed for long periods.

Since 1985 state procurement of agricultural products has undergone changes that perhaps look more revolutionary than they in fact are. Except for certain stipulated products, state quotas for the delivery of products at state-fixed prices have been abolished and replaced by a system of contracts signed between state purchasing agencies and family tenant farmers. Any surplus remaining after the negotiated delivery targets have been met can be sold at market prices. For grain and other products formerly subject to state monopsony ("unified purchase"), the contract price is supposed to be the weighted average made up of 30 percent of the compulsory quota price and 70 percent of the higher above-quota price. It should be noted that between 1978 and 1985 both the quota and above-quota prices for grain and other unified purchase items had been significantly raised to reflect costs better than before.[19] Even though these increases in state procurement prices, reflected in today's contract prices, were in part intended to serve a limited allocative function by increasing peasant incentives and evoking a larger supply, there is evidence that the new contract prices remain coercive and depart from free prices formed by demand and supply on the market. Contract prices for staple grain crops—rice, wheat, and soybeans— and cotton were said to be about half the market price in 1987. Under those conditions, given the producers' right to sell these goods on the free market, family tenant farmers are not likely to sell these commodities to the state. They have no right *not* to sign a contract, however; they must sign the contract or lose their land.[20]

In reality, therefore, price negotiations between the state and the family farmers are not negotiations between rough equals, but— as of old, if more benignly—vertical, unequal treaties. Consequently, state contract prices, even though formally performing limited allocative functions, remain in essence Group 1 prices, like their predecessors, the quota procurement prices. Notice also that state retail prices for staple foods in urban areas are even lower than the purchase contract prices in the countryside. The cost to the state budget was 20 billion yuan in 1984.[21] Given the fact that nonstaple food prices are now largely decontrolled, family tenant farmers have been turning wheat and rice fields over to growing more profitable free market nonstaples (like vegetables) and engaging in sideline activities like poultry raising, or feeding surplus wheat to pigs, which they then sell on the free market. This practice has prompted calls in some leadership quarters for greater "discipline," that is, inducing farmers through administrative pressures to grow more grain.[22] Others, however, advocate the complete abandonment of the contract price system, allowing prices of staple crops to rise to their market-clearing level and the imposition of a land tax to subsidize urban staple food prices.[23]

Group 3 Prices. Group 3 prices perform allocative functions. They are of two kinds: (1) market prices for consumer goods on rural and urban fairs and for materials and producer goods sold by state and cooperative enterprises over and above the plan; and (2) black market prices, including currency exchange.

For much of the post-1949 period free market prices in China were severely repressed in both their legal and their illegal forms. The scope and coverage of such pricing have expanded after 1978 to include some basic and intermediate materials and capital goods. According to one report, "Sales of [industrial] commodities with prices fixed by the state account for only 40 percent of the country's total sales volume. The prices of more than 1,000 kinds of small commodities have been decontrolled." Looked at another way, "Of total retail sales, the state commerce share dropped from 90 percent in 1978 to 40 percent [in 1986]; the collective share (including the rural supply and marketing cooperatives) rose from 7.4 percent to 36 percent; and that of private and other business jumped from 2 percent to 24 percent."[24] State authorities, however, especially at the local level, do not leave the free markets alone. "No units or individuals shall go their own way," writes one authority. "It is necessary to rigorously tighten price controls and to strengthen supervision and inspection in this regard. It is absolutely impermissible for any unit or person to boost prices at will by taking advantage of the reform. . . . Those who commit such actions should be sternly dealt with."[25]

The retention of subsidized prices for staple foods and some nonstaples sold in state retail outlets in urban areas and the introduction of wholesale markets for materials and producer goods side by side with identical state-distributed and priced items means that today China operates on a double-track price system. Basic goods are available from the state at low fixed prices and on the free market at high fluctuating prices. A ton of steel, for example, reportedly sold at one time for 600 yuan at the fixed state price and for 1,300 yuan on the open market. The double-track system's disadvantages probably outweigh the benefits; for one thing, the system does not improve defective economic calculation.[26]

One suspects that the wariness with which free market pricing has always been approached in Socialist China derives not only

215

from the philosophical implications of such pricing but also from a very imperfect understanding of how the free market system works. Those who advocate price reform as the centerpiece of all economic reform may not understand that price flexibility is not a one-time shot but that to efficiently allocate resources, the process must be ongoing and spontaneous. Price flexibility is still equated in China with "profiteering," "arbitrariness," "blindness," "anarchy," and an obsessive fear of inflation.[27] Moreover, price flexibility must extend to factor markets: to wages, interest, and rents, which means freeing labor, capital, and land. Today, however, most industrial labor in China is still allocated administratively by state labor bureaus, and the mobility of rural labor is restricted by prohibitions against migration to the larger cities. These prohibitions, however, are breaking down. In the past they had contributed to what Claude Aubert calls a "massive [rural] underemployment, a frightening misutilization of manpower in the countryside disguised under the 'full employment' achieved by the agricultural collectives."[28] Capital markets are in a state of infancy. Although enterprises now have to obtain a part of their capital from banks at a 3–6 percent annual rate of interest, rather than as a free nonreturnable grant from the state, the interest rate does not even remotely mirror the relative scarcity of capital: it is a capital charge, a tax of quite limited allocative usefulness.

Price Policy

Two broad policy conclusions emerge from the review of China's price system over most of the post-1949 era. First, more than in other Socialist countries, except for Khmer Rouge Cambodia, the price system in China played a modest allocative role, a bit part. Even those prices that theoretically were supposed to perform partial allocative functions in support of the plan's physical rationing prescriptions saw their allocative capacity paralyzed much of the time. Retail prices and wages, as we have noted, remained unchanged over as much as two decades, and above-quota agricultural procurement prices stayed fixed over similarly long stretches of time. In addition, legal free markets, when not interfered with by local authorities, were severely repressed, as during the Great Leap Forward and the Cultural Revolution. Information on the history of illegal markets in China is scarce. Together with legal free markets, they play an important reallocative role in all centrally planned economies—to the point, indeed, where the plan would probably be unworkable without them. Granted the scantiness of the material on the second economy in China and on black market pricing, one still gets the impression that, at least after 1951–1952 and before 1978, underground markets were hunted down with resolve as ideologically and politically counterrevolutionary phenomena, and that in consequence of this their allocative importance in China's economy has perhaps been less than elsewhere. In short, until 1978, prices in China in all three groups were comparatively unimportant as institutional arrangements for the generation, conveyance, and processing of information about relative costs and utilities in the system; as coordinating devices; and as incentives to effort, especially efficient effort. Their very presence, of course, meant that they exerted some allocative influence, that they were not completely passive. But by reason of the prices' divorce from actual relative scarcities in the system, more often than not this influence was negative, encouraging even more wasteful resource use. This has been true of some fuels, residential rents, and transportaton charges, among others.

Second, the relationship of Chinese prices to current production costs was much of the time very loose, not just because of the conceptually defective computation of costs inherent in the labor theory of value, but because cost calculations were labeled manifestations of bourgeois mentality. From 1958 until 1978, with only a brief interruption in 1961–1962 Chinese economic policy was not only highly politicized but also disdainful of costing and economic accounting in general. So Group 1 prices, the so-called "cost-plus" prices, honored cost computations mostly in the breach.

Because prices were unreliable, not just with respect to measurement of opportunity costs but with regard to accounting costs as well, their usefulness to the planners as measurement and control instruments must surely have been questionable also. Nevertheless, control and measurement, together with income distribution, were what prices were used for in China at least some of the time. (Since no comprehensive statistics were published from 1959 through the late 1970s, one may question how important the measuring function of prices—measurement of economic activity—really was.)

Wages were used by the planners, through the central determination of job grades and wage scales on the Soviet model, for income distribution purposes. One of the policy objectives entering into wage determination was control of inflation in the setting of a full employment constraint and low priority assigned to the production of consumer goods. Although between 1957 and 1978 industrial employment expanded very significantly, industrial wage rates remained by and large unchanged, except for some upward adjustments in the lower wage grades and some reductions in the highest grades. Bonuses, when not abolished, tended to be distributed equally to all workers, as simple wage supplements. Retail prices were also used to implement an income distribution philosophy noted much of the time for its egalitarian tenor. Not only were prices of basic necessities kept low in the cities, but also prices of the few "luxuries," as defined by the planners, carried often considerable profit margins (the profits being appropriated by the state); this combination worked in favor of real income being even less unequal than the already not very differentiated money income. When cost reductions occurred in the production of basic necessities, they were used to reduce the state's subsidy burden. When cost reductions applied to planner-designated "luxuries," they were to be passed to the users at the planners' discretion: with a lag (longer or shorter, depending on the degree of "luxuriousness" of the good), in part, wholly, or not at all.[29]

Price Policy since 1978. It has been mentioned earlier that policy may be ordinary, essentially a repair or improvement of the existing institutional arrangements within the limits allowable by an updated, "revisionist" economic philosophy. Or policy may be reformist if it brings about fundamental changes in the system's institutions and economic philosophy, including the abandonment of any or all of the institutions and philosophy. Reformist policy may be either adopted as a package or evolved incrementally from ordinary policy.

Apparently, China's post-1978 agricultural price policy is reformist. At first there was only adjustment; procurement prices were raised sharply by various amounts. This had a positive incentive effect on output and labor productivity in agriculture, and much of the gain in the peasants' money income so far is no doubt attributable to this rather simple upward price adjustment. Subsequently, more far-reaching changes were made in the property structure of agriculture: de facto privatization of property rights in land through the family tenancy system and decollectivization of ownership in other means of production, such as draft animals, farm machinery, and implements, and in means of transport. In addition, beginning in the 1980s the prices of most nonstaple foods were deregulated, and the scope of free market prices was extended. The gradual abolition of the state's monopsony with regard to staples such as grain and oil-bearing crops, as well as cotton, implied a movement toward the marketization of the agricultural price system. Peasants did, in fact, respond to market price signals in their decisions about what to grow and how much. Continued marketization of the agricultural price system together with consolidation of de facto private property rights to assets is essential to the further rationalizaton of China's agricultural economy.

There are indications, however, that the price reform movement is in danger from at least three directions. First, the great official fear of even short-run inflation is behind the continued heavy subsidization of food prices in the cities and contributes to the contract prices' being below market prices for the same products. The size of the food subsidy represents the cost of the failure of agricultural price reforms. Charged to the commercial sector, the subsidy has contributed in the past to the negative growth rates of that sector. An element of coercion still enters into the agricultural price determination process, creates a two-track price system, and distorts economic calculation and decision making. Moreover, the deregulated part of the agricultural price system has been deregulated only partly: floating and guided prices for many nonstaples do not leave the price-forming process completely to demand and supply forces in the market.

The state also can and does intervene in agricultural retail price formation through ad hoc regulations such as imposition of price ceilings and price inspections. Local authorities opposed to "unjustified" profits derived by some peasant families from market operations and market prices have been known to skim off a portion of those profits through various more or less arbitrary levies. Second, even the present incomplete marketization of agricultural prices has brought about increased income differentials in the countryside, both within localities and among regions.[30] This disparity will tend to increase in the absence of an effective redistributive tax system (one that, however, does not destroy production incentives) as Chinese agriculture begins to experience the need to move on to the second stage of farm development through improved technology, necessitating farm mergers. Income and wealth differentials—a necessary part of market calculation—are an extremely sensitive issue in China. Future attempts to narrow such differences through a rollback of the current reformist policies cannot be discounted. Third, the semi-marketized agricultural price system operates in conjunction with much less marketized and privatized industrial price and property arrangements. This contradiction does not promote rational economic calculation. It is likely to exert additional strains on the relatively marketized agricultural price system, which can be saddled by its opponents with responsibility for various allocative distortions. True, the advocates of price system reform can blame the relatively unreformed industrial price system for the same thing. All this, however,

219

helps factionalize political discourse, produces zigzag motion, and conveys the impression that the reform lacks a sense of direction. A practical example of the uneasy coexistence of partly marketized agriculture and a still highly socialized, government-controlled industrial price system is the sale of pesticides, chemical fertilizers, fuel, and other inputs to tenant family farmers. Selective pricing of these inputs by the state quasi-monopolist can be used to try to enforce the state's preferences with respect to the volume, composition, and pattern of farm production, against the interests of the peasants as indicated by market prices. In a larger sense, it is by no means clear that the so-called "price scissors" (rural-urban terms of trade), which for years operated against the peasants, have been either fully eliminated or reversed, particularly when account is taken of all the overt and covert price subsidies to urban workers extended since 1978.[31]

Industrial policy has remained, by and large, ordinary rather than reformist.[32] It is true that the number of commodities subject to central allocation has been drastically reduced: only twenty-six materials are reportedly sold nowadays at prices fixed by the central government and only sixty final products.[33] There has been a shift toward "guidance" planning in this regard, but to Chinese officials guidance planning seems to mean mandatory planning at lower administrative levels.[34] Many if not most of the deregulated prices of goods other than "small" ones, including prices of above-plan materials and capital goods traded on wholesale markets in some cities, are floating prices subject to some regulation and suasion, or they are the outcome of bureaucratic bargaining in a setting of local protectionism and monopoly.[35]

As part of the initial ordinary policy, industrial money wages were raised, and overtime and bonus payments were reinstituted. The bonus funds for firms were linked to profits, and profits were no longer taxed at 100 percent. Attempts have been made to introduce a labor responsibility system, whereby basic wages and bonuses are linked to workers' productivity performance rather than seniority. The Soviet-type eight-grade tariff wage system is to be abolished in state firms, firm managers are to have more control over wage determination, and total payrolls are to be allowed to float according to individual enterprise performance as measured by profits. To be effective, such practices require the freeing of industrial labor so that labor can move spontaneously and freely in response to fluctuating wage differentials. So far this has not happened except at the margin. The *danwei* (work unit) remains a semifeudal arrangement that, in addition to its production and income distribution functions, is also the principal agent of the workers' social welfare. Wage increases and bonus payments are often treated by the *danwei* as welfare payments to be distributed equally or according to seniority rather than effort.

Overall, post-1978 policy recognizes the importance of economic levers (as against administrative levers) in the management of the economy, first and foremost prices—including wages, interest rates on loans, and foreign exchange rates, but not rents—as well as taxes, profits, and other financial or quasi-value magnitudes. Ordinary policy, which interprets management in the narrow sense of planners' directives, aims at improving such management by making greater use of prices and their derivatives, basing prices on the "law of value," and paying more attention to supply and demand. This Marxist formulation intends to use prices as more active and accurate backup planning devices and implies more attention to cost calculations $(c + v)$ in the determination of Group 1 prices, and greater marketization of Group 2 (and some Group 1) prices. Attention to cost calculations has provoked considerable discussion of the mechanics and accounting components of production costs and profit rates—something the Soviets had gone through in the 1960s and again in the early 1980s, with indifferent effects on the quality of allocation. Reformist policy—implemented in part in agriculture, proposed and then stalled in industry—interprets management in a wider and qualitatively different sense. It regards prices as the principal institutional arrangements of information coordination, and incentive in the system and as quantitative expressions of many competing decision-making centers.

Reduction of static inefficiencies and shortages and more lively innovation in the system's civilian sector will depend on whether prices continue to gain in allocative power and, more important, whether they become the quantified expression of autonomous buyer and seller demands and offers in a workably competitive market. The resolution of the plan's three major problems requires not just resort to price levers as bonded servants of the state, but the rule of prices that synthesize in mathematical terms a widespread freedom to choose and the sovereignty of consumer preferences.

13
Why China's
Economic Reforms Fail

China's economic changes took off in 1979 to the acclaim of the masses and a still traumatized Party. Some initial spectacular output, income, and productivity records were set in agriculture and consumer goods, but then the reforms sputtered and stalled. After mid-1988 they began to be pushed back to the accompaniment of much tinkering with the parts and to the drumbeat of political turmoil.

In this chapter I examine why economic reforms fail in China (as they also seem to do in other Socialist countries), focusing on systemic reasons. In the first part, I consider these general concepts: China's economic problems around 1978, the origins of these problems, possible policy and structural remedies for the problems, the kind of reform, requirements for market-type reform, and requirements for a successful market system. Next I look at China's reforms since 1979, specifically the chronology and results. The final section draws conclusions and suggests possible pointers to the future.

China's Economic Problems around 1978

Like other Socialist centrally planned economies, the Chinese economy in the late 1970s suffered from four major problems that made it nonmodern: chronic shortages of wanted goods, both consumer and producer goods—in fact, shortages of everything useful; massive waste, that is, static misallocations of resources; stagnation of research, development, innovation, and diffusion of modern technology; deficient incentives to labor, management, and entrepreneurship contributing further to low productivity. The four add up to one overall problem—the *quality* of economic performance.[1]

222

Origins of Problems. There are three related causes of China's quality problem. First are the objective causes such as the country's huge absolute size and rapid incremental population increase (about twenty-six additional people per minute to be fed, clothed, housed, educated, and eventually employed), the shrinkage of farmland (about one million acres a year), energy shortages, and the weight of tradition. These are "acts of God"—something can be done to alleviate them (through family planning, soil conservation and reclamation, and the like) but not much right away.

Second are the policy errors, the Party's favorite explanation and excuse for minor and major disasters. Policy errors are also known as mistakes of "work style," usually made by subordinates who allegedly either misunderstand or distort (with ulterior motives) correct instruction from above. Sometimes such mistakes are made by people on top: rightists, leftists, revisionists, dogmatists ("capitalist roaders," for example, or the Gang of Four). Everyone makes mistakes. Some are big ones—as the Great Leap Forward that resulted in widespread famine and an absolute drop in population of more than 13 million (probably double that) in just two years[2]—and merge with acts of God to upset the ecological balance. Others, like farm collectivization, ruin the incentive system.

Third is the system itself and the implicit assumption behind the policy errors argument that China's economic system is all right, that mistakes have simply been made within a basically sound structure. The "system-at-fault" argument, in contrast, is that problems are caused by a bad system and to address them effectively one cannot merely make repairs. One must dig up foundations, tear down the building, and replace both with a different structure. The policy errors diagnosis was dominant in China from 1976 through most of 1978. The economic difficulties, it was contended, were due to "left errors" committed by the Gang of Four, even by Mao after 1957. The view that there may have been policy errors but that the primary causes of China's troubles were to be found in its economic system gained ground in the course of 1978 and came to dominate economic analysis thereafter. But with regard to the political system, despite some temporary, largely rhetorical leadership concessions ("without political reforms, economic reforms cannot succeed in the end"), the errors-of-policy diagnosis has held the high ground all along.

Possible Policy and Structural Remedies

The remedy for policy errors is policy *adjustment*. Adjustments are intrasystemic remedies. They consist of measures such as raising or lowering the obviously more distorted relative prices of individual goods (what is often erroneously called price "reform"), reordering economic priorities (that is, reshuffling the order of planners' preferences in favor of agriculture and industrial consumer goods, for example), and—a perennial favorite—administrative reorganization (reassigning the bureaucrats).

The remedy for systemic ills is *reform* of the foundations and structure of the system, a much more radical (but not necessarily violent) transubstantiation of the two main components of the economic system, which are institutions and ideas.

The *institutions* of an economic system are the agreed upon and legally sanctioned and protected ways of doing things, such as allocating relatively scarce resources among possible alternative, competing uses, or ends. These institutions comprise information about relative (opportunity) costs to producers and utilities (use values) to users, that is, information about the relative scarcity (supply-demand) relationships within the system; coordination of allocative decisions made by consumers and producers; motivation of economic agents (workers, managers, entrepreneurs, planners) to engage efficiently in income-generating activities; and legal rights with regard to property in goods and services.

The ideas of an economic system, its doctrines or theories, comprise two groups: (1) positive or analytical theories that explain how the institutions of the system correlate and work and how they can be influenced without being distorted or destroyed; and (2) normative theories of desirable behavior, or a code of economic ethics. A system is an integrated, internally consistent whole made up of interrelated, interacting, and mutually compatible institutions and ideas, the purpose of which is the optimal allocation of resources among alternative, competing ends. It is a package governed by an inexorable internal logic, not a loose collection of randomly assembled parts. It rejects transplanted organs that are not compatible with its binding logic.

If Reform, What Kind of Reform?

Once it is acknowledged that chronic shortages, waste, technological turpitude, and the breakdown of incentives are due more to systemic causes than to policy errors and that, therefore, systemic reform is needed, the question is posed, What kind of reform?

There are two answers, the first being now and for some time to come impracticable—that is, perfect electronic *centralization*.[3] This would involve mathematical modeling and the central solution of a very large and exponentially growing number of dynamic, ever-changing variables by resort to supercomputers, resulting in perfect dictatorship. The second way is economic (as distinct from administrative) *decentralization,* that is, adoption of the market system. This is the only practicable and civilized way available at present to solve the central planning system's quality problems. Transformation of the Socialist economy's administrative central command system into the market system requires fundamental changes in institutions and ideas.

The *institutions* have to be marketized and privatized. Marketization means the replacement of command (whether physical specifications of inputs and outputs, or expressed in centrally determined political prices) by institutional arrangements based on the principle of economic freedom. Economic freedom means that decisions on resource allocation (what to buy and sell, when, where, from and to whom) are vested in individuals and freely constituted associations of individuals (partnerships, firms, or corporations). Transaction relations are horizontally inclined, tending toward rough equality of bargaining power between buyer and seller and are incompatible with hierarchical relations of dependence of one party on the other (political bargaining, monopoly, monopsony). Privatization means to vest in individuals as a matter of fundamental principle, not expediency, and in freely constituted associations of individuals; it implies very broad (but not unlimited) legal rights to the use, transfer (buying, selling, renting, leasing), and income from goods and services. Systemic consistency requires that these three rights be vested together, as a package, not selectively and disjointedly.

Ideas have to be fundamentally changed, both economic analysis and economic ethics. Marxist economic theory and its latter day (Leninist, Stalinist, Maoist) annotations, extensions, and "creative" elaborations have to be abandoned and replaced by market theories. The Socialist ethical code (including the imperatives of egalitarian income distribution, guaranteed full employment irrespective of performance, no firm bankruptcies, and stability of the price level, among others) has to be replaced by ethical prescriptions of the marketplace. The ideas that undergird the market system are:

- individualism—the individual's or household's inherent right to make decisions
- voluntariness—the ability to make exogenously unconstrained decisions
- individual responsibility for decisions taken
- competition—the presence of alternatives

225

- horizontality of transactions—absence of hierarchical relationships

Such deep changes in institutions and philosophy are, of course, extremely difficult to bring about, particularly when the reform movement is initiated from above and because, in traditionally autocratic sociopolitical systems, the changes necessitate the self-liquidation of the ruling class (that is, the Communist party and its monopolistic "leading role").

Requirements for Market Reform

What is required to bring about market reform? This issue may be addressed in the questions and answers below.

Q: How far?

Theoretical Ideal: All the way to the market system; no compromise; no ifs, buts, or in-betweens. The half-and-half compromise of market socialism or Socialist market is theoretically deficient. In practice, the best it can produce is Yugoslavia. "All the way" means that market institutions (including private property) are clearly dominant in the system.[4]

Practical Compromise: As in the theoretical ideal.

Q: How fast?

Theoretical Ideal: At once. Postponement of reforms courts stagnation and invites eventual recidivism, because: (1) postponement stretches out the period during which market institutions are incomplete and unconnected and not strong enough to do the quality job of allocation expected of them; at the same time the partially dismantled institutions of the plan no longer work (hence, wrongly, reforms become discredited in popular perception); (2) postponement enables the opposition to regroup (mainly adversely affected special interests), organize, and counterattack; and (3) postponement creates unnecessary disruptions, malformations, bottlenecks, and pain, causing panic.

Practical Compromise: Whatever the political traffic will bear, which depends on the threshold of tolerance in a society. A certain minimum critical mass of reforms must, however, be introduced at once, and the reform momentum has to be sustained. Short-run disruptions (for example, inflationary pressures, widening income disparities) must be accepted if they are due to system restructuring and not to postponement of restructuring (that is, incomplete, disjointed reform) or policy errors on the way to the market.

Q: How much?

Theoretical Ideal: Reform must be comprehensive and synchronized, not selective with bits and pieces of the market system literally "being used" to "perfect" the plan (using capitalism to make socialism work better).

Practical Compromise: A certain minimum critical, integrated mass of reforms is required to constitute the kernel of a substitute system.

Q: What relation to the political order?[5]

Theoretical Ideal: The market system is by definition incompatible with a totalitarian polity. The only equilibrium position is the combination of the market system with political democracy (without any qualifying adjectives that demean it, such as "Socialist" democracy).

Practical Compromise: The market system can coexist, albeit uncomfortably, with political authoritarianism of various degrees of severity. Such combinations, however, are precarious and unsteady and require evolution toward a natural equilibrium of market system and democracy if retreat into economic command is to be avoided.

Requirements for a Successful Market System

A market system that will successfully deal with the four quality problems that characterize central planning must fulfill seven conditions.[6]

• There must be free markets for goods and factors (land, labor, capital, and entrepreneurship). Market freedom means free entry and exit for buyers and sellers, no physical rationing of inputs and outputs, and an absence of exogenous compulsion to enter into transactions. In sum, voluntariness is the governing principle.

• Prices must reflect relative scarcities in the system, that is, relative changing costs and utilities (opportunity costs). Prices must be the core decision-making device for information, coordination, and incentives, and there must be a tendency toward a single market price for each commodity.

• There must be workable (not textbook-perfect or pure) competition between and among buyers and sellers, that is, the availability of alternative courses of action. With a few strictly circumscribed exceptions, there can be no monopolies or monopsonies, private or public, central or local.

• There must be maximizing (rational) behavior by buyers and sellers within the limits set by competitive market prices. Buyers

227

must seek to maximize their utilities under given price and income constraints, and sellers must seek to make profits.

• Private property rights must be dominant. This means that very broad, legally sanctioned and protected rights of use, transfer, and income from goods and services are vested in individuals and free assocations of individuals. The three rights (use, transfer, and income) must go together. Among others, private property rights are necessary for the free mobility of factors.

• There must be rule of law or a legal order (not just laws) that applies equally to all without exception, government included.

• Macroeconomic monetary and fiscal instrumentalities of government intervention in the market process must be in place, as well as arrangements designed to remedy market failures (for example, unemployment compensation and social security schemes, provisions for the supply of public goods). Laissez faire never advocated the absence of government, merely the government's limited economic role; nor did it ever claim that the market system was faultless.

China's Reforms since 1979

China's economic reform reveals three distinct periods: (1) 1979 to 1984—mainly agricultural changes (first emphasizing policy adjustments, for instance, procurement price increases, and then structural reforms in property rights and in the locus of decision making); (2) 1985 to September 1988—mainly changes in industry; and (3) September 1988 to the present—a freezing of reforms and growing signs of retreat.

In addition, from 1979 through mid-1989, an "open-door" strategy was followed with regard to China's external economic relations. This, too, proceeded from adjustment (increased foreign trade and borrowing) to reform (active courting of private foreign investment and acceptance of a variety of forms in which this investment materialized—joint ventures, wholly owned foreign-invested firms, and the like).

Positive and Negative Results. By and large, the period 1979–1984 was marked by success in agriculture. Specifically, farm output, labor productivity, and per capita peasant income significantly increased. The period 1985–September 1988 saw the emergence of troubling problems in both industry and agriculture, specifically:

• overheating of the industrial economy
• loss of control over industrial investment accompanied by stagnating investment in agriculture

228

- loss of control over social consumption (consumption by ministries, departments, bureaus, and other official organizations at all levels)
- inflation (approximately 30 percent in 1988)
- erosion of the living standards of large segments of the urban population
- increasing income inequalities
- increasing difficulty experienced by the government in paying cash to peasants for contractual deliveries of produce
- turning of the terms of trade against the peasantry
- open unemployment and rising labor unrest
- rampant corruption, particularly of officials at all levels of the state and Party apparats

As noted earlier, some of these problems are inevitable to a certain degree and, indeed, necessary accompaniments of structural reform of an economy in which chronic excess demand was the natural condition. Much of the problem and its severity, however, was due to the disjointedness and incompleteness of the less-than-half reform effort. In the most general terms, the problems that emerged after 1984—many of them from their formerly suppressed state—were caused by reform measures that did not go all the way to the market system, did not proceed fast enough, were not comprehensive enough, and were not accompanied by any substantive political changes.

Specific Reasons for Negative Results. The reform-tending measures undertaken since 1979 violated the seven conditions for a successful market system.

Free markets. The measures introduced partly free markets for some agricultural commodities and some industrial goods, but practically no free markets for factors. There is no market for land, except for a small portion of urban apartment space and real estate in the special economic zone of Shenzhen; an above-quota, residual market in capital goods exists in a few cities (for instance, in Shanghai and Shenyang); and there is a very restricted, very imperfect market for labor. Agricultural labor can move from fieldwork in specialized farm-related or neoindustrial occupations in the countryside but cannot legally move into the cities, although some of it does. Most industrial labor is still allocated by state labor bureaus and works under a state-determined tariff-plus-bonus wage system, the correspondence of which to marginal revenue product is purely coincidental. An increasing portion of industrial labor works under a contract system concluded between workers and their employing enterprises

229

and is compensated under a more flexible wage system, "according to work." Both types of labor are still very much tied to the work place *(danwei)* in terms of housing and social benefits of all kinds. Labor mobility in the state sector remains nominal, and this is true of both unskilled and skilled workers including managers and technicians. Personnel turnover rates are extremely low (around 3 percent per annum for scientific and engineering staff).

Notice that in neither agricultural nor industrial labor does the principle of voluntariness hold, or it applies only in small part. Thus, the rural household production responsibility system is not voluntary. In order to obtain partial legal use rights to its land allotment (what to produce or sell, to whom, and at what price), a household must sign a contract under which a designated portion of a designated output must be sold to the state at state-set contractual prices, which are normally well below the market prices for the same goods.[7]

Prices. The present price arrangement is one of multiple-track prices that bear varying relations to relative scarcities in the system, or none at all. Thus, some prices of some goods are more or less free, still interfered with by officials on the lookout for profiteering (when the price constellation does not benefit them personally).[8] Most of these quasi-free prices are for above-contract foods, some manufactured consumer goods that find their way to the free market, and consumer services like repairs or restaurants. Other prices are "floating," that is, essentially not allowed to exceed officially set ceilings. Still other prices are fixed by the state—most of these apply to "strategic" and "basic" commodities. Agricultural staple commodites such as grain, vegetable oils, and cotton are purchased by the state at negotiated prices and resold to urban consumers at lower, state-fixed retail prices, necessitating a huge agricultural subsidy. Some industrial wages are fixed, some floating—for equivalent labor. There is one set of input prices for domestic firms and another set for foreign ventures. There is one official exchange rate for the renminbi and another for foreign exchange certificates (FECs). In addition, there exists a thriving black market in FECs and foreign currencies.

In those circumstances, prices do not reflect relative scarcities and therefore cannot indicate to decision makers the rational choice of alternatives, that is, an optimal—or even an internally consistent— pattern of resource allocation. In such a setting, giving enterprises decision-making autonomy makes no allocative sense since profit is not necessarily an indicator of social profitability. There is no reconciliation of individual and social interests that a competitive market equipped with free prices normally brings about. Profitable enterprises, as often as not, are socially harmful. The waste goes on. And because of allocatively distorted price signals, adaptations of supply to changed levels and patterns of demand (as well as changes in demand itself), when they occur, are suboptimal, often significantly and grostesquely so.

In sum, failure to install a system in which prices indicate relative scarcities and are the core information, coordination, and incentive device perpetuates allocative irrationality, disinformation, supply bottlenecks, and inflation and invites distorted economic behavior and corruption.

Competition. There is no market competition to speak of in the semireformed Chinese economy. Five developments in this connection should be noted. First, there has been regionalization, a far-reaching administrative decentralization of the economy. Indeed, this has a long history going back to 1957–1958 and the Cultural Revolution. Administrative decentralization involves the devolution of many key allocative decisions to government organs at a lower, usually provincial or municipal, level of the state organization. It is a redistribution of power among bureaucrats, differing from economic decentralization in that it does not vest any significant allocative decisions in private persons and privately owned firms. Regionalization of the planning bureaucracy normally results in local quasi-autarkies and encourages regional protectionism and local monopolies. By the same token, it militates against the nationwide marketization and monetization of the economy and is generally strongly anticompetitive. One result of China's reforms so far has been the further splitting up of such national markets as did exist into many protected local units and subunits, sometimes with only barter relations among them. Moreover, the intraregional links are bureaucrat-to-bureaucrat, that is, highly politicized.

Second, the central government (sometimes provincial-level governments) remains a monopolist in several important respects. It continues to prepare material balances for some sixty key commodity groups and through its Bureau of Supplies distributes about thirty strategic materials, including 60 percent of capital goods, 60 percent of steel products, and 45 percent of coal. Such extensive physical rationing of inputs and outputs violates a central requirement of market competition. Of particular interest and impact is the government monopoly in supplying family tenant farms with important productivity-enhancing inputs such as farm machinery, diesel fuel, electricity, chemical fertilizers, pesticides, and plastics and—through its subservient banking system—the provision of agricultural credit. These can and have been used to put additional pressure on peasant producers to do the state's bidding in such matters as the proportion of sown area devoted to grain. Deliveries of chemical fertilizers and other inputs are often linked to administratively determined farm production patterns, which is equivalent to disguised collectivization.

Third, there is a central monopsony under which the government remains the most important buyer of a number of farm products including grain, oils, and cotton. Fourth, competition for labor among enterprises is practically unknown, although some informal luring away of skilled workers surely goes on as it does in all Socialist countries. More generally, lateral competition among firms in output, price, quality, product differentiation, or anything else is notable for its near absence. (There are a few exceptions, as in the case of some bicycle lines, for example, but they are few and far between.)

Fifth, roughly half the imports are still subject to the administrative command plan, purchased to make up shortages of domestically produced goods and priced the same as domestically produced goods. The rule of thumb is import what is short, export what is long. Thus, these imports do not have a competitive effect on domestic production through undercutting domestic prices. In sum, market competition is inhibited in China to the point where one might say it hardly exists. Its place is taken by competition for official favors and competitive markets for bribes, gratuities, and other palm-greasing emoluments; it is a neomercantilistic phenomenon of mutual back-scratching, political bargaining, and, as the Chinese say, "big fish eating small fish."

Maximizing rational behavior. The market system for its successful operation requires not just maximizing behavior by economic actors but also *rational* maximization. This means behavior designed to achieve optimal resource allocation under any given set of constraints. This in turn, requires rational indicators (competitive market prices) that accurately reveal the opportunity costs in the system. In the absence of such indicators, with markets for the most part unfree and competition political, maximizing behavior by buyers and sellers does not harmonize individual and social benefits—the invisible hand is invisible because it is not there. The allocatively wrong things are maximized, firms are rewarded for producing goods that are not wanted, and the behavior of one and all is distorted. What is maximized is a disjointed collection of microbenefits reaped through market cornering, true profiteering, and squeeze.

232

Property. Like the price system, property under the reform takes multiple forms with state ownership, however, remaining dominant. The multiple track arrangement characteristic of market freedom and prices applies equally to property rights. In agriculture the *baogan daohu* (household production responsibility) formula has vested partial rights to land use in the private family unit. The family determines the use of land once the contract-induced use of the land has been settled—that is, some land use is determined by the need to fulfill the delivery terms of the contract. There is no de jure right of private transfer of the family land parcel. The land is rented from the authorities and its legal ownership remains vested in the state. Private rights of transfer are limited to the purchase and sale of use rights through the instrumentality of land-use certificates. This constitutes an extremely narrow interpretation of transfer rights. Similarly, private rights to draw income from the land are partial, limited to that portion of income generated by above-contract sales on the free market.[9]

The property picture is equally muddy outside agriculture. There have been some (now suspended) experiments with stockholding in state-owned firms, limited for the most part to the issue of stock to the firms' workers and in rare instances to the general public. The stocks are more like bonds carrying fixed yields, and their trading is inhibited by the very underdeveloped, primitive state of China's financial markets. There has also been some movement toward the collectivization of state-owned firms. In the absence of a rational price system, this relative diminution in state controls over such firms amounts to nothing more than administrative decentralization. The expansion of the truly private property sector, while spectacular given its point of departure—zero—represents a mere blip on China's property landscape. It is limited almost exclusively to consumer (and a few producer) services, mainly retail trade and some house construction, and the manufacture of simple consumer goods such as furniture.

Rule of law. Despite the proliferation of laws after 1978, there is still no rule of law. Decisions are made "in accordance with laws," but the law remains an instrument of Party convenience. What has been done is to fill what was formerly a legal vacuum with traffic rules that help move transactions and perhaps temporarily reassure foreign lenders, investors, and other persons of good will but that do not in any fundamental respect alter the essential lawlessness of the land.

233

Macroeconomic instrumentalities. Because of the six conditions just discussed, no system-compatible, market-type instrumentalities of government intervention in the economy exist in the present neither-this-nor-that, halfway nonsystem. Monetary policy cannot be effectively employed because of the near absence of financial markets, the shortcomings of the multitrack price structure, and the status of the central banking authority as a subordinate organ of the state. Hence there is loss of control over the money supply.

Fiscal policy cannot be used because of the absence of a coherent tax system that could help combat, for example, the increasingly skewed distribution of income and correct China's budgetary deficits. The administrative decentralization of the economy has been particularly far-reaching in the fiscal area. Extrabudgetary revenues controlled by provincial and local governments are today equal to budgetary resources.[10] The result has been a segmentation of what was never a satisfactory national system of taxation and a weakening of the central government's capacity to intervene fiscally in the economy to correct disequilibriums.

The serious deficiencies of both instrumentalities of market-type intervention make it practically impossible for the authorities to combat inflation, except by resort to remnant instruments of the plan consisting primarily of administrative prohibitions. These, however, have been considerably weakened both by the partial dismantling of the institutional structure of the plan and by administrative decentralization. Not only do they not work as intended, but when they do work they tend to add to the indicator confusion and make matters worse.

So far no progress has been made toward the elaboration of a system of unemployment compensation and social insurance that would help cushion the effects of enterprise bankruptcies and structural unemployment that inevitably and necessarily attend reform toward the market system. The *danwei* remains an all-purpose organization performing a variety of functions of which efficient production is one and not the most important.[11] It cannot be made into the basic economic unit without the establishment of a social infrastructure that, for one, would enable workers to collect their unemployment compensation in ways other than wages. A particularly relevant social infrastructure for future economic modernization, one which has been neglected both in funding and freedom, is education. It has been devastated, again, by the events of the spring and summer of 1989 in the most profound sense of deep and perhaps irrevocable alienation of the intellectuals, young and old, from the system.

Conclusions

While objective causes and policy errors contributed to the Chinese centrally planned economy's problems of shortages, waste, technological sluggishness, and deficient incentives, the main reasons have been systemic. To remedy these system-based problems, measures were taken after 1978 to marketize and privatize partially the institutions that made up the system and simultaneously to dismantle partially the institutions of central, administrative, command planning. Little, however, was done to replace the positive and normative theories of central planning with market analysis and market ethics.

This "quiet revolution," as some have termed it, was also an unfinished one. It stopped less than halfway to the market system, further along in agriculture than in industry. Indeed, the reform was never intended to go all the way to the market system but only to a vaguely conceived halfway construct of socialism with Chinese characteristics. The aim was not to replace central planning with the market and socialization with private property but merely to use selected and pasteurized elements of the market and private property to make the Socialist system work better. Progress toward that compromise objective was to be slow and pragmatic ("crossing the river while groping for the stones"). Because of this slowness, which was translated into postponements and partial retreats, and the unwillingness to accept the implications of the market idea[12] and go all the way, the reform—after some initial successes—created more problems than it solved. It brought some formerly suppressed disabilities into the open (for example, inflation, unemployment, and real income disparities) without the ability to master them. The essential cause of the disarray after 1984 has been the disjointedness and incompleteness as well as hesitant pace of the changes resulting in the emergence of a nonsystem that has unintegrated, often incompatible, and internally inconsistent and unrelated parts of market and plan.

Chances are that in such conditions, the easy way—one that comes naturally to the now underemployed planners—is to revert to central administrative command. Indications are that since September 1988 and until the political upheavals of May–June 1989, this was indeed the path chosen by China's policy setters. With the political turmoil, of course, all bets are off. This much, however, can be confidently stated: recidivism—a return to even updated central planning—will certainly not solve China's problem of quality. It will, as certainly, by reason of technological lag ensure that China is permanently mired in third world status and that the distance separating it from the world's dynamic market democracies will inevitably and rapidly increase. This condition of self-imposed poverty and retardation is unlikely to be tolerated for long by China's young and talented population. The only answer is for the reforms to go all the way to the market system at both the levels of institutions and ideas. This once unthinkable thought, though temporarily repressed and shunted aside in China, is no longer as strange and alien as it once was.

14

The Economic Consequences of Tiananmen Square

In the early morning hours of June 4, 1989, acting on orders from China's paramount leader Deng Xiaoping, President Yang Shangkun, and Premier Li Peng, soldiers of the Chinese People's Liberation Army (PLA) rolled tanks and armed personnel carriers into Tiananmen Square in the center of Beijing. The PLA shot and killed hundreds, possibly thousands, of unarmed young people who had for several weeks peacefully demonstrated for democracy and an end to rampant official corruption. The massacre took place in full view of hundreds of foreigners, including foreign newspaper correspondents and television reporters, and much of the butchery was recorded on camera and viewed instantly by millions of people around the world.

The Tiananmen Square massacre was followed by mass arrests, interrogations, beatings, torture, show trials, imprisonment, and executions of students, young workers, and intellectuals. The leadership reimposed mind-numbing thought control and Marxist-Leninist orthodoxy on universities just beginning their recovery from the holocaust of the Cultural Revolution. The leadership remuzzled the media, which, for a short time, had spoken with many voices.

The repression continues unabated, albeit without the fanfare of international publicity given at the beginning. The square and the surrounding boulevards, streets, and alleys have been hosed down. Selected foreign "friends," concerned tour operators, and school children dressed in pretty red scarves and ribbons have been guided (courtesy of the PLA) through Tiananmen Square to show that things have been normalized. The children express gratitude to the government and the PLA for safeguarding their Socialist future. The tourists look sheepish and the tour operators nervous, but that is not unusual. At least one of the Communist regime's foreign admirers who worked there a long time, William Hinton, left China with all the appearances of disgust after decades of faithful service. But what of the businessmen?

How Ethical Are Capitalist Ethics?

Some academics in comparative economic systems think that the market system is the "best" because it does what an economic system should do: provide ordinary people with increasing quantities and qualities of goods, which they want, at prices they are able and willing to pay. The best economic system should do this efficiently, with the least possible resource waste. Unquestionably, the market system does this better than any other known system. Moreover, the market system has a way of exerting persuasive pressures for political democracy.

Our problem with the "best" system is market ethics. (Some academics argue that it should not really be considered a problem at all.) In the spontaneous market order, competition, combined with the principle of voluntariness of transactions, ensures the operation of the "invisible hand," a transformer of individual "selfish" strivings to public benefits. Indeed, capitalism, in the simplest and most accurate terms, is a system of voluntary transactions that leave those engaging in them better off; it is an essentially meliorist arrangement.

The automatic, free-wheeling reconciliation of private and social interests—with occasional exceptions caused by market failures—is absent from every other economic system where it is deliberately formulated by some superior authority (a government, a party, or a church) and enforced by political, administrative, and judicial means. The historical record shows clearly that the ethics of pre-capitalist systems like slavery, feudalism, and mercantilism are no better. Socialism—capitalism's contemporary—has not demonstrated an ethical high ground. Most of the time socialism's functioning ethics are inferior to the morality of the marketplace.

The problem with the "best" system, if it is one, is in the way market ethics are expressed. Market prices are the market's language, and this language articulates the principles governing its positive operation and normative conduct. Indeed, the phrase "price system" is used as a synonym for market system. Prices are expressed in money terms, and, for the producer, they translate into an accounting of profits and losses. For the market system to do its job of efficient resource allocation, producers must make profits and consumers must strive to maximize their satisfactions.

Put simply, what makes money is good and should multiply; what loses money is bad and should wither. As an evolving organism, anything in the market system is justified if it results in the propagation of its own genes. This factor is a source of problems for people who understand the market system and support it. For reasons stemming from instinctual, traditional, nonrational (in the economic sense), or transcendent processes, the market's narrow interpretation of the moral imperative leaves these market proponents in a moral malaise.

Social commentator Peter Berger recognizes that, taken by itself, the market system

> fosters both the virtues and the vices of salesmanship. Among the virtues are risk-taking, initiative, and innovation, and at least a rough egalitarianism (everybody's money has the same color). Among the vices are the tendency to assess human success in purely monetary terms ("how much is it worth?"), an extension of competitiveness and achievement-orientation into non-economic spheres of life (notably the sphere of intimacy), and a disparagement of what the Greeks called the "theoretical life."[1]

Socialist enemies of the market system have been quick to notice the free marketeers' moral ambivalence. They scoff at the market's driving ethic of greed. Capitalists, they say, must buy and sell. They will sell their grandmothers if the price is right, that is, market clearing. In the meantime, however, it is interesting to note that Socialist East Germany is reducing old-age pension rolls by selling its grandmothers to West Germany for hard currency—so many deutschemarks per granny.

We shall soon see how these ethical speculations relate to the Western business world's decisions about whether to do business in post–Tiananmen Square China or to stay out of China altogether. First, however, let us look at the Chinese side of the economic ethics question.

Socialist Ethics

The Communist regime has its own ethics problems. Contrary to "bourgeois logic," the main issue now dividing the Chinese leadership is not the moral question one might think ensued following orders for wholesale murder of students. Leaders, like Party Secretary Zhao Ziyang or Defense Minister Qin Jiwei, who had reservations about the revolutionary correctness and political expediency of massacre orders, have been purged and put under arrest. The question nagging China's doddering autocrats today is if they should continue with the market-oriented economic reforms blamed for the recurrent demands for democratic reforms or if they should retreat to the familiar economic inconveniences of a central plan under which people are kept politically in line.

Complicating this question, posed on the high moral plane of Socialist revolution and Party dictatorship, is a personal moral conundrum facing the top leaders, Deng Xiaoping and Yang Shangkun prominently included. They and their many relatives have materially benefited from the current halfway economic nonsystem in which dictatorial political power is exercised in crevices between disjointed markets. After a decade of halfhearted marketizing and privatizing changes in the centrally planned, Soviet-type economy, China today does not have an economic system but rather a jumble of unfinished markets and partly dismantled plans working at cross-purposes. In this confusion, the elite members of the monopoly Communist party make their daily killings—their Socialist market profiteering, which had been one of the targets of the Tiananmen protestors. The Party elite has benefited from a market in which competition takes the form of lucrative personal and political connections, nepotism, clientism, patronage, influence peddling, graft, theft, embezzlement, kickbacks, gifts, tributes, favors, intimidation, squeeze, extortion, and brutalism—from each according to his ability, to each according to his greed.

Transition to a full market system accompanied by democratic political control would clean up much of this official filth. Retreat to the central plan will push the muck below ground and cut off many of the most profitable opportunities that are directly associated with the privileged stratum's foreign trade and currency dealings available through their current "open-door" policy.

For the leaders feeding at the semireformed economy's trough, the only question is a pocketbook one: whether to leave the door open or to close it. Not surprisingly, they have decided to leave it open, for now at least. Over and above personal considerations, a return to central planning and an embrace of the USSR would be ill-advised on every count, especially when everyone is jumping the Socialist ship. Will joint-venture capitalists and other hard currency rich foreign devils keep walking through China's open door?

The Stakes

Can one put dollar figures on what is at stake? It seems one can because the World Bank requires the recipients of soft loans to clean up their statistical act as a first condition of creditworthiness. China had received $8.5 billion in low-interest World Bank loans over the past nine years and $3.4 billion of that was interest free.

Even the gerontocratic members of Deng's advisory commission, including Chen Yun, Bo Yibo, Peng Zhen, and Li Xiannian, should recognize that China needs massive infusions of foreign know-how and technology. These infusions are needed simply to decrease the distance now separating their country from the advanced market democracies of the West and the dynamic newly industrializing market economies on the east Pacific rim. They probably recognize that these infusions have to be accomplished through China's growing involvement in international trade and finance.

China's foreign trade jumped to $100 billion in 1988, a staggering figure considering that the foreign trade from 1966 to 1978 added up to only $9.4 billion. Today that $100 billion is nearly one-third of China's national income, a large share for such a big country. In 1988 China's exports and imports were $48 billion and $55 billion, respectively. From 1979 through 1988 the cumulative contract value of foreign loans came to $47 billion, of which $33 billion was actually delivered. The value of contracted direct foreign investment came to $28 billion, of which $11.6 billion was delivered, about 10 percent of all domestic state investment in fixed assets during this period.

China's primary trading partner is Hong Kong. Approximately 30 percent of China's trade and half the direct foreign investment come from Hong Kong. Hong Kong firms employ 3 million Chinese workers in Guangdong province. Direct investments over the past two years have totaled $7 billion.

One would think it might make good sense for China not to frighten the Hong Kong business community by, for example, killing masses of people in Tiananmen Square in front of cameras and then blithely denying its actions. From 1981 to 1986 China's technology purchases from advanced capitalist countries added up to more than $9 billion, one-fifth each from Japan and the United States and two-fifths from the European Economic Community. Borrowing abroad resulted in the accumulation of a Polish-sized hard currency debt estimated at $42–44 billion, half of it denominated in Japanese yen, with a debt-service ratio (the ratio of debt repayments to hard currency export earnings) of about 15 percent, and rising. The trade

241

balance has been negative since 1984. At the end of March 1989 foreign exchange reserves were $17.5 billion (compared with Taiwan's $76 billion), or roughly three months' worth of imports at rates projected for the year.[2] All of this indicates China's increased involvement in and dependence on the international market economy, particularly on that economy's advanced components. Closing the door to the outside world would have dire consequences for China at this stage.

The material stakes, given what has already been sunk into the Chinese economy since the door's opening in the late 1970s, are quite high for both foreigners and China. As for future growth and modernization of the economy, it would seem indispensable for China to continue and, indeed, to expand its recent involvement in international trade, finance, and worldwide division of labor. But it takes two to tango. How will the foreign business community respond?

The Capitalist's Dilemma

The present poverty (like Zambia, a $300 total annual income per capita) aside, China's potential, by virtue of the massiveness of its population and the vastness of its territory, has always hypnotized foreign traders in search of profit and missionaries in search of souls. The vision of a billion customers, each buying a box of detergent, is like opium for the capitalists and a clear triumph of hope over reason and experience.[3] For the Japanese, guilt about what the Imperial Armies did to China from 1937 through 1945 mixes with hope. For overseas Chinese hope mixes with nostalgia and cultural chauvinism.

For Hong Kongers, a third ingredient is apprehension of the 1997 turnover to Chinese control. Hence the more affluent pillars of the community try to curry favor with their future masters by endowing schools, hospitals, and the like on the mainland. They cater to the material fantasies of chief executive officers of phony mainland Chinese companies, like the one run by Deng Xiaoping's no. 1 son, Deng Pufang, out of Hong Kong. Deng Pufang was crippled by the Red Guards during the Cultural Revolution. Upon his father's return to power, he was appointed Head of the China Welfare Fund for the Handicapped. He subsequently also became the CEO of the Kanghua Development Corporation based in Hong Kong. After this corporation was found to have had shady financial connections with the Welfare Fund ("management irregularities" was the official euphemism), most of its operations were closed down in October 1988. But the junior Deng was not brought to whatever justice his father's regime dispenses. On the regime's own admission, more than 10,000 "companies"—some real, most not—have privileged links with high Communist party bureaucrats. Nearly 150 of them carry top officials—of ministerial rank or equivalent—on their payrolls.

A British businessman puts the foreign capitalists' case this way: "You're not in it for the money. . . . [You're in it for the] immense potential [and] the celebrated intangible good will."[4]

As demonstrated by Liu Xiangdong, director of the Department of Policies and Structural Reform under the Ministry of Foreign Economic Relations and Trade, the Communist authorities encourage sentiments like: "China's market has tremendous potential. People who abandon this market today will regret their action tomorrow."[5] The liquidation of the "shocking counterrevolutionary rebellion," say the authorities, in no way affects the open door policy insofar as China is concerned, especially since "there was no 'massacre' of the sit-in students on the Square, and no one died there."[6] Zheng Tuobin, minister of foreign economic relations and trade, says: "I expect that all businessmen will be back very soon since security is now no problem for them."[7] Security is only a problem for Chinese dissenters. The handling of the security problem by the government is none of the foreign businessmen's business.

Zheng may well prove to be right in his predictions, judging by a remarkable article published by the *Wall Street Journal* sixteen days after the Tiananmen killings.[8] The article, written by the executive vice president of an international real estate firm based in Atlanta, Georgia, translates a capitalist ethic into guidelines helpful to a Western China trader in the fastidious pursuit of turning the bottom line black. There are four criteria, he says, which must be met before his company returns to China: (1) safety of the company's expatriate workers; (2) a stable and productive environment for the company's work; (3) advice from the company's Chinese partner to come back; and (4) an official statement from the local municipality that the city is safe and open to foreign interests. These criteria "appear to have been met in Shanghai, and we most likely will return this week."

There is more. Because the Chinese authorities clearly desire the return of foreign business to China, the capitalist mentality predicts that the Chinese "may be willing to concede a few points in order to do so." Good business sense dictates that the Chinese be pressed on the following points: (1) before returning, the foreign investor should attempt to expand the term of his venture, double its duration if possible; (2) negotiate a reduction in the venture's taxes (what better time to ask?); (3) ask for more control in the venture's management; (4) ask for help in solving the foreign exchange conversion problem "so that earned local currency can be reasonably converted and remitted efficiently"; (5) encourage Chinese officials to undertake a "promote China" campaign aimed at tour operators, businessmen, and tourists ("selling a safe, stable image of the country"); and (6) urge officials to make special appeals to overseas Chinese (especially those in Hong Kong, Taiwan, Singapore, and the United States) "not to give up on the homeland."

A growing number of Western businessmen have acted on this advice. The Chinese authorities, with some reservations and fuzzy ambiguities, have acceded to this type of manipulation. For example, the American MGM Development Company headed by Mohammad Malekpour signed a contract just two months after Tiananmen to develop an industrial zone in Tianjin. The Chinese side obliged by extending the time period for payment by the company of a seventy-year lease ($17.2 million for two square miles) from eighteen months to three years. The Chinese expect profits to be 10 billion yuan a year. For what it is worth, the Chinese also changed the original agreement, originally under negotiation for two years, to read that if at any time during the seventy years of the lease the country should become too unstable for foreign businesses to make money, the People's Republic would compensate foreign investors with a "fair price." Since nearly all the banks, companies, developers, and original potential investors backed out fast after Tiananmen, the Malekpour deal is a significant contribution to luring them back. In the *International Herald Tribune* Malekpour said, "So we told the Chinese about the fears of foreign investors and said they would have to make the terms better. They agreed."[9]

MGM Development's initiative notwithstanding, some investors' fears are not easily allayed. Hong Kong investors have been promised capitalism for fifty years after China's takeover of the colony. This is not very different from the promise of seventy-year stability and "fair price" compensation if things turn sour on the Tianjin zone investors. Rather than pulling out their investments from China, Hong Kong professionals are pulling out of the city in ever-greater numbers. Instead of buying good will in China, they now buy passports of convenience and real estate in Canada.

There is the very real prospect of the Communists inheriting an empty shell in Hong Kong, a lot of cathedrals of profit, bricks, and mortar, with all the faithful gone. Even before that, many might-have-been projects will go by the board. Hong Kong money men were planning to finance highway, electric power, and airport projects in Hong Kong and China. It now looks as if these ventures will not materialize unless a miraculous transformation occurs in Hong Kong's shocked psyche between now and 1997.

Many Taiwanese entrepreneurs who put in at least $1 billion last year in various labor-intensive, low-tech projects in Guangdong and Fujian provinces appear to have had second thoughts about both the profitability of their investments and the sociopolitical utility of what they were doing: an attempt at political reconciliation between the two Chinas. This reminds one of Adam Smith's observation in *The Wealth of Nations:* "I have never known much good done by those who affected to trade for the public good. It is an affectation, indeed, not very common among merchants, and very few words need be employed in dissuading them from it." The Taiwanese merchants, like their Hong Kong cousins, cannot readily pull out the money they have already invested. But they do not have to throw good money after bad.

The market system's ethical concerns raised earlier are being translated through the agency of the potential investors' rational profit-and-loss expectations into market language. Private capital does not shun risk, but it abhors political volatility and erratic behavior, precisely what China exhibited in June. Old capital sunk into projects that are now operational will stay for the most part, but new capital is more hesitantly committed and offered at interest rates calibrated to the foreign investors' perceptions of greater risk and dimmer prospects. Japanese companies invested $200 million in China last year. This year the figure is expected to be about half that amount. Before June 1989, five Fortune 500 companies were gearing up to channel $650 million into the Chinese economy. As of August, only one of them was prepared to proceed. The tourist trade, which brought in more than $2 billion in badly needed hard currencies in 1988, has been a shambles since last June. Convertible currency earnings from that source are likely to be less than half last year's figure.

It is not just political instability—including the possibility of more turmoil as old Deng goes to see Marx—causing China's economic problems. While the events of April–June 1989 were indeed prompted by political rot, serious economic problems were also at work. The reforms begun in 1978 ran out of steam by 1985, for the reason that systemic changes were only partially carried through. This gave rise to severe structural collisions between the remnant institutions of the central plan and the emergent imperfect, partial, and disjointed markets. For one thing, while there were markets

245

for some individual goods, there were practically no markets for labor, capital, and land. Supply could not elastically respond to changes in the demand for the marketized goods. A dual price system made nonsense of any semblance of rational calculation.

Many factors have eroded the urban living standards and distorted the pattern of income distribution. These include inflation fed by budgetary deficits, runaway money pumped into the economy by a highly politicized banking system responsive to provincial and other local authorities' hunger for investment funds, a vicious cycle of subsidies to consumers of about 40 billion yuan a year, and bailouts of money-losing state firms.

Administrative retrenchment measures adopted by the center in the summer of 1988 are being evaded at the provincial level and below. The measures are well on the way toward inducing stagflation. There is widespread unemployment, both open and hidden. For their contractual (that is, compulsory) food deliveries, the government is paying peasants with worthless IOUs known as "white slips" and rapidly depreciating cash. The peasants complain of being overcharged by the state on their purchases of chemical fertilizer, plastics, and farm machinery. When they threaten to withhold supplies, hardline authorities threaten them with the grim prospect of recollectivization. The coastal provinces are the worst off, because they were once the standard bearers of reform and, indicatively, the recipients of solicitous attentions from the now disgraced Party General Secretary Zhao Ziyang.

Government and International Agency Sanctions

Adding to the problems are economic sanctions imposed by some Western governments and international aid agencies. The World Bank has put a hold on some $780 million in low-interest loans. Following the Tiananmen thuggery, the Japanese government postponed a $3.3 billion loan that was to have been disbursed over seven years. Smaller loans have been withheld, for the time being, by Italy and Belgium. The United States suspended military sales.

By and large, Western governmental reactions to the June events in China have been noticeably restrained. The flow of trade and credit may be expected to resume, albeit at a higher cost to China and in perhaps somewhat smaller volume for a while. The governmental equivalent of the businessmen's, perhaps mythical, estimate of China's huge economic potential is the vision of China as an emerging regional power that should not be pushed too hard lest it cozy up to the Soviets and upset the delicate political-military power balance in east Asia.

British Prime Minister Margaret Thatcher is concerned about the possible dissolution of her 1984 preemptive surrender of Hong Kong to China and the peaceful invasion of Britain by several million Hong Kong citizens. President Bush considers himself an old China hand on the strength of a brief official sojourn in Beijing (1974–1975) and admits to his friendship with the present Chinese leaders. Thatcher and Bush have been leading the forces of moderation, not to mention outright mushiness, on the issue of economic sanctions. Mrs. Thatcher is on record as opposing "too precipitate" sanctions that could "cause great panic in Hong Kong."

A free society does not react monolithically to even the most repulsive events. When the old men in Beijing kill their grandchildren, terrorize society, or have their soldiers beat up Tibetan monks and desecrate their monasteries while the tourists are out to lunch, capitalist businessmen look to their profit-and-loss accounts, balance sheets, the bank rate, and stock market quotations and formulate responses consonant with these indicators. If they are right, they make money: if they are wrong, they lose it, exit from the marketplace, and that is the end of it.

In formulating their response, the governments of free societies need not, nor should they, confine themselves to the profitability dictates of the market. They can go beyond the bounds of the narrow market ethic and articulate their political constituents' moral revulsion (or the absence of it) and in their response take into account the broad political, economic, and strategic dimensions of the relationship of their polities to the government responsible for the abomination.

The academic and other autonomous estates within the free society (for example, the press) can take their own positions, independent of and often at variance with those of the business community and the government. They are less hamstrung than the entrepreneurs and the government by the cash nexus, the constraints and immediate policy-making repercussions of their opinions. They can be unambiguous in their moral stand, an opportunity that unfortunately they often fail to grasp (as in their almost total lack of condemnation of the barbarities committed against the Chinese people in general and the intellectuals in particular by Mao's hooligans during the Cultural Revolution of the 1960s and 1970s).

The Bush and Thatcher responses to the Tiananmen tragedy have been too restrained, weak, and cautious and too concerned with the danger of "losing" China by taking a clear principled stand

247

on fundamental questions of human rights. In particular, calls on the butchers of Tiananmen to put an end to the arrests, tortures, deportations, and killings after June 4 have lacked strength, conviction, and the muscle of effective political and economic sanctions. What seems not to have been understood is that the present leadership has, by its misguided actions, lost much of China, particularly the thinking class without which the country can never modernize. To appease the men now in charge, whom the prominent Chinese dissident Liu Binyan describes as "cruel, hypocritical, incompetent, and extremely mean," is a sure way for the West to lose the real and decent China.

The cruel, hypocritical, incompetent, and extremely mean old men who rule a resentful nation by the gun quickly detected the lack of backbone and resolve in the Western (especially American, British, and Japanese) response. Their actions conform to the Chinese saying: "molest the weak and fear the strong" because there is no strength to fear abroad. They have interpreted as timorousness the kid-glove treatment accorded them by the West and the timidity that prompts it, and they have responded accordingly: with arrogance, abuse, lies, and undiminished barbarity.

Moreover, the Chinese government has gained stature by the presence in their midst, actual or scheduled, of foreign individuals who were once high public officials in their own countries or are relatives of public figures. Among these are Henry Kissinger, Alexander Haig, Richard Nixon, and Prescott Bush, the incumbent president's brother. Despite their current status as private businessmen and investors in China, most of them continue to make public analyses of international affairs, China prominently included, and exert considerable influence on public opinion in their countries.[10] The line separating a person's private business interests in China and his public analysis of China's society, politics, economics, and foreign relations is not always as clearly traced as one would hope.

Longer-Term Consequences

All these, however, are fairly short-run consequences. Chances are that the businessmen and bankers who flew away when the shooting began will return to China; like the Ancient Mariner wiser and sadder perhaps, but with the lure of profit (preferably in dollars and yen) alive, if a bit tarnished. That is their destiny and their function in life, and one should not blame them for doing what they must. Western governments, too, will relent; they usually do where left-wing regimes are concerned. Moreover, the moral memory span of their voters tends to vary inversely with geographical distance. Like Mayor Marion Barry of Washington, D.C., China's leaders can always say that "outside the killings, we have one of the lowest crime rates."

Check-happy functionaries of international aid agencies will be back spending other people's money: that, too, is their job. They are, in fact, in the process of unfreezing their credits. So, the perpetrators of the Tiananmen horror are probably right to tough it out. But what are the longer-term consequences of June's massacre?

The consequences are, I think, very serious for China's economic modernization. The consequences are so serious that one can legitimately wonder whether that objective will ever be accomplished. As Professor Yuan-li Wu, a leading American expert on the Chinese economy, once put it, "Some countries muddle through; others muddle but not through." China appears to belong in the latter category.

Steeped in the Enlightenment's intellectual tradition of reason overcoming all obstacles and an addiction to happy endings, it is extremely difficult for Westerners in general and Americans in particular to accept the idea, despite recurrent evidence to the contrary, that some problems cannot be solved.

The events of Tiananmen Square have brought to the surface two issues that are bound to have profound consequences for China's economic future.

The first is the alienation of the intellectuals, young and old alike. Without them China's economic modernization will go nowhere. Thousands have been killed, imprisoned, or sent to do menial work in the remote countryside; tens of thousands have decided to delay, perhaps forever, their return from abroad; millions of bright young minds are being befuddled daily by Marxist blather. China is loaded with prohibited talents and unrealized intellectual potential, a resource that will remain untapped so long as the Communist system—not just the present kleptrocratic *lumpen* element in the leadership—is around.[11] The repression of Tiananmen is the proximate cause of the estrangement of China's intellectuals from the system, but the real cause runs deeper. Considering itself to be the absolute truth revealed by history, communism has at all times treated the free intellect with unabashed hostility, cruelty, and witlessness. This, ultimately, will be communism's undoing. The system will perish of its own stupidity.

The Socialist economic system of central administrative command planning is deeply flawed, as nearly everyone nowadays (Castro excepted) recognizes. The system is based on an intellectual error and fails in practice to address the problem of efficient resource allocation. Communism does not supply wanted goods at prices people are willing and able to pay. To correct the situation, the system must be thoroughly changed at both the philosophical and the institutional levels. Nothing short of complete transition to the market system will do. Body shuffling and other halfway exercises in hybrid market socialism are not enough. In fact, they are in many respects worse than no medicine at all. But that is precisely what the Dengist semireforms amount to.

The nightmare of the Communist leadership, in China as elsewhere, is the conjunction of political ideas about freedom and economic grievances, or to put it another way, the alliance of the intellectuals and the working classes, peasants included. In its present state of systemic disarray, the Chinese economy both lacks automatic adjustments and eludes planned control. Neither market-type means of intervention nor central administrative commands work. This means that inflation continues to erode urban living standards at an accelerating clip. The workers are unhappy with this. The first result of the austerity measures applied since mid-1988 has been, as mentioned earlier, to make it difficult for state purchasing agencies to pay the decollectivized peasants for the produce they are supposed to supply under delivery contracts concluded with the government. The peasants are unhappy with this. They are also unhappy with the high prices the government is charging them for essential farm inputs.

When economic grievances of workers and peasants combine with the students' demands for intellectual freedom and representtive government, the resulting mixture will be highly explosive. Retreat into central planning will not solve anything. It will merely prolong China's present status of third world dictatorship propped up by the army, wallowing in elite corruption, going nowhere. The only way out is real economic reform: changeover to the market system, accompanied by the withering away of political absolutism. This may still perhaps be brought about peacefully, but the odds against a peaceful revolution are growing with time. But then, nothing at all may happen, and China may just keep muddling along.

PART FOUR

Comparative Economic Development in Three Chinese Entities

15

The Economies of Taiwan
and Mainland China

Under the scrutiny of every major indicator of performance, the economy of Taiwan over the past three and a half decades has been a resounding success, a triumphal march from poverty to prosperity. In real terms, between 1952 and 1985 product growth on Taiwan has been nearly twice that on the mainland (table 15–1).[1] When other dimensions of growth are taken into account, the comparison is less favorable to the mainland than table 15–1 suggests.

The Economies Compared

First, Taiwan's growth has been the addition of useful output. A sizable part of mainland growth has been useless because the goods

---

TABLE 15–1

INDEXES OF GROSS NATIONAL PRODUCT AND NATIONAL INCOME,
TAIWAN AND THE MAINLAND, 1952 AND 1985

(1952 = 100)

Year	Gross National Product of Taiwan	National Income[a] of the Mainland
1952	100	100
1985	1,544.2	820.2

NOTE: For Taiwan, 1981 prices; for the mainland, "comparable prices."
a. National income, mainland definition. This consists of the sum of values added by the "productive" (material) sectors of the economy and is roughly equivalent to net material product.
SOURCES: For Taiwan, *Taiwan Statistical Data Book 1987*; for the mainland, *Statistical Yearbook of China 1986*.

produced were of poor quality, of the wrong assortment, in the wrong locations, or not needed. This system-related problem of coordination is shared by all centrally planned Soviet-style Socialist economies without exception. For example, in 1987, despite an acute shortage, 30 million bicycles were in government warehouses because they could not be sold; they could not be sold because they did not work.

Second, despite Taiwan's sensitivity to economic fluctuations beyond the island's shores, especially in the United States, Taiwan's growth has been relatively smooth. Long-term growth on the mainland, in contrast, has been very uneven. This unevenness includes one mega-sized depression (1959–1962), as a result of which the number of people on the mainland dropped by 13½ million in two years (1960 and 1961), according to official figures—but probably more.[2]

Third, Taiwan's growth has been balanced with industry, agriculture, transport, communications, commerce, and other service trades working in concert. By contrast, in line with the Soviet-style system's developmental philosophy, growth on the mainland has been highly skewed, resulting in large inter- and intrasectoral imbalances. Among the more important has been neglect of consumption in favor of accumulation, of agriculture and the consumer goods industry compared with heavy industry, and of investment in "nonproductive" construction such as housing relative to "productive" construction such as factories. These imbalances had disincentive effects on the labor force and thus on labor productivity, confirming Milovan Djilas's characterization of the Soviet-style Socialist economy as "a nonmarket, bureaucratic economy . . . where all real values, including the value of work, are lost."

Fourth, Taiwan's growth has been modernizing in three senses: (1) the growth has been intensive, that is, attributable mainly to improvements in factor productivity; (2) it has raised the technological level of the economy—from tennis shoes to customized computer chips—so that today Taiwan is on the verge of joining the select community of the world's high-tech producers; and (3) the growth has restructured the composition of domestic product and employment, away from agriculture and toward industry, commerce, and financial and other services. After 1956, and until 1980, this modernizing process of growth was much less evident on the mainland:

- Output growth was obtained mainly by extensive means, that is, through addition of factors, especially labor and capital—in terms of domestic product, there was an annual decline of factor productivity between 1957 and 1982 of 1.1 percent.[3]

- The technological level of the economy stayed stagnant.
- Despite industrial advance, both the domestic product and the employment of the mainland remained deeply marked by agriculture, while the share of commercial and other services was in retreat (table 15–2).

In 1985, on the mainland, 63 percent of the labor force was employed in agriculture, down from around 80 percent in 1952. In 1985, on Taiwan, 35.7 percent of the labor force was in agriculture, down from 56 percent in 1952.

Fifth, the benefits of growth have been equitably shared in Taiwan, increasingly so as the economic pie grew larger.[4] While the inequality of income distribution on the mainland is low, in fact, one of the lowest in the world,[5] three qualifications should be noted: (1) partly because of the comparatively sluggish product growth over the years, partly because of a low-incomes policy pursued during

TABLE 15–2

SECTORAL ORIGIN OF NET DOMESTIC PRODUCT (TAIWAN)
AND NET MATERIAL PRODUCT (MAINLAND), 1952 AND 1985
(percentage shares)

	Taiwan		Mainland	
	1952	1985	1952	1985
Agriculture	35.7	6.9	57.7	41.4
Industry	13.5	40.2	19.5	41.5
Construction	4.4	5.0	3.6	5.5
Transport[a]	3.8	5.5	4.3	3.5
Commerce	23.9	15.3	14.9	8.1
Other[b]	23.9	27.1	N.A.	N.A.

N.A. = not applicable.
a. For Taiwan, transport and communications.
b. Banking, insurance, real estate, government services, and other services.
SOURCES: See table 15–1

the Maoist period, the relative equality of income on the mainland amounts to poverty equally shared; (2) as with product growth, the degree of inequality has fluctuated in the distribution of income, depending on changes in institutional property relations in agriculture and industry and in policy regarding growth; and (3) enormous inequalities between the privileged class of power holders and everyone else have always existed on the mainland in regard to the distribution of the material "rents" extracted by the privileged class of party cadres and state apparatus bureaucrats from the public assets under their control and the nonmaterial perquisites accruing to them from the political power monopoly of the Communist party. In autocratic regimes, especially the really thorough Communist autocracies, this "power income" aspect of overall income distribution is of particular significance. After all, at the time of his death, Mao was reportedly earning less than 500 yuan ($250) a month.

Taiwan has become one of the world's leading traders: the twelfth largest trading country in the world in 1987 and the fifth most important trading partner of the United States. Per capita foreign trade, which was $38 in 1952, came to $5,571 in 1988, in current prices. For a variety of reasons, including bouts of xenophobic self-imposed self-sufficiency, mainland China has been slow to emerge from its cocoon to take advantage of wealth-promoting international specialization (table 15–3). Taiwan's trade since the mid-1970s has been consistently in surplus, resulting in accumulations of huge foreign exchange reserves—in 1987, at $75 billion, the world's second largest after Japan. Since its emergence as a trader on world markets in the early 1980s, the mainland has had varying trade surpluses and deficits reflected in wide fluctuations of its foreign exchange reserves.

Taiwan's rate of natural population increase fell slowly from 3.3 percent in 1952 to 1 percent in 1986. This decline, like that of Japan earlier, was the spontaneous byproduct of modernizing economic growth: of voluntary decisions made by urbanized families to have fewer children. The mainland, after following see-saw policies on the issue, reduced its rate of increase from 2.3 percent in 1953 to 1.4 percent in 1986. The decline occurred largely because of the implementation of Draconian birth control measures (the one child per family policy), which has earned mainland China criticism from many quarters for violation of basic human rights.

The Record since 1979

Three years after Mao's death, mainland China began to move away from the Maoist variant of the Soviet-style economy and, indeed,

TABLE 15–3

FOREIGN TRADE, TAIWAN AND THE MAINLAND, 1952–1988

(in billions of U.S. dollars)

	Taiwan[a]				Mainland[b]			
Year	Total	Exports	Imports	Balance	Total	Exports	Imports	Balance
1952	0.31	0.12	0.19	−0.07	1.94	0.82	1.12	−0.30
1960	0.46	0.16	0.30	−0.14	3.81	1.86	1.95	−0.09
1965	1.01	0.45	0.56	−0.11	4.25	2.23	2.02	0.21
1970	3.00	1.48	1.52	−0.04	4.59	2.26	2.33	−0.07
1975	11.26	5.31	5.95	−0.64	14.75	7.26	7.49	−0.23
1979	30.87	16.10	14.77	1.33	29.33	13.66	15.67	−2.01
1980	39.54	19.81	19.73	0.08	37.82	18.27	19.55	−1.28
1985	50.82	30.72	20.10	10.62	69.61	27.35	42.25	−14.90
1986	64.01	39.84	24.17	15.67	73.85	30.94	42.91	−11.97
1987	88.57	53.61	34.96	18.65	82.65	39.44	43.21	−3.77
1988	110.24	60.59	49.65	10.94	102.90	47.60	55.30	−7.70

a. Customs statistics.
b. Figures before 1980 are from Ministry of Foreign Trade. Figures after 1981 are from Customs Statistics, according to the *Statistical Yearbook of China 1986*.
SOURCES: For Taiwan, *Taiwan Statistical Data Book 1989*; for the mainland, *China Statistical Yearbook, 1988; Beijing Review*, February 6–12, 1989.

perhaps from the Soviet-style centrally planned system itself. This movement has had three major components:

• an incentives-related change of policy regarding the neo-Stalinist priorities of the economy—a movement away from the three imbalances discussed earlier, toward emphasis on consumption, agriculture and light industry, and "nonproductive" construction
• an institutional reform stressing markets and de facto privatization of property rights—particularly in agriculture but since 1984 also in industry and the urban sector in general, involving attempts to introduce elements of factor and financial markets
• an opening up to the world market, including relatively generous provisions for foreign investments on the mainland

Looked at another way, developmental strategy since 1979 has shifted from near autarky to a combination of import substitution and export promotion with growing emphasis on export promotion. Perceiving a not-too-distant threat to its traditional exports from the mainland's rapidly growing involvement in world trade (and the mainland's comparative advantage in labor costs), Taiwan—which has a long record of correct and timely anticipation of trends in the international economy—initiated steps in the early 1980s to upgrade the structure of its economy toward higher value-added, high-technology goods and the development of financial services, partly perhaps in the expectation that Hong Kong will likely decline in the 1990s as one of East Asia's leading financial centers. To blunt the protectionist blow from abroad (especially from the United States), Taiwan has also begun to moderate, if not yet abandon, its long-standing policy of export-promotion-cum-import substitution by taking various measures to liberalize imports and the export of capital.[6] These economic steps were accompanied by political liberalization of genuine democratic content, exceeding quantitatively and qualitatively the quite marginal political adjustments made by the mainland since the Thirteenth Congress of the Communist Party in 1987. In this way, Taiwan's image as a model not only of materially successful but also of politically progressive development is brightened.

The data on per capita GNP or national income in Taiwan and on the mainland suggest that since 1979, when mainland economic changes took off, Taiwan has more than held its own; in fact, the gap has grown larger than ever before. Nevertheless the growth performance of the mainland economy since 1979 has been creditable (table 15–4), approaching the dynamism of the four East Asian tigers: Taiwan, South Korea, Hong Kong, and Singapore. Taiwan's precautionary steps appear well founded, assuming that the mainland changes will continue in the general direction they have taken so far.

With the adoption of the open-door policy, mainland China rapidly increased its foreign trade turnover. Between 1979 and 1986 mainland exports rose 2.3 times and imports 2.7 times. During the same period Taiwan exports rose 2.5 times and imports increased 1.6 times (table 15–3), resulting in the massive accumulation of foreign exchange reserves, the bulk of them held in U.S. dollar securities. This "mountain of gold" is causing Taiwan more trouble than perhaps it is worth by, among others things, fueling protectionist sentiments in the United States. Some academic economists on Taiwan have argued for a reduction of the reserves through import liberalization, relaxation of restrictions on private investments abroad, and encouragement of domestic consumption, an argument government policy makers seem increasingly to listen to.[7] Neobullionist sentiments, however, die hard, and the advice to keep the reserves large in case of military emergency remains persuasive to some in positions of influence. The mainland's problem since the late 1970s has been to prevent recurrent massive hemorrhaging of

TABLE 15–4

ANNUAL GROWTH RATES
OF REAL GROSS NATIONAL PRODUCT (TAIWAN)
AND NATIONAL INCOME (MAINLAND), 1979–1988
(percent)

Year	Taiwan	Mainland
1979	8.46	5.0
1980	7.13	0.4
1981	5.71	2.5
1982	3.30	6.4
1983	7.88	8.3
1984	10.52	11.7
1985	5.08	3.5
1986	11.64	1.4
1987	11.90	9.0
1988	7.30	11.2[a]

NOTE: Taiwan, at 1981 constant prices. Mainland, at current prices adjusted for annual inflation rate. National income defined as in table 12–1.
a. Gross national product.
SOURCES: For Taiwan, *National Conditions of the Republic of China,* Autumn 1986, 1987, 1988; for the mainland: *Statistical Yearbook of China 1986; Beijing Review,* February 9, 1987, p. 24; ibid., March 2, 1987, p. 20; ibid., January 11–17, 1988, p. 27; ibid., February 6–12, 1989, p. 21.

its hard currency reserves, such as occurred in 1978–1980 and again in 1984–1986. The 1978–1980 problem was caused primarily by ignorance. Liberated from Mao's "all-round" self-sufficiency, mainland buyers acted like children in a candy store, their prodigality necessitating a painful retrenchment and the cancellation of several large import-based investment projects. The 1984–1986 seepage, caused mainly by the center's loss of control over hard currency imports by local authorities and enterprises, was a phenomenon spurred by the system's chronic investment hunger.[8]

While the long-run (1952–1986) quantitative growth record of Taiwan is obviously much better than that of the mainland—domestically and in external trade, in general as well as per capita—the more significant difference between the two economies is in their qualitative performance, particularly regarding the quality of goods and services produced, the attention to consumer welfare, and the modernization of growth. Much of the effort of the mainland's economic reformers since 1979 has been to reduce this quality difference between mainland and island growth. The success to date has been greater in agriculture than in industry. Spectacular output increases in agriculture have been obtained with a smaller labor force and the use of a smaller farm area than previously. Some 80–100 million farm workers have been made superfluous, and most of them have been absorbed by rapidly expanding rural industries. Increases in industrial output, in contrast, have been obtained in the old way, primarily through additions of capital and labor. Between 1978 and 1983 factor productivity in state sector industry declined. A 28 percent growth of net output came about through a 49 percent increase of capital and a 17 percent increase of labor.[9]

The qualitative difference between Taiwan and the mainland derives largely from a difference of systems. Centrally planned Socialist economies have in the past exhibited fast rates of growth in domestic product and foreign trade but they were, and remain, inferior to the market system in three qualitative respects:

- They are enormously wasteful.
- They neglect demand, treating the consumer as a means rather than the end of economic activity.
- They suffer from arthritic technological innovation and diffusion, which, together with consumer neglect, contribute to low factor productivity, including widespread labor apathy.

These disabilities are traceable to the system's defective institutional arrangements of information, coordination, motivation, and property.[10] These defects can be overcome by structural reform, that is, by a change of system. Taiwan provides a model for such systemic turnaround.

Taiwan as a Systemic Model

It is argued in some quarters that Taiwan cannot serve as a model of exemplary economic or political growth because it is too small, because it has a peculiar history, because it received generous U.S. aid, or for any number of other reasons that allegedly make it a "special case." Such argument is erroneous. Of course, no model can be transferred bodily without some adjustment and modification. Even on that score it could be contended that Taiwan and the mainland have a common history, culture, and language, which should make model transfers easier than in other instances where these commonalities are lacking.

What matters most, however, are the systemic arrangements: the economic institutions that deal with information about relative marginal costs and utilities in the system, the coordination of allocative decisions, the incentive structure, the nature and distribution of property rights to goods and services, and the products of those goods and services. These institutional arrangements, through which economic policy is pursued, are based on an economic philosophy composed of economic theory and economic ethics. An economic system is essentially a set of interrelated, internally consistent ideas about what should be done, by whom, for whom, and how—ideas embodied in the rule of law. It is a logical whole, individual parts of which cannot be lifted out of context and grafted onto another, different, perhaps opposite, system. If intersystemic transfer is to take place, one system must be substituted for another. Moreover, such total substitution necessitates the transfer of the sociopolitical environment within which the system that is adopted has been conceived and nurtured. It is impossible, for example, for a centrally planned economy, if it is to benefit from the market system's superior institutional arrangements with respect to static and dynamic efficiency and material plenty, to (1) use bits and pieces of the market and some privatization of property but reject the market as an organic whole; (2) adopt the institutions of the market system but reject the market philosophy in either its theoretical or ethical form (adopt the market system, but use a Marxist theory of value to explain it and "Socialist morality" to sustain it, for example); and (3) adopt market institutions and philosophy but reject the sociopolitical culture that gave rise to those institutions and philosophy. One has to buy the whole package or nothing. And that is the fundamental reason why voluntary, peaceful intersystemic transfers are so difficult to accomplish.

I would suggest that in the case of Taiwan and mainland China, where the superiority of the island system has been so clearly demonstrated over nearly four decades, the transfer of the Taiwan model to the mainland, while certainly not easy, is perhaps relatively easier than the adoption, say, of Western European capitalism by the Soviet Union. That seems to be so not only because of the shared history, language, and culture and the dire straits to which Socialist economics (pushed to its extreme by Mao) had brought the mainland but also because Taiwan's market system has absorbed those elements of the Confucian tradition and Sun Yat-sen's Three Principles of the People that are compatible with and supportive of the dominant free market institutions and free market philosophy.[11] In this sense, Taiwan's market system has truly Chinese characteristics, besides being effective in providing the people with an abundance of goods and facilitating the emergence of an increasingly pluralistic and democratic society and polity. What the mainland has to come to terms with, if it is serious about overcoming its chronic shortages, static misallocations, and dynamic inefficiency and their many negative derivatives, is capitalism with Chinese characteristics. This model is what Taiwan has to offer and, as a natural extension of it, political democracy with Chinese characteristics. Such acceptance on the part of the mainland (certainly difficult, but not impossible eventually) would produce the only viable solution: not of "one country, two systems," but of one country, one system.

Before taking a closer look at the Taiwan model of a market economy with Chinese characteristics, we must mention one contributory factor to Taiwan's success. Although U.S. aid and the U.S. military shield were important in permitting the system to take root and develop in the early years, more important by far has been the easy access to the huge American market provided by the United States to Taiwan since the beginning. This liberality, greater than that of any other developed capitalist country or region (Japan or Western Europe, for example), has made it possible for Taiwan's export promotion policy to succeed and has been a key element in enabling the market system of Taiwan to show what it can do. If reciprocity is secured, there is no reason why this liberal attitude should not continue in a wider context of one China, one system.

Taiwan is a model of a market system with private property as the dominant form of ownership and state intervention in behalf of the market and private property. The underlying philosophy is that of individual economic freedom, voluntary transactions, and competition. Taiwan subscribes with Confucian decorum to Adam Smith's dictum that "consumption is the sole end and purpose of all production; and the interest of the producer ought to be attended to only so far as it may be necessary for promoting that of the consumer." The presence of an interventionist government is sometimes cited to dispute the free market–private property characterization of Taiwan's economic system. This, however, is based on a misunderstanding. Capitalism is what people (perhaps with the exception of the Russians) do when they are left alone. The essence of laissez faire is precisely to leave people alone to do their buying and selling and to maximize their satisfactions and their profits as best they see fit, on the basis of information supplied by workably responsive market prices. Laissez faire never meant the absence of government from the picture. It meant the limitation of the government's economic functions to certain tasks needed to protect competition and private property rights, including the provision of a legal order (protection of contracts), external defense (critical in the case of Taiwan), money, and public goods to tackle externalities and to take care of those who cannot take care of themselves.[12] It does not preclude the government from taking steps to initiate and foster economic growth and development through, for example, land reform that encourages more widespread private ownership, research and development expenditures designed to promote an up-market restructuring of the economy, even temporary (but they must be temporary) policies of sheltered growth for infant industries, export promotion, support for education (provision of equal opportunity for all at the start), and correction of highly skewed, politically explosive income disparities where these arise from market imperfections.

That the government on Taiwan has acted in the promarket, proprivate property spirit is evidenced by its declining ownership of industrial output: in 1952 the state owned 57 percent of industrial output; by 1962 its share had fallen to 46 percent, 19 percent by 1972, 14 percent by 1982, and 10 percent today.[13] By contrast, the first economic function of government on the mainland has been to severely limit and control, when it was not bent on destroying, the market and private property, an attitude that has changed only recently but has not been totally reversed. The government of Taiwan encouraged development through its policies of import substitution (1950s), export promotion (1960s and 1970s) and, more perilously from the U.S. perspective, export promotion with import substitution through the mid-1980s. It set an example for others to follow in creating a climate favorable to export-oriented investment on the island and lately has begun a process of import liberalization, encouragement of domestic consumption and investment, liberalization of capital exports, and technologically upward restructuring of the economy. In general, the government's policies have been pragmatic, guided by capitalistic financial discipline and the principle of market economics in command of politics.

Taiwan's market institutions and market philosophy dovetail into Sun's key principles of "people's livelihood" (attention to consumption), "land to the tillers" (Taiwan's exemplary land reform, which provided one of the foundations of the island's industrialization), government intervention to facilitate intersectoral capital transfers from land to modern industrial uses, and the view that international trade and financial relations are not inherently exploitative.

I believe it is by now understood on the mainland, certainly by the brighter academic economists and some economist-officials, that much can be learned from Taiwan. What is not so clearly understood is that to solve the mainland's structural problems properly, Taiwan's systemic model has to be adopted in its entirety, including the system's economic philosophy and environmental political culture of pluralism and expanding democracy. Even if understood, such a package deal is extremely difficult for a monopoly autocratic party staffed by a multimillion-member privileged class to accept. Partial transplants will not do, and wholesale rejection of the model will ensure that the mainland's structural defects will continue to stall the economy, frustrate consumer aspirations, and lead to competitive decadence with other reform-resistant Socialist economies, if any are left. The Chinese characteristics of Taiwan's capitalist model may ease somewhat the painful decisions that mainland leaders have to make on what to do with their obsolete and unworkable centrally planned system. In any event, the Taiwan model is available for the asking: its institutions, its theory, and its economic ethics. Perhaps it may yet be adopted by the mainland out of sheer historical necessity, under growing popular pressure.

For Taiwan the first task ahead seems to be to continue on its way toward greater riches. Snobbish governments may not diplomatically recognize, but cannot ignore, a country with a per capita GNP that by the turn of the century, given current growth rates, will reach $17,000 or thereabouts. Taiwan's second task is to maintain social peace and political stability, while modernizing its polity in a democratic direction—a difficult but not impossible assignment. Its third task is to avoid being lured into ever more intimate economic relations with the mainland without concrete evidence, carefully inspected, that each step in the growing intimacy is attended by market-oriented structural changes of the mainland's economic system. Without such common-sense caution, Taiwan, for all its riches and temporal success, could slide into the tragedy of a one country–one system situation—the system being socialism with Soviet characteristics.

16
U.S. Economic Relations with Taiwan since the Taiwan Relations Act

Since 1979, the year in which the Taiwan Relations Act was passed, economic relations between the United States and the Republic of China (ROC) on Taiwan have prospered as never before.

Achievements of the U.S.-ROC Economic Relationship

Two-way commodity trade, which was $9 billion in 1979, reached $36 billion in 1987, an increase of four times. Taiwan became the world's twelfth largest trading country and the fifth largest trading partner of the United States. The U.S. share of Taiwan's total trade rose from 29 percent in 1979 to 33 percent in 1988. Over these years American consumers greatly benefited from the massive importation of relatively cheap, relatively high-quality Taiwan-made goods. About 7 percent of those goods were sell-back items from Taiwan-based firms that had American equity—roughly ·15 percent if the original equipment manufacturer condition is taken into account. Due largely to export-oriented policies of development and U.S. cooperation, the material welfare of ROC citizens progressed rapidly during the period. Between 1979 and 1988 real national income per capita grew at an annual rate of 6.5 percent. By 1988 per capita income was in the neighborhood of $7,000. Unemployment rates were kept low throughout, and income distribution was comparatively equitable.

In 1979 U.S. private investment in Taiwan had been $80 million. In 1988 it was $135 million. During the ten years of 1979–1988 U.S. private investment in the Taiwan economy amounted to $1.8 billion, nearly 40 percent of total foreign private investment. In the eight years preceding 1979, total U.S. private investment in Taiwan was only $343 million, accounting for 34 percent of all private foreign investment.

The U.S.-ROC trade and investment relationship during the years following the U.S. "derecognition" of the ROC and the enactment of the Taiwan Relations Act has not only generally benefited the economies of the two countries but also contributed importantly to the promotion of world trade and the international division of labor. The phenomenal expansion and progressive liberalization of the world market have, in turn, contributed to the preservation, indeed sharpening, of competition in the domestic economies of the world's advanced capitalist countries and the modernizing, rational restructuring of those economies, resulting in increased comparative advantage. The superior dynamic efficiency of the world market system compared with the system of central planning is thus largely attributable to the growth of increasingly uninhibited international trade and finance.

The U.S.-ROC economic relationship has been, moreover, the principal concrete expression of a shared cast of mind that sees trade among nations not as an adversarial contest in which one side inevitably loses but as the pursuit of mutual advantage and emphasizes the primacy of free enterprise, the free market principle, and private ownership, without denying the need for government intervention in behalf of the market and private property. According to this philosophy, free markets and private ownership are the necessary conditions of political freedom and democracy. Not only has Taiwan done the American thing by turning itself from a loser into a winner, but also it has conclusively demonstrated the close connection between economic and political freedom. The ROC serves as a systemic model that others, bent on modernization, can profitably follow. The philosophical U.S.-ROC symbiosis is worth preserving and nurturing, no matter what the temporary irritants. It is, indeed, central to the continued expansion, liberalization, and multilateralization of trade and finance, the prosperity of market societies, and the containment of the impoverishing system of central command planning and Communist party monocracy.

Problems in the U.S.-ROC Economic Relationship

By now the major problems attendant on the U.S.-ROC economic relationship are widely known, partly because of their growing magnitude and partly because they have been inserted into the U.S. political process. The satisfaction both sides can take from the felicitous development of trade and investment since 1979 has to be qualified by an examination of individual issues and closer scrutiny of the overall data.

At the center of the problem are the growing U.S. trade deficit with the ROC and the corresponding growth of ROC foreign exchange reserves, which make the ROC appear to some like a throwback to bullionism. The explosive growth of the overall U.S.-ROC commodity trade since 1979 (from $9 billion to $36 billion in 1988) has been fueled by ROC exports to the United States ($5.7 billion in 1979, $23.4 billion in 1988), while ROC imports from the United States progressed at a more leisurely pace (from $3.4 billion to $7.7 billion in 1987 and then a sudden jump to $13 billion in 1988 as American anger rose). During the 1979–1987 period the annual growth rate of Taiwan exports to the United States was almost twice the rate of increase of Taiwan imports from the United States. The U.S. trade deficit with the ROC, which had been $2.3 billion in 1979, came to $16 billion in 1987—more, if U.S. figures are accurate. It was driven down to $10.4 billion in 1988. At the close of 1988 the ROC's trade surplus with all countries was more than $11 billion, 91 percent of it from trade with the United States alone. Although not quite of the same magnitude, Taiwan is today, with Japan and Western Europe, one of the foremost contributors to the U.S. trade deficit of roughly $130 billion in 1988. Taiwan's contribution to that deficit is nearly 8 percent of the total. In 1979 less than a quarter of Taiwan's imports came from the United States. This ratio remained unchanged ten years later.

The trade deficit problem has been argued back and forth, some of the arguments revolving around questions of principle, others concentrating on more technical problems. While there has been consensus in the United States and the ROC on each side of the argument, there has not been unanimity. On the American side the range of argument has been from Taiwan bashing to Taiwan idealizing. On the ROC side there has been self-criticism on the one hand, mainly by professional economists, and protestations of injured innocence on the other, mainly from government officials. By and large, the argument has been conducted with decorum, and it has been accompanied by generally constructive policy action. It remains emotionally charged and politically sensitive, however, and for it not to get out of hand—with injury to all—the mutual understanding needs to be reflected in hard trade figures.

Certainly on the American side, the range of disagreement has been narrowed in the past year or so, and I believe the same to be true of Taiwan. The effect of the mutual narrowing of disagreement has been convergence and thus a new opportunity for resolution of the problem. Despite political pressures, the general drift of the argument in the United States has been toward hard-headed review of the facts. I think something similar has been happening in Taiwan, despite the 1987 nationalistic flap over the alleged beer, wine, and tobacco surrender, and other kinds of U.S. "bullying." So far at least, the superprotectionists have not done well in either country.

The American position since 1979 is, as I see it, summed up in the following general propositions: First, the United States subscribes to an open-market philosophy, is eager to promote a multilateral world trading system by applying and extending GATT rules, and insists on removing, through bilateral negotiations with its trading partners, those practices it considers to be in restraint of trade. Of these, removal of trade restraints has near-unanimous support of the U.S. administration, Congress, and business. It applies particularly to Japan, the European Economic Community (especially Germany), Korea, and Taiwan. The association of Taiwan with Japan in the minds of many Americans as the villains of the deficit piece is unfortunate, since Taiwan has been more accommodating and responsive to American concerns in this regard than has Japan. Nor are the orders of magnitude of, respectively, the Japanese and the ROC contributions to the U.S. deficit comparable—not yet at any rate. In contrast, partly because of the lesser appreciation of the new Taiwan dollar (NT$) against the U.S. dollar since 1985 (indeed, the reluctance of ROC authorities to allow the NT$ to find its "natural" exchange rate), the Taiwan portion of the U.S. deficit has been comparatively more resistant to efforts at compressing it.

Regarding open markets and extending the GATT, the American position is that, with few exceptions, the United States actually practices what it preaches. The United States has been, it is claimed, and continues to be more liberal in allowing entry by foreigners into its domestic market than America's leading trade partners have been. Many contend that the exemplary success of the Taiwan economy is largely a result of the ready access Taiwan has had in the past, and still has today, to the huge American market. This access has enabled Taiwan to take advantage of economies of scale and thus to compete effectively in the world market for manufactures. America's extention of trade enhancement measures to Taiwan, including the generalized system of preferences and most-favored nation treatment, has facilitated that access. Easy entry into the U.S. market by the ROC has probably been a more important ingredient in the Taiwan economic "miracle" than outright U.S. aid, which was phased out in the 1960s. It is reasonable to argue that in the future continued easy access to the U.S. market will be important for the ROC as it endeavors to restructure and upgrade its economy and begins to engage in high-technology production and trade. Taiwan's past efforts to sell goods on the Japanese and West European markets have not been very successful. In 1979, 13.7 percent of Taiwan's exports went to Japan and 5 percent to West Germany. In 1988 the respective ratios were 14.5 percent for Japan, and 4 percent for Germany. A simple but accurate explanation is that Japan and Germany are less liberal about foreigners' entering their home markets than is the United States.

Second, the American argument is that, while the trade imbalance between the United States and the ROC is attributable to many policy and structural causes (including the enormous appetite of Americans for consumption and the deficiency of domestic savings for investment), one important and remediable cause is Taiwan's reluctance to allow American exports to enter the Taiwan market as easily as Taiwan's exports enter the U.S. market. In the 1950s, with American encouragement, Taiwan followed an import substitution policy of high tariffs, quantitative import restrictions, and overvalued exchange rates. In the 1960s this policy gave way to one of export promotion, the keystone of which was substantial reduction in the overvalued NT$ exchange rate. Export promotion, however, was not accompanied by the abandonment of import substitution (protectionism). On the contrary, the two went hand in hand until very recently. Indeed, it could be argued that they have not been separated to this day, even though the protectionist impulse has been on the wane, partly as a consequence of outside pressures and partly because of criticism by influential Taiwan economists.[1] Americans request neither the immediate nor the total elimination of ROC-made barriers to American business activities in the Taiwan market. They ask only for a level playing field consonant with the mutually espoused free trade philosophy and commensurate with what they consider to be the wide opportunities offered Taiwan business interests in America. They are interested in seeing the depreciation of the U.S. dollar relative to the currencies of America's major trading partners reflected more faithfully in the US$-NT$ exchange rate—a sensitive issue for the ROC.[2] Rightly or wrongly, they ascribe the recent divergent movements in the U.S. trade deficit with Japan and Taiwan in large part to the undervaluation of the

NT$—designed, they suspect, to give Taiwan a temporary competitive edge against Japan, protect domestic export concerns that are too small to survive competition in the new low-value U.S. dollar international setting, and postpone the necessary but painful restructuring of Taiwan's industry. The field-leveling request goes along with the hope that the ROC will initiate appropriate policies to stimulate domestic demand for imports and consumption, a sentiment the United States has conveyed to others—notably Germany and Japan—with varying success (more success in Japan than in Germany).

Third, while acknowledging that American consumers have benefited from the trade deficit, as have some multinationals and corporate investors, and that the competitive pressure of imports from abroad has been domestically invigorating, and insofar as it mirrors actual (not rigged) comparative costs and comparative advantages in the global market, has contributed to a rationally defensible long-term restructuring of the U.S. economy, Americans note that the situation since 1979 has not been without its dark side. The most obvious negative impact of the Taiwan import surge has been on certain U.S. industries: machine tools, hardware fixtures, and bicycles, to name a few. These sectoral and geopolitically localized problems translate into powerful political pressures on the Congress and the administration to "do something about it," the "it" being what those adversely affected perceive to be "unfair" trade practices by Taiwan. Beyond these micro-difficulties there looms a larger problem of perhaps less immediate popular concern, but worrying the specialists, about the dangers for the United States inherent in large and chronic trade deficits financed by foreign sellers.

Fourth, Americans agree on the need for trade deficit reduction, a process already set in motion by the falling U.S. dollar. They may not fully appreciate, however, the painful adjustments in their own economy that trade deficit reduction (even more, a reversal) will necessitate, including higher prices to consumers for formerly low-priced imported goods and more pressure on workers and managers in export industries to compete successfully on world markets. America's major trading partners are keenly aware of the painfulness of the adjustment required of them: a $130 billion turnaround, including $10 billion for Taiwan.[3] That is perhaps why they want to postpone the process or stretch out the pain. For the ROC, whose exports are about 60 percent of gross national product and which typically devotes 15–20 percent of its national income and half its annual savings to the accumulation of foreign exchange assets, the pain of adjustment will be particularly acute and easily politicized. The social peace and political legitimacy of Taiwan are more closely tied to economic health and economic health to the successful performance of the export sector than in any other country, Korea included.[4]

Work to Be Done

Social peace on Taiwan and the political sovereignty of the Republic of China are of vital interest to the United States. This long-term strategic interest must be kept in mind in the course of negotiations aimed at deficit reduction. It is important not just that the deficit reduction talks and the measures that emerge from them be guided by current economic need but that they be fitted into a more lasting and broader framework resting on shared philosophical foundations and emphasizing the desirability of preserving and consolidating U.S.-ROC understanding and friendship.

It is this strategic vision and the need to avoid distraction or even separation by keenly felt but minor irritants that demand attention, need nurturing, and call for an enormous effort of education in both countries. Indeed, the vision is poorly focused, and the legacy of understanding and friendship is being eaten away by many corrosives, not just economic irritants—changes since 1979 on the mainland of China, for example. It is imperative that Americans and Chinese on Taiwan alike understand what has been done so far by both sides to lessen the frictions inevitable in any lively business relationship and, more important, that they comprehend this relationship as part of a general concept that goes well beyond trade and financial considerations. Without a clear understanding of the proper general concept, deficit reduction measures will tend to be piecemeal, to lack orientation, and to give the impression of opportunistic maneuverings. In such a conceptual vacuum, the United States might be tempted to turn up the heat on Taiwan to levels unacceptable to the government of the ROC and the people on Taiwan, and Taiwan may be tempted to take action in the name of trade diversification, that it, the United States, and the rest of the free world would later regret. I have in mind a slide into the economic embrace of the "motherland," accompanied by stepped-up economic relations with other parts of the Socialist world: the USSR and Eastern Europe. Such action would find some supportive constituencies within Taiwan among businessmen concerned about losing out to competition on the mainland market, among some politicians, and perhaps among some American-trained academics.[5] It would be applauded by certain segments of American public opinion, particularly by those who wish to see "the Taiwan problem get off our backs" and to see "the Chinese settle their differences among themselves."

Studies made by Chinese economists on Taiwan show that Taiwan-mainland indirect trade has long been vigorous, significant, and rising, with, of course, Taiwan registering a surplus.[6] Indirect two-way trade in 1988 was nearly $3 billion, certainly much more if undocumented, including illegal direct trade is considered. Taiwan's surplus was estimated at $720 million.[7] Taiwan-mainland indirect trade in 1987 was, however, a small proportion of total Taiwan trade: 1.4 percent—perhaps two or three times that if all transactions were properly accounted for. The same holds for Taiwan's exports to the mainland. In addition, a number of small and medium-sized Taiwan firms (the big firms tend to be government-owned) have invested in plants and equipment on the mainland, presumably to take advantage of the comparatively low labor costs there, the potential market, and the economic inducements offered by the People's Republic of China to "compatriots from Taiwan."[8] In 1988 such direct Taiwan investments on the mainland were estimated at more than $1 billion.

The ROC has also been moving toward more active trade with the Soviet Union and Eastern Europe. Direct trade with Eastern European countries is to be legitimized, whereas formerly only indirect trade was allowed (total indirect trade of $121 million in 1986, $270 million in 1987). It is unlikely that by trading with the Russians, Eastern Europeans, and mainland Chinese, the Taiwan economy will upgrade itself technologically—which is what ROC economists and officials think has to be done in the coming years—and restructure its manufacturing firms to keep up with the competition on sophisticated world markets. Taiwan's new Socialist partners have delicate problems with generating and applying technological innovation to their civilian economies and converting their domestic currencies into goods and hence into hard foreign money. They are not models of modernization, and many are rapidly jumping the Socialist ship.

The extent of Taiwan's involvement in trade and investment with mainland China, the Soviet Union, and Eastern Europe is, of course, for the people on Taiwan and their government to decide. They will, no doubt, weigh the benefits of trade diversification (which Americans have been urging on them) against the inconveniences of trade with Socialist economies and compare both with the gains and annoyances of the extensive trade with the United States. In this calibration a carefully thought-out conception of the ROC's long-term strategic interest in prosperity, political survival, and freedom, and how these are related to the ROC's American connection, would be of inestimable value. As Taiwan's trade surplus difficulties with the United States show, the insulation of economics from politics is easier to verbalize than to carry out. It is much more difficult to keep the two apart when problems arise in economic relationships with Socialist polities.[9]

Some in the United States have suggested that the most effective way to translate the long-term strategic interests of the United States and the Republic of China into present economic reality is to negotiate the establishment, under the authority of the Taiwan Relations Act, of a free trade area (FTA) between the United States and Taiwan, precedents for which exist in the U.S.-Canada and U.S.-Israel FTAs.[10] Others have urged, more modestly, commitment by both sides to trade and investment liberalization measures in a specified time frame.[11] There are also those who oppose the FTA solution on various grounds.[12] I have expressed my hesitations on the subject, for both practical and theoretical reasons, and remain to be persuaded that the FTA idea will accomplish more than the proposal for a memorandum of understanding on the need for and time schedule of trade and investment liberalization.[13]

Finally, while it is imperative to propagate the common long-term interest of the United States and the Republic of China in resolving their economic differences through a progressive removal by both sides of the remaining obstacles to the free flow of trade and investment, and not allowing the deficit problem to become the only determinant of U.S.-ROC relations, the American public and the people on Taiwan must be informed about how much has already been accomplished in mutual trade and investment liberalization. Indeed, of America's major trading partners, Taiwan has been among the more cooperative and forthright in this respect. The reduction and elimination of tariffs and quantitative restrictions, the opening up of the Taiwan market to American banking, insurance, and other services in which the United States is highly skilled and competitive, the crackdown on the infringement by Taiwan businessmen of foreign (mainly American) intellectual property, the "buy American" missions, and many more should be repeatedly put before the American public as evidence of Taiwan's good faith. At the same time, the protectionist thesis, on both sides, should be refuted by patient and meticulously documented argument.

The many steps taken in the past by Taiwan to accommodate the U.S. request for leveling the playing field—steps that some Americans believe to have been taken only under extreme duress to defuse an explosive situation—have been lately buttressed in Taiwan by arguments of economic principle. It is now openly acknowledged by Chinese scholars and officials that the much advertised Taiwan policy of export promotion was, in fact, one of export promotion-cum-import substitution and that the neobullionist drive to pile up dollar-denominated foreign exchange assets that depreciate before one's very eyes, both in domestic currency and in purchasing power, is as irrational today as it had been in the sixteenth century.[14] Because of this recognition of principle, future ROC actions in trade, investment, and the encouragement of domestic consumption will tend to be less in the nature of ad hoc responses to current and shifting emergencies and become more attuned to longer-range themes of a common U.S.-ROC interest. Despite occasional outbursts of nationalistic temper, the record of U.S.-ROC economic relations since the Taiwan Relations Act has been a positive one, marked by an effort at understanding rendered easier by a commitment to a shared set of philosophical postulates. Given the strength and dynamism of the two economies and of the market system to which both belong, there is every reason to be optimistic about the future evolution of the U.S.-ROC relationship.

Bibliography

Cheng, Chu-yuan. "United States–Taiwan Economic Relations: Trade and Investment." *Columbia Journal of World Business,* vol. 21, no. 1. (Spring 1986).

Conference on U.S.-Taiwan Economic Relations. Taipei: Chungwa Institute for Economic Research, 1985.

Flowers, Edward B. "The Pattern of Taiwan's Foreign Direct Investment in the United States." Paper presented at the Annual Meeting of the North American Economics and Finance Association, Boston Park Plaza Hotel, March 10–12, 1988.

Lasater, Martin D., ed. *U.S.-Republic of China Economic Issues: Problems and Prospects.* The Heritage Lectures, no. 150. Washington, D.C.: Heritage Foundation, 1988.

Pye, Lucian W. "Taiwan's Development and Its Implications for Beijing and Washington." *Asian Survey,* vol. 26, no. 6 (June 1986), pp. 611–29.

"ROC-US Trade: 1987 in Review." *Free China Journal,* December 14, 1987.

Simon, David. "Recent Trade Law Issues between the United States and the Republic of China." Paper presented at the 29th Annual Meeting of the American Association for Chinese Studies, Washington, D.C., October 24, 1987.

Stoltenberg, Clyde D. "Republic of China Export Incentives and U.S. Countervailing Duty Law." Paper presented at a Conference on United States–Republic of China Relations, University of California, Berkeley, November 2–4, 1987.

Wheeler, Jimmy W., and Perry L. Wood. *Beyond Recrimination: Perspectives on U.S.-Taiwan Trade Tensions.* Indianapolis, Ind.: Hudson Institute, 1987.

Wu, Chung-lih. "Some Measures to Promote a More Balanced Bilateral Trade Relationship between the ROC and the USA—Economic and Political Implications." *Economic Review,* The International Commercial Bank of China, Taipei, no. 241 (January–February 1988), pp. 5–20.

Wu, Yuan-li. "U.S.-Taiwan Trade Relations and the U.S. Dollar–New Taiwan Yuan Exchange Rate." Paper, Hoover Institution, October 23, 1987.

17

The Hong Kong Agreement and Its Impact on the World Economy

Jane said passionately: "What's needed is a new heaven and a new earth! And you sit there eating kidneys!?"
AGATHA CHRISTIE, An Overdose of Death

To Lord Palmerston in the mid-nineteenth century, Hong Kong was "a barren island with hardly a house upon it," and perhaps also the added inconvenience that there was nowhere to play cricket.[1] Some hundred years later, after the Japanese imperial armies had finished with it, Hong Kong was "a run-down, war-damaged, pre-industrial society with no very evident future."[2] Sixteen years after that, in 1961, with a half-million refugees from Communist China and many more on the way, it was "dirty, overcrowded, often very thirsty, and obviously fighting hard for 'a place in the sun.'"[3] More recently, Hong Kong has been described as "sometimes chaotic and always opportunist . . . [It] is at all levels . . . permeated with the idea of working and making money. . . . There is not much sympathy or public support for those who do not or cannot work."[4] In the words of one of its native sons, Hong Kong is "a money-making machine."[5] It is that, but it is also more than that.

To the student of politics, it is a singular colonial city state, which, when compared with most postcolonial states, splendidly illustrates Joan Robinson's proposition that "the misery of being exploited by capitalists is nothing compared to the misery of not being exploited at all."[6] It is a Chinese city with British law and, more important, the British instinct for the rule of law. For the humanist it is not just a place where, if we had a hedonimeter, it would register—on a scale of 0 to 10—Hong Kong man at 9.9. It is also a city of refugees, the largest of its kind in the world: of family

276

loyalties and sacrifices, not just of competition but of that other indispensable ingredient of the free competitive society, voluntary cooperation.

For the economist Hong Kong is the nearest living thing to Adam Smith's "obvious and simple system of natural liberty," or laissez faire, a credit to the idea of the competitive market and the presumption against government involvement in what Alfred Marshall has called "the ordinary business of life."[7] Although the Hong Kong phenomenon is not as simple and obvious as it is sometimes made out to be, it is still the most obvious and simplest of the lot.[8] Under the Hong Kong government's policy of active nonintervention, the greater part by far of the ordinary business of life is left to individuals and families to do with as they please. The government has limited its actions to the three duties of the sovereign listed in the *Wealth of Nations* and the fourth duty added, curiously enough, by Milton Friedman.[9] These are protection of society from the violence and invasion of other independent societies; protection of every member of the society from the injustice or oppression of every other member of it, or the duty of establishing an exact administration of justice; the provision of "public works," which might not "be for the interest of any individual or small number of individuals to erect or maintain . . . though it may frequently do much more than repay it to a great society"; and, the Friedman duty, protection of members of the community who cannot be regarded as responsible individuals.[10] Even the harsher critics of the Hong Kong government would, I think, agree that these four duties, quite narrowly interpreted, have been discharged in an exemplary manner over the years, under the most trying conditions. While the private sector has had its share of disorder and crime and the public sector its scandals, by and large it has been an orderly society with an administration both apolitical and relatively uncorrupt.[11] It will be difficult to replicate this combination.

Under this benevolent nonrule, where "every man . . . [is] left perfectly free to pursue his own interest his own way, and to bring his industry and capital into competition with those of any other man," Hong Kong has grown and prospered.[12] With refugees from China arriving in staggering numbers, it has, in the 1960s and 1970s, increased its per capita gross national product (GNP) at an average annual rate of 7 percent, surpassed in the whole (non–oil-exporting) world only by Singapore, with 7.4 percent. By 1987 its per capita GDP (gross domestic product) reached $8,070, putting it among those the World Bank calls "high income economies," roughly on par with New Zealand. In those terms, Hong Kong is the second most materially comfortable place in Asia, well behind Japan ($15,760 GNP in 1987) but right in front of Singapore ($7,940 GNP in 1987). By comparison, Communist China's per capita GNP in 1987 was $290, comparable to Somalia or Togo.[13]

Data on the distribution of income and wealth in Hong Kong are largely, but not altogether, impressionistic. The impression conveyed by one long-time observer is that

> The contrast between the lives of the wealthy and the lives of the poor is very great, and this contrast is unusually evident in Hong Kong where there are many people and little room, so that no one can hide himself away or separate himself from his fellow citizens for very long. But although the contrast is obvious, it is not so extreme or disagreeable as in many countries. On the one hand the rich are rarely idle; and on the other poverty is seldom abject or degrading. . . . Between the new and the old and the rich and the poor there is an enormous volume of plain but evidently quite tolerable living, geared to modern patterns of work and consumption.[14]

Less impressionistic investigations suggest that income distribution in Hong Kong has been relatively equitable: relative even to the more redistributively inclined industrial market economies like Britain and France.[15] The findings of technical income distribution analysis for Hong Kong are indirectly confirmed by the leading social indicators, such as life expectancy, infant mortality, calorie intake, education, adult literacy, and the physical quality of life index, all of which have shown dramatic improvement since the early 1960s.[16]

Hong Kong's movement toward middle-class prosperity among the nations of the world has not only been rapid and comparatively equitable but also modern, as export-oriented industrialization has progressively emphasized higher value added through increasing intensity of skills and rising technological level ("going up market," as this is sometimes called). In this way Hong Kong has managed to keep a step or two ahead of the competition on the world market coming from the low-income economies, which are now in the cheap garments and plastic flowers business, whereas Hong Kong increasingly works for the fashion houses of Europe and America and is producing fairly complex electronics. Hong Kong's economy has also been modernized by its expanding tertiary sector, including the provision of sophisticated banking, financial, and professional services. In 1980 manufacturing contributed 22 percent of Hong Kong's gross domestic product (GDP); transport, financial, real estate, and business services, 27 percent; the distributive and catering trades, 23 percent; and ownership of premises, 10 percent.[17] In short, "services" account for 60 percent of GDP.

Looked at from a different, causal angle, this modern economic performance is attributable largely to the unfettered exercise of choice by private economic agents. This freedom and the pressures that go with it have given Hong Kong a flexibility and a quickness of response to changing conditions in the world market that are without equal.[18] They have also contributed importantly to the nervousness, speculativeness, and volatility of the economy and its very erratic upward course.[19]

The tension in the Hong Kong psyche bears significantly on the city's future. Of course, fascination with risk, speculative activity, the cycles of exuberance and anxiety, impatience, and frayed nerves are among the facts of life of any free market. In Hong Kong they are merely carried to something like near extreme. The people there, it has been said, have "difficulty finding middle ground between smugness and panic."[20] If Hong Kong is, as some have suggested, money and if money is confidence, then the slightest change in the complex and delicate pattern of factual information, rumor, and interpretation on which confidence rests will have instant large multiplier effects on decisions to consume, save, invest, stay put, or leave for more congenial climes.[21] Like its owners, big money is extremely mobile. It is the perception of events by financial and mercantile decision makers, both domestic and foreign, that is a key determinant of Hong Kong's economic viability in the future. Although domestic and foreign money work in tandem, it is the domestic component of the combination that is the more influential, if simply by reason of numbers. Only 10 percent of investment in Hong Kong is foreign.[22] The rest is local Chinese money, much of it big. Practically all local Chinese money belongs to people who either are themselves refugees from China or are descended from refugees. This cannot but influence the perception of events, and hence Hong Kong's economic future.[23]

Hong Kong and the World Economy

Thus far we have concentrated on the meaning and significance of Hong Kong to itself: as a place to live, work, and make money in. But what does Hong Kong mean to the outside world? How important is it in this wider context?

Hong Kong's merchandise trade with the outside world in 1987 was 265 percent of Hong Kong's gross domestic product.[24] Hong Kong exports about 98 percent of what it manufactures.[25] It is one of the top twenty trading countries in the world. Its exports exceed those of China, which has 200 times more people and 9,600 times more territory. It is the world's largest exporter of garments, plastic toys, and watches and among the world's larger exporters of electronic products (transistor radios, cassette recorders, computer memory systems, calculators, transistors, circuits, semiconductors, electronic modules, TV games, and assembled TV sets),[26] photographic equipment, textile yarns, fabrics, electric household goods, polyvinyl chloride-back materials for use in upholstery, clothing, floor tiles, and indoor paneling, metal manufactures, and travel goods. It has a lively reexport trade in textiles, clothing, precious stones (especially diamonds), watches, clocks, and electric machinery. Its entrepôt trade with China is significant and growing. It is a communications center serving southeast Asia, a major foreign exchange market, and an important regional center for fund management. It is home to a large number of financial and other companies, local and foreign, including 800 American corporations with offices, factories, or joint ventures.[27] It is Asia's leading center for the setting of precious stones and one of the world's largest gold markets. And it is, of course, a great tourist city: 3.2 million visitors in 1984, 20 percent of them American and another 20 percent Japanese.[28]

Not included in this impressive, if somewhat promotional, list is Hong Kong's reputation for pirating intellectual property in a perfectly nonchalant and even-handed way. While the press is free and lively, Hong Kong is not otherwise noted for extraordinary literary or artistic accomplishment.

This wide-brush, broad-stroke portrait of tiny Hong Kong as a world-class economic heavyweight is, on closer examination, somewhat deceiving. Hong Kong's permanent case of nerves is not altogether paranoid in origin. It is, on the contrary, rationally justified on at least three grounds, two of which predate the agreement between Britain and China, the third consisting of some troubling questions and uncertainties raised by the agreement itself.

The Preagreement Vulnerability of Hong Kong

In an article commenting on the unenviable situation in which the Mexican middle class finds itself, Mary Walsh, a reporter for the *Wall Street Journal,* says something that without much stretching also applies to Hong Kong: "The rich . . . have the savvy and political clout to stay rich; the poor stay poor no matter what. But the middle class bounces up and down with each new jolt of the economy. Its morale is shot."[29] The fact that Hong Kong has reached an upper-middle income status among the nations of the world, while laudable and fairly unusual, puts it in an ambivalent position. It is not poor enough to elicit the kind of benevolent feelings in the governments of the industrialized nations and world bankers inspired by the likes of Ethiopia and other unfortunate or mismanaged economies, and it is not rich enough to have any kind of credible political or economic clout in world affairs. Its reputation for being a money-making machine does not help: nobody loves a slot machine. The emotions it arouses are anger and resentment when things go wrong, as when the bottom falls out of the local real estate market or when U.S. and Western European textile and garment workers are put out of work by what they and their unions perceive to be unfair Hong Kong competition. In fact, nobody anywhere outside Hong Kong really cares what happens to the place so long as the money is safe and can be profitably turned over or pulled out fast enough. Much investment in Hong Kong, foreign as well as domestic, is relatively short term: it can be recouped in five years or less, with handsome profits in the bargain. As one *New York Times* reporter put it, "Almost everybody agrees that there is that much time, perhaps more, before the shadows of 1997 cast a pall."[30] The old Chinese saying, "Drink your wine today and get drunk," applies exceptionally well to Hong Kong before and after the agreement. Naturally, bankers lead the cheering section. A survey of 194 top bank executives in east and southeast Asia, excluding Japan, revealed that 41 percent of them thought Hong Kong would show the "most dramatic banking growth" in the next ten years, exceeded only by Tokyo (57 percent), but well ahead of Singapore (27 percent) and Sydney, Australia (24 percent).[31] (Leading bank executives also thought that Brazil, Mexico, and Poland were good credit risks.) In the meantime, the smart long-term money is finding a niche in the real estate market of Vancouver, British Columbia, which is fast becoming a barometer of the fluctuating state of confidence in Hong Kong.

The second preagreement vulnerability of Hong Kong has been the colony's lack of diversification or, conversely, its reliance for its commodity exports on a relatively few light industrial products, concentration on a few export markets where buyer tastes are fickle, dependence on China for essentials such as water and food, and the large role played by U.S. capital in the colony's foreign investment picture.

Although Hong Kong's economy has diversified, both deepening, with an increase in technical sophistication and skill, and widening, with the growing importance of services in GDP, manufacturing exports continue to be dominated by apparel and textiles; they account for more than two-fifths of total export value and employ two-fifths of the manufacturing labor force. Garment and textile exports are highly recession sensitive, and they are the favorite targets of protectionists in the importing countries. It has been estimated that the "Jenkins Bill," vetoed by President Reagan, would have caused a 12 percent reduction in Hong Kong textile exports to the United States (70 percent for exports not covered by the Multifiber Agreement), resulting in foreign exchange losses to Hong Kong of $1 billion.[32]

Almost half of Hong Kong's commodity exports go to one market: the United States. Another 20 to 30 percent go to the European Economic Community (EEC), mainly to West Germany and the United Kingdom (about 10 percent to each).[33] This is not an altogether satisfactory situation, particularly in view of the large U.S. trade deficit with Hong Kong.[34] It is the kind of thing that raises protectionist ire despite free trade arguments that stress the benefits gained by American consumers from importing goods from Hong Kong cheaply.[35] Hong Kong's import sources are more diversified but are still dominated by China and Japan, each of which contributes roughly one-quarter of Hong Kong's imports, with China's share rising in recent years. Almost half of all foreign investment in Hong Kong is American. Japan is second with about one-quarter, and Britain, a distant third with 6 percent.[36] China's relative share is growing fast. Despite recurrent jitters, foreign capitalist investors, especially Americans, keep coming in. This strikes some Chinese in Hong Kong as the "entrepreneurial equivalent of rats swimming toward a sinking ship."[37] As noted already, however, a good deal of that investment is liquid and short term. Besides, some of the bigger money has already either migrated or diversified. Jardine Matheson has moved its corporate headquarters to Bermuda, and the Hong Kong & Shanghai Bank, which derives 60 percent of its earnings from business in Hong Kong, now has 70 percent of its assets outside the colony, mainly in North America (over 40 percent).[38] So the real direction of the swim is not so clear-cut as might at first appear.

What all this means is that the United States, Western Europe, Japan, and increasingly China are very important to the Hong Kong economy but that the reverse is much less true, except for China. Big trader that it certainly is, Hong Kong is only tenth among America's trading partners (1988). Imports of Wisconsin ginseng, Florida oranges, and cufflinks notwithstanding, Hong Kong is not a significant buyer of U.S. products. It is handy as a stepping stone for U.S. business dealings with China, assuming that Chinese development continues along the lines traced over the past several years by the Deng Xiaoping regime.[39] To the industrialized countries (essentially the United States, EEC, and Japan), Hong Kong is useful and convenient as a place to do business and make fast profits, but it is not indispensable. Garments, plastic dolls, watches, and home computers can be made and imported from elsewhere without much disturbance of comparative advantage. There are many third world countries and a few newly industrialized countries waiting to take over chunks of the Hong Kong trade in goods and services, including offshore banking, should Hong Kong turn from a newly industrialized country, into what Chalmers Johnson calls a collapsing recently industrialized country.[40] The real loser would be China. But China has survived the domestication of Shanghai, although to this day it has not properly understood what has been lost in proletarianizing that international city.[41] If to the industrialized market economies Hong Kong is useful but replaceable, to Hong Kong the industrialized countries—essentially the United States, Western Europe, and Japan—are the world in which Hong Kong has prospered. The alternative world of Communist China is unattractive: a darkness, perhaps under some future less benevolent Chinese Communist leader, a *Kristallnacht*.

Vulnerability under the Agreement

After the British preemptively surrendered to the Chinese in October 1983, things became much more amiable around the negotiating table. With insouciant bonhomie the Chinese now promised almost everything short of a three-week, all-expense-paid vacation in Bermuda for each and every Hong Kong compatriot.[42] "Paper," Stalin once said, "will put up with anything written on it." The terms of the agreement are generally known.[43] On the question of what to make of the assurances contained in the document, there are three schools of thought: those who take the promises seriously, those who think that to believe them is like believing that Calcutta has a brilliant future, and those in between. I am inclined to take the third position. Wu Yuan-li says,

> It is a mistake to look for the economic consequences of the Agreement per se. In a sense, the terms of the September Agreement are really quite irrelevant because no one, not even the PRC (People's Republic of China) leaders, can say for certain today whether the terms will be honored. All they can tell us, and have been telling us, is their present intention to honor these terms if nothing untoward happens. In addition, all parties agree that as of now it is in

the PRC's economic self-interest to leave Hong Kong as it is. Beyond this one cannot really be sure of anything.[44]

Prediction is a dicey affair. "Heaven," says Mencius, "does not speak."

The problem can be broken down into two parts. There is, first of all, the question of the intent by the people now in power in the PRC. And here, I think, one can give them the benefit of the doubt. They are, as Communist leaders go, level-headed and down-to-earth people who perhaps mean it when they say they want to leave Hong Kong much as it is—for a while anyway. It is undoubtedly in the present economic self-interest of the PRC to do so. The economic benefits derived by China from Hong Kong are many, not limited to the earning of a substantial portion of China's hard currencies. As Frank Ching points out, the PRC

> can expect to learn modern management methods, import Western technology, and attract funds for investment. . . . Many foreign companies with offices in China prefer to bring in staff from Hong Kong rather than hire unskilled and unreliable personnel in China or bring in expensive expatriates from their own countries. Tour guides in the major tourist centers in China have had to learn Cantonese because of the big influx of free-spending Hong Kong visitors.[45]

If Hong Kong falters, however, its 5 million people—deprived of their captialist soul (freedom) and their cathedrals of profit emptied of priests (the skilled professionals)—will be a drain on China's meager purse. Since 1979 Hong Kong's trade exchanges with the PRC have risen dramatically and are today roughly one-fourth of Hong Kong's foreign trade turnover. Exports to China rose eighteen times (albeit from miserly levels) and imports four times. The Bank of China has become an increasingly influential presence in the city, slowly displacing the Hong Kong & Shanghai Banking Corporation once known as "the Bank." Beijing money has propped up the failing, locally founded Ka Wah Bank and bailed out Conic Investments Ltd., a major manufacturer of TV sets, radios, and electronic components. Beijing's China Resource Holding Company has invested heavily in Hong Kong businesses and now controls more than 300 firms in the territory, encroaching on the preserves of traditional British "hongs" such as Jardine Matheson and Swire Pacific Ltd. China has a substantial interest in the newly founded Dragon Airlines (Sir Yue-kong Pao, chairman), which competes with Swire's Cathay Pacific Airways and intends to cash in on Beijing's takeover of Hong Kong's Kai Tak airport. China has also invested heavily in the territory's real estate market. It owns some choice properties in downtown Victoria, including the site of the seventy-story Bank of China building designed by I. M. Pei. Hong Kong investors have been active in China's special economic zones, especially Shenzhen.[46] Already Hong Kong's economy is being restructured away from the traditional export industries and redirected from its cosmopolitan orientation toward rustic China. Hong Kong is reverting to its traditional role as an entrepôt and a conduit for China, but on a larger scale.

Even if one grants the sincerity of the PRC's present intent with respect to the economic configuration of Hong Kong, troubling questions remain. Economic self-interest is for Beijing a necessary but not a sufficient condition for what it does. The insufficiency stems from Chinese nationalism and from Leninism. During the early stage of the negotiations, the British and some Hong Kongese let it be bruited about that the most rational way for the Chinese side to demonstrate its grasp of what China's economic self-interest meant would have been to throw a big party at which Chinese sovereignty over Hong Kong would have been vociferously acknowledged and then quietly to let the British run the place as they used to. This sentiment was not lost on Beijing, which interpreted it as implying that Chinese were not capable of running Hong Kong. The raw nerve of Chinese cultural nationalism was touched to the quick, and, as Chalmers Johnson has shown, it right away mousetrapped Hong Kong.[47]

Whatever it was that the British were or were not suggesting, the real point surely is that communism is incapable of running a market economy. Once offended nationalism insinuated itself into the argument, however, the idea of Chinese-sovereignty-cum-British administration was dead. Beijing not only thinks it can run Hong Kong but also argues that without China's help in food, water, labor (albeit of the refugee variety), and the China market, Hong Kong would not have survived. This Sino-centric understanding of international commercial interdependencies is not new. Lin Zexu, Imperial Commissioner at Canton, appointed to that post in 1839 by the Dao Guang emperor, composed a letter to Queen Victoria pointing out Britain's dependence on Chinese rhubarb, without which the English would die of constipation.[48] Margaret Thatcher has been censured for unnecessarily raising the question of sovereignty and so provoking a rebuff. However that may be, politics in command of economics, though not very Marxist, is very Leninist indeed, and Leninism is what counts. Thatcher's gaffe or not, the political issue could not be avoided. It was decisive. In this respect, the Chinese Communist leadership acted in a perfectly orthodox, predictable,

285

and Party-correct way. But what this does is raise serious questions about the validity of the economic self-interest *über Alles* argument. So there is a problem even on the side of China's present intent.

The real problem, however, is on the side of the execution of the intent. And here profound skepticism is in order. First, the actuarial tables are against Deng Xiaoping's presiding for very long over pragmatism in China. His appointees lack the prestige and power bases that Deng possesses. A rather large and strong political constituency does not like what goes on in China today. Within that constituency, the neo-Stalinist conservatives like Chen Yun and Deng Liqun have demonstrated uncommon staying power. In addition, many frustrated Maoists are now lying low.[49] Second, China's track record of policy stability has been, to put it mildly, disquieting. So the present intent could simply be thrown away somewhere down the road in accordance with the ancient law that things that happen once may happen twice.[50] But these are subsidiary matters. Something else, permanent and important, argues persuasively against the future fulfillment of present intent: the nature of the Socialist system.

The Socialist system is constitutionally incapable of leaving people alone. Capitalism (which the agreement promises to keep in Hong Kong for fifty years—why not seventy-five?) is what people do when left alone. Socialism—Stalinist, Maoist, and Dengist—is in different degrees the antithesis of the noble quality of laissez faire. The triumph of an idea over common sense, it will not let things be. The Socialist administrative command economy, which despite some modifications is still what China has, rests on philosophical premises and demands intellectual qualities and temperamental predispositions of its operators that are fundamentally and irreconcilably at variance with the premises, qualities, and temperament of the free market economy. The command economy and the market economy do not mix. "Market socialism," now being touted in China under the appellation of "socialism with Chinese characteristics," is a contradiction in terms, like Australian cuisine.[51] Instead of socialism with Chinese characteristics, what the Chinese are getting on the mainland is mercantilism with corrupt characteristics. So it is not the deliberate repudiation of the agreement's promises that is the main threat to Hong Kong but the ineluctable damage done to markets when Leninists lay their hand on the delicate mechanism that freedom of economic choice represents: "A speck of rat's dirt will spoil a bowl of rice," as the Chinese say.

It is easy to "muck up" Hong Kong. There is a strong case to be made that such mucking up will occur naturally and effortlessly, certainly after 1997, probably before, by reason of the structure and inner dynamics of the Socialist system, despite contrary present intent.[52] The history of Marxism everywhere has been that of a dream destructively applied.

Conclusion

So what happens if Hong Kong is mucked up? From the standpoint of the world economy, nothing much. It will be an inconvenience. Other great business and financial city states disappeared in the past without pulling the mercantile world down with them. Some newly industrialized countries may benefit, if they are quick enough to pick up the pieces by liberalizing their still rather restrictive financial and banking arrangements. The big loser will be mainland China, but the damage will not be lethal: more of a shame than a loss. The biggest loser will be Hong Kong.

PART FIVE

Conclusion

18
The Transition from Socialism to Capitalism

Like other social organisms, an economic system is an internally logical whole of interdependent, interacting, compatible, integrated institutions and ideas, a holistic operation, not a random collection of parts. Institutions are socially agreed-on and legally recognized and protected ways of doing things: in this instance, of allocating land, labor, capital, and entrepreneurship among competing alternative uses.

Economic, Noneconomic, and Antieconomic Systems

The ideas of an economic system consist of positive and normative theories. Positive theories, or economic analysis, explain the way the system works: what is. Normative ideas, or economic ethics, set down rules of proper conduct: what should be. The requirement of interdependence, interaction, compatibility, and integration applies not only to the system's component institutions but to its positive and normative theories and to the relationship between the system's institutional framework and its explanatory and ethical ideas.

In addition, an economic system functions in a broader context of politics, law, culture, and other systems with which it must act compatibly. The market system, for example, is cosubstantial with the rule of law.

The institutionalized allocative process requires choices, not just of what to produce, how, and for whom, but who the choice makers are, that is, whose preferences prevail. The scarcity relationship between means and ends constitutes the economic problem, and the purpose of an economic system is to address that problem, to alleviate scarcity. Indeed, the fundamental purpose of an economic system is to produce goods that people want at prices they are willing and able to pay. That seems like a straightforward, common-sense proposition; yet history is full of systems that, although called economic, did not address the economic problem at all or did not do so effectively or, in fact, added to rather than subtracted from scarcity. An economic system cannot banish scarcity, of course, merely reduce it. Systems, like those based on Marxism, the normative ideas of which posit a utopian state of earthly plenty and equity, encourage and justify mischievous, even villainous, means (Leninism, Stalinism, Maoism) on the way to an impossible end. Their spotless intentions are sullied in practice. Systems that do not address the problem of relative scarcity are noneconomic. Examples of noneconomic systems include bullionism, which made the piling up of specie synonymous with wealth creation; mercantilism, which focused on the enhancement of the power of the emerging nation-state through regulation and protectionism designed to yield a perpetual positive balance of external trade; and national socialism, a variant of central administrative command, which aimed at maximizing armed force for world conquest in the cause of racial superiority.

Central administrative command planning, or real socialism, does not address the scarcity problem effectively. The system is, thereby, noneconomic. In fact, its ineffectiveness makes scarcity worse. In 1989, meat consumption in Poland was at the level of 1979, pork production at the level of 1973, and milk output at the level of the 1960s. While Poland's plight is severe, it is not atypical. The system produces, as a normal outcome of its operations, chronic shortages of useful goods side by side with permanent surpluses of useless goods—a coexistence of shortage and waste, an endless sellers' market or condition of excess demand. The Hungarian economist János Kornai ascribes this outcome to the financial irresponsibility of Socialist firms or the "soft budget constraint." In the Socialist system no state-owned business unit is subject to the burden of proof. Unlike the market system's private firms, the Socialist enterprise is not obliged to prove its economic viability by making profit within a rational system of opportunity cost prices to continue functioning. According to this view, the economically absurd result is unintended.

Others, for instance the Polish economist Jan Winiecki, see chronic excess demand under socialism as deliberately created. In a regime of chronic excess demand, intermediate and final users are reduced to the status of supplicants. The planning authorities, in accordance with the autocratic political leadership's scale of preferences, can then decide who has access to goods. The sovereignty of allocative choice is removed from consumers and vested in the Communist party elite. Indeed, in the Socialist antieconomic system, both in its Marxist inspiration and in its Leninist-Stalinist practice, buying and selling are largely demonetized and turned into clumsy barter, internally within each country and externally among members of the Socialist international community. "In the traditional Marxian view," says the late J. Wilczynski in his *Comparative Monetary Economics*, "money is the ultimate source of social evil." Access to goods becomes a function of political clout and connections, rather than money. The demonetization of the economy under socialism, where money does not buy goods but political influence and hierarchical status do, is one aspect of the system's regressiveness or antimodernism.

Another aspect of socialism's antimodernism is the system's demonstrated inability to make the transition from extensive to intensive growth. Extensive growth is growth achieved through the addition of production factors of a known technological level, while intensive growth is growth generated by improvements in factor productivity. Such improvements stem from technological innovation of both the engineering and the social kind. UCLA's Ivan Szelenyi thinks that socialism's crisis is neither cyclical nor general but transitional: the system experiences serious problems with shifting from extensive to intensive growth in a maturation process. He believes the problem can be overcome by plastic surgery of the market Socialist "mixed" type.[1] I argue that the problem goes much deeper and is malignant. It derives from a fundamentally flawed view of man's nature and place in society, expressed in Marx's dialectical and historical materialism, and of the economizing process presented in his theory of surplus value, a feel-good theory for aspiring revolutionaries but useless in optimizing resource allocation. This view manifests itself in socialism's antieconomism combined with its antimodernism. Intersystemic grafts cannot cure these deficiencies. The Socialist system, insofar as it grapples with the economic problem, is statically and dynamically inefficient—grossly so. It operates deep inside its production possibility frontier, finds it extremely difficult to move onto the frontier, and is apparently unable to push the frontier outward, that is, to increase its capacity to produce goods over time without any increase in factor inputs. It is, in other words, an economic dead end, a revolution of falling satisfactions.

The reasons for the system's static and dynamic inefficiencies, the high and ultimately fruitless and self-destructive cost of its operations, are embedded in the system's ideas and institutions. The neglect of useful goods—that is, of goods people want—like fresh meat, or any meat for that matter, decent clothing, civilized housing, and consumer durables that actually endure—and the frenetic accumulation of machine tools and such, most of them with military and police applications, are traceable to the perception of the individual human person as a derivative of the group, as a cog. Cogs are not moral beings; they have no civil rights. The individual does not and cannot know what he wants but must be told by the Leninist keepers of the sacred flame what it is that history and society have decreed he should have in the interest of his distant descendants' final dissolution in full communism. It is in essence a theory of the individual as nerd. In the system individuals have ends imposed upon them by an authority they did not freely select and that they do not respect. This misconceived and arrogant approach to the human person finds quantified expression in the Socialist state's *ex ante* pricing. Anything the central planners decide to include in the plan is by definition socially necessary and is assigned a value in the form of a state-set price, irrespective of whether the thing is of any use whatsoever to anyone at all. The more useless things are planned and produced, the higher the growth rate measured in such worthless prices, and the greater the waste and the lunacy of it all.

The second of several fundamental theoretical errors of socialism is the assumption about the nature of the economy, a fatal conceit pointed out by Friedrich A. von Hayek. The mistaken assumption is that a rational complex structure can be deliberately constructed at all, that one can dispense with the "natural, spontaneous, and self-ordering process of [market type] adaptation to a greater number of particular facts than any one mind can perceive or even conceive."[2] More eyes see more. In a recent essay, Soviet economist Larissa Popkova-Pijasheva writes:

> The experience of all socialist countries that have done their best to put into effect Marx's idea of a planned economy has corroborated only too well the thesis put forward as early as the 1920s by B. D. Brutkus, who held that the economic problem was in principle insoluble under Marxist socialism. His central idea was that economic life cannot be planned in advance, as the very development of the human organism cannot be, nor can that of any evolutionary process in nature itself.[3]

Popkova's colleague, Vasily Selyunin, writing in the May 1988 issue of *Novy Mir*, agrees:

The problem here lies not in individual mistakes but in the mistaken idea that you can prescribe from above, more or less in detail, the proportions and priorities of economic development and the scale of production of even the most important products.

To this, one might add the impossibility of prescribing from above which are the most important products. According to Soviet economists Nikolai Shmelev and Vladimir Popov in their book *The Turning Point: Revitalizing the Soviet Economy,* in 1987—two years into *perestroika*—Soviet planners were mistaken in predicting the direction of change in eleven out of sixteen cases. In 1986–1987 the average deviation between actual and planned growth ranged between 90 and 167 percent.

Socialism's apparent inability, not so much to generate technological innovation—after all the Rubik cube is a Hungarian invention—but to diffuse and apply innovation to the production of useful civilian goods is an organic part of socialism's intellectual contempt for and restriction of individual free search and discovery, the dialogical learning process as Don Lavoie calls it, which is the mainspring of any dynamic social system.[4] Freedom is the scarcest and most adulterated commodity in a regime of Socialist central planning. Accurate information, which in a dynamic order must be freely and continuously available to all, is regarded by the planners and their hierarchical superiors as state property—that is, their own and their relatives'—to be rationed on a need-to-know basis, the need being determined by themselves. Most of the information that does circulate in the system is defective because either it is based on wrongheaded theories (as, for example, the relative values of goods calculated according to the Marxist notion of socially necessary labor expenditure) or it results from deliberate lying. Individual initiative cannot thrive in what is in essence a militarized peacetime regime obsessed by secrecy. In such a setting to come up with smart, novel ideas—worse still, to try to apply them—is to be charged with insubordination and counterrevolutionary chutzpah; also there is no money in it. And, in any case, money does not count except in the form of hard currencies when it can buy the torch bearers.

Because it misunderstands the individual human person and the complex social orders established by such persons through trial and error, particularly the economic order, socialism motivates people in perverse ways. It adds to the waste and confusion of what was originally conceived to be orderly central planning. Not only does its incentive system encourage antieconomic behavior in economic agents but because Marxist theory and Leninist practice consign the individual to the status of mindless pupil in the school of communism, it morally corrupts whomever it touches. The Socialist system is not only inefficient but morally bankrupt. What in the market system is competitive striving becomes in socialism destructive envy. The Communist ideal of the eradicated ego, empathy, equality, and joyful merging of the individual in the collective becomes in Socialist practice slovenliness, envy, and greed. What decency is left retreats into the cellular societies of family and close friends. "Below the crust of Soviet society," says Soviet economist Andrei Kuteinikov, "an enormous and radicalized mass of poor people seethes with discontent."[5]

In the Kurgan bus factory, workers take partially assembled GAZ 53 trucks from the Gorky car factory and smash them to pieces with sledgehammers, except for the chassis. They then take the chassis, the only part of the trucks they need, and use them to make buses. Why not send just the chassis from Gorky to Kurgan?

> Because the state all-union standards board (GOST) says that trucks have to be made with all the bells and whistles on, even if all that is required is the chassis to make a bus.[6]

"It is much harder to change GOST," says Nikolai Shmelev who reports on this cap-and-bells economics, "than to swing a sledgehammer."[7] This is not some arcane, atypical bit of Marxiana turned into a Marx brothers night at the bus factory farce, but standard Socialist systemic procedure. It is, or should be, known in the literature as rational maximizing behavior within an irrational, allocatively worthless, incentive structure. The planners are not lunatics, nor are the workers and managers at the Kurgan plant stark crazy. It is the system that is deranged, specifically in its heady abstractions that do not comprehend what motivates human beings and so fail to resolve, at the source, the conflicting interests of order givers and order getters.

Now, if the Socialist system because of its erroneous theory and institutions is antieconomic and regressive, what *is* its rationale? Ideological propaganda to the contrary, the fundamental purpose of the Socialist system is the establishment and preservation of the monopoly power ("leading role") and class privileges of the Communist party elite, the top 2–3 percent of the *nomenklatura* and their hordes of retainers. When the system can no longer deliver the goods or safeguard the leading role of the Party elite, genetic decomposition sets in, and the system falls apart.

The Question of Mixture

No system is pure, except at the level of absolute abstraction. All operational real-life systems are "mixed." Elements of the market system are present in central administrative command planning and vice versa. That is not, nor has it ever been, in dispute. The notion of laissez faire, for example, says simply that to do their economizing job well, people should be left alone as a matter of general principle, not in every detail. Like all social organisms, the market system has its share of failures, some of them serious (for example, negative externalities, inability to detect needs not backed by purchasing power, provision of public goods, and so on). Some of them can be overcome only by resort to extramarket means of intervention in the market process. Similarly, absolute command or perfect dictatorship comprises dictatorial failures and bureaucratic errors that have to be remedied by resorting to markets.

Granted this, the crucial question is one of proportions in which the elements of the mixture are combined. A system has to be an internally consistent whole of compatible institutions and ideas operating within a larger symbiotic political, legal, and cultural environment. As an absolute condition the system must have a certain minimum critical mass of such internally consistent institutions and principles that clearly and unequivocally determine the rules of the game. For the system to retain its identity and purpose, systemic borrowings cannot be so great that they paralyze the functioning of the system's own institutions and invalidate its explanatory theories and ethics:

> The real issue is the relative strength of the components of the mixture. Although there are no exact measures, I venture the following proposition. The frequency and intensity of bureaucratic intervention into market processes have certain critical values. Once these critical values are exceeded, the market becomes emasculated and dominated by bureaucratic regulation.[8]

And the same applies to the incursion of market institutions and ideas into bureaucratic command planning. The really big trouble arises at the systemic border, which, despite the efforts of econometricians, mathematical economists, and other surveyors, has not been exactly laid out. This area has been described by visionary explorers in terms as elegant and effusive as they are misconceived and irrelevant, notably by Oskar Lange before he returned at the end of

World War II to Poland from the University of Chicago.[9] It has been given the name of market socialism or Socialist market: an efficient Socialist utopia. In practice, the nearest thing to it is the Yugoslav mess.

Theoretically, market socialism is supposed to be a balanced organic fusion of opposing principles of freedom (the market) and command (the plan), with private and state property rights fairly evenly balanced. The basic idea seems to be that the market mechanism would be used to reduce the high transactions costs associated with central planning but would not generate spontaneous economic processes.[10] This half-and-half construct keeps cropping up in the literature in various guises: as Lange's market socialism, Jaroslav Vanek's involuntary labor managed market economy, Jan Drewnowski's dual preference system, Jan Tinbergen's market planning, and so on. Most proponents of these intellectual hybrids reside in Western market democracies and tend to expend much of their ingenuity on the analysis of market failures. They are impelled to do so, I think, primarily by what they believe to be the market system's ethical shortcomings, its unfairness, and by the unimpeachable desire to prevent nuclear confrontation. They are for the most part people of professional standing and good will, not, as is sometimes alleged, stretch limousine liberals. The same, unfortunately, cannot be said of the many quick-change artists and self-recycled Communist apparatchiks in Eastern Europe and the Soviet Union. Threatened in their rents, sometimes in their lives, by the rising tide of popular wrath, they busy themselves by repackaging the old wares and offer them as cure under the label of humane democratic socialism or socialism with a human face. According to this formula, humanity and democracy are to spread by injecting markets and private property into what through a historical quirk had become inhumane and undemocratic socialism, not at all the way it should have been. This is the opposite of the prescription offered by Western market Socialists and others—John Kenneth Galbraith's parlor Socialists, for example—who hope to humanize and democratize the market system by treating it with a dose of socialism.

In addition to abstract faults with market socialism, the idea cannot work for down-to-earth reasons. First, in the market Socialist model, the government planners are conceived of as legal-rational Weberian types, scholar officials, "reincarnations of Plato's philosophers, embodiments of unity, unselfishness, and wisdom . . . satisfied with doing nothing more than enforcing the 'Rule,' adjusting prices to excess demand."[11] This is nonsense. Bureaucrats are not like that, certainly not Communist party–bred bureaucrats who reach their positions at the end of a process of reverse social Darwinism. At the very least, bureaucracy is compulsively, hyperkinetically interventionist, especially at the micro level. It will go after anything that so much as stirs of its own accord, including prices. Second, market socialism creates, in Kornai's words, a condition of "dual dependence" where firms depend vertically on the bureaucracy and horizontally on their suppliers and customers. In this condition, vertical dependence prevails often as a result of counterstrategies adopted by firms that find state intervention opposed to their interests. Horizontal competition between buyers and sellers becomes politicized bargaining between hierarchical levels of the bureaucracy and between the firm and its administrative superiors. In such a mixture, the odds against optimal resource allocation are about the same as those against a monkey's producing the complete works of Shakespeare by banging away at a typewriter keyboard.

What Kornai calls "Galbraithian socialism," the rage of American liberal literary salons of the 1950s, is the legitimation of the Socialist *status quo ante—ante* the East European people's revolution of 1989:

> [The Galbraithians] justify the dualities of the present system: the coexistence of public and private sectors, bureaucracy and market, large and small firms, provided that the first component in all these pairs has the undisputed upper hand.[12]

The Galbraithian cocktail will do nothing for socialism. Imbibed by capitalism, it will cripple it.

In summary, socialism is an economic failure, because the imposition of an economic design on extended, evolving social orders, with mistaken ideas regarding human beings as moral entities, is simply not feasible. Such errors are translated into clumsy and cruel institutional arrangements that add to scarcity and that in the end fail to ensure even central control and uncontested rule by the Communist party elite, always their main concern. Added to economic and political failure are the system's cultural stodginess and sterility. Attempts to square the circle through halfway market Socialist pseudo-reforms merely add wasted motion to an already enormous accumulation of lost resources and unrealized potential. Readings in Galbraith and his followers can only set one back.

To Market

Socialism cannot deliver the goods. "Even if Stalin had never existed," as *The Economist* put it, "communism stands condemned as a historically unnecessary stage on the road from capitalism to capitalism. It promised the moon. It cannot even deliver a pair of jeans."[13] It would seem that the citizens of Moscow, 30,000 of them on McDonald's opening day, demonstrated that what Russia needs is less Marxism and more Big Macs. It is really that simple. A banner carried at a huge Moscow protest rally on February 4, 1990, read: "72 Years on the Road to Nowhere." There is just so long one can quench thirst by contemplating plums, as the Chinese say. Substituting bads for goods to quench the thirst will not do. In the ten years before Gorbachev (1974–1984) most of the increase in the Soviet Union's national income was attributable to increased sales of vodka. The only remedy is to cross clear over to the market and democracy, to a system of economic and political freedom: all the way, not one-third of the way, or halfway, but all the way across. The movement forward has to be brisk, like the West Germans' in 1948, and one has to have a clear idea where one is going.[14]

There is no need to know the exact topography, however, just the general direction and the destination. While it would be ideal to have a map, a ready-made general theory of systemic transition—and its absence is sometimes cited as a serious obstacle to reform—such a theory is not essential. A more important obstacle is irresolution, which comes partly from bad mental habits acquired through Marxist teaching: a private property phobia and the equating of all price increases with profiteering, of income differences with economic injustice, and of individual initiative and spontaneity with chaos. Socialism's success in befuddling the citizenry, at least temporarily, is reflected in some opinion surveys made when the movement to abandon socialism was young. In the Soviet Union, for example, almost 60 percent of the population thought that the best solution to shortages of consumer goods was administrative rationing. Only 6 percent approved of free pricing, without which there can be no market reform.[15] In December 1989, a poll taken in Czechoslovakia showed that 47 percent wanted their economy to remain state controlled, while 43 percent wanted a mixed economy. Only 3 percent said they favored capitalism, in sharp contrast to the Poles who will have no truck with socialism, mixed or not, but are yet to rid themselves of the Communist establishment in control of the police and the army.[16] Rapid economic deterioration has been changing Russians' minds, however, and taking some of the illusory sheen off Czech Dubčekism.

The transition has to be to market democracy: an economic order determined by voluntary, competitive transactions between buyers and sellers; responsive to accurate, flexible, freely flowing, scarcity price information; under the rule of law, with broad and dominant private property rights, free markets, for goods and factors and free entry and exit; and equipped with fiscal and monetary instruments of mostly indirect, macrointervention by a market-supportive, democratically elected government accountable to its electorate. The transition is not to a rarified, atomistic, Walrasian, rational equilibrium, the market equivalent of Marx's Communist utopia but to a working system that has proved it can both provide sausage and care for the blind. It is even better for flowers than socialism. This working system of advanced democratic capitalism lays heavy store by efficiency, without which the implementation of the system's ethic of gentleness and kindness is hampered and impoverished by waste and unrealized growth potential, and is ultimately unrealizable.

The Socialist countries, without exception, have emphasized—at least since Stalin's death—the ethical imperative of security and equity, that is, protection of its members from physical and social risks and the guarantee of distributional fairness. In the end physical and social security has been provided for most people at levels qualitatively so demeaning as to completely discredit the noble goal. The average Soviet state pension is 84 rubles a month, or $12.50 at the realistic black market exchange rate. Retired members of the *nomenklatura* elite, however, collect pensions of up to 500 rubles a month with access to the privileged distribution channels they had used when working, which is the only way the rubles can buy anything useful.

Advanced democratic capitalism is a system with both large and small firms, but the size distribution of firms does not paralyze interfirm competition. The system has both private and state property, with the property of the state playing a relatively minor role. Responsiveness of firms, including large ones, to domestic and international market prices is generally strong, and the budget constraint of firms is generally hard, that is, persistent losses entail bankruptcy. The government intervenes in the system primarily through indirect macroeconomic means. The interventions are not designed to alter fundamentally the market's *modus operandi* but rather to correct market errors and compensate for market failures. The intervention supports the market system as an allocative device and protects private property, which is indispensable to the functioning of that device. The system does exhibit supply and demand disequilibriums but not chronic shortages. The major problem in this regard is excess supply: the market system is a buyers' market. The principles governing the system are the individual's inherent right to make self-interested decisions; free entry and exit; personal responsibility for decisions; voluntariness of transactions; competition—that is, the presence of alternative courses of action and the absence, with very few and well-defined exceptions, of monopolies, monopsonies, and other concentrations in restraint of production and trade, be they private or public; and the absence of hierarchical relationships.

The transition to such a system must be not only rapid but orchestrated. It has to be a quick thrust along the whole front: the simultaneous and comprehensive recasting of all institutions and ideas. All the critical decisions must be taken away from the planners and vested in autonomous economic agents acting through the market and private property. These decisions concern entry and exit, credit, investment, ouput, and wages. To borrow a Socialist phrase, the *nomenklatura* must be eliminated as a class, not in the Stalinist way, of course, but by pensioning off its members or reforming them through honest labor in the market ("to each according to his marginal productivity"). The many steps that have to be taken simultaneously all hinge on the prior decommunization of the Communist *nomenklatura* as a social category, not just the individual Jaruzelskis, Gysis, and Modrows. This cleansing operation should be like the denazification of West Germany after World War II, only more thorough. The workers' militia must be disbanded and Party cells in factories abolished. The voters must vote out the Party. Otherwise, there will be endless delays, obstructionism, red herrings—like heading for market socialism—and attempts at a comeback. Systemic reform will be turned into aerobics on a treadmill leading nowhere, or worse. Worse would be a return to central administrative command, like China's after the Tiananmen massacre. Winiecki warns that the *nomenklatura* mafia, most of them opportunists whose opportunities ran out with the system, are trying to buy on the cheap, through special channels, the state companies they formerly mismanaged, turn them into private businesses, and themselves into a Socialist bourgeoisie. He calls the process the "enfranchisement of the *nomenklatura*." Others, however, see such enfranchisement as a necessary if sleazy step on the way to a free market economy, a way for the former ruling class out of political defeat.[17]

The transition from socialism to capitalism requires continuous, vigorous pressure from below in support of reform. The ambivalence of popular opinion on capitalism is a passing phenomenon. Decades of Socialist propaganda about the Dickensian evils of private property and free markets have left some mental scars. While theories of market socialism and other in-between states disseminated by concerned Western Marxist professors and others in affluent capitalist countries may for a time throw people off the capitalist road, they will not for long. The great majority of people who have had the misfortune to live under real socialism reject that system in its rotten totality. Their more recent familiarization with the successful and by and large humane economizing process of modern democratic capitalism will ensure that the journey toward market democracy is completed despite the hardships that will inevitably attend it. At the end of the road lies not a utopian vision but a working system that actually delivers the goods without maiming the people.

Notes

CHAPTER 1: FOUNDATIONS OF THE CRISIS

1. Kenneth J. Arrow, *The Limits of Organization* (New York: Norton, 1974), p. 23.

2. *Los Angeles Times*, December 26, 1980.

3. In the absence of the money illusion, that is, if consumers and workers are not fooled by the low prices of often unavailable goods and by pockets stuffed with cash, because they implicitly assign a price to waiting in line and fighting their way to the communal kitchen and bathroom in their home, raising retail prices to market equilibrium levels—that is, telling the truth—could boost labor productivity, since time lost in queueing and devising scenarios of bribery could be put to more productive use in the factory or office.

4. *Economist* (London), January 30, 1982, p. 29. In 1982 state meat prices in Czechoslovakia were raised by 137 percent. In Romania (1982), sugar, rice, cooking oil, and some other state prices of staples were increased by 100 percent. Most blue-collar workers received wage increases averaging 16.5 percent and a 35 percent increase in state child support allowances. *Wall Street Journal*, February 11, 1982.

5. Under the Soviet antiparasite laws, any able-bodied person who is out of work for more than four months in the year is liable to imprisonment of up to two years.

6. Tom Bethell, review of *Karl Marx—Friedrich Engels: Selected Letters* (edited by Fritz J. Raddatz; Little, Brown, 1982). *Wall Street Journal*, February 8, 1982.

7. "Revising Stalin's Legacy," *Wall Street Journal*, July 23, 1980, and "Excerpts from the Trial of a Soviet Dissident," *Wall Street Journal*, January 18, 1982.

8. Anthony Lewis, "Act of Despair," *New York Times*, December 14, 1981.

9. Herberto Padilla, "After 20 Cuban Years," *New York Times*, September 17, 1981.

10. Werner Gumpel, "Die wirtschaftlichen Grenzen des Sowjetstaates" [The Economic Frontiers of the Soviet State] *Politische Studien*, no. 253 (1981), pp. 518–19.

11. For starters, in the early months of 1982, banks in Sweden and France extended $350 million in credits to the USSR for the purchase of industrial

equipment. The credits were reportedly granted on "easy terms." In March 1982, while U.S. commercial banks were becoming hesitant about further involvement in loans to the USSR, a farmers' cooperative bank in Denver lent the Soviets $6.5 million to buy U.S. grain. Poland's 1981 debt ($2.4 billion due that year) was rescheduled over seven and one-half years in April 1982.

CHAPTER 2: REFORM, FREEDOM, DEMOCRACY

1. Leonard Schapiro, *Russian Studies* (London: Collins Harvill, 1986), p. 31.

2. Paul Johnson, *Modern Times* (New York: Harper & Row, 1983), p. 84.

3. Leszek Kolakowski, "Marxist Roots of Stalinism," in Robert C. Tucker, ed., *Stalinism: Essays in Historical Interpretation* (New York: Norton, 1977), pp. 283–98.

4. The Socialist centrally planned economy may be defined in the following way: the setting of mandatory general and specific goals by government officials regarding production, exchange, and distribution, as well as the outlining of procedures for attaining those goals (the goals and procedures being expressed in physical-technical and financial terms and enforced primarily by administrative means). All significant means of production are government owned, either directly (nationalization) or indirectly (nominal cooperativization). Jan S. Prybyla, *Market and Plan under Socialism: The Bird in the Cage* (Stanford: Hoover Institution Press, 1987), p. 4.

5. Janos Kornai, *Economics of Shortage* (Amsterdam: North-Holland, 1980). After forty years of socialism, bread is rationed in Romania and tree bark is an officially recommended dietary supplement. Manuela Hoelterhoff, "Romania's Restructuring: No Perestroika," *Wall Street Journal*, May 19, 1988, p. 34.

6. The *rentier* class argument is made by Jan Winiecki, "Why Economic Reforms Fail in the Soviet-Type System: A Property Rights-based Approach," Seminar paper no. 374 (1986), Institute of International Economic Studies, University of Stockholm.

7. David K. Shipler, "In Soviet, Change Struggles to Emerge," *New York Times*, May 8, 1988.

8. *Chronicle*, Emperor Han Gaozi, 202–195 B.C. I owe this quotation to Lyman Miller.

9. Jan S. Prybyla, "The Soviet-Type Economic System: Strong or Weak?" *Issues & Studies* (Taipei), vol. 22 (November 1986), pp. 80–96, esp. pp. 86–96 (on the public security and military economies under socialism).

10. Igor Birman, "The Soviet Economy: Alternative Views," *Russia*, vol. 12 (1986), pp. 60–74.

11. Joseph S. Berliner, "Managing the USSR Economy: Alternative Models," *Problems of Communism*, vol. 32 (January–February 1983), pp. 40–56.

12. Birman, "The Soviet Economy," pp. 66, 70.

13. Translation of L. Popkova's letter to *Novy Mir* may be found in *Foreign Broadcast Information Service–USSR (FBIS-USSR)*, May 13, 1987, Annex. Similar, if not identical, sentiments have been expressed by others, for example, Nikolai Shmelyov (*Novy Mir,* June 1987).

14. Tadeusz Kowalik, *On Crucial Reform of Real Socialism,* Forschungs-berichte, no. 122 (Wiener Institut für Internationale Wirtschaftsvergleiche, 1986), p. 66. "If modern communist societies are to develop, it is an elementary condition that the function of the state should be drastically limited, command planning be given up, hierarchically structured rigid economic links be replaced by the money-commodity relations." Ibid., p. 52. Kowalik works at the Institute of History of Science Education and Technology of the Polish Academy of Science.

15. Oleg Bogomolov, "The World of Socialism on the Road of Perestroika," *Kommunist* (November 1987), p. 99. Bogomolov is director of the Institute of the Economy of the World Socialist System.

16. James Bovard, "The Hungarian Illusion," *World & I* (April 1987), p. 125.

17. Mark D'Anastasio, "Dwayne Andreas Gains an Apparent Position as Kremlin Favorite," *Wall Street Journal,* December 26, 1986. Compare "German Banks Increase Loans to Soviets and Introduce Moscow to Bond Markets," *Wall Street Journal,* May 16, 1988.

Chapter 3: The Fifth Modernization and the Other Four

1. Amnesty International Report, August 13, 1987, as reported in the *New York Times,* August 14, 1987.

2. *Beijing Review,* June 29, 1987, p. 15, reporting on Deng's remarks made on December 30, 1986. This report looks like a cleaned-up version of Deng's views on this matter reported by the *International Herald Tribune* on January 14, 1987: "Look at Wei Jingsheng. We put him behind bars and the democracy movement died. We haven't released him, but that did not raise much of an international uproar."

3. G. Warren Nutter, *Political Economy and Freedom* (Indianapolis, Ind.: Liberty Press, 1983), p. 50. The "minimum principle" of classical liberalism has been that "government should exercise the minimum of coercion required to minimize coercion."

4. "Historically, modernization is the process of change towards those types of social, economic, and political systems that have developed in western Europe and North America from the seventeenth century to the nineteenth." S. N. Eisenstadt, *Modernization, Protest, and Change* (Englewood Cliffs, N.J.: Prentice-Hall, 1966), p. 1.

5. Leonard Schapiro, *Russian Studies* (London: Collins Harvill, 1985), p. 31.

6. Jacques Raiman in the *Wall Street Journal,* June 15, 1988.

7. Adam Smith, *The Theory of Moral Sentiments* (1759) (New York: Augustus M. Kelley, Reprints of Economic Classics, 1966), p. 337.

8. See Irving Kristol, "Adam Smith and the Spirit of Capitalism" and "Rationalism in Economics," *Reflections of a Neoconservative* (New York: Basic Books, 1983).

9. Peter L. Berger, "The Market, Morals and Manners," *Wall Street Journal,* July 14, 1988. See also his *The Capitalist Revolution: Fifty Propositions about Prosperity, Equality, and Liberty* (New York: Basic Books, 1988).

10. János Kornai, *Economics of Shortage* (Amsterdam: North-Holland, 1980).

11. Jan S. Prybyla, "Socialist Economic Reform, Political Freedom, and Democracy," *Comparative Strategy,* vol. 7, no. 4 (1988).

12. *Economist* (London), April 30, 1988.

13. *Far Eastern Economic Review,* January 8, 1988, p. 118.

14. *Plan Econ Report,* vol. 5, nos. 19–20, May 19, 1989, p. 1.

15. Question: . . . would you say that resource misallocation is a serious problem in the Hungarian economy?

Answer: This must be the case, but this is difficult to evaluate because we cannot calculate the opportunity cost.

John B. Hall, "Plan Bargaining in the Hungarian Economy: An Interview with Dr. Laszlo Antal," *Comparative Economic Studies,* vol. 28, no. 2 (Summer 1986), p. 58.

16. Claude Aubert, "Rural Capitalism versus Socialist Economics? Rural-Urban Relationships and the Agricultural Reforms in China" (Communication for the Eighth International Conference on Soviet and East European Agriculture, University of California-Berkeley, August 7–10, 1987, mimeographed), pp. 11–12.

17. *Economist,* May 21, 1988.

18. *New York Times,* July 8, 1988, and June 29, 1988.

19. Smith, *The Theory of Moral Sentiments,* p. 337.

20. K. C. Yeh, "Macroeconomic Changes in the Chinese Economy during the Readjustment," *China Quarterly,* no. 100 (December 1984), table 6, p. 711.

21. *New York Times,* June 24, 1988.

22. Arthur Koestler, *The Invisible Writing* (Boston: Beacon Press, 1954), p. 59.

23. *Wall Street Journal,* October 14, 1987.

24. *New York Times,* June 8, 1988.

25. F. A. Hayek, *Law, Legislation and Liberty* (Chicago: University of Chicago Press, 1976).

26. Because this [bourgeois] society proposes to make the best of this world, for the benefit of ordinary men and women, it roots itself in the most worldly of common human motivations: self-interest. It assumes that, though only a few are capable of pursuing excellence, everyone is capable of recognizing and pursuing his own self-interest. This 'democratic' assumption about the equal potential of human nature, in this limited respect, in turn justifies a market economy in which each individual defines his own well-being, and illegitimizes all the paternalistic economic theories of previous eras. One should emphasize, however, that the pursuit

of excellence by the few—whether defined in religious, moral, or intellectual terms—is neither prohibited nor inhibited. Such an activity is merely interpreted as a special form of self-interest, which may be freely pursued but can claim no official status. Bourgeois society also assumes that the average individual's conception of his own self-interest will be sufficiently 'enlightened'—that is, sufficiently far-sighted and prudent—to permit other human passions (the desire for community, the sense of human sympathy, the moral conscience, etc.) to find expression, albeit always in voluntaristic form" (Kristol, *Reflections of a Neoconservative*, p. 29).

27. *Economist*, May 7, 1988.

28. On the theoretical shortcomings of the market Socialist model, see Don Lavoie, "The Market as a Procedure for Discovery and Conveyance of Inarticulate Knowledge," *Comparative Economic Studies*, vol. 28, no. 1 (Spring 1986), pp. 1–18.

29. Jan S. Prybyla, *Market and Plan under Socialism: The Bird in the Cage* (Stanford, Calif.: Hoover Institution Press, 1987).

30. Ludwig von Mises, *Human Action*, 3d rev. ed. (Chicago: Henry Regnery, 1963), p. 195; Larissa Popkova, letter to *Novy Mir*, May 1987 (translation in *Foreign Broadcast Information Service–USSR*, May 13, 1987, Annex).

31. Kristol, *Reflections of a Neoconservative*, p. 167.

32. *The Thirteenth Party Congress and China's Reforms* (Beijing: Beijing Review Publications, 1987), p. 31.

33. *New York Times*, July 8, 1988.

34. *The Thirteenth Party Congress*, pp. 46–47.

35. "Deng Xiaoping on Upholding the Four Cardinal Principles," March 30, 1979, *Beijing Review*, February 9, 1987, p. 31.

36. Jan S. Prybyla, "Mainland China and Hungary: To Market, to Market . . . ," *Issues & Studies*, vol. 23, no. 1 (January 1987), pp. 43–85; *Market and Plan under Socialism: The Bird in the Cage*, chap. 10, "Neoclassical Liberal Plan"; *Issues in Socialist Economic Modernization* (New York: Praeger, 1980).

37. Edward A. Gargan, "As China's Economy Grows, So Grows Official Corruption," *New York Times*, July 10, 1988.

38. Edward A. Gargan, "China Nods Sagely at Soviet Changes," *New York Times*, July 4, 1988.

39. Jan S. Prybyla, "The Hundred Flowers of Discontent," *Current History*, vol. 80, no. 467 (September 1981), pp. 254–57, 274.

40. *The Thirteenth Party Congress*, p. 35. Compare this with the statement by Oleg Bogomolov, one of Mr. Gorbachev's spokesmen for "socialist pluralism": "Socialist pluralism is not the notorious 'free play' of political forces, but an expansion of the platform of national unity under the leading role of the party." *Kommunist* (1987), p. 99.

41. *Beijing Review*, June 29, 1987, p. 15.

42. *Beijing Review*, February 9, 1987, p. 32 (Speech of March 30, 1979). See also, "In reality, without the Chinese Communist Party, who would organize the socialist economy, politics, military affairs and culture of China, and who would organize the four modernizations? In the China of today

we can never dispense with leadership by the Party and extol the spontaneity of the masses," p. 33; and "While propagating democracy, we must strictly distinguish between socialist democracy on the one hand and bourgeois individualist democracy on the other. We must link democracy for the people with dictatorship over the enemy, and with centralism, legality, discipline and the leadership by the Communist Party," p. 35.

43. Paul Johnson, *Modern Times* (New York: Harper & Row, 1983), p. 581.

CHAPTER 4: MAN AND SOCIETY IN CHINA

1. Alexander Orlov, *The Secret History of Stalin's Crimes* (New York: Random House, 1953), pp. 129–30.

CHAPTER 5: STRONG OR WEAK?

1. The government that owns the means of production and distribution is totalitarian: the product of a nonelectoral, self-nominating, self-perpetuating process or imposed by outside force.

2. It is legitimate to compare (1) ideal systems (theoretical systemic constructs) among themselves; (2) actual economic systems among themselves; and (3) an actual system with its own ideal. It is not legitimate to compare an actual economic system with the ideal construct of a different system. Gregory Grossman, *Economic Systems,* 2d ed. (Englewood Cliffs, N.J.: Prentice-Hall, 1974), p. 4.

3. The two groups are largely expositional and are not cast in concrete. Technological innovation and diffusion, for example, were in the past put in the less conventional group, but no longer. See Paul R. Gregory and Robert C. Stuart, *Soviet Economic Structure and Performance,* 3d ed. (New York: Harper & Row, 1986), pp. 363–64.

4. On the influence of these "environmental ecosystems" on economic modernization in China, see the excellent study by Richard Baum, "Science and Culture in Contemporary China: The Roots of Retarded Modernization," *Asian Survey,* vol. 22, no. 12 (December 1982), pp. 1160–86.

5. Kanji Haitani, *Comparative Economic Systems: Organizational and Managerial Perspectives* (Englewood Cliffs, N.J.: Prentice-Hall, 1986), p. 7. Add to this the difficulty of finding acceptable measures of performance under each heading.

6. Other reasons for disagreement and controversy include ideological preference. This seems to be the case with Victor Perlo, as in his and Ellen Perlo's *Dynamic Stability: The Soviet Economy Today* (New York: International Publishers, 1980). For the occasional acrimony, see Frank Durgin's extraordinarily discourteous review of Marshall I. Goldman's *USSR in Crisis: The Failure of an Economic System* (New York: W. W. Norton, 1983), in the *ACES Bulletin,* vol. 26, no. 2–3 (Summer–Fall 1984), pp. 99–110; Goldman's reply, ibid., pp. 111–16.

7. Among the more qualified analyses is Joseph S. Berliner's "Managing the USSR Economy: Alternative Models," *Problems of Communism*, vol. 32, no. 1 (January–February 1983), pp. 40–56.

8. In addition to Marshall Goldman's book mentioned above, the thesis of systemic collapse is implicit in, among others, Sven Rydenfelt's *A Pattern of Failure* (New York: Harcourt, Brace, Jovanovich, 1984); and in my *Market and Plan under Socialism: The Bird in the Cage* (Stanford, Calif.: Hoover Institution Press, 1987); and "The Dawn of Real Communism: Problems of COMECON," *Orbis*, vol. 29, no. 2 (Summer 1985), pp. 387–402. Compare, "Listen to a Polish intellectual describe Mikhail Gorbachev's efforts to knock Soviet communism into shape. 'He is perched on a dead whale. No matter how hard he tries, he can't move it. He can whip it, he can yell at it, he can tell it to be more disciplined, and he can make it stop drinking, but it is still a dead whale.'" Frederick Kempe in the *Wall Street Journal*, July 3, 1986.

9. Jan S. Prybyla, "Mainland China and Hungary: To Market, to Market . . ." (Paper presented at the Fifteenth Sino-American Conference on Mainland China, Taipei, Taiwan, June 12, 1986); chap. 7 in this volume.

10. Mervyn Matthews, *Poverty and Patterns of Deprivation in the Soviet Union*, Berkeley-Duke Occasional Papers on the Second Economy in the USSR, paper no. 6, June 1986, p. iii; ibid.,*Poverty in the Soviet Union* (London: Cambridge University Press, 1986).

11. Gregory Grossman, *The Second Economy in the USSR and Eastern Europe: A Bibliography*, Berkeley-Duke Occasional Papers on the Second Economy in the USSR, paper no. 1, September 1985, and subsequent papers.

12. *Economist*, May 27, 1982, p. 40; *Wall Street Journal*, June 11, 1982; "The Black Economy," *Newsweek* (International Edition), June 30, 1986, pp. 20–26.

13. *New York Times*, December 16, 1983; and August 7, 1983; W. T. Lee, "Soviet Military Spending Still Growing," *National Security Record* (Heritage Foundation, Washington, D.C.), no. 91 (May 1986), p. 5.

14. Mikhail Augursky, *The Soviet Military-Industrial Complex* (Jerusalem: Magnes Press, the Hebrew University, Jerusalem Papers on Peace Problems 31, 1980), p. 25. Some other useful sources: Abraham S. Becker, *The Burden of Soviet Defense. A Political-Economic Essay*, Rand Corporation, R-2752-AF, October 1981; Michael Checinski, "The Military-Industrial Complex: Planned and Non-Planned Consequences of CMEA Defense Spending," in *The CMEA Five-Year Plans (1981–1985) in Perspective* (Brussels: NATO Economics and Information Directorates, 1982); ibid., *The Military-Industrial Complex in the USSR: Its Influence on R&D and Industrial Planning and on International Trade*, no. AZ2303, Stiftung Wissenschaft and Politik, Ebenhausen, FRG, September 1981; Steven Rosefielde, ed., *World Communism at the Crossroads: Military Ascendancy, Political Economy, and Human Welfare* (Boston: Martinus Nijhoff, 1980); David Holloway, "Innovation in the Defense Sector," in R. Amann and J. M. Cooper, eds., *Industrial Innovation in the Soviet Union* (New Haven, Conn.: Yale University Press, 1982), pp. 276–367; Henry S. Rowen and

Charles Wolf, Jr., eds., *The Future of the Soviet Empire* (San Francisco, Calif.: Institute for Contemporary Studies, 1986).

15. A dissenting view is presented by Robert Campbell, "Management of Spillovers from Soviet Space and Military Programs," *Soviet Studies*, vol. 23, no. 4 (1972).

16. Augursky, *Soviet Military-Industrial Complex*, p. 31.

17. Robert Delfs, "Swords into Bicycles," *Far Eastern Economic Review*, August 25, 1983, pp. 91–92.

18. Augursky, *Soviet Military-Industrial Complex*, p. 31.

19. Ibid., p. 21.

20. In 1984, in even the relatively liberal Hungarian plan, legally sanctioned private investment opportunities were minimal. A private investor could acquire up to five kinds of utility and construction bonds at six to eight years maturity and an annual yield of 7–11 percent. The total value of the bonds so available, however, was under 300 million forints, or less than 0.04 percent of recorded savings deposits in Hungary (which are probably vastly understated). Rudolf L. Tokes, "Hungarian Reform Imperatives," *Problems of Communism*, vol. 33, no. 5 (September–October 1984), p. 7. As of mid-1986, only about 30,000 people in Hungary bought such bonds. There are some interesting wrinkles. To help modernize its telephone equipment, the Hungarian Postal Administration offered bonds paying 10 percent. The purchaser was also given a guarantee that his telephone would be installed within two years, instead of the usual ten—the normal waiting time. Since the guarantee applies only to the original bond purchaser, the price of the bond on the secondary bond market dropped by one-fourth of its issue price. Michael T. Kaufman, "Hungarians Clip Coupons and Call It Communism," *New York Times*, July 8, 1986.

21. Prybyla, "Mainland China and Hungary," note 9.

22. According to Augursky, *Soviet Military-Industrial Complex*, pp. 11–12, the military receives: (1) materials of the highest quality; (2) parts banned by special regulation for civilian production; (3) more generous funds for the acquisition of new equipment; and (4) a higher wages fund.

23. Aron Katsenelinboigen and Herbert S. Levine, "Some Observations on the Plan-Market Relationship in Centrally Planned Economies," *Annals of the American Academy of Political and Social Science*, no. 434 (November 1977), p. 194. See also the discussion of R & D in the Soviet military economy by Augursky, *Soviet Military-Industrial Complex*, pp. 10–11.

24. "Secrecy requirements mandate that the real names of military products may not appear in writing, even those stored in the KGB department, and that they should not be pronounced anywhere, even at closed meetings. . . . The general intent is that the employees of one department be unaware of what employees in other departments are doing. . . . Every Soviet scientific and technical journal . . . requires that every author furnish a certificate issued by experts of his own organization vouching that the publication does not reveal any secrets, including patented information, and a note from the author himself guaranteeing that no secrets are contained

in his article. . . . In the military industry the [clearance] procedure lasts several months." Augursky, *Soviet Military-Industrial Complex*, p. 15.

CHAPTER 6: CHANGES IN CHINA AND THE SOVIET UNION

1. Jan S. Prybyla, "China's Economic Reforms," *Journal of Comparative Social and Economic Systems* (Beijing), no. 3 (1988), pp. 36–40.

2. "The Other Gorbachev," *Economist* (London), December 10, 1988, p. 9.

3. *The Thirteenth Party Congress and China's Reforms* (Beijing: Beijing Review Publications, 1987), pp. 31, 32, 35.

4. Since in an economy of chronic shortage money is not readily convertible into goods, narrowing down money income inequalities is meaningless. What really counts is access to desirable goods, and this is a function of political connections and hierarchical positioning, which are very unequally distributed.

5. Peter Gumbel, "Soviets Rethink Plan for Reform of Economy," *New York Times*, December 2, 1988.

6. Gertrude Schroeder, "Anatomy of Gorbachev's Economic Reform," *Soviet Economy*, vol. 3, no. 3 (1987), pp. 219–41.

CHAPTER 7: REFORM IN CHINA AND HUNGARY

1. For discussion of plan and market systems, see chaps. 1 and 2.

2. "Since 1956, when compulsory deliveries to the state were abolished, government control of agricultural producer cooperatives [in Hungary] has been indirect, rather than direct, yet its influence remains considerable. The state maintains control of prices of outputs and inputs; and while cooperatives aim at profit maximization and can use internally-generated funds for expansion, large investment projects require credit which, again, is subject to state control. By not cooperating with the government and ignoring its requests, the cooperative might lose its 'creditworthiness' and therefore be unable to acquire the chronically scarce capital goods its needs." A. L. Muller, "The Hungarian Socialist Market Economy (Review Note)." Review of P. G. Hare, H. K. Radice, and N. Swain, *Hungary: A Decade of Economic Reform* (London: Allen & Unwin, 1981), in *The South African Journal of Economics*, vol. 50, no. 3 (1982), p. 274.

3. Támás Bauer, "The Hungarian Alternative to Soviet-Type Planning," *Journal of Comparative Economics*, vol. 7, no. 3 (September 1983), p. 305.

4. Bela Balassa, *Reforming the New Economic Mechanism in Hungary* (Washington, D.C.: World Bank, Staff Working Papers no. 534, 1982), pp. 1–11; Laszlo Racy, "On the New Price System," *Eastern European Economics*, vol. 12, no. 1 (Fall 1981), pp. 49–69.

5. János Kornai, "Hungary's Reform: Halfway to the Market," *Challenge* (May–June 1985), p. 31; Bauer, "The Hungarian Alternative to Soviet-Type Planning," p. 312.

6. János Kornai, "The Dilemmas of a Socialist Economy: The Hungarian Experience," *Cambridge Journal of Economics*, vol. 4, no. 2 (June 1980), p. 151. Kornai describes the new coordinating mechanism in the following terms:

> There is not one central planning authority, but many subcenters—one for prices, another for foreign trade, a third for banking, one for customs—and their decisions are often mutually inconsistent, and even contradictory. The bureaucratic bargaining that goes on now is not about physical targets and quantitative inputs; it is bargaining about subsidies, or tax exemptions or the price to be set for administratively priced goods, or customs and tariffs. There are hundreds of specific import licenses or export promotions. There are hundreds of small affairs where you as a producer are more interested in getting support from the bureaucracy than from the buyer in the marketplace. This excessive vertical intervention diverts the attention of producers from the market (Kornai, "Hungary's Reform," p. 26).

7. These points are made by James Mulick, *The New Economic Mechanism in Hungary. A True Reform?* (M.A. paper in Economics, Department of Economics, the Graduate School, Pennsylvania State University, 1984), pp. 11–12.

8. Zhang Jiachi and Chen Jianfa, "The Decisionmaking Power of Enterprises and Free Prices—Eyewitness Account of Hungary's Economic Reform," *People's Daily*, April 4, 1983, in *Foreign Broadcast Information Service (FBIS-China)*, April 7, 1983, H4.

9. Kornai, "Hungary's Reform," p. 20.

10. János Kornai, "Comments on the Present State and the Prospects of the Hungarian Economic Reform," *Journal of Comparative Economics*, vol. 7, no. 3 (September 1983), p. 231.

11. Bauer, "The Hungarian Alternative to Soviet-Type Planning," p. 314.

12. Frederick W. Crook, "The *Baogan Daohu* Incentive System: Translation and Analysis of a Model Contract," *China Quarterly*, no. 102 (June 1985), p. 295. In 1984–1985, 30 percent of grain was bought by the state at the quota price and 70 percent at the higher above-quota price. Zhao Ziyang (Chao Tzu-yang), "Why Relax Agricultural Price Controls?" *Beijing Review*, February 18, 1985. Quota and above-quota procurement prices were increased by nearly 48 percent between 1979 and 1983 (or over 8 percent per annum). Nicholas R. Lardy, "Consumption and Living Standards in China, 1978–83," *China Quarterly*, no. 100 (December 1984), p. 861. Since urban retail prices of staples were kept unchanged, the agricultural subsidy in 1984 was estimated at 20,000 million yuan. Ibid., p. 905.

13. Zhao Ziyang, "Why Relax Agricultural Price Controls?"; "Market to Replace the Quota System," *Beijing Review*, January 14, 1985.

14. Tian Jiyun (T'ien Chi-yun) (vice-premier), "On the Present Economic Situation and Restructuring the Economy," *Beijing Review*, February 10, 1986.

15. Jan S. Prybyla, "The Chinese Economy: Adjustment of the System or Systemic Reform?" *Asian Survey*, vol. 25, no. 5 (May 1985), p. 565.

16. Christine Wong, "Material Allocation and Decentralization: Impact of the Local Sector on Industrial Reform," in Elizabeth J. Perry and Christine Wong, eds., *The Political Economy of Reform in Post-Mao China* (Cambridge, Mass.: Harvard University Press, 1985); Prybyla, "The Chinese Economy," pp. 568–69.

17. Zhao Ziyang, "Report on the Seventh Five-Year Plan" (Delivered at the 4th Session of the 6th National People's Congress, March 25, 1986), *Beijing Review,* April 21, 1986.

18. *Beijing Review,* October 29, 1984.

19. On the various industrial price categories: "Questions and Answers on Prices," *Chung-kuo fa-chih pao,* November 11, 1985, in *Inside China Mainland* (Taipei), March 1986, pp. 16–17. The problem of the spillover effect of irrational prices on the price structure as a whole is similar to that experienced in Hungary. See note 9 above.

20. "As for the more important means of production, such as raw and semifinished materials and steel, the price for that amount required for planned distribution remains basically unchanged, while the remaining portion can be sold at market prices." See note 14 above. On emerging markets for the means of production in mainland China, see William Byrd, "The Shanghai Market for the Means of Production: A Case Study of Reform in China's Material Supply System," *Comparative Economic Studies,* vol. 27, no. 4 (Winter 1985), pp. 1–29.

21. Abram Bergson, "A Visit to China's Economic Reforms," *Comparative Economic Studies,* vol. 27, no. 2 (Summer 1985), p. 79.

22. "More than 80% of the population functions in a private enterprise environment. And the sphere of private enterprise is growing rapidly and vigorously." William Hinton, "Which Way China? December 1985 Observations," *Far East Reporter* (March 1986), p. 31. Hinton is not sympathetic to the marketizing changes.

23. For example, William Hinton, "Responsibility and Enterprise: A New Leap or a New Elite," ibid., pp. 3–9; Hinton, "An Analysis of the Responsibility System: Where Will the New Polarization Lead?" ibid., pp. 10–17.

24. Victoria Pope, "Hungary Braces for Austerity Plan," *Wall Street Journal,* July 2, 1983.

25. Frederick Kempe, "Budapest's Economic Changes Prompt Concern of Hungarian, Soviet Officials," ibid., April 1, 1985.

26. Bela Balassa, "Reforming the New Economic Mechanism in Hungary," *Journal of Comparative Economics,* vol. 7, no. 3 (September 1983), pp. 264–67. Mulick, *The New Economic Mechanism in Hungary,* p. 23.

27. Istvan Kemeny, "The Unregistered Economy in Hungary," *Soviet Studies,* vol. 34, no. 3 (July 1982), pp. 349–66.

28. "State Council Provisional Regulations on Greater Decision-Making Powers of State-Owned Industrial Enterprises," *Beijing Review,* June 18, 1984, pp. 10–11; Zhao Ziyang's speech to the National Committee of the Chinese People's Political Consultative Conference, January 1, 1985, *Beijing Review,* January 7, 1985, p. 15.

29. On the various taxes in mainland China, see Christine Wong, "The Second Phase of Economic Reform in China," *Current History* (September 1985), pp. 260–62; Barry Naughton, "False Starts and Second Wind: Financial Reform in China's Industrial System," in Perry and Wong, eds., *The Political Economy of Reform in Post-Mao China*.

30. Kornai, "Hungary's Reform," pp. 27–28. A fuller statement of the soft budget constraint problem may be found in his *Economics of Shortage* (Amsterdam: New Holland, 1980).

31. Hinton, "An Analysis of the Responsibility System."

32. This presupposes the emergence of democratically constituted village or township councils—an unlikely event in the present political temper of mainland China.

33. This is to be accompanied by a far-reaching delegation of supervisory and advisory functions from the central to local governments. James P. Sterba, "Central Control Subdued under Peking's Plan," *Wall Street Journal*, April 15, 1986.

34. József Macsáry, "Centralization of the Hungarian Enterprise System and Its Impact on the Efficiency of Production Control and the Regulatory System," *Eastern European Economics* (Winter 1982–83), pp. 34–61; Márton Tardos, "The Increasing Role and Ambivalent Reception of Small Enterprises in Hungary," *Journal of Comparative Economics*, vol. 7, no. 3 (September 1983), pp. 277–87.

35. Statistical data documenting the performance of mainland Chinese and Hungarian economies under the post-1978 changes (China) and the post-1968 NEM (Hungary) may be found in a number of sources. For example, for China: *Statistical Yearbook of China*, compiled by the State Statistical Bureau of the People's Republic of China (especially from 1983 onward); Li Chengrui, "Economic Reform Brings Better Life," *Beijing Review*, July 22, 1985, pp. 15–22, which contains useful tables and diagram comparing the situation in 1978 with that in 1984; Richard Critchfield, "China's Agricultural Success Story," *Wall Street Journal*, January 13, 1986; U.S. Department of Agriculture, Economic Research Service, *China: Outlook and Situation Report* (Washington, D.C., July 1985); USDA, *Agricultural Statistics of the People's Republic of China, 1949–82* (Washington, D.C., October 1984); U.S. Congress, Joint Economic Committee, *China: Economic Performance in 1985* (Washington, D.C., 1986). For Hungary: World Bank, *World Development Report 1985; Statistical Pocket Book of Hungary* (annual), (Budapest); and *Statisztikai eykonyv* (Statistical yearbook), annual (Budapest).

36. Peter Murrell, "Hungary's Hidden Economic Handicaps," *Wall Street Journal*, October 22, 1984.

37. Kornai, "Hungary's Reform," pp. 31, 26. Compare, "The general principle is to give more power to the role of market forces while upholding the country's planned economy," Zhao Ziyang, *Beijing Review*, January 14, 1985, p. 8.

38. On being caught between market and plan institutions, see Gertrude Schroeder, "The Soviet Economy on a Treadmill of 'Reforms,'" in U.S. Con-

gress, Joint Economic Committee, *Soviet Economy in a Time of Change* (Washington, D.C.: U.S. Government Printing Office, 1979), pp. 312–40, and Schroeder, "Soviet Economic 'Reform': More Steps on the Treadmill," in U.S. Congress, Joint Economic Committee, *Soviet Economy in the 1980s: Problems and Prospects* (Washington, D.C.: U.S. Government Printing Office, 1982), Part 1, pp. 65–88.

39. Kornai, "The Dilemmas of a Socialist Economy," p. 148.

40. Ibid.

41. Kornai, "Hungary's Reform," p. 31.

42. One of the exceptions is Ivan Volgyes. See his "Kadar's Hungary in the Twilight Era," *Current History* (November 1984), pp. 361–64, 386; Volgyes, "Hungary: A Malaise Thinly Disguised," *Current History* (November 1985), pp. 365–68, 388; Victor Pope, "Hungarians Show Discipine and Old World Restraint," *Wall Street Journal*, March 7, 1983; Jan S. Prybyla, "The Hundred Flowers of Discontent," *Current History* (September 1981), pp. 254–57, 274.

43. The note, however, is depressing primarily in a relative sense. Compared with the darkness of Stalinism and Maoism, the alienation of the half-plan half-market, neither-plan-nor-market society may be seen as a development toward moral health, the beginning of the shedding of Marxist-Leninist hypocrisies among the people and segments of the Party, and a rejection of ideological inanities. There is in it an element of overcompensation for past material privations, a feverish quest for moneymaking, and an impatient desire to start living with some degree of physical comfort. There is not much inherently wrong with that, except its denial by the purist guardians of official morality.

CHAPTER 8: THE POLISH ECONOMY

1. Poland's 1985 per capita gross national product (as given by the World Bank) was $2,050, comparable to Mexico ($2,080) and Panama ($2,100).

2. "Quality deterioration caused by shoddy workmanship and the use of substandard material inputs passes undetected, and forced replacement purchases of such goods (because of their rapid deterioration) are counted as volume growth of production and/or consumption." Jan Winiecki, "Are Soviet-Type Economies Entering an Era of Long-Term Decline?" *Soviet Studies*, July 1986, p. 344.

3. *PlanEcon Report*, PlanEcon Inc. (Washington, D.C.), April 24, 1987, p. 6.

4. Jack Bielasiak, "Economic Reform versus Political Normalization," in Paul Marer and Włodzimierz Siwiński, eds., *Creditworthiness and Reform in Poland: Western and Polish Perspectives* (Bloomington: Indiana University Press, 1988), p. 110.

5. Michael T. Kaufman, "Secret Poll Is Said to Have Found Gloom in Poland about Economy," *New York Times*, January 27, 1986.

6. Wojciech Pruss, "Ile Kosztuje Równowaga" (How much does balance cost), *Zycie Gospodarcze* (Economic life), July 3, 1988, p. 1.

7. Winiecki, "Soviet-Type Economies," p. 332.

8. Anonymous, "Notes on Poland's Economic Situation: An Inside View," *Radio Free Europe Background Report (Poland)*, August 9, 1978, p. 7.

9. Pruss, "Ile Kosztuje Równowaga," p. 1.

10. Jan Czekaj and Stanisław Owsiak, "Dokąd Zmierza Gospodarka Socjalistyczna?" (Which way is the Socialist economy headed?), *Życie Gospodarcze*, August 7, 1988, p. 10.

11. Irena Dryll, "Robotnicy w Reformie" (The role of workers in reform) *Życie Gospodarcze*, July 3, 1988, p. 7.

12. Listy, *Życie Gospodarcze*, July 10, 1988, p. 6.

13. Wolfgang Quaisser, "Agricultural Price Policy and Peasant Agriculture in Poland," *Soviet Studies*, p. 578.

14. Barry Newman, "Slovenes Acquire Taste for the Good Life: But Party May Be Over," *Wall Street Journal*, September 7, 1986.

15. Zdzislaw Sadowski, "The Philosophy of the Reform," *Polish Perspectives*, no. 1, 1988, p. 6.

16. Włodzimiers Brus, "The Political Economy of Reform," in Marer and Siwiński, eds., *Creditworthiness and Reform in Poland*, p. 66.

17. Ibid., p. 70.

18. Ibid., p. 71.

19. Ibid., pp. 71–72.

20. Benedykt Askanas, Halina Askanas, and Friedrich Levcik, "The Economies of the CMEA Countries in the Second Half of the Seventies," *Eastern European Economics* (Fall 1979), p. 32.

21. Zbigniew Kamecki, "On the Current State of the Economy," in Marer and Siwiński, eds., *Creditworthiness and Reform in Poland*, p. 61.

22. Danuta Wanicka, "Kompromis a Pluralizm" (Compromise and pluralism) *Życie Gospodarcze*, August 8, 1988, p. 4.

23. Krzysztof Fronczak, "Halo, Mówi sié . . ." (Hello, speaking. . . .), *Życie Gospodarcze*, August 7, 1988, p. 1.

24. Dryll, "Robotnicy w Reformie," p. 6.

25. *PlanEcon Report*, April 24, 1987, p. 12.

26. Zbigniew Fallenbuchl, "Present State of the Economic Reform," in Marer and Siwiński, eds., *Creditworthiness and Reform in Poland*, pp. 125–26.

27. Winiecki, "Soviet-Type Economies," p. 327.

28. Peter Truell, "Caught in the Scissors: A Continent in Trouble," *Wall Street Journal*, September 9, 1988.

29. Brus, "The Political Economy," in Marer and Siwiński, *Creditworthiness and Reform in Poland*, p. 125.

30. Anonymous, "Notes on Poland's Economic Situation," p. 7.

31. Sadowski, "The Philosophy of the Reform," p. 10.

CHAPTER 9: ECONOMIC REFORMS

1. An allocatively rational (scarcity) price system is composed of prices that may be expressed as follows:

$$\frac{MSC_a}{MSC_b} = \frac{P_a}{P_b} = \frac{MSU_a}{MSU_b}$$

where *MSC* is marginal social cost, *MSU* is marginal social utility (use value), *P* is price, and *a* and *b* are commodities. The notion of social cost and use value covers private and external costs and use values. Prices are allocatively irrational where either the cost or the use value side of the equation does not hold. Where allocatively irrational prices exercise any allocative influence at all (as they do under the regime of central planning), resource allocation will tend to be wasteful.

2. I take "market" to mean voluntary, contractual, competitive, horizontal transactions carried out by individual, autonomous, property-owning units for utility or profit-maximizing purposes, by consulting spontaneously generated price signals, through the disbursement of money votes. More concisely, the market is an open contest of alternatives. See Jan S. Prybyla, *Market and Plan under Socialism: The Bird in the Cage* (Stanford, Calif.: Hoover Institution Press, Stanford University, 1987), p. 4.

3. Voluntariness, horizontality, and competition in exchange transactions need not be theoretically perfect. They need merely be workable.

4. The Hungarians introduced a progressive income tax and a value-added tax. The problem is that these taxes have been introduced into a setting that is neither market nor plan. To achieve the regulatory benefits expected of the new tax system, markets would simultaneously have to be made much freer than they are and marketizing reform of the price system (wages included) would have to be pressed much farther than it has. See "Hungary Takes Another Leap into the Unknown," *Economist* (London), October 31, 1987, pp. 45–46.

5. "Rationality and Market Failure," in Andrew Schotter, *Free Market Economics: A Critical Appraisal* (New York: St. Martin's Press, 1985), chap. 4.

6. "Consumption is the sole end and purpose of all production; and the interest of the producer ought to be attended to only so far as it may be necessary for promoting that of the consumer." Adam Smith, *The Wealth of Nations* (1776), Edwin Cannan edition, New York: Random House, Modern Library, 1937), p. 625.

7. F. A. Hayek, *Law, Legislation and Liberty* (Chicago: University of Chicago Press, 1976).

8. See János Kornai, *Economics of Shortage* (Amsterdam: North-Holland, 1980); and his "Resource-constrained versus Demand-constrained Systems," *Econometrica*, vol. 47 (1979), pp. 801–19.

9. If the terms "private" and "privatization" in relation to property are offensive to some, they can be rephrased without trouble. "Economic decentralization" or "marketization" of property rights are acceptable substitutes. What is important is the substance, not the phraseology, of pluralism in property as in prices.

10. *China Daily* (Beijing), January 3, 1988.

11. For example, "Letter from Candidate of Economic Sciences, L. Popkova," under the rubric "From the Editorial Mailbag: Where Are the Pies Bigger and Better?" *Novy Mir* (Moscow), no. 5 (May 1987), pp. 238–40, 241. "Have a look," says Popkova, "at what is happening in developing countries from the 'plan or market' angle, and you will see how fast we are being caught up by those who have opted for the market, and how hungry are they who approach the market with suspicion and fear and where they treat it without any particular ceremony. . . . Look, finally, at the socialist countries: wherever there is more market, the pies are bigger and better."

12. *The Thirteenth Party Congress and China's Reforms* (Beijing: Beijing Review Publications, 1987), pp. 31, 32, 35.

13. "The Rev in Revolution," *Economist* (London), November 7, 1987, pp. 13–14.

14. Támás Bauer, "The Hungarian Alternative to Soviet-Type Planning," *Journal of Comparative Economics*, vol. 7, no. 3 (September 1983), pp. 304–16; János Kornai, "The Dilemmas of a Socialist Economy: The Hungarian Experience," *Cambridge Journal of Economics*, vol. 4, no. 2 (June 1980), pp. 147–57.

15. These adjustment insufficiencies and the need for thorough systemic reform have been recognized by the peaceful Hungarian revolution of late 1989.

CHAPTER 10: FROM MAO TO MARKET

1. Mao's New Democracy was an attempt to combine Communist dictatorial political forms with emasculated and restricted manifestations of political pluralism in a united front of Communists and non-Communist "patriotic personages." New Democracy was envisaged by Mao as a transitional phenomenon, the main function of which was to prepare the ground for proletarian dictatorship by the Communist party. Like the transitional arrangements in the economy before 1953, it was a mix of incompatible elements. See Mao Tse-tung, "On New Democracy" (January 1940), in *Selected Works of Mao Tse-tung*, vol. 2 (Beijing: Foreign Languages Press, 1965), pp. 339–84.

2. Total factor productivity is defined as the output per unit of labor and capital combined. For a discussion of factor productivity, see K. C. Yeh, "Macroeconomic Changes in the Chinese Economy during the Readjustment," *China Quarterly* (London) (December 1984), pp. 705–13.

3. See table 6, "Annual Rates of Growth of Domestic Product, Factor Inputs and Productivity, Selected Periods," in ibid., p. 711.

4. Ibid.

5. The following is just one of many examples of ecological abuse. In Inner Mongolia (Nei Monggol), the plowing up of grasslands during the Cultural Revolution's "take grain as the key link" campaign turned 967,000 acres of good pastureland into desert and resulted in the invasion of 1.9 million acres by sand. Between 1966 and 1978, the number of livestock

in this autonomous region declined by half. *Renmin Ribao* (Beijing), January 23, 1979; and Nei Monggol Regional Radio Station (Hohhot), January 26, 1979, trans. in *Foreign Broadcast Information Service, Daily Report: China* (Washington, D.C.—hereafter *FBIS-CHI*), February 2, 1979. For an overview of the ecological disaster in China wrought by leftward adjustments, see Vaclav Smil, *The Bad Earth: Environmental Degradation in China* (Armonk, N.Y.: M. E. Sharpe, 1984).

The educational damage inflicted by the Cultural Revolution was both quantitative and qualitative. "Educational work suffered great setbacks during the 'cultural revolution' in the years 1966–76, and has not to this day fully recovered from the evil consequences" (*Beijing Review,* January 1, 1981, p. 8). According to Hu Yaobang, general secretary of the Central Committee of the Communist party of China, 160 million youths who were between the ages of 8 and 18 in 1966 (at the outset of the Cultural Revolution) received substandard, indeed "poisonous," education during the years of turmoil. Another 210 million teenagers in primary and secondary schools around 1980 were being given deficient education as a result of the destruction wrought by the Cultural Revolution (ibid., April 14, 1980, p. 15). In 1978, in a population exceeding 960 million, China had a total of 4.3 million scientific and technical personnel in engineering, scientific research, agriculture, public health, and teaching. The only relatively reliable ones were those whose skills were acquired before 1966. State Statistical Bureau, *Statistical Yearbook of China 1983* (Hong Kong, Economic Information and Agency, 1983), pp. 103, 525. For an update on the educational situation, see Marianne Bastid, "Chinese Educational Policies in the 1980s and Economic Development," *China Quarterly* (June 1984), pp. 182–219.

6. The transformation thesis explicitly rejects the convergence notion of market socialism in which market and plan harmoniously fuse in roughly equal proportions, the one aiding and rounding off the other. I find the convergence notion to be theoretically unsound and operationally unattainable.

7. See Robert Michael Field, "Changes in Chinese Industry since 1978," *China Quarterly* (December 1984), p. 742.

8. As explained more fully in the text below, by resort to capitalist social techniques is meant the use of prices (including wages and interest rates), profits that depend on prices and taxes to motivate workers and managers and to influence the spending patterns of consumers and investors, and the use of exchange rates in transactions with foreign countries. It also means that broad property rights with regard to assets are vested in the actual users of those assets. In a capitalist (market) economy, these techniques arise from competitive, lateral, buying and selling transactions concluded by freely choosing economic units. In a command economy, only the form of these techniques is used, without the substance. Thus, prices in a command economy setting are not the mathematical expression of costs and utilities in the system and do not even remotely indicate allocative rationality. Rather, they are accounting devices denoting—very roughly and

imperfectly—production costs plus an arbitrary margin of profit. Property rights in assets vested in enterprise managers are subject to administrative restrictions regarding their value, size, use, and so on.

9. The ethical principles of a Socialist economy are listed by the Hungarian economist János Kornai as: (1) Socialist wage setting (to each according to his work and equal pay for equal work); (2) solidarity (help the weak to rise rather than punish them through capitalist-like competition); (3) security (full employment guaranteed by society); and (4) priority of general interest over partial (individual) interest. See János Kornai, "The Dilemmas of a Socialist Economy: The Hungarian Experience," *Cambridge Journal of Economics* (Cambridge, Eng.) (June 1980), p. 149. Kornai rightly concludes that conflicts are inevitable between these four ethical principles and the five conditions for economic efficiency, which are: (1) an incentive system to stimulate better performance from all individuals participating in production; (2) careful calculation of costs and benefits and termination of nonefficient production activities; (3) fast and flexible adjustment to the current situation and external conditions; (4) entrepreneurship; and (5) personal responsibility.

10. On the Soviet and East European borrowing of capitalist social techniques and its efficiency results, see Jan S. Prybyla, *Market and Plan under Socialism: The Bird in the Cage* (Stanford, Calif.: Hoover Institution Press, 1986).

11. "The Retreat from Marx," *Economist* (London), October 27, 1984. In China, "the assigned profit margin for making hot rolled steel is now ten times as high as for cold rolled steel. So the hot sort is naturally in surplus while the cold has to be imported at great cost. Yet rolled steel is one of the products [that] will stay subject to administrative decree" (ibid.).

12. For example, it has been reported that since August 1984, 1,000 customs and security officials have manned around the clock the perimeter of the Shenzhen Special Economic Zone (near Hong Kong). *South China Post* (Hong Kong), May 29, 1985.

13. Tariff or basic wages and salaries are laid down—on the Soviet model— by the central authorities in schedules that are mandatory on state-sector enterprises. There are several such schedules. Industrial workers in China are generally subject to an eight-grade schedule, the skill and basic wage rate being spelled out for each job grade. State employees are under a different schedule containing roughly thirty salary grades. There are separate schedules for engineering and technical personnel, teachers, etc. See Jan S. Prybyla, *The Chinese Economy: Problems and Policies*, 2d ed. (Columbia: University of South Carolina Press, 1981), pp. 150–63.

14. The *xiafang* movement, which peaked in the late 1960s and early 1970s, involved the compulsory transfer of educated urban youths (mainly middle-school graduates) to the countryside. Between 1968 and 1978, about 20 million urban youths were so relocated. The policy of rustication was quietly phased out in 1978–1979, following the National Conference on Rusticated Youth Settling in the Countryside held in Beijing, October 31 to December 10, 1978. Although most of the "sent down" youths returned to their home

towns after this time, many apparently still remain stranded in the country-side, caught in inextricable red tape. See Charles Hoffman, "Urban Unemployment in China," *Asian Thought and Society* (March 1984), pp. 32–37.

Rightist labels were attached to many people, mainly intellectuals, during the Anti-Rightist Campaign of 1957 that followed the aborted Hundred Flowers Campaign. The consequences for an individual of being branded a rightist were terrifying. See, for example, Ruth Earnshaw Lo and Katherine Kindermann, *In the Eye of the Typhoon* (New York: Harcourt Brace Jovanovich, 1980). Removal of rightist labels was ordered in 1975, but the order was countermanded by the left faction within the leadership. The removal process was resumed shortly after the arrest of the so-called Gang of Four in late 1976. See "Last Rightists Have Their Designation Removed," *Beijing Review*, November 24, 1978.

Urban unemployment, according to Hoffman (note 14, table 2, p. 33), probably peaked at 13 percent of the urban labor force in 1979. The precise youth component of the 15 million urban unemployed in that year cannot be known with certainty, but it could be as high as three-fifths. According to Li Xiannian (Report to a working conference of the Party's Central Committee, April 25, 1979), the urban unemployment at that time stood at 20 million. *Ming Pao* (Hong Kong), June 14, 1979. See also John Philip Emerson, "Urban School-Leavers and Unemployment in China," *China Quarterly* (March 1983), pp. 1–16.

15. For example, gross agricultural output rose from 128.5 billion renminbi in 1976 to 164.6 billion renminbi in 1980. Over the same period, gross industrial output rose from 321.9 billion renminbi to 499.2 billion. See *Statistical Yearbook of China 1983*, pp. 149, 215.

16. For a discussion of this view among youth, see Stanley Rosen, "Prosperity, Privatization, and China's Youth," *Problems of Communism* (March–April 1985), pp. 1–28.

17. "Decision of the Central Committee of the Communist Party of China on Reform of the Economic Structure, Adopted by the 12th Central Committee of the CPC at Its Third Plenary Session on October 21, 1984," *Beijing Review*, October 29, 1984. See also *FBIS-CHI*, October 22, 1984. For a discussion, see the *New York Times*, October 21, 1984.

18. A literal translation of *baogan daohu* is "full responsibility to household."

19. Two major differences between *baogan daohu* (1985) and the household contract system of 1961–1965 should be noted. First, the 1961–1965 system was less prevalent than the present one. Second, in a significant proportion of cases, the 1961–1965 system involved payment in workpoints to the household by the contracting team or brigade *(baochan daohu)*, whereas no workpoints are involved in the present system *(baogan daohu)*. In other words, the present arrangement represents a more widespread and profound decollectivization than did its 1961–1965 predecessor (denounced during the Cultural Revolution as an evil creature of Liu Shaoqi).

20. Yak-Yeow Kueh, "China's New Agricultural Policy Program: Major

Consequences, 1979–1983," *Journal of Comparative Economics* (December 1984), pp. 354–61, esp. table 1, p. 356, and table 2, p. 357.

21. A useful source is Frederick W. Crook, "The *Baogan Daohu* System: Translation and Analysis of a Model Contract," *China Quarterly* (June 1985), pp. 291–303.

22. Du Runsheng, "Second Stage Rural Reform," *Beijing Review,* June 24, 1985; Zhao Ziyang, "Why Relax Agricultural Price Controls," ibid., February 18, 1985.

> Starting this year [1985], Chinese farmers will no longer be obliged to sell a portion of their harvest to the state. Instead, they will depend primarily on contracts and the market demand to determine which crops they will grow. . . . Through contracts with farmers, the government will purchase large amounts of grain and cotton at preferential prices and leave the rest of the crop to be regulated by the market. When the market price goes low, the state will purchase the grain or cotton from the farmers at a protective price higher than market price. On the other hand, when the market price goes high, the state may sell its reserves in big quantities to bring the price back down. By buying and selling the government can control the wide fluctuations in the market.

See also "Market to Replace the Quota System," ibid., January 14, 1985. As part of the "second stage" (1985) agricultural changes, and reflecting the growing monetization and commercialization-specialization of the rural economy, the agricultural tax, formerly paid in grain, will henceforth be settled in cash in the "reverse ratio" of 3:7, that is, 30 percent of the tax grain will be valued at the former state monopoly (quota) price, and 70 percent at the former (higher) above-quota price. *Xinhua* (Beijing), May 24, 1985, in *FBIS-CHI,* May 29, 1985.

23. Estimates of grain production in 1985 put grain output at about 27 million tons below the 1984 record of 407 million tons. See John F. Burns, "Facing a Decline in Its Grain Fields, China Retreats on Policy," *New York Times,* January 1, 1986.

24. For example, grain production in China increased from 284.5 million metric tons in 1975 to 407.1 million metric tons in 1984. *Statistical Yearbook of China 1983,* p. 158; and State Statistical Bureau, "Communiqué on Fulfillment of China's 1984 Economic and Social Development Plan," *Beijing Review,* March 25, 1985.

25. According to Fei Xiaotong, "More than one-third of the total rural labor force in southern Jiangsu [Province] has given up farming" ("Surplus Rural Labor Put to Work," *Beijing Review,* May 27, 1985). According to a *New York Times* report, "Apart from peasants who have switched to growing cotton and other crops [rather than grain], about 50 million have cut back or abandoned farming to go into the fastest growing sector of the economy, rural industry." Such a comparatively low figure would constitute roughly 15 percent of the total agricultural labor force. See John F. Burns, "China Grain Crop Dips: Setback Seen for Policy," *New York Times,* December 23,

1985. The Beijing *China Daily News* (New York ed.) of October 9, 1985, puts the number of "surplus laborers" in China's contryside at 120 million, which is expected to reach some 230 million by the turn of the century. Sixty million surplus farm workers were employed in rural industries in 1985. There are indications that the rural industries are being developed too fast. There is also talk of "wasted funds, raw materials, and energy [which] greatly dampen the enthusiasm of the masses." Commentator's article, *Renmin Ribao*, June 3, 1985, trans. in *FBIS-CHI*, June 7, 1985. See also Robert Delfs, "The Rural Uprising," *Far Eastern Economic Review* (Hong Kong), July 11, 1985, pp. 56–57.

Per capita income in 1984, according to a sample survey of peasant households, came to 355 yuan, an increase of 160 percent over 1978, or 100 percent when price increases are taken into account. *Beijing Review,* April 22, 1985. A note of caution: knotty statistical problems are involved in the sample surveys of peasant incomes. These include the questionable reliability of the price deflator in the countryside; the representativeness of the samples drawn on an unspecified but nonrandom basis; the question of collectively supplied consumption goods (not taken into account by the income data); and the propensity of local officials to "overfulfill" the statistical plan, that is, the tendency to inflate statistics so as to show that what the leadership wants (that the peasants should grow rich) is, in fact, happening instantaneously. On the technical problems involved in rural income sampling, see Nicholas R. Lardy, "Consumption and Living Standards in China, 1978–83," *China Quarterly* (December 1984), pp. 851–52.

26. See, for example, Chen Yun's speech to the National Party Conference (September 23, 1985), in *Beijing Review*, September 30, 1985; and Tian Jiyun, vice-premier of the State Council, "Price System Due for Reform," ibid., January 28, 1985.

27. In early May 1985, the prices of 1,800 food items were partially deregulated in Beijing. Although the average price increase was said to have been 50 percent, beef prices went up 130 percent, and many vegetable prices doubled. Concerned about possible adverse reactions by urban workers to the price hikes, the government awarded every Beijing resident a subsidy equivalent (at present) to U.S. $2.19 a month. The total cost of this subsidy (about U.S. $140 million a year) is roughly equal to the subsidy formerly paid by the government on food purchased from peasants and resold to urban consumers at lower prices. In December 1985, Deputy Prime Minister Li Peng announced that this subsidy would be raised in order to "stabilize" the situation in Beijing, and that there would be no major price changes in 1986. *New York Times*, December 23, and May 10, 1985; *Ta Kung Pao* (Hong Kong), May 31, 1985, in *FBIS-CHI*, May 31, 1985. A contingent of 11,000 government price inspectors was deployed in Beijing to prevent price gouging (some would say, to prevent prices from finding their market equilibrium level). In 1984, a decision was made to partially deregulate the prices of certain raw materials and energy. This resulted in a sharp increase in factory production costs. The factories affected by the rise were not, however,

permitted to pass on their increased costs in the form of increased prices of their products. Very few went out of business. The great majority were kept afloat by new government subsidies. *Wall Street Journal*, April 1, 1985.

28. Following are two examples of the cadres' deficient theoretical grasp of how a market price system operates. In Urumqi, a meeting of cadres concluded that "commodity price departments must straighten out prices so as to conform to the law of prices. Prices which should be changed must be resolutely changed. Those which should be controlled must be strictly controlled. Prices which are not allowed to be raised, resolutely must not be allowed to be raised." (Xinjiang Regional Radio [Urumqi], May 30, 1985, trans. in *FBIS-CHI*, June 4, 1985). Consider also the statements of a *Renmin Ribao* commentator:

> At present a small number of state commercial units in some cities and rural areas still show no interest in market conditions. Some of them are merely hankering after profits. When more products are supplied, they force down the prices at the expense of the producers; and when products are in short supply or in great demand, they raise prices willfully at the expense of the consumers. . . . The authorities concerned should strengthen effective management and supervision over the market and should strictly ban willfull price hikes in violation of state regulations.

("State Commerce Should Learn to Participate in Market Regulation," *Renmin Ribao*, May 28, 1985, trans. in *FBIS-CHI*, May 28, 1985.) The commentator would have flunked Economics 101.

29. On the unauthorized and uncontrolled movement of rural labor to the cities, see Christine Wong, "The Second Phase of Economic Reform in China," *Current History* (September 1985), p. 262. In the Chinese conception of the market, labor and natural resources (for example, land) are not "commodities," hence they are not subject to market transactions that are concerned only with commodities. Capital goods produced by state firms are presently in a theoretical twilight zone. Some, like trucks and tractors, have been reclassified from noncommodities to commodities. See Robert C. Hsu, "Conceptions of the Market in Post-Mao China: An Interpretive Essay," *Modern China* (October 1985), pp. 438–40.

30. "When Party and government organs and cadres use their influence to set up enterprises . . . all the profits are siphoned off into the pockets of individuals or small groups. . . . These malpractices mar the reputation of the reform. . . . They contaminate the organism of the Party. The new malpractices are all associated with money. Some cadres and Party members are . . . blinded by lust for gain. . . . They have become slaves to money" (*Zhibu Shenghuo* [Beijing], no. 5, 1985, trans. in *Inside China Mainland* [Taipei] [August 1985], pp. 15–17). See also *Beijing Review*, April 1, 1985, p. 7. To date the biggest scandal, on Hainan Island, involved 690 parties who pocketed 2.1 million yuan (U.S. $720,000). Between January and March 1985, 872 more-or-less phony companies were set up by eighty-eight government departments and others (even schools and kindergartens). Contraband vehi-

cles and sixteen other luxury goods imported from Hong Kong and other capitalist places were resold at hefty profits on the domestic market. See the *Asian Wall Street Journal Weekly* (Hong Kong), August 19, 1985.

31. Barry Kramer, "Oriental Tradition—Chinese Officials Still Give Preference to Kin, Despite Peking Policies; Favoritism Stirs Resentment but Curb Isn't Enforced; A Job for a Son of Deng," *Wall Street Journal,* October 29, 1985.

32. As noted earlier, "value" instruments of control in a centrally planned economy are norms expressed in financial terms (for example, profit, sales targets), the "values" being based on allocatively irrational, planner-determined prices.

33. *Beijing Review,* October 29, 1984, puts the reduction at from 120 to 60. Some aggregation in the remaining balances of items that were listed separately before may be involved.

34. Abram Bergson, "A Visit to China's Economic Reforms," *Comparative Economic Studies* (Summer 1985), p. 76. A secretary of the Lingui County (Guanxi Province) Party Committee told bankers who were reluctant to lend money for building some questionable town and township enterprises: "We are not in charge of personnel administration, but your 'party tickets' are in our hands. . . . You don't have to follow the leadership of the county government. . . . You refuse to give help. In the future don't call on us when you have problems." The bankers got the message and gave the loan. *Renmin Ribao,* June 5, 1985, trans. in *FBIS-CHI,* June 7, 1985. In the first six months of 1985, the Agricultural Bank lent 2 billion yuan to rural industries run by local authorities under guidance planning, a figure originally targeted for the whole year. Vigor Fung, "China Seeks to Slow Economy without Reversing Reforms," *Asian Wall Street Journal Weekly,* August 19, 1985.

35. Since deregulation, some local governments have refused to decontrol and have used their power to monopolize the timber trade and exploit forest farmers. *Renmin Ribao,* May 28, 1985, trans. in *FBIS-CHI,* June 3, 1985. Local leaders have reportedly been restricting the marketizing changes promoted by the center by, for example, limiting the availability of open spaces and enclosed areas where market transactions are authorized, collecting unwarranted fees and fines ("squeeze"), suspending or confiscating business licenses, and capriciously occupying private business premises. Shandong Provincial Radio Service (Jonan), June 9, 1985, trans. in *FBIS-CHI,* June 11, 1985. On the frequent verticality ("commandism") of what are supposed to be lateral, mutually arrived-at *baogan daohu* contracts, and the great number of levies and surtaxes imposed locally by cadres hostile to the *baogan daohu* system, see Ts'ai Ming-ch'in, "The Burden on the Peasantry: An Analysis of Mainland China's Rural Economy," *Issues and Studies* (Taipei) (April 1984), pp. 30–47.

36. Gertrude E. Schroeder, "The 1966–67 Soviet Industrial Price Reform: A Study in Complications," *Soviet Studies* (Glasgow) (April 1969), pp. 462–77; and Jan S. Prybyla, "Soviet Economic Reforms in Industry," *Weltwirtschaftliches Archiv* (Kiel), vol. 107, no. 2 (1971), pp. 272–316.

37. "Tian Jiyun on Commodity Prices," *Banyue Tan* (Beijing), no. 9, May 10, 1985; trans. in *FBIS-CHI*, June 5, 1985.

38. For a discussion of some of the experiments, including the use of job markets for nationwide placement, see *Asiaweek* (Hong Kong), September 6, 1985.

39. Hunan Provincial Radio Service (Changsha), May 18, 1985, trans. in *FBIS-CHI*, May 21, 1985.

40. New Year's speech by Zhao Ziyang, premier of the State Council, to the National Committee of the Chinese People's Political Consultative Conference in Beijing, January 1, 1985, in *Beijing Review*, January 7, 1985.

41. Zhao Ziyang, "Report on the Work of the Government," delivered at the Second Session of the Sixth National People's Congress on May 15, 1984, in *Beijing Review*, June 11, 1984.

42. "Decision of the Central Committee of the Communist Party of China on Reform of the Economic Structure," adopted by the Twelfth Central Committee of the Communist Party of China at its Third Plenary Session on October 20, 1984, in *Beijing Review*, October 29, 1984.

43. See notes 40 and 41.

44. Zhao Ziyang, "Report on the Work of the Government." On the problem of runaway consumption and investment in late 1984 to mid-1985, see An Zhiwen, "A Year in Which Marked Progress Was Made in the Reform of the Economic Structure of the Cities," *Renmin Ribao*, May 13, 1985, trans. in *FBIS-CHI*, May 22, 1985, pp. K/6–11, esp. p. K/10. Western economists estimate the 1985 inflation rate in the urban areas of China at 10 to 15 percent, with the Shanghai rate put at 17 percent. Leonard Silk, "China Hits Its Stride," *New York Times*, October 27, 1985.

45. Wong, "The Second Phase of Economic Reform," p. 279.

46. *Hong Kong Evening Standard*, June 4, 1985. In 1984, gross wages in Beijing rose 500 million yuan. Of this, more than 80 million yuan was paid out in in-kind and money bonuses, including bonuses for worn-out shoes. *Ming Pao* (Hong Kong), May 17, 1985, in *FBIS-CHI*, May 22, 1985.

47. Wong, "The Second Phase of Economic Reform," p. 262, and Christine Wong, "Ownership and Control in Chinese Industry: The Maoist Legacy and Prospects for the 1980s," in U.S. Congress Joint Economic Committee, *China in the 1980s* (Washington, D.C., U.S. Government Printing Office, 1985).

48. *Statistical Yearbook of China 1983*, p. 120; and *Beijing Review*, March 25, 1985.

49. Barry Naughton, "False Starts and Second Wind: Financial Reform in China's Industrial System," in Elizabeth J. Perry and Christine Wong, eds., *The Political Economy in Post-Mao China* (Cambridge, Mass.: Harvard University Press, 1985).

50. Alec Nove, *The Soviet Economic System*, 2d ed. (Boston and London, George Allen & Unwin, 1980); Marshall I. Goldman, *USSR in Crisis: The Failure of an Economic System* (New York, W. W. Norton, 1983); and Prybyla, *Market and Plan under Socialism.*

51. See William G. Rosenberg, "Observations on the Soviet Incentive System," *The ACES Bulletin* (Bloomington, Ind.) (Fall–Winter 1977), pp. 27–43; and Prybyla, "Soviet Economic Reforms in Industry." After-tax profits of Soviet state enterprises are allocated, in accordance with centrally determined formulas, among three major enterprise funds (also known as "economic stimulation funds"): the material incentive fund; fund for social-cultural measures; and production development fund. Monies from these funds may be disbursed by enterprises (with the approval of their supervisory ministries) for various enterprise-related purposes.

52. On the various types of new taxes, see Wong, "The Second Phase of Economic Reform"; and Naughton, "False Starts and Second Wind." On broader issues involved in the change, see Nina P. Halpern, "China's Industrial Economic Reforms: The Question of Strategy," *Asian Survey* (Berkeley) (October 1985), pp. 998–1012.

53. What is "undeserved" is sometimes difficult to define in the much-plan, some-market context. For example, many local firms have jumped in on the booming market in herbal medicines and cigarettes, allegedly reaping windfall profits from these addictions, while supplying inferior products.

54. This is a graduated progressive tax that had long been imposed on collective enterprises and is now extended to state enterprises.

55. See notes 40 and 41. Under the former system, enterprise managers—who were appointed by superior administrative-party authorities—had very limited rights with respect to the hiring and dismissal of workers in their enterprises. In conformity with the Socialist ethical principle of job security (see note 9 above), it became almost impossible to fire incompetent (much less, superfluous) state-sector workers. The phenomenon goes by the name of the unbreakable "iron rice bowl." In Kaifeng, Henan Province, for example, of 400 large factories, 110 were at one point operating below capacity or had ceased operations altogether, while keeping everyone on the payroll. *Beijing Review,* May 25, 1979.

56. These various rights are listed in *Beijing Review,* June 18, 1984, in a report on the May 10, 1984, "State Council Provisional Regulations on Greater Decision-making Powers of State-owned Industrial Enterprises." For some recently aired innovative proposals on micro-autonomy, see Mary Lee, "Prescription for Health: Reform Highlights Management Problems in China," *Far Eastern Economic Review,* September 12, 1985.

57. In Hebei Province, between 1980 and 1984, some enterprises paid only 30 percent of the taxes due by them. Officials at various levels have been accused of "lowering tax rates at random, widening the range of tax exemptions, even regarding taxation as an obstacle to reform." *Renmin Ribao,* May 24, 1985, trans. in *FBIS-CHI,* May 28, 1985; *Xinhua* (Beijing), May 27, 1985, trans. in *FBIS-CHI,* May 31, 1985. See also Marlowe Hood, "China Learns a Capitalist Lesson: Tax Evasion Goes with the Game," *Wall Street Journal,* November 16, 1985.

58. For example Gertrude Schroeder, "The Soviet Economy on a Treadmill

329

of 'Reforms,'" in U.S. Congress Joint Economic Committee, *Soviet Economy in a Time of Change* (Washington, D.C., U.S. Government Printing Office, 1979), pp. 312–40; and "Soviet Economic 'Reform': More Steps on the Treadmill," in U.S. Congress Joint Economic Committee, *Soviet Economy in the 1980s: Problems and Prospects* (Washington, D.C., U.S. Government Printing Office, 1982), Part I, pp. 65–68.

59. See footnote 9.

CHAPTER 11: BACK FROM THE MARKET?

1. Liu Guoguan, "A Sweet and Sour Decade," *Beijing Review* (Beijing), January 2–8, 1989, pp. 22–29.

2. Jan S. Prybyla, "China's Economic Experiment: From Mao to Market," *Problems of Communism* (January–February 1986), p. 29.

3. "China's Seriously Distorted Pricing System Has Not Been Fundamentally Changed," *Beijing Review,* September 26–October 2, 1988, p. 7.

4. Liu, "A Sweet and Sour Decade."

5. State Statistical Bureau, "Rural Reform," *Beijing Review,* September 26–October 2, 1988, pp. 31–32; Ding Shengjun, "Projected Changes in Chinese Consumption," ibid., October 3–9, 1988, pp. 24–25.

6. State Statistical Bureau, "The Industrial Economy," *Beijing Review,* October 3–9, 1988, pp. 27–30.

7. "High-Pressured, but Out of Steam," *Economist* (London), November 12, 1988, p. 38.

8. China's Statistics Consulting Service Centre & CITIC Research International Branch, *China's Latest Statistics* (Shenzhen, Hong Kong: October 1988), part 2, p. 28.

9. "Sliding into Recession," *Far Eastern Economic Review* (Hong Kong), November 10, 1988, p. 95; *Liaowang Zhoukan* (Beijing), no. 23 (June 26, 1988), pp. 6–10, in *Inside China Mainland* (Taipei), November, 1988, p. 15.

10. Li Yungi, "Freeing the Banks from Beijing's Grip," *Asian Wall Street Journal* (Hong Kong), November 7, 1988, p. 13. Li is an economist with the People's Bank of China.

11. Retail food prices in state food stores are not only below free market prices for comparable goods but also below the purchase prices paid by the state to peasants under the system of contractual deliveries.

12. Li, "Freeing the Banks," p. 13.

13. Ibid.

14. "Chicken Feed," *Economist,* November 26, 1988, p. 38.

15. "Straining at Beijing's Tether," *Economist,* December 10, 1988, p. 31.

16. Yang Xiaobing, "China's Battle against Corruption," *Beijing Review,* January 16–22, 1989, p. 20. According to the *People's Daily,* peasants in Jiangsu province in the first half of 1988 spent 1.5 billion yuan on "sympathy gifts" for officials. For China as a whole, such bribes increased by 30 percent compared with the same period of 1987. *China News Analysis* (Hong Kong), no. 1371 (November 1, 1988), p. 4.

17. "Rolling Back the Years," *Asiaweek* (Hong Kong), November 18, 1988, p. 26.

18. Jan Winiecki, "Why Economic Reforms Fail in the Soviet-Type System: A Property Rights-Based Approach" (Seminar paper no. 374, Institute of International Economic Studies, University of Stockholm, 1986).

19. Private communication to the author from a Chinese economist in Beijing, December 20, 1988.

20. "China, arthritic after 40 years of central planning, still finds the idea of market prices hard to understand. Some of its leaders, the collective rhetoric notwithstanding, would prefer to return to the old ways, when prices were controlled, supply fixed, and demand ignored." "Freeze a Bit, Melt a Bit, Stir," *Economist*, July 30, 1988, p. 34.

21. James Buchanan, "Man and State," in Svetozar Pejovich, ed., *Socialism: Institutional, Philosophical, and Economic Issues* (Boston, Mass.: Kluwer Academic Publishers, 1987), pp. 3–9. On market failures, see Andrew Schotter, *Free Market Economics: A Critical Appraisal* (New York: St. Martin's Press, 1985), chap. 4.

22. "The right solution was prescribed long ago by the logical economists who ran the great postwar economic miracles in West Germany and Japan: instantly free all prices, mercilessly control the money supply, and keep the currency undervalued." "High Pressured, but Out of Steam," *Economist*.

23. Liu Guoguan, "A Sweet and Sour Decade," p. 25. One suggestion for moving to a full market system may be found in Jan S. Prybyla, "China's Economic Reforms," *Journal of Comparative Social and Economic Studies* (Beijing), no. 3 (1988), pp. 36–40 chap. 9 in this book.

24. For example "China's State-owned Enterprises Will Never Be Privatized," Zhao Ziyang, "Report to the Third Plenary Session of the Thirteenth CPC Central Committee," (September 26, 1988), *Beijing Review*, November 14–20, 1988, p. v. On systemic transition, see Jan S. Prybyla, "The Chinese Economy: Adjustment of the System or Systemic Reform?" *Asian Survey*, vol. 25, no. 5 (May. 1985), pp. 553–86.

25. Jin Qi, "Factory Directors' Worries," *Beijing Review*, October 3–9, 1988, p. 7.

26. "I used my money to buy his power, and then used his power to make myself more money," said a "business operator" caught bribing a supply official. *Liaowang* (Beijing), no. 37 (September 12, 1988), pp. 10–12, in *Inside China Mainland* (Taipei), January 1989, p. 22.

27. Bela Balassa, "China's Economic Reform in a Comparative Perspective," *Journal of Comparative Economics*, vol. 11, no. 3 (1987), pp. 410–26.

28. Ge Wu, "Policy of Reform and Openness Remains Unchanged," *Beijing Review*, October 31–November 6, 1988, p. 7.

29. Ibid., p. 7.

30. Robert Delfs, "Property to the People!" *Far Eastern Economic Review* (Hong Kong), December 22, 1988, pp. 12–13; Adi Ignatius, "Chinese Policies Run at Cross Purposes in Fumbled Attempt to End Farm Crisis," *Wall Street Journal*, October 26, 1988.

31. Adi Ignatius, "Beijing's Two Top Economic Thinkers Reflect Leadership's Broader Divisions," *Wall Street Journal*, October 26, 1988.

32. Liu, "A Sweet and Sour Decade," p. 26.

33. Delfs, "Property to the People," p. 12.

34. "Farmers sneak out at night to bypass the authorities. Regional protectionist measures, such as internal tariffs seemingly similar to the *likin* transit taxes of the last century, are fragmenting China into a country of warring economic fiefdoms." Louise do Rosario, "China's Price Pirates," *Far Eastern Economic Review*, October 13, 1988, p. 96.

35. Zhao, "Report of the Central Committee," pp. i–iii.

36. Ge, "Policy of Reform and Openness," p. 7.

37. Zhao, "Report of the Central Committee," p. iv.

38. Louise do Rosario, "Peking's Growing Pains," *Far Eastern Economic Review*, January 5, 1989, pp. 54–55.

39. Ignatius, "Chinese Policies."

40. Adi Ignatius, "Millions Are Expected to Lose Jobs As China Implements Its Austerity Plan," *Wall Street Journal*, January 27, 1989.

41. Jan S. Prybyla, *Market and Plan under Socialism: The Bird in the Cage* (Stanford, Calif.: Hoover Institution Press, 1987).

42. Liu, "A Sweet and Sour Decade," pp. 26–28.

CHAPTER 12: PRICE REFORMS

1. On this analytical formulation, see Jan S. Prybyla, *Market and Plan under Socialism: The Bird in the Cage* (Stanford, Calif.: Hoover Institution Press, 1987).

2. In the centrally planned system the choice and ranking of goals are the translation into economics of the political Party line. The methods used to reach the goals represent the planning and managerial bureaucracies' "style of work."

3. See Zhang Weiying, "On the Role of Prices," *Zhongguo Shehui Kexue*, no. 3 (1985), in *Social Sciences in China (SSIC)*, vol. 6, no. 4 (December 1985), p. 193. "China has not only preserved a natural economy in agriculture, but also created to a certain extent an 'industrial natural economy' ('great and comprehensive,' 'small and comprehensive')," ibid., p. 186. The inclination toward natural economy is accompanied by an antimoney bias.

4. The assumption here is that reform of the planner-determined price system excludes perfect electronic centralization of the system:

> Even if we were able now to establish great mathematical systems comparable to economic activities and theoretically were able to figure out the price and quantity of all commodities and labor, assuming that all gaps and parameters in the formula have been filled in, this would still prove to be futile. The determination of price, particularly relative price, is subject to the influences of the specific information possessed by each participant in an economic activity and the influence of numerous external variables and random factors . . . all of which can change the structure of relative

prices. At the present level of economic mathematics any attempt to build up such an all-inclusive mathematical model that can also accurately, quickly, and economically reflect the complete process of the movement of the national economy is an utterly unrealistic notion (Yang Zhongwei and Li Bo, "Pricing and Price Reforms," *Zhongguo Shehui Kexue*, no. 5 [1985], in *SSIC*, vol. 7, no. 1 [March 1986], pp. 71–72).

5. Price subsidies for consumer basics appear to be part of a package that the Hungarian economist Janos Kornai designates as principles of Socialist ethics (Socialist wage-setting—to each according to his work; solidarity; security; and priority of the general interest). These ethical principles, according to Kornai, conflict with "five conditions for efficiency": proper incentive system, cost-benefit calculation, fast and flexible adjustment mechanisms, entrepreneurship, and personal responsibility. Janos Kornai, "The Dilemmas of a Socialist Economy: The Hungarian Experience," *Cambridge Journal of Economics*, vol. 4, no. 2 (June 1980), pp. 148–49. For a critical appraisal of this formulation, see Bartlomiej Kaminski, "Pathologies of Central Planning," *Problems of Communism*, vol. 36, no. 2 (March–April 1987), p. 90.

6. The five economic laws of capitalist self-destruction derived from the (labor) surplus value theory are: (1) capital accumulation and the declining rate of profit; (2) concentration and centralization of capital and wealth; (3) capitalist crisis and business cycles; (4) reserve army of the unemployed; and (5) immiseration of the proletariat. If the surplus value theory does not hold, neither do the laws. The Marxist thought system, not capitalism, self-destructs.

7. In Marxist theory, cost of production is composed of constant capital (*c*) and variable capital (*v*), or $c + v$. Constant capital represents the amount of socially necessary past labor embodied in materials used up in the production process (that is, depreciation plus material cost). Variable capital represents the amount of current labor (the wages bill). In practice, the one exception to the absence of interest is the counting of interest charges on borrowed working capital as part of production cost. See Yuan-li Wu, *The Economy of Communist China: An Introduction* (New York: Praeger, 1965), p. 57. Some "contend that those who accept the concept that capital creates value are worshippers of dead labor, or commodity fetishism. It is true, that the bourgeoisie trumpets the productiveness of capital in order to downgrade the productiveness of live labor. Indeed, we should expose and criticize capitalist tricks." Lin Wenyi and Jia Lurang, "The Law of Supply and Demand and Its Role in a Socialist Economy," *Jingji yanjiu*, no. 9 (1981), in *Chinese Economic Studies (CES)*, vol. 18, no. 2 (Winter 1984–85), p. 35.

8. Lu Lijun, "A Discussion of Sun Yefang's Economic Theories by Chinese Economists," *SSIC*, vol. 5, no. 4 (December 1984), p. 19. Compare E. G. Liberman, "The Plan, Direct Ties, and Profitability," *Problems of Economics*, January 1966, pp. 27–31, and Liberman, "Profitability and Socialist Enterprises," *SSIC*, March 1966, pp. 3–10.

9. "Since the early 1960s the Soviet Union and some Eastern European countries have devoted major efforts to the implementation of planned optimum mathematical methods. . . . However, the problems of low microeconomic benefits, slow technical progress, inferior product quality and limited variety still remain to be solved; furthermore, it frequently happens that the production of consumer goods and construction of basic installations lag far behind the social needs." Yang Zhongwei and Li Bo, "Pricing and Price Reforms," p. 71.

10. "Planning comes first, and prices second. This calls for first drawing up plans in accordance with social needs; the next thing is to set rational prices for various products, and to see that these prices serve our plans, rather than separating the two." Hu Qiaomu, "Observe Economic Laws, Speed Up the Four Modernizations," *Renmin Ribao,* October 6, 1978, cited by He Jiangzhang, "More on Planned Economy and Market Regulation," *SSIC*, vol. 3, no. 4 (December 1982), p. 49. He thinks that "in accordance with social need" refers to the requirements of the basic economic law of socialism and those of the law of planned and proportionate development of the national economy. To set "rational prices for various kinds of products" refers, according to He, to compliance with the requirements of the law of value—a not very enlightening prescription for optimization.

11. Wang Zhenzhi, Wang Yongzhi, and Jia Xiuyuan, "A Summary of the Discussions on Price Theory during the Past Few Years," *SSIC*, vol. 3, no. 3 (September 1982), pp. 16–34.

12. N. Fedorenko explicitly advocated the application of marginalism to costing and the use of relative utility in pricing. N. P. Fedorenko, *Ekonomika i matematika* (Moscow: Znaniye, 1967), pp. 9–25, 41–44, 55–57. A useful source on this and the work of Novozhilov and Kantorovich is J. Wilczynski, *The Economics of Socialism,* 4th ed. (London: George Allen & Unwin, 1982), pp. 137–39. In Russia Novozhilov had argued for the introduction of the notion of marginal cost pricing through the recognition of a socially necessary limit to production costs: that is, the price should cover the firm's costs of producing a product that is socially desirable (demanded)—it should cover marginal cost. A similar idea is present in the following statement by Chinese economists Gu Shutang and Yang Yushuan:

> When demand exceeds supply by an overwhelming margin and social need cannot be met by commodities produced under inferior or even the most inferior [marginal] conditions, the social value of commodities will be determined by the inferior or even the most inferior production condition and their market price will be higher than social value. . . . It is evident that social need has a regulatory effect on production conditions determining the commodity value and thus has a direct-bearing on value determination.

Gu and Yang, "A Further Inquiry into Value Determination and the Law of Value," *Jingji yanjiu,* no. 12 (1981), in *CES,* vol. 18, no. 1 (Fall 1984), p. 69.

13. Prybyla, *Market and Plan under Socialism*, figure 2.1, p. 18. The categories of Chinese prices, beginning in the early 1950s, have followed closely those earlier introduced in the Soviet Union. Compare Chu-yuan Cheng, *China's Economic Development: Growth and Structural Change* (Boulder, Colo.: Westview Press, 1982), pp. 226–27, and Paul R. Gregory and Robert C. Stuart, *Soviet Economic Structure and Performance*, 3rd ed. (New York: Harper & Row, 1986), pp. 193–202.

14. Commentator, "Lead the Reform as We Lead an Ox by the Halter," *Liaowang*, May 27, 1985, p. 4, in *Foreign Broadcast Information Service—China (FBIS)*, June 11, 1985, p. K17. Unchanged housing rents are "a tremendous obstacle to the solution of the housing problem in urban areas." "The pricing system currently practised in our country is very unreasonable. The prices of many commodities reflect neither their value nor the relationship between supply and demand." He Jiangzhang, *Renmin Ribao*, May 24, 1985, p. 5, in *FBIS*, June 4, 1985, pp. K4 and K5.

15. Another category of prices that should be included in Group 1 are factory prices: the sum of planned factory cost and planned factory profit. These are used for internal accounting only. Chu-yuan Cheng, *China's Economic Development*, p. 226.

16. Liu Guoguang, "Price Reform Essential to Growth," *Beijing Review*, no. 33 (August 18, 1986), p. 16.

17. Prices in the first subgroup of Group 2 prices were changed quite infrequently in the past (before the 1980s). One Chinese economist explains it this way:

> We should note that two important reasons why fixed prices have lasted for decades in China (notwithstanding their increasing unreasonableness) are technological stagnation and the slow growth of people's income. Technological stagnation meant relatively unchanging production costs. The slow growth of income meant the demand structure was relatively stable. Furthermore, the objects of consumption were mainly daily necessities with little demand elasticity (for which the rationing system could be easily applied). As autonomy expands, technological progress will speed up and the relative cost of products will rapidly change. Consumers' income will rapidly rise, consumer goods will improve in quality, and consumption choice will tend to diversify. Thus goods will have to be continually replaced by newer and more fashionable ones and the structural balance point [demand-supply equilibrium] like a heated molecule, will be in incessant motion. Under these circumstances, any attempt to protect an unchanging price system will be as fruitless as the attempt to use the Great Wall to defend against a modern enemy's attack.

Zhang Weiying, "On the Role of Prices," pp. 181–92.

18. In 1985 "the government introduced new policies for the purchase and sale of pigs and pork products, and gave *localities* the go-ahead to fluctuate prices on vegetables and other fresh non-staple products." Tian

Jiyun, "China Sets to Improve Price Mechanism," *Beijing Review*, no. 6 (January 27, 1986), p. 16 [emphasis added].

19. Between 1980 and 1985 procurement prices for all crops were raised 54 percent, and 98 percent for grain.

20. "A Survey of China's Economy," *Economist*, August 1–7, 1987, p. 7. The state (at least in 1985–1986) committed itself to purchase any surplus grain (as well as oil-bearing crops and cotton) offered by the peasants at "protective" prices—higher than the market price—whenever market prices "go low" (below the old quota price). On the other hand, when the market price "goes high," the state will sell appropriate quantities of its reserves on the market to bring the price back down. Zhao Ziyang, "Why Relax Agricultural Price Controls?" *Beiling Review*, February 18, 1985, p. 17. On the question of coerciveness of the contract price, see Jean C. Oi, "Peasant Grain Marketing and State Procurement: China's Grain Contracting System," *China Quarterly*, no. 106 (June 1986), pp. 272–90. The family farm contractual obligations (prices included) usually are arrived at by bureaucratic bargaining: between the village bosses and the state purchasing departments.

21. After deregulation of vegetables, meat, eggs, poultry, aquatic products, and other nonstaple foodstuffs state subsidy on such goods was reduced from 1.2 billion yuan in 1984 to 700 million yuan in 1986. Following sharp increases in the deregulated prices in the towns, however, "the government has demanded that suburban areas guarantee a certain acreage for vegetable farming, and that state-owned groceries control most of the sources for ordinary vegetables in order to ensure a continuous supply and stable prices. The state-owned groceries were also instructed to introduce a ceiling price on certain vegetables," Tian Jiyun, "China Sets to Improve Price Mechanism."

22. "Chen Yun's Speech," *Beijing Review*, no. 39 (September 30, 1985), pp. 19–20.

23. "A Survey of China's Economy," *Economist*.

24. Gao Shangquan, "Progress in Economic Reform (1979–86)," *Beijing Review*, no. 27 (July 6, 1987), pp. 20, 22.

25. "Tan Jiyun on Commodity Prices," *Ban Yue Tan*, no. 9 (May 10, 1985), in *FBIS*, June 5, 1985, p. K13. "Governments at various levels have established and strengthened organs for exercising supervision, examination, and control over the market prices. Their work in these fields has been systematized." *Liaowang*, May 27, 1985, p. 4, in *FBIS*, June 11, 1985, p. K17: "Producers and consumers are still unfamiliar with the market's regulatory role." Xue Muqiao, "Socialism and Planned Commodity Economy," *Beijing Review*, no. 33 (August 17, 1987), p. 18.

26. "In recent years, as central planners have eased their grip on the economy, raw materials increasingly have been supplied in free markets and prices have risen rapidly. To protect enterprises, [Shanghai] city officials have been purchasing large amounts of raw materials at high, free market prices, and selling them to enterprises at lower state-set prices." James R. Shiffman, "Shanghi Firms Reject Contract System," *Asian Wall Street Jour-*

nal, August 25, 1987. For other distortions caused by the coexistence of multitrack price systems, ibid., p. 1, 4.

27. How is this for an understanding of market pricing?

> At present a small number of state commercial units in some cities and rural areas still show no interest in market conditions. Some of them are merely hankering after profits. When more products are supplied, they force down the prices at the expense of the producers, and when products are in short supply or in great demand, they raise prices willfully at the expense of consumers. . . . The authorities concerned should strengthen effective management and supervision over the market and should strictly ban willful price hikes in violation of state regulations."

Commentator's article, "State Commerce Should Learn to Participate in Market Regulation," *Renmin Ribao,* May 28, 1985, p. i, in *FBIS,* May 28, 1985, pp. K15–K16. In fairness, the analysis may reflect concern with the widespread prevalence of local monopolies in China, that is, protection of "their" industries by local authorities from outside competition. Although China has a significantly smaller industrial concentration ratio than other Communist economies, it does not have much more competition.

28. Claude Aubert, "Rural Capitalism versus Socialist Economics? Rural-Urban Relationships and Agricultural Reforms in China" (Communication for the Eighth International Conference on Soviet and East European Agriculture, University of California, Berkeley, August 7–10, 1987, Mimeographed), p. 12.

29. Jan S. Prybyla, *The Chinese Economy: Problems and Policies,* 2d. ed. (Columbia: University of South Carolina Press, 1981), pp. 127–29. See also the seminal study by Justin Yifu Lin, "Rural Factor Markets in China after the Household Responsibility System Reform" (Paper presented at Third International Congress of Professors' World Peace Academy, Manila, the Philippines, August 24–29, 1987, Mimeographed).

30. For a Maoist view of this question (cast in terms of the reemergence of "rich peasant" classes), see Michel Chossudovsky, *Towards Capitalist Restoration? Chinese Socialism after Mao* (London: Macmillan, 1986), pp. 62–65.

31. Nicholas Lardy, "Consumption and Living Standards in China, 1978–83," *China Quarterly,* no. 100 (December 1984), p. 862, and his *Agriculture in China's Modern Economic Development* (New York: Cambridge University Press, 1983).

32. This view does not seem to be shared by the survey of China's economy published by *Economist,* August 1–7, 1987, especially pp. 9–10. I do not find the argument of a "disguised" industrial price reform persuasive.

33. Ibid., pp. 16, 19.

34. Abram Bergson, "A Visit to China's Economic Reforms," *Comparative Economic Studies,* vol. 27, no. 2 (Summer 1985), p. 79.

35. The following prediction is made by the China Institute of Social Sciences, Price Reform Group:

[Over the next four years] floating and market prices will become the central nucleus of the pricing model. Their scope will increase to cover as much as 70% of all produce, while unified [state-fixed] prices will apply to only 30%. . . . Unified prices cannot possibly be totally eliminated and will continue to apply to a large proportion of products. They will mainly key national investment industries and monopolies which require compulsory planning and resource management. . . . The proportion of market prices subject to intervention will gradually increase over the next four years, probably at greater pace than that of market prices subject to no controls ("Prices: Thoughts on Further Reform," *Jingji yanjiu*, no. 4 [1987], pp. 15–20, in *Inside China Mainland* [Taipei] [August 1987], p. 12).

CHAPTER 13: WHY REFORMS FAIL

1. How economists preoccupied solely with quantitative growth failed to factor in the crucial dimension of the quality of growth is revealed by CIA economic analysts studying the growth performance of the Soviet economy. In the twenty years leading up to the mid-1980s, they found that the average Soviet money wage doubled, social security incomes tripled, but retail prices (fixed by the government) increased by only 10 percent. Conclusion: during this period the Soviet real wage rose two to three times. Right? Wrong. Why? Because in line with chronic shortage and waste, few if any extra useful goods were produced (that is, goods people wanted and were willing and able to pay for with their money). Hence the only thing that happened was that the money supply increased two to three times, stimulating suppressed inflation. The lines outside the stores became longer, the black market more rampant, and official corruption more widespread and grasping. The wage earner's currency remained by and large inconvertible into useful goods.

2. State Statistical Bureau, *Statistical Yearbook of China*, 1987, p. 67.

3. One would hope always, because it is morally disgusting.

4. What constitutes clear dominance is quantitatively difficult to pinpoint with econometric exactitude—percentage of national income attributable to government? ratio of private to government output? or of the value of privately owned to socially owned assets?—but work is being done on it.

5. Jan S. Prybyla, "Socialist Economic Reform, Political Freedom, and Democracy," *Comparative Strategy*, no. 4 (December 1988), pp. 351–60; "China: The Relationship between the Fifth Modernization and the Other Four," in *Politics of Modernization in East Asia* (New York: St. John's University, forthcoming). The possibility of a coexistence between a market economy and an authoritarian policy (formerly exemplified by South Korea and Taiwan, but no longer) has been seized upon in China in the year of trouble, 1989, to produce an instant "theory" of the new authoritarianism.

6. Jan S. Prybyla, "Policy Measures to Open China's Economy: A Rational Development Strategy?" (Paper presented at the international symposium "China's Contemporary Economic Reform as a Development Strategy" at the University of Duisburg, West Germany, June 1989) forthcoming in confer-

ence proceedings from the Research Institute on Economic-Technical Developments in Japan and the Pacific Region, University of Duisburg.

7. According to *People's Daily*, the state-paid delivery price for grain purchased under the household production responsibility contract in May 1989 was only one-third of the market price. (*China Daily* [Taipei], May 20, 1989, p. 3).

8. For example, farmers in Hebei Province are forbidden to sell their above-contract produce to Beijing consumers nearby. See Roseanne E. Freese, "The Mixed Blessings of Agricultural Reform," *China Business Review* (November–December 1988), p. 34.

9. In 1988–1989 contractual deliveries of produce to the state were often paid for by worthless IOUs because the state was in a financial bind. In other words, it amounted to outright confiscation (ibid.).

10. Nicholas R. Lardy, "Economic Developments in the People's Republic of China," and Joseph Fewsmith, "Chinese Economic Reform: Intellectual Approaches and Political Conflict" (Papers presented at the Eighteenth Sino-American Conference, Hoover Institution, Stanford University, June 1989).

11. Andrew G. Walder, *Communist Neo-Traditionalism: Work and Authority in Chinese Industry* (Berkeley: University of California Press, 1986).

12. In the war of ideas between reformers and their adversaries, the most threatened reformist positions have been those of the think tanks such as the Economic System Reform Institute and the Agriculture Development Institute of Rural Policy Research.

Chapter 14: Effects of Tiananmen Square

1. Peter L. Berger, "The Market, Morals, and Manners," *Wall Street Journal*, July 14, 1988.

2. *Economist* (London), June 10, 1989, p. 22; Sheryl WuDunn, "China's Ability to Pay Debts: Damaged but under Control," *Wall Street Journal*, August 14, 1989; Jan S. Prybyla, "Policy Measures to Open China's Economy: A Rational Development Strategy?" (Paper presented at Duisburg University, West Germany, June 1988), forthcoming in the conference proceedings.

3. Graeme Browning, *If Everybody Bought One Shoe: American Capitalism in Communist China* (New York: Hill & Wang, 1989). For more than a century now, Western businessmen have thought of China as a potential enormously lucrative market. If only each and every Chinese bought one item of what each seller had to sell, great fortunes could be made. Unfortunately, so far, the potential has not materialized. The disposable income of each Chinese is below $300, and three-fifths of that is spent on rice and Chinese cabbage. If the present leadership's recentralizing and anti-intellectual policies continue to be pursued for any length of time, the long-awaited potential will certainly not be realized for decades to come. But the businessmen's hope remains undimmed.

4. William Fisher, "When a Firm Unreels Secrets of Soviet Joint Ventures," *Wall Street Journal*, August 28, 1989. Fisher refers to the Soviet potential

market, but his remarks apply with even greater force to China's perhaps mythical potential.

5. Liu Xiangdong, director of the Department of Policies and Structural Reform under the Ministry of Foreign Economic Relations and Trade, in *Beijing Review,* July 24–30, 1989, p. 18.

6. "VOA Disgraces Itself," *Beijing Review,* June 26–July 2, 1989, p. 13.

7. "Turmoil Won't Close Open Door," *Beijing Review,* June 26–July 2, 1989, p. 11.

8. A. J. Robinson (executive vice president of Portman Overseas, Atlanta, Georgia), "Strategies to Get Business Back to Normal in China," *Wall Street Journal,* June 20, 1989.

9. Mohammad Malekpour, cited in *International Herald Tribune,* August 12–13, 1989.

10. John J. Fialka, "Mr. Kissinger Has Opinions on China—And Business Ties. Commentator-Entrepreneur, In Wearing Two Hats, Draws Fire from Critics," *Wall Street Journal,* September 15, 1989; Adi Ignatius, "Bush's Brother, Other Americans Are Talking Business with China," *Wall Street Journal,* September 18, 1989. Former Secretary of the Treasury William E. Simon heads an investor group that owns several banks in Hawaii and is interested in acquiring a stake in a Chinese bank. Associated Press, September 11, 1989.

11. Although the problem is particularly acute in China, it is systemwide. In East Germany, portrayed by some Westerners as the economically best of a bad lot, playwright Juergen Gross's play *Reviso oder Katze aus dem Sack* (a parable on Nikolai Gogol's "Revisor") was shut down after only three performances at the Potsdam Hans-Otto Theater. One of the characters in the play says,

> Die Staat macht seine Diener dumm.
> Der Dumme haut den Klugen krumm.
> Die Kuenstler brauchen wieder Mumm.
> Und Morgen macht Europa bumm.
> (Die Welt am Sonntag, June 18, 1989, p.2)

Roughly translated:

> The State makes its servant's dumb.
> The dumb ones tear the wise ones down.
> The artists must again keep mum.
> And tomorrow Europe will just go boom.

CHAPTER 15: TAIWAN AND THE MAINLAND

1. The validity of table 15–1 rests on an enormous act of faith in the veracity and technical competence of the China mainland figures. Given the checkered history of mainland China's statistical services, the belief may well be misplaced. The quality of Taiwan's statistics is equal to that of the most advanced market democracies.

2. *Statistical Yearbook of China 1986,* p. 71.

3. K. C. Yeh, "Macroeconomic Changes in the Chinese Economy during

the Readjustment," *China Quarterly*, no. 100 (December 1984), table 6, p. 711. The average annual growth of labor productivity in agriculture from 1957 through 1978 has been estimated at 0.2 percent (almost nothing), 2.8 percent in construction, and 1.2 percent for services. Ibid., table 4, p. 706.

4. Yuan-li Wu, *Income Distribution in the Process of Economic Growth of the Republic of China* (Baltimore: University of Maryland School of Law, Occasional Papers/Reprints Series in Contemporary Asian Studies, no. 2, 1977).

5. Irma Adelman and David Sunding, "Economic Policy and Income Distribution in China," *Journal of Comparative Economics*, vol. 11, no. 3 (September 1987), pp. 444–61.

6. Jan S. Prybyla, "United States–Republic of China Economic Relations since the Taiwan Relations Act: An American View" (Paper presented at the Symposium on ROC–US Relations under the Taiwan Relations Act: Practice and Prospect, Institute of International Relations, Taipei, April 5–6, 1988).

7. S. C. Tsiang, "The ROC's Balance of Trade Problem and Trade Dispute with the US," *Economic Review* (The International Commercial Bank of China, Taipei), no. 241 (January–February 1988), pp. 1–4.

8. "If you can wangle an investment project you also become a more important factory with bigger bonuses, even if the production from the new investment is not needed." "One Awful Communist Example," *Economist* (London), April 2, 1988, p. 40. The investment allocation, incidentally, is a free good—a nonreturnable grant from the state.

9. Gene Tidrick, "Productivity Growth and Technological Change in Chinese Industry," *World Bank Staff Working Paper*, no. 761, Washington, D.C., 1986.

10. Jan S. Prybyla, *Market and Plan under Socialism: The Bird in the Cage* (Stanford, Calif.: Hoover Institution Press, 1987).

11. Like the so-called "Protestant ethic," Confucian teachings are supportive of the work ethic required by the market system. Sun Yat-sen's teachings do not constitute a complete economic system, institutionally or philosophically. They can be used as supplements to the existing economic systems of socialism and capitalism—more logically to the latter. A. James Gregor with Maria Hsia Chang and Andrew B. Zimmerman, *Ideology and Development: Sun Yat-sen and the Economic History of Taiwan* (Berkeley, Calif.: University of California, Institute of East Asian Studies, Center for Chinese Studies, 1981).

12. Adam Smith, *The Wealth of Nations*, bk. 5; Milton Friedman and Rose Friedman, *Free to Choose* (New York: Harcourt Brace Jovanovich, 1980), pp. 29–33. The Friedmans reject protection of infant industries as a legitimate function of government in a market system.

13. The 10 percent, however, includes such strategic goods as steel, petroleum, petrochemicals, electric power, and shipbuilding (*Economist*, March 5, 1988, p. 13).

CHAPTER 16: RELATIONS WITH TAIWAN

1. S. C. Tsiang, "The R.O.C.'s Balance of Trade Problems and Trade

Dispute with the U.S.," *Economic Review* (Taipei), no. 241 (January–February 1988), pp. 1–4; S. C. Tsiang, Wen Lang Chen, and Alvin Hsieh, "Progress in Trade Liberalization, Taiwan, Republic of China," ibid., no. 230 (March–April 1986), pp. 5–10.

2. Nelson Chung, "Debate over New Taiwan Dollar Swirls On; Exporters Nervous," *Free China Journal*, December 14, 1987, p. 4.

3. Philip Revzin, "As Trade Gap Closes, Partners of U.S. Face End of the Gravy Train," *Wall Street Journal*, March 17, 1988.

4. Roy A. Werner, "Taiwan's Trade Flows: The Underpinnings of Political Legitimacy?" *Asian Survey*, vol. 25, no. 11 (November 1985).

5. "More than 43 percent of the people on Taiwan think the government should liberalize trade with mainland China, according to a recent survey. . . . The island-wide survey of 1,178 adults over twenty showed that 43.3 percent thought the government should allow local businessmen to do business with their counterparts on mainland China. About 17 percent were against doing business with the mainland, and 12 percent adopted a wait-and-see attitude." *Free China Journal*, February 29, 1988.

6. Yu Teh-pei, "An Analysis of Economic Ties Linking Hong Kong, PRC, and ROC—with Special Reference to Trade," *Issues & Studies* (Taipei), vol. 22, no. 6 (June 1986); and Ronald Hsia, *The Entrepôt Trade of Hong Kong with Special Reference to Taiwan and the Chinese Mainland* (Taipei: Chungwa Institute for Economic Research, 1984).

7. *Free China Journal*, January 11, 1988; December 21, 1987.

8. During my one month's teaching stint at Nankai University, Tientsin (December 1987–January 1988), I read and heard several complaints about the low quality of Taiwan-made consumer goods, or perhaps goods pawned off on the mainlanders by Hong Kong intermediaries and labeled as having been made in Taiwan. I found that the relatively low costs of mainland labor (not so low when all the hidden subsidy-like costs are factored in) tend to be less attractive than they appear, by reason of socialist work attitudes of the mainland manufacturing workforce (deficiency of the instinct of workmanship). It is sobering to remind oneself, in the midst of the euphoria about Chinese economic reforms, that the mainland is still (as Milovan Djilas calls socialism) "a non-market, bureaucratic economy . . . where all real values, including the value of work, are lost."

9. "Premier Yu (Kuo-hwa) said the government will not mix economics with politics in competing with Communist-controlled China in the international arena. One move in that direction, he said, may see the government allowing the private sector to trade directly with East bloc countries." *Free China Journal*, February 29, 1988. "A delegation of Hungarian businessmen on a visit to Taiwan has informed Republic of China authorities that the ROC doesn't have to compromise its anticommunist stance in doing business with Hungary. 'We are a socialist nation, not a communist nation,' said Sandor Demjan, president of the Hungarian National Bank" (*Free China Journal*, February 29, 1988).

10. Edwin J. Feulner and Richard V. Allen, "The Case for a U.S.-Taiwan

Free Trade Area," in Martin L. Lasater, *The Two Chinas: A Contemporary View* (Washington, D.C.: Heritage Foundation, the Heritage Lectures, no. 55), pp. 36–40.

11. Joseph Kyle, "The Economic Situation on Taiwan," in ibid., pp. 40–53.

12. For example, Michael Aho, "Most Bilateral Trade Pacts Carry a Penalty," *Wall Street Journal*, March 18, 1988. Aho would restrict the FTA solution to Canada and Israel, and possibly Mexico.

13. Jan S. Prybyla, "Economic Developments Affecting the Taipei, Peking, Washington Triangular Relationship," *American Asian Review*, vol. 5, no. 1 (Spring 1987), pp. 89–146; and Prybyla, "United States Trade Relations with the Republic of China on Taiwan: The Vexed Nexus" (Paper presented at a Conference on United States–Republic of China Relations, University of California, Berkeley, November 2–4, 1987).

14. Tsiang, "The R.O.C.'s Balance of Trade Problems," pp. 1–4.

CHAPTER 17: THE HONG KONG AGREEMENT

1. Cited by Hugh D. R. Baker, "'Greatness Thrust upon Them': Hong Kong before and after the British," *Asian Affairs*, vol. 16, part I (1985), p. 47.

2. A. J. Youngson, *Hong Kong Economic Growth and Policy* (Hong Kong: Oxford University Press, 1982), p. 2.

3. Ibid., p. 7.

4. Ibid., p. 19.

5. Frank Ching, *Hong Kong and China: For Better or for Worse* (New York: China Council of the Asia Society and the Foreign Policy Association, 1985), p. 60.

6. Joan Robinson, *Economic Philosophy* (Chicago: Aldine, 1963), p. 45.

7. Alfred Marshall, *Principles of Economics* (1890; reprint, London: Macmillan, 1949), p. 1.

8. On the less than obvious and simple role of government in Hong Kong in the areas of education, health care, transport, housing, land, money, rents, and rice, see Youngson, *Hong Kong Economic Growth and Policy*, pp. 119–36; and Hugh D. R. Baker, "Life in the Cities: The Emergence of Hong Kong Man," *China Quarterly*, no. 95 (September 1983), pp. 469–79.

9. Adam Smith, *The Wealth of Nations*, ed. Edwin Cannan (New York: Modern Library, 1937), p. 651.

10. Milton Friedman and Rose Friedman, *Free to Choose: A Personal Statement* (New York: Harcourt Brace Jovanovich, 1979, 1980), pp. 32–33.

11. "The Hong Kong China Needs," *Economist*, October 1, 1983, pp. 8–9.

12. Smith, *Wealth of Nations*, p. 651.

13. World Bank, *World Development Report 1988* (New York: Oxford University Press, 1988).

14. Youngson, *Hong Kong Economic Growth and Policy*, pp. 52–53.

15. Steven C. Chow and Gustav F. Papanek, "*Laissez-faire*, Growth and Equity—Hong Kong," *Economic Journal*, vol. 91, no. 362 (June 1981), pp.

466–48. See also, World Bank, *World Development Report 1984*, table 28, p. 273 (data for 1980).

16. World Bank, *World Development Report 1984*, tables 23, 24, and 25, pp. 263, 265, 267. John A. Mathieson, *The Advanced Developing Countries: Emerging Actors in the World Economy* (Washington, D.C.: Overseas Development Council, Development Paper no. 28, November 1979), table 4, p. 21. The physical quality of life index is a composite indicator giving equal weight to life expectancy, infant mortality, and literacy. It is measured on a scale of 0 to 100, with 0 representing worst possible performance and 100 representing best possible performance. In the mid-1970s the index was 87 for Hong Kong (95 for the IMEs and the United States).

17. Census and Statistics Department, Hong Kong, *Hong Kong in Figures 1989.*

18. Willard Sharpe, Hong Kong area economist for Chase Manhattan Bank, lists ten ingredients for Hong Kong's success: free enterprise, market-determined pricing, free movement of goods and people, market access for Hong Kong goods, the British legal system, freedom of information, free movement of funds, an independent currency, a range of financial institutions, and a simple, low tax structure. Kevin Rafferty, "Hong Kong," *Asia and Pacific 1984*, p. 140.

19. For a more exhaustive analysis of the internal and external causes of Hong Kong's success, see Jan S. Prybyla, "The 'Gang of Four's' Economic Miracle: Hong Kong, Singapore, South Korea, Taiwan," in *America's New Pacific Era: Five Lectures on U.S.-Asian Relations* (Washington, D.C.: Heritage Foundation, Heritage Lectures, no. 43, 1985), lecture 3, pp. 53–90. On the erratic path of Hong Kong's growth, see Youngson, *Hong Kong Economic Growth and Policy*, table 1.1, p. 8.

20. Robert Keatley, "Jittery Hong Kong Frets about Its Future," *Wall Street Journal*, August 30, 1982.

21. Y. C. Yao,"The 1997 Issue and Hong Kong's Financial Crisis," *Journal of Chinese Studies*, vol. 2, no. 1 (April 1985), pp. 124, 131–32, 140; Frank Ching, *Hong Kong and China*, pp. 12–13.

22. James P. Sterba, "Hong Kong's Chinese Fearing '97 Takeover, Seek Capitalist Havens," *Wall Street Journal*, June 22, 1984.

23. The influence, however, is not as straightforward as it might seem. Some of Hong Kong's leading capitalists (for example, Sir Yue-kong Pao, the shipping and real estate magnate) have been assiduously courting Beijing, building luxury hotels in China and endowing universities in their places of birth. In their view, the best insurance policy for *nous après le déluge* survival is a network of highly placed personal connections (*guangxi*) with the men in charge in Beijing. They also seem to believe, despite the Shanghai precedent, that they can "educate" China's communist leaders in the capitalist mechanics and ethics of Hong Kong. Feelings of Chinese patriotism also enter into this delusion. See "The Rich Folk Go Courting Peking," *New York Times*, December 29, 1985.

24. World Bank, *World Development Report.*

25. Len Dunning, executive director, Hong Kong Trade Development Council, *Wall Street Journal*, June 21, 1982.

26. Reacting to quotas and other trade restrictions imposed by the IMEs, Hong Kong's textile and garment industries have moved up market and many of them are now working for Pierre Cardin, Calvin Klein, Fiorucci, and Yves St. Laurent. Hong Kong boosters hope that the electric and electronics industries will follow the same path. One obstacle is that most of the 1,300 Hong Kong electronics workshops are very small: 80 percent of them employ fewer than 100 workers each. They compete on their own against government-aided or otherwise subsidized Singapore firms and Taiwan's government-supported push toward high technology (Kevin Rafferty, "Hong Kong," p. 139).

27. James P. Sterba, "Although Hong Kong Reverts to China Soon, U.S. Influence Prevails," *Wall Street Journal*, October 10, 1985.

28. Hong Kong, Census and Statistics Department, *Hong Kong in Figures 1985.*

29. Mary Williams Walsh, "Mexico's Middle Class Blames Government for Economic Crunch," *Wall Street Journal*, December 30, 1985.

30. John Burns, "Hong Kong Savors Its Interlude," *New York Times*, December 29, 1985. "For the last two decades, Hong Kong has been a place where investors could pour capital into hotels, office blocks, and cross-harbor tunnels and retrieve it with a profit in as little as three to five years," ibid.

31. *Wall Street Journal*, December 10, 1985.

32. *Asian Pacific Monitor* (Washington, D.C.), December 1985, p. 1.

33. Hong Kong, Census and Statistics Department, *Hong Kong in Figures 1985.*

34. International Monetary Fund, *Direction of Trade Statistics Yearbook*, various years.

35. The Hong Kong Trade Development Council took out an advertisement in the *New York Times* (November 18, 1985) to educate Americans in the benefits they derive from their Hong Kong connection. While the textile problem was skirted and the pirating not mentioned, two themes were stressed. The first was the importance to the United States of exports to Hong Kong: $3.1 billion in 1984 (nearly one-third reexported to China), with Hong Kong being the leading global importer of U.S. razors and razor blades, ginseng from Wisconsin, dressed poultry, cigarettes, buttons, studs and cufflinks, oranges, lemons, and $70 million worth of diamonds and other precious and semiprecious stones (making Hong Kong the third largest customer in the world for New York dealers and cutters in this trade). The theme is appealing and stimulating, especially the ginseng part of it, but it is not convincing. For one thing, U.S. exports to Hong Kong represented in 1984 just 1.4 percent of total U.S. exports. The second theme was the importance of Hong Kong's role as an intermediary with China for U.S. goods and other exports.

36. *Wall Street Journal*, June 22, 1984, and October 10, 1985; T. B. Lin, "Foreign Investment in the Economy of Hong Kong," United Nations, *Economic Bulletin for Asia and the Pacific*, vol. 35, no. 2 (December 1984), pp. 96–106.

37. Ibid., June 24, 1984, p. 13.

38. Ibid.

39. See, "Big Business Sees Profit in a Chinese Flag over Hong Kong," *Business Week*, October 8, 1984, p. 55.

40. Chalmers Johnson, "The Mousetrapping of Hong Kong: A Game in Which Nobody Wins," *Asian Survey*, vol. 24, no. 9 (September 1984), p. 887.

41. Throughout the Sino-British negotiations, Beijing kept repeating that "if we can rule Shanghai, we can surely rule Hong Kong," without realizing what this was doing to Hong Kong's Hang Seng Index, the exchange rate of the Hong Kong dollar, and the curbside passport market. See "Hearts Ill at Ease," *Far Eastern Economic Review*, March 17, 1983, pp. 43–45.

42. A Hong Kong businessman interviewed by Frank Ching put it this way: "If I were looking for a job, and I know I'm worth $30,000, but they offer me $60,000, I'd think there was something fishy" (Ching, *Hong Kong and China*, p. 43).

43. See, for example, the Symposium on Hong Kong 1997, with articles by Hungdah Chiu, Y. C. Yao, and Chu-yuan Cheng, in *Journal of Asian Studies*, vol. 2, no. 1 (April 1985), pp. 95–163, available also in *Occasional Papers/Reprints Series in Contemporary Asian Studies*, vol. 68, no. 3 (1985) (Baltimore: University of Maryland School of Law, 1985).

44. Yuan-li Wu, "The Future of Hong Kong before and after 1997," *American Asian Review*, vol. 2, no. 4 (Winter 1984), p. 13. At one point in what, with poetic license, might be called the negotiations on the future of Hong Kong, Deng Xiaoping tried to reassure nervous investors in the colony. He told them that with him in charge they could put their hearts at ease. That caused immediate panic for, among other things, it was not their hearts the investors were worried about.

45. Ching, *Hong Kong and China*, p. 60. A good source for the economic relationship between China and Hong Kong is A. J. Youngson, ed., *China and Hong Kong: The Economic Nexus* (Hong Kong: Oxford University Press, 1983).

46. Louise de Rosario, "Into the Red Zone," *Far Eastern Economic Review*, September 19, 1985, p. 61.

47. Johnson, "The Mousetrapping of Hong Kong," n. 40.

48. Baker, "'Greatness Thrust upon Them,'" *Asian Affairs*, p. 46, citing Arthur Waley, *The Opium War through Chinese Eyes* (London, 1958), p. 33.

49. From an interview of Hu Yaobang by Hong Kong journalist Lu Keng, on May 10, 1985, *Paittsing* (Hong Kong), no. 97, June 1985, pp. 3–16, in *Foreign Broadcast Information Service–China*, June 3, 1985:

> LU: I would like to tell you some reactions in overseas areas, and please do not take offense. Outside people are worried that once Mr. Deng [Xiaoping] goes to see Marx, some Army generals may try to emerge, big and strong, and our General Secretary Hu [Yaobang] may not have peremptory command of the Army!
> HU: This is not quite right!
> LU: Another point is linked to policies. Everyone holds that in the economic reform, the old gentleman Chen Yun opposes the reform policy of the revered Deng.

Hu: That is not true.

Lu: I do not believe it much either. However, this is what people say: "Chen Yun, Peng Zhen, and Wang Zhen oppose the revered Deng. . . ."

Hu: Our Comrade Chen Yun . . . has been in poor health for the past two years and his energy has flagged a bit. . . .

50. John F. Burns, "China on the Move: Will the Changes Last?" *New York Times Magazine*, December 8, 1985, pp. 38–42, 86–94; and Burns, "China Grain Crop Dips; Setback Seen for Policy," *New York Times*, December 23, 1985.

51. On the theoretical deficiency and impracticality of market socialism, see Jan S. Prybyla, *Market and Plan under Socialism: The Bird in the Cage* (Stanford, Calif.: Hoover Institution Press, 1986). Compare Don Lavoie, *Rivalry and Central Planning: The Socialist Calculation Debate Reconsidered* (New York: Cambridge University Press, 1985).

52. The mucking up has already begun. Timid British attempts to translate *gangren zhigang* (Hong Kong people ruling Hong Kong) into something more than a cardboard Socialist united front slogan have met with hardly disguised Communist fury. See Emily Lau, "No More Velvet Glove," *Far Eastern Economic Review*, September 19, 1985, p. 27; and Lau, "Long, Slow March . . ." *Far Eastern Economic Review*, October 31, 1985, p. 18. Also see John Burns, "Hong Kong Has Seen the Future and Has Doubts," *New York Times*, January 7, 1986. The precedent of preemptive surrender set by the British in the negotiations leading to the agreement is being followed by influential sections of Hong Kong society as they kowtow to what they perceive to be the wishes and *modus operandi* of the new masters in Beijing. Hong Kong's independent journalism has "begun to steer clear of politics and concentrate on less controversial subjects, such as juvenile delinquency or bus-fare increases." This voluntary abdication of freedom of speech is one of many incremental accommodations to Socialist rule, the pace and scope of which may be expected to accelerate and expand as the countdown to 1997 proceeds. See Julia Leung, "Hong Kong Press Cooling Criticism of Peking Rulers," *Wall Street Journal*, February 7, 1986.

CHAPTER 18: FROM SOCIALISM TO CAPITALISM

1. Ivan Szelenyi, "Eastern Europe in an Epoch of Transition: Toward a Socialist Mixed Economy?" in Victor Nee and David Stark, eds., *Remaking the Economic Institutions of Socialism: China and Eastern Europe* (Stanford, Calif.: Stanford University Press, 1989), pp. 208–32.

2. Friedrich A. von Hayek, *The Fatal Conceit: The Errors of Socialism* (Chicago: University of Chicago Press, 1988), p. 73.

3. Larissa Popkova-Pijasheva, "Why Is the Plan Incompatible with the Market?" in "Privatizing and Marketizing Socialism," *Annals of the American Academy of Political and Social Science*, January 1990, p. 84.

4. Don Lavoie, "Computation, Incentives, and Discovery: The Cognitive Function of Markets in Market Socialism," *Annals*, January 1990, pp. 72–79.

5. Andrei Kuteinikov, "Soviet Society Much More Unequal than U.S.," *Wall Street Journal,* January 26, 1990.

6. "In the Lunatic Bus Factory," *Economist* (London), November 25, 1989.

7. Nikolai Shmelev and Vladimir Popov, *The Turning Point: Revitalizing the Soviet Economy* (New York: Doubleday, 1989).

8. János Kornai, "The Hungarian Reform Process: Visions, Hopes, and Reality," in Nee and Stark, eds., *Remaking the Economic Institutions of Socialism,* p. 48.

9. Oskar Lange and Fred M. Taylor, *On the Economic Theory of Socialism* (Minneapolis: University of Minnesota Press, 1938).

10. Stark and Nee, "Toward an Institutional Analysis of State Socialism," in Nee and Stark, eds., p. 17.

11. Kornai, p. 84.

12. Ibid., pp. 89–91.

13. "The Hard Road from Capitalism to Capitalism," *Economist,* November 18, 1989.

14. Christian Watrin, "Transforming the Command Economies," *The World & I,* November 1989, pp. 93–105; Enno von Loewenstern, "The Man Who Pulled West Germany Out of Poverty," *Wall Street Journal,* November 21, 1989.

15. Andrei A. Kuteinikov, "New-Look Socialism for Soviets," *Wall Street Journal,* December 4, 1989.

16. Steven Greenhouse, "Czechs Fault Policies of Hard-Line Communists as Cause of Industrial Lag," *New York Times,* December 1, 1989.

17. "Enter Comrade Capitalist," *Economist,* August 26, 1989.

Acknowledgments

CHAPTER 1, "Foundations of the Economic Crisis of State Socialism," was first published in an expanded version in *Orbis*, vol. 26, no. 4 (Winter 1983), pp. 869–87 as "The Philosophical and Institutional Foundations of the Economic Crisis of State Socialism." Reprinted with permission.

CHAPTER 2, "Socialist Economic Reform, Political Freedom, and Democracy," originally appeared in *Comparative Strategy*, vol. 7, no. 4 (1988), pp. 39–49. Reprinted with permission.

CHAPTER 3, "The Relationship between the Fifth Modernization and the Other Four in China," was first given as a presentation at the Sixth Annual Asian Conference, Institute of Asian Studies, St. John's University, New York, September 23, 1988. It appeared in Cynthia L. Chennault, ed., *Modernizing East Asia: Economic and Cultural Dimensions of Political Change* (New York: Institute of Asian Studies, St. John's University, 1989).

CHAPTER 4, "Some Reflections on Man and Society in China," was the commencement address at Behrend College, Pennsylvania, May 25, 1975. It was published in *Vital Speeches of the Day*, vol. 31, no. 18 (July 1, 1975), pp. 551–55.

CHAPTER 5, "The Soviet Type of Economic System Strong or Weak?" first appeared in *Issues and Studies* (Taipei), vol. 22, no. 11 (November 1986) pp. 80–96. Reprinted with permission.

CHAPTER 6, "Similarities and Differences of Economic Changes in China and the Soviet Union," first appeared as "Economic Changes in China and the Soviet Union: Similarities and Differences," in *The American Asian Review*, vol. 7, no. 2 (Summer 1989), pp. 1–18. Reprinted with permission.

CHAPTER 7, "Mainland China and Hungary—To Market, to Market," was first published in *Issues and Studies* (Taipei), vol. 23, no. 1 (January 1987), pp. 43–83. Reprinted with permission.

CHAPTER 8, "The Polish Economy—A Case Study in the Structure and Strategy of Disaster," first appeared in *Comparative Strategy,* vol. 8, no. 1 (1989), pp. 191–203.

CHAPTER 9, "China's Economic Reforms" appeared in the *Journal of Comparative Social and Economic Systems* (Beijing), no. 3 (1988), pp. 36–40. Full original text.

CHAPTER 10, "China's Economic Experiment—From Mao to Market," was originally published in *Problems of Communism,* vol. 35, no. 1 (January–February 1986), pp. 21–38. Reprinted with permission.

CHAPTER 11, "China's Economic Experiment—Back from the Market?" was first published in *Problems of Communism,* vol. 38, no. 1 (January–February 1989), pp. 1–18. Full original text. Reprinted with permission.

CHAPTER 12, "Price Reform in the People's Republic of China," was first printed in W. Klenner, ed., *Trends of Economic Development in East Asia: Essays in Honor of Willy Kraus* (Berlin: Springer Verlag, 1989), pp. 353–369, under the title "On Some Questions concerning Price Reform in the People's Republic of China."

CHAPTER 13, "Why China's Economic Reforms Fail," © 1989 by the Regents of the University of California. Reprinted from *Asian Survey* vol. 29, no. 11 (November 1989), pp. 1017–32. Reprinted by permission.

CHAPTER 14, "The Economic Consequences of Tiananmen Square," was first published in the *International Freedom Review,* vol. 3, no. 1 (Fall 1989), pp. 27–41. Reprinted with permission.

CHAPTER 15, "The Economies of Taiwan and Mainland China," was first published in *Issues and Studies* (Taipei), vol. 24, no. 12 (December 1988) pp. 12–28. Reprinted with permission.

CHAPTER 16, "U.S. Economic Relations with Taiwan since the Taiwan Relations Act," was first printed in *Issues and Studies* (Taipei), vol. 24, no. 11 (November 1988) pp. 70–82. Reprinted with permission.

CHAPTER 17, "The Hong Kong Agreement and Its Impact on the World Economy," originally appeared in *Issues and Studies* (Taipei), vol. 22 no. 6 (June 1986), pp. 92–110. Reprinted with permission.

Index

Adjustment, economic
in China, 146–47, 148–50
defined, 120, 147
in Hungary, 144–45
Agricultural Bank of China, 195
Agricultural sector, China
credit source for, 195
decollectivized program for, 99–101
economic change in, 80–81, 82, 186–87
growth of output in, 174–75
incentives in, 99–101
market system and privatization in, 186–87
performance from 1978 to 1988 in, 151–55, 174, 180–81, 228
policy response to reform in, 195–96
privatization of property rights for, 106–8, 140, 143–44
problems of, 180–81
reform in price system of, 93–95
reform proposals for, 143–44
See also Contract system; Property, China
Agricultural sector, Hungary
incentives for, 98–99
price system for, 89–90
property privatization for, 108–9
Agricultural sector, Soviet Union, 82
Amnesty International, 29
Andreas, Dwayne O., 27
Arrow, Kenneth J., 4
Aubert, Claude, 216
Augursky, Mikhail, 67–68

Balassa, Bela, 188
Banking system, China, 178, 192, 195, 234
Barter system, 35, 293
Berger, Peter, 32, 239
Bergson, Abram, 97
Berliner, Joseph, 22
Birman, Igor, 22–23
Black market. *See* Underground economy
Bogomolov, Oleg, 26

Bonner, Yelena, 63–64
Bonus funds, China and Hungary, 104
Bo Yibo, 241
Brezhnev, Leonid, 78, 82
Brus, Wlodzimierz, 124–25
Bureaucratic system
behavior in free market environment of, 167–68
control of innovation by, 14–15
cost of information in, 12–13
effect on agricultural sector of, 15
Bush, George, 247
Business work partnerships (BWP), Hungary, 111

Cambodia, 4
Capital markets, Hong Kong, 281
Catholic church in Poland, 132
Central bank, China. *See* People's Bank of China (central bank)
Chen Yun, 86, 241, 286
Ching, Frank, 284
Civilian market economy, Soviet type, 64, 66–68, 70–71
Commodity (market) economy. *See* Market system
Competition, 24, 190–92, 231–32
Contract system, China, 151–53
Cooperatives
in China, 81, 163
in Hungary, 111
Corruption, China, 181–83, 198–99, 229
Council of Mutual Economic Assistance (CMEA), 85
Cultural Revolution, 41, 78, 79, 146, 147, 157, 216
Czechoslovakia, 33

Debt, external (China), 241
Decentralization, administrative (China), 231
Democracy, 25
defined, 17, 37

351

market system as condition for, 38–39, 238
suggestion in China for, 29–30
See also Freedom, economic; Freedom, political
Demonetization, 35, 293
Deng Liqun, 286
Deng Pufang, 242–43
Deng Xiaoping, 16, 17, 28, 30, 40, 42–43, 73, 80, 193, 197, 200, 237, 240, 286
Djilas, Milovan, 20
Drewnowski, Jan, 298
Dyadkin, Iosif, 8

Economic philosophy
components of, 203
price system in, 204–7
See also Leninism; Market system; Marx, Karl; Marxism; Socialism
Economic policy, 203–4
Economic system
adjustment vs. reform for, 223–28
comparison of China and Hungary, 86
comparison of China and Taiwan, 253–64
components of, 120, 203
conditions for modern, 30–37, 43, 291–92
differences in Chinese and Soviet experience with, 78–83
incentive system for centrally planned, 98–106
indicators for economic performance, 59–60
performance of, 559–60
recipe for reform: China and Soviet Union, 83–84
structure of, 203
See also Adjustment, economic; Market system; Price system; Reform, economic
Economic system, China
change for, 40–41, 43–45
change in 1979–88 period, 171–74
changes in, 72–75
choice between plan or market system for, 199–202, 239–40
current status of change for, 186–93
formula for change in, 78–83
limitations to change for, 183–85
performance up to 1978 for, 222–23
periods of reform for, 228–36
policy response to reform effects, 194–98
post-1978 move toward reform for, 150–57, 228–36, 235, 245–46, 257–60

requirements for reform of, 135
shift from Mao-style economic planning, 147–50, 256–60
social and political organization in, 47–50
Socialist economic system in, 32–33
Economic system, Hong Kong
as example of laissez-faire concept, 276–77
performance of, 277–80
Economic system, Hungary
disequilibrium in, 114–16
experimentation with, 85–89
underground economy of, 66, 71, 112
Economic system, Poland
attempts at reform for, 120–23
effect of flawed policy on, 122–29
proposals for reform for, 131–32
requirements for reform of, 131
trends and crises in, 118–19, 123–29
Economic system, Socialist
creation and development, 17–18
failure to modernize, 32–37
problems of, 18–21, 249–50
proposed reform of, 36–37
requirement for modernization of, 38–39
Economic system, Soviet type
economic performance of, 60–63
interactions of subeconomies of, 64–71
Economic system, Soviet Union
changes for, 72–75
formula for changes in, 78–83
military-public security economy of, 64–71
planned civilian economy of, 64–69, 71
underground economy of, 64–69
Economic system, Taiwan
as model, 260–64
performance of, 253–60
Economic system, Yugoslavia, 145
Economic zones, special (SEZs), China, 197
Education, China, 234
Enterprise business work partnerships (EBWP), Hungary, 111
Ethiopia, 61
Europe, Eastern, 272
Exchange rates
See Foreign exchange certificates (FECs)
Exchange rates, China, 230
Export promotion
in China, 257
in Taiwan, 258, 274

Factor markets, China and Soviet Union, 76
Financial markets, China, 187, 192, 234
Foreign exchange certificates (FECs), China, 230
Four Modernizations (China), 28–29, 42, 72
Freedom, economic, 24–25
  as element of reform in economic system, 136
  in modern economic system, 31–32
Freedom, political
  defined, 16–17, 25
  in democracy, 37
  in market system, 38–39
Free trade area (FTA), 273
Friedman, Milton, 277

Galbraith, John Kenneth, 298, 299
Gargan, Edward A., 41
General Agreement on Tariffs and Trade (GATT), 268
Germany, East, 32
Ge Wu, 188
Gierek, Edward, 126
Glasnost, 26, 34–35, 80
Gomulka, Wladyslaw, 124, 126
Gorbachev, Mikhail, 26, 33, 73, 78
Government
  in China, 231–32
  in market system, 31
  role in free market economy of, 24
Government intervention
  under capitalism, 301–2
  in China, 158–62
  in Hungary, 159
Great Leap Forward, 28, 41, 79, 147, 157, 216, 223
Grossman, Gregory, 64

Harding, Harry, 42
Hayek, Friedrich von, 294
Hinton, William, 238

Import substitution
  of China, 257
  of Taiwan, 258, 274
Income distribution
  in China, 179–80, 181–82, 229
  in Hong Kong, 278
  in Socialist economies, 178–79
Industrial sector, China
  degree of privatization in, 109–10
  effect of economic changes for, 81
  effect of reform on, 142–43
  growth in, 175–76

performance from 1978 to 1987 in, 175–76
  post–central plan move toward reform for, 155–57
  price system reforms for, 95–98
Industrial sector, Hungary
  easing of state control for, 110–12
  price system for, 90–93
  public-private property enterprises, 111–12
  wage incentives in, 101–3
  See also Managers, state sector: Hungary
Inflation, China, 176–78, 181, 187, 198, 229, 246
Information
  in China, 86–87, 96, 98, 137
  cost in bureaucratic system of, 12–13
  creation and transmission of, 11
  in free market system, 168
  in Hungary, 86–87, 91, 115
  in Poland, 130
  rationing of, 34
  sources in market and centrally planned economies, 208–9
Innovation
  effect of bureaucratic system on, 14–15
  lack of climate for, 20–21
  in Socialist economic system, 33–34
Interest rates, China, 162, 196–97
Investment, direct foreign
  in China, 164, 241
    See also Joint ventures, foreign
  in Hong Kong, 281
  of PRC in Hong Kong, 284–85
  in Taiwan, 265–66

Japan, 268
Johnson, Chalmers, 283, 285
Johnson, Paul, 17–18
Joint ventures, foreign (China), 164, 175

Kamenev, Lev, 51–52
Katsenelinbogen, Aron, 70
Koestler, Arthur, 34
Kolakowski, Leszek, 4, 50
Kopelev, Lev, 9–10
Korea, North, 32
Kornai, János, 85, 92–93, 106, 114, 115, 292, 299
Korolenko, Vladimir, 55
Kowalik, Tadeusz, 26
Kristol, Irving, 16

Labor force, China
  imperfect market for, 229–30, 232

mobility in public and private sectors for, 229–30, 161–62
unemployment and underemployment in, 180, 182, 187, 192, 197–98, 229
Labor force, Socialist economies, 6
Laissez-faire doctrine, 31
Lange, Oskar, 115–16, 297–98
Lavoie, Don, 295
Law on the State Enterprise (Soviet Union), 81
Lenin, Vladimir, 12, 16, 17–18, 164
Leninism
  necessity to renounce tenets of, 199
  party control concept in, 169–70
  price system philosophy of, 204–5, 207
  reform undermines philosophy of, 182
Levine, Herbert, 70
Liberman, Yevgeni, 104
Liberman experiment (Soviet Union), 81–82, 143
Lin Piao, 46
Li Peng, 237
Liu Binyang, 248
Liu Guoguang, 171–73, 186, 190, 201
Liu Xiangdong, 243
Li Xiannian, 241
Li Yining, 189–90, 194
Li Yungi, 178

Macroeconomic policy, China, 192, 234
Malekpour, Mohammed, 244
Managers, state sector: China
  effect of changes in responsibility of, 104–6, 140, 142–43
Managers, state sector: Hungary
  changes in economic system for, 104–6, 140
Maoism, 2–4, 5
Mao Zedong, 12, 16, 28, 48, 49, 193
Markets, illegal. See Underground economy
Market system
  China's incomplete transition to, 199–202, 229–30, 235–36, 240
  complete transition to, 83–84
  components of free, 24–25
  conditions for, 31–37, 185–86, 227–28
  control mechanisms embedded in, 183–84
  philosophy and ethics of, 136–37, 225–26, 238–39, 266
  political freedom in free, 25
  price system in, 208

role of property rights in, 31
  See also Price system
Marshall, Alfred, 277
Marx, Karl, 12, 16, 51, 56
  labor theory of value of, 8, 33, 82, 137, 204, 206, 207
Marxism
  class hatred in, 7–9, 10, 169
  economic system of, 292
  effect of ideology on economic reform, 168–69
  emasculation of the individual in, 9–11, 17–18
  necessity to renounce tenets of, 199, 225
  price system philosophy of, 204–5
  relativity of truth in, 3–7
Marxist-Leninist doctrine, 59
MGM Development Company, 244
Military–public security economy, Soviet type, 64–71
Mill, John Stuart, 50–51, 55, 183
Mironov, L. G., 51–52
Mises, Ludwig von, 37
Monetization, China, 178
Money supply, China, 178
Murrell, Peter, 114

New Democracy era, China, 146
New Economic Mechanism (NEM), Hungary, 66, 87, 91
  incentives for agricultural sector in, 98–99
  incentives for industrial sector under, 101–3
  incomplete privatization reforms of, 144–45
New operational systems (NOS), Hungary, 111–12

Padilla, Heberto, 10–11
Parallel economy. See Underground economy
Peng Zhen, 241
People's Bank of China (central bank), 195
Perestroika, 26, 82, 184
Poland, 61
Political system, China
  choice of socialism or capitalism for, 78, 199–200
  policy response to reform effects, 197
  proposals for reform, 141–42
  rationale for change in, 41–45
Political system, Soviet Union
  change with economic reform of, 78
Popkova-Pijasheva, Larissa, 23, 294
Popov, Vladimir, 295

Population
in China, 256
in Taiwan, 256
Poverty
in China, 147, 198, 242
in Soviet Union, 62
Price system
components of Socialist and capitalist, 204
effect of multiple-track, 135, 231
fallacies of Socialist, 204–7
in Poland, 129–31
Price system, China, 93–98
allocative role of, 216–17
analysis of policy for, 216–21
current status of change for, 187–90
effect of distortion in, 104–6
with household contract system, 151–55
industrial and agricultural, 80–82, 87–89
policy response to reform effects, 194
policy since 1978 for, 218–21, 230–31
price control in, 181
proposed reform for, 135–39, 142
readjustment and reform for, 75–76, 160–62
requirement and purpose for reform of, 135–36, 137, 142, 188–89
three groups of prices in, 209–16
Price system, Hungary, 89–93
for agricultural and industrial products, 87–89
effect of distortion of, 104–6
price control in, 92
Price system, Soviet Union
lack of reform for industrial, 82
reform for, 75–76
revision of wholesale price structure of, 159
See also Foreign exchange certificates; Information; Underground economy
Privatization, China
attempts, 86–87
of property, 189–90
of property in agricultural sector, 106–9
of property in industrial sector, 109–12
Privatization, Hungary
in agricultural sector, 106–9
attempts, 86–87
in industrial sector, 109–12
Profit motive
in China, 104–5, 165
in Hungary, 104–5

Property
defined, 106, 139–40
Property, China
mixed forms for, 81, 162–64
post-1978 move to reform for, 233
privatization for, 106–8, 151–53, 189–90
privatization in industrial sector for, 109–10
proposals for reform of, 139–41
rights to, 80–81, 142–43
Property, Hungary
privatization in industrial sector for, 110–12
privatization of, 108–9
Property rights
in free market economy, 24
as incentive in China and Hungary, 98–101, 142–43
reform in China and Soviet Union for, 76–77
in Socialist economic system, 33
Protection, trade (Soviet Union), 83

Qin Jiwei, 240

Rationing
in China, 88–89, 187, 194–95
in Hungary, 88–89
nonprice, 19
in Soviet Union, 82
Reform, economic
in centrally planned economy, 121
defined, 120, 147
See also Adjustment, economic; Agricultural sector; Economic system; Industrial sector; Political system
Reform, economic: China
potential of contract system for, 151–55
problems and effects of, 166–70, 171–83
proposals for, 135–41, 185–98
Regional administration, China. See Decentralization, administrative
Robinson, Joan, 276
Romania, 32, 61
Rule of law, 31, 184
in China, 233
effect of absence of, 123
role in market system of, 31, 184, 291
See also Government; Market system

Sadowski, Zdzislaw, 121–22, 132
Sanctions against China, 246–48
Selyunin, Vasily, 34–35, 294–95

SEZs. *See* Economic zones, special (SEZs), China

Shadow economy. *See* Underground economy

Shenzhen SEZ, 285

Shmelev, Nikolai, 295, 296

Shortages, 18–20, 22, 32

Smith, Adam, 16–17, 31, 32, 277

Socialism
 attempt to change reality of economic system, 25–27, 204–5
 defined, 16
 ethical principle of, 77, 115–16, 168–69, 225, 238, 239–40
 failure of, 292–300
 incompatibility with free market system of, 23
 See also Leninism; Marxism

Socialist ethical code. *See* Socialism

Social justice concept. *See* Catholic church in Poland

Social techniques, capitalist
 in China, 148–50
 use in planned economies of, 148

Social welfare programs
 in China, 234
 effect of bureaucratic system on, 13–14

Solzhenitsyn, Alexandr, 10, 55, 56

Soviet Union
 Socialist economic system in, 33
 trade policy of Taiwan with, 272

Special Economic Zones (SEZs), China, 98, 150, 197–98, 229

Stalin, Josef, 16, 51–52, 59

Stalinism, 204–5

State-owned enterprises, China, 81
 bail-outs for, 246
 increased autonomy for, 164–66

State-owned enterprises, Hungary, 110–11

Stock exchange, China, 187

Stock ownership, China, 81

Subsidies
 in China, 105–6, 176–77, 192, 246
 in Hungary, 105–6
 in Soviet Union, 82

Szelenyi, Ivan, 293

Taiwan Relations Act (1979), 265, 266, 273, 274

Tax system, China, 234
 to correct price distortion, 104–6, 165–66

Tax system, Hungary
 to correct price distortion, 104–6

Thatcher, Margaret, 247, 285

Tiananmen Square massacre, 237, 241, 247–48

T'ien Chi-Yun, 85

Timmerman, Jacobo, 20

Tinbergen, Jan, 298

Totalitarianism, 50–54

Trade, international
 U.S. position on, 268–71

Trade, international, China, 83
 performance of, 241–42, 257–60
 since 1979, 256–58

Trade, international, Hong Kong
 performance of, 279–80
 with trading partners, 83, 282

Trade, international, Taiwan, 257–58
 with Eastern Europe, 272
 with mainland China, 272
 with United States, 265–74

Trade, international, world
 U.S. promotion of, 268

Transactions in free market, 24

Treml, Vladimir, 64

Underground economy
 in China, 109–10, 156, 176, 216–17, 230
 in Hungary, 66, 112
 in Poland, 130
 of Soviet type, 64–66, 68

United States
 relations with Taiwan of, 265–71
 trade relations with Hong Kong of, 282

Vanek, Jaroslav, 298

Vietnam, 61

Voluntariness, 24, 34

Wage structure, China
 effect of control for industrial, 161–62
 incentives in system for industrial, 103–4
 in inflationary environment, 176–77
 policy response to reform effects, 197

Wage structure, Hungary
 incentives in, 98
 incentives in system for industrial, 101–3

Walesa, Lech, 4

Walsh, Mary, 280

Warsaw Pact, 85

Waste, 20

Wei Jingsheng, 29–30

Wilcynski, J., 293

Winiecki, Jan, 292

World Bank, 241, 246

Wu Jinglian, 190

Xue MuQiao, 203

Yang Shangkun, 237, 240
Yuan-li Wu, 283–84

Yugoslavia, 145

Zhao Ziyang, 193, 194, 197, 240
Zheng Tuobin, 243
Zhou Enlai, 28

About the Author

Born in Poland and educated in England, Ireland, and France, Jan Prybyla is professor of economics at Pennsylvania State University. He is the author of numerous articles on Socialist economies, with special reference to China, and on comparative economic systems; editor of *Comparative Economic Systems* (1969); and author of several books, including *The Political Economy of Communist China* (1970), widely considered a classic treatment of the subject, *The Chinese Economy: Problems and Policies* (1978, 1981), *Issues in Socialist Economic Modernization* (1980), *Market and Plan under Socialism: The Bird in the Cage* (1987), and *China and the Crisis of Marxism-Leninism* (1990, co-authored with Franz Michael, Jurgen Domes, and Carl Linden).

He has taught at Nankai University's Institute of Economics (Tianjin, 1987–1988) and lectured at the Shanghai Academy of Social Sciences (1988). He was a visiting scholar at the Institute of International Relations, National Chengchi University, Taiwan, in 1989.

Dr. Prybyla is a contributing editor of *Current History* and member of the editorial advisory board of *Occasional Papers/Reprints Series in Contemporary Asian Studies,* University of Maryland School of Law. From 1982 to 1989 he was on the board of directors of the American Association for Chinese Studies. He is currently president of the Conference on European Problems.